The
SHRINK
in the
DRINK

ANDREW HILL-SMITH

UK Book Publishing.com

DEDICATION

To my dad, who loved to travel.

Illustrations by Fiona Macpherson

Editing, design, typesetting and publishing by UK Book Publishing

www.ukbookpublishing.com

ISBN: 978-1-917329-52-1

www.laseraroundtheuk3.uk
www.facebook.com/laseraroundtheuk
www.youtube.com/@andrewhill-smith9535

The
SHRINK
in the
DRINK

ACKNOWLEDGEMENTS

I would like to thank Liz, my wife, for tolerating my mad adventures. I would also like to thank her for being the tracker supervisor, distance monitor, and for appreciating that my decision making was reasonably sensible.

I would like to thank Sam, my eldest child, for his invaluable support in editing, and posting videos throughout the trip.

Thanks go to Neil Peters, Ken Fowler and Paul Walker who offered invaluable advice and support throughout the trip. A big thank you goes to Ron Pattenden for being the first to go round GB in a Laser, and for coming up with the rolling fender idea. May he rest in peace.

Huge thanks go to all the wonderful people who supported me along the way, fed and watered me, welcoming me with open arms on so many occasions. In particular I would like to thank Alastair and Cat, Geoff and Alison, Ditta and Philip, Colin and Martha (plus Willow the dog), Jacqui and Guy, and so many others.

A big thank you goes to all those who donated so generously to my chosen charities. Many thanks to the Andrew Simpson Foundation, Place2Be, and Motor Neurone Disease Association, for their support in setting up fundraising.

Many people have been wonderfully supportive in the preparation of the manuscript. It has been an equally huge and daunting task for me. Special thanks go to Liz for being endlessly encouraging, to Judith and Steve for their commentaries, and especially to Anne Sharp for her detailed feedback.

And lastly, a huge thank you goes to you, the reader. I hope you enjoy the journey as much as I have done.

CONTENTS

CHAPTER 1

In the beginning

* * *

"I think there's a 95% chance of you coming back," said Liz. Calm, clear, without jest or malice, this was my wife's actuarial estimation of risk for the journey.

"That's not very encouraging," I replied. However, I knew better than to ask for any more support, since I was already rationed to five minutes' talk about my round the UK trip per day, a rule that was invariably broken on a regular basis.

I could imagine a few ways that my life could come to an end on this particular self-imposed enterprise, all of which concluded with the final common path of drowning – not my preferred way of exiting the world. For instance, a knockout blow to the head from the boom, or falling overboard and being lost at sea, maybe the boat sinking, or perhaps being run over by a ship. There was even talk of being sucked down in a whirlpool in the gulf of Corryvreckan on the west coast of Scotland. Drowning can take as little as two minutes and maybe ten if you half do it, so there would be plenty of opportunity throughout the 600 hours at sea. If you get imaginative, I suppose there is the 'trashed on the rocks' option as well, which might not involve drowning, but come to think of it, that does not sound very comfortable either. All of these end points were best avoided, I thought.

"You're mad," everyone else concluded. At least it got people talking, preferably in appropriate company. All the aghast reactions had the inevitable effect of social encouragement, which added layers of planning detail, and before I knew it, the idea was gathering unstoppable momentum.

By the end of the journey, I had fallen out many times, lost or broken pieces of kit, been stranded for hours in the Thames, marooned near Aberdeen, rescued at Blackpool and smothered in fog on the south coast. Looking back, I loved every minute of it, especially the bad bits, since the bad bits made the good bits even better. Through it all, people were so incredibly kind and supportive, I couldn't help falling in love with human nature.

Background

By chance I had come across Stick Daring's 2019 Laser around the UK story, via Facebook. My initial thoughts were that his journey was crazy, and extremely uncomfortable, but really cool. There was an early video of Stick illuminated by torchlight in his flapping tent, camping near Dover in a storm, with little prospect of respite. It looked to me like a terrible way to spend the night. I later learnt that Stick had one or two other bits of terrible advice, mostly uncomfortable sleeping arrangements. Little did I know it at the time, but I would end up following in his footsteps.

Stick is a great raconteur, who invited you into the messiness of his adventure with a daring by name and daring by nature candour that made it feel like the journey was both possible and impossible, all at the same time. As a lake sailor the sea was strange to me. As a mediocre club sailor, I had no idea whether I had the skills required to follow along Stick's awesome path. As a determined but cautious adventurer, I needed to find out.

I love sailing, and have loved it for years and still do. The simplicity of air and water coming together to make movement in a controllable direction, is so repeatably reinforcing, and yet so endlessly variable, that there is almost no limit to its joyousness. Provided, of course, that the fear of being in the water does not overcome the pleasure of being on it.

I also needed an escape. Escape from repetition of work. From ageing. From time.

Yes, of course, you can't escape time, but that is the way I saw it. Whilst the hands march inexorably around the clock, my clumsy chronometric calculations for task completion, jumbled with competing social needs and personal expectations, clatter relentlessly round in my head. At the end of each day, those ruminations come to a juddering halt at the 13th hour when a cacophony of alarms are sounded, coupled with a flashing sign saying "you should have done all that, but you have run out of time. Failed again".

There are things like dyslexia, and the lesser described dyscalculia, for those who are not so good at maths. I reckon there should be a dystemporalia for those who struggle with time estimation. I mean like, why not? Time is everywhere, all the time. And some people are better than others at avoiding the ticking bomb of expired seconds, coupled with the more complex task of deciding how much you can squeeze into scarce minutes, without everything blowing up.

For the less well endowed, this presents a problem. I used to introduce myself as a doctor, with the added descriptor of being usually late. Fortunately, the NHS and the fearsome reputation of unpunctual doctors, provided cover for my ineffectual time keeping, though these failings have become less and less acceptable over the years.

Liz, my wife, does not suffer the same fate. On one occasion, she cunningly added an appointment to a school parents' evening schedule. The first slot at time minus 10 minutes, was with one, Dr B. Early. I did not recognise this person's name. I did attend the appointment, more or less on schedule. It worked a treat, much to Liz's amusement, and mine for that matter. Unfortunately, like setting a watch five minutes early, you can't play the same trick too many times, so I was left with an endlessly losing battle against the clock.

Having launched the idea in my head, I figured I should do some research. I went to meet Stick in the autumn of 2021. It was a lovely late summer's afternoon near Eastbourne, and Ron came to join us for a beer at Stick's workplace. Ron arrived on his bicycle and I in my car, having stopped on the journey to buy a couple of boat parts.

Ron was the first person to sail round GB in his Laser, taking the budget approach to travel. He took a leaky tent, refused accommodation when it was offered, and used laminated sections of an AA road atlas, and a compass, to guide his travels. He stuffed empty lemonade bottles in the boat hull to provide extra buoyancy. His one enduring invention was to use a boat fender, to help roll the boat up the beach. Ron and Stick both sailed at Pevensey Bay Sailing Club, on the south coast, so they had met. Stick was inspired by Ron's adventure.

Stick and Ron had a great time recounting mainly scary stories of their journeys, and miserable remote camping spots, and I had a not-so-great time feeling increasingly uncomfortable about what I was intending to do. Stick told a tale of sailing round the Mull of

Kintyre with "waves as big as that house over there". He had then seen a coastal rescue type craft, surfing down the back of a wave, as you might. It then simply disappeared into the back of the next water monster, never to be seen again, not by Stick at least.

I left with a small supply of tips, a modest supply of beer in my belly, and a large supply of fun. Perhaps the most important thing was feeling part of a team. "Maybe I could become number 3," I mused as I drove back home. "Maybe it's possible to become the third person to sail around mainland GB in a Laser."

I had set my sights on NHS retirement at age 60, so I still had two years to go. There was plenty of preparation to be done, like obtaining a VHF licence, getting a boat, sorting the luggage, practising some launching and landing, to name but a few.

I also needed to find out what it was like, sailing on the sea. In 2020, I had completed a sail around the Isle of Wight on a Laser, travelling with two other dinghies (Liz was on one of them), blessed with the company of a safety boat. Liz and I had also sailed across to the Isle of Wight at Bembridge, and out to the Needles from Lymington on another occasion. These had acted as helpful tasters of sea sailing, rather than anything extensive – no cross-channel yacht journeys, or offshore sailing for me.

One of Ron's pieces of advice was to take a rivet gun. That's because "a drill is relatively easy to find," he said, when asking helpers, "but a rivet gun could be scarce. You'll need it to mend your mast." Ron had also taken a metal sleeve to fit inside the tube if it snapped, so that he could end to end the aluminium mast, and still have a functioning boat. I was not so sure I liked the idea, preferring to keep my mast intact, but needed to find out how to avoid those unwelcome crashes.

Bracklesham Beach was one of the nearest launching practice points on the South Coast. On a wet and windy day, I headed down with my original Laser called Lulu, to try out some launching. As well as getting used to the waves, I wanted to test a system to minimise boat scratches. I had prepared a fender for the front of the boat and some foam matting, thinking that I could rest my precious craft on the smooth surface, before easing us all into the sea. How naïve was I?

Waves breaking on the shingle were exciting for surfers, but definitely not in the "nice" category for me. I was pushed and dragged around the shoreline with each incoming bundle of foam fun, with the boat thrown left and right and occasionally over my head, as I was unceremoniously dumped into the water. After a few minutes, my pieces of pretentious foam matting and spare string were disparagingly discarded onto the shingle. Onlookers tried to help, thinking that I was escaping the sea, but soon stood back when they realised my mad mission, as I was tossed about in front of them like a discarded rag doll.

Persistence paid. After about an hour of exhausting struggle, I managed to launch, only to fall out about 100 metres offshore, when seaweed tangled in my main sheet. I heard later that someone was about to call the coastguard. However, when they saw me reboard the boat, and come zooming in to shore, for what in hindsight was a pretty impressive and unplanned landing, their phone pistol was returned to its holster. I trudged my way back to the car park and homewards, both knackered and a bit disheartened.

Given that nothing was irreparably broken on the boat or about my person, there was only one course of action available to me, which was to try again.

The next visit to Bracklesham was much more successful. And the third, well, awkward, because I broke my mast.

My learning points from these trips were as follows:

1. It's best to avoid shore break if you can.
2. The shore break is usually much less if the tide is out and the beach less steep.
3. A Laser is not a surfboard, so should not be used as one, at any time.
4. If a breaking wave catches the back of the boat, it's really difficult to prevent a capsize.
5. And if the mast so much as touches the ground, whilst a wave is pushing the boat, the mast is likely to snap.

So that's what happened. One sheepish sailor returned home with fractured aluminium tube and ripped sail, with his tail between his legs.

Oh, and one final learning point:

6. This whole enterprise was going to be tricky.

But the idea kept gnawing away at me. Moments of busyness or frustration at work, would tempt me to wander to the sea, to problem solve some possibilities, or devise a plan to overcome a potential obstacle.

I spoke to my colleague Louise about my incessant draw to this absurd adventure, so she gave me a collegiate consultation. "Do you think it's a search for freedom?" she asked.

Is that what my heart was looking for? Was it really as simple as that? Maybe so.

Whatever the motivations, my mind was set.

I needed to do some full-blooded practice to see what I could manage.

As COVID lockdowns were easing in 2021, I ventured out along the coast, again setting out from Bracklesham, but this time going east as far as I could. This was a proper test run, with tent, radio, without rescue cover, just as it would be. It was a chilly windy April, with dry bright days, making the photographs look like it was warm, when it wasn't. Many of the South Coast facilities were still closed, or shunned listless customers from indoor spaces, for fear of contagion.

Afterwards, I wrote pages and pages of reflections, and listed rows of actions, based on errors or eventualities that I had not considered. Two learnings stood out. The first was, when travelling into the wind, not only is boat speed limited, but also you have to travel 40% extra distance, because of the zig zagging. Bizarrely, I had discounted this obvious fact when calculating my estimated distances for the day. And second, it can be lonely.

With that in mind, I resolved to build a rota of willing callers, with whom I could speak each night once I had landed, as a way of feeling connected and yes, grounded. Lonely, tired, maybe scared, could be potential showstoppers, all feeding into an unmotivated feeling. Those unquantifiable and unpredictable emotions could end up being as variable as the weather, so something to mitigate the risk was needed. My good planning paid off, because the call rota worked really well.

Undeterred by my first practice trip, I set out in July of the same year, this time from Cornwall. It was gorgeous sunny weather, and I had a lovely time bimbling along the south Cornwall and Devon coast, mixing with sweaty holidaymakers as they roasted themselves on the beaches. I managed to grab two tows from passing boats, and also had a lovely time in Salcombe, meeting up with friends and relatives.

The highlights from this summer sojourn were that:

1. My estimation of achievable distance in a day was still hopelessly optimistic.

2. There is no such thing as a sea breeze in the UK – it was roasting hot and not a whisper of wind appeared.
3. Paddling is painfully slow, but it is still possible to make ten miles in a day.
4. I hadn't been put off.

By now I had settled on a few key ingredients that were essential for a successful voyage.

These were:

1. A six-month slot in the summer was needed, to catch longer days and avoid time pressures.
2. Which would mean a formal end to working.
3. A functioning body.
4. Avoid frightening myself.

Boats and packing and stuff, I could sort out over time. The awkward issues of sailing competence and navigational nous would hopefully solve themselves through learning on the job. A little risky you might say, but it wasn't a race. I knew that Stick was a Laser sailor of international standing, but Ron wasn't, and I reckoned I didn't need to be.

To confirm my incompetence, I joined in with the Laser, or ILCA (International Laser Class Association) nationals in the summer of 2022. I was delighted that I avoided coming last, but it was close.

When 2023 came around, I became one of the lucky bunch of 60-year-olds who had retired. We were part of a cohort of millions of healthy able people whom Jeremy Hunt, as the then chancellor of the Exchequer, was trying to entice back into the workplace. His approach made absolute economic sense for the nation. Unfortunately, the opportunity to start a new life as a 60-year young person, plus the luxury of a comfortable pension, provides little incentive to return to regular employment. My strong social conscience continued to cajole me into reactivating my medical skills, so maybe later.

The march of time gets the better of all of us in the end. For me, whilst being reasonably physically fit, there were plenty of niggles appearing, mainly on the musculoskeletal front. Patches of osteoarthritis crept around my body, flaring up at points, then subsiding into a creaky stiffened joint. An arthritic foot nearly stopped me walking for a few months in the previous year, and I am fairly one eyed. "Maybe in five years' time, I would be simply too unfit to consider the challenge," I thought.

The march of time also got the better of my mother. For 18 months she complained in her wonderfully frank way, that she just wanted to die.

She had had enough and was not enjoying life, though was still living independently on her own. "Don't be 92," she would often say when I visited, to which there was no useful reply.

Even better than that, was her cake cutting wish, when young and old were gathered in anticipatory silence to hear what she had to say at her 91st birthday party. "Not to have another birthday," was the immortal line. We could only laugh at her preposterous bluntness. She meant it though, and said so, many times afterwards.

And yet, when briefly admitted to hospital to help with leg cellulitis, just as COVID was surging across the land, she brought in a Greek textbook in order to take another step forward with her crossword solving skills. 'Independent, pragmatic and brave, right to the very last,' as my middle sister, Katie, had said at our mother's funeral. And she was.

Not that we knew it at the time, but a huddled Christmas, just fitting within gathering guidance, was to prove her last before her wish was granted. She got what she wanted, but we didn't.

CHAPTER 1

At least we were able to have a socially distanced send off in her local church, as COVID restrictions were closing in again. At the funeral, the vicar recounted some more forthright bluntness. Mum had advised him not to play bridge. When asked why, she said, "Well, you wouldn't be very good at it, if you are only just learning how to play!"

We were also lucky to have a dry day for the funeral. We were able to gather outside the crematorium after the service, and pay our respects in the chill winter sunshine. It had been so much worse for so many others.

I am the third child and only son, out of four surviving siblings. Two brothers were born before my time, both named Anthony. The first died aged two from food poisoning, and the second from childbirth. Mercifully, my parents selected a different Christian name for me. My sisters accused me of being a favourite, presumably their reaction to my parents' response to their tragic losses. I can't say I ever noticed being treated any differently.

Going to boarding school at age eight didn't feel special. It was meant to be the route to a great education back then. Years later, as a child psychiatrist, I sometimes recommended the away-from-home education option, for some of the more disturbed and disturbing young people under my care, and it felt strange to think that I too had followed a similar route. I didn't think I was that bad!

My career choice came through at an early age. I often relayed my decision-making steps at careers fairs, making the point to attentive students that choices are not always logical, but can turn out to be just fine. My story went like this.

At the age of six, I thought I wanted to be God. "I mean why not?" I thought. "It sounds like the best job." But then I realised that was taken.

"Hmmm, so what about Jesus?" It turned out that role was taken as well, which was disappointing. Undeterred on this theme, I persisted. Jesus, to my understanding, was a preacher, a teacher, and a doctor. I didn't fancy being a preacher since I tended to tune out during church sermons. "Teachers are great but they can also be annoying," I thought, so that didn't sound very attractive. That left me with the last option of being a doctor, and I couldn't see anything wrong with that. So being a doctor was what it was going to be. Over time I realised I liked helping people, and fixing things, which seemed to fit the role well enough, and so the aspiration stuck.

Life was full of good fortune in many ways. Well cared for, well supported and well educated gives you freedom. Rubbing shoulders with other Etonians at secondary school gave me a sense of the possible. It remains incredible that so many prime ministers have come from the same establishment. Boris Johnson must have been there at a similar time to me, but I don't recall seeing him, other than a vague memory of his distinctive blond mop.

It was not the first time I had failed to recognise a famous person. A cringeworthy story has been gleefully retold by Liz to many friends. It related to a time when our family was making a trip to Althorp House, the home of the Spencers (as in Charles and Diana). Standing with my family, we were surveying the local collection of Venetian pigs, when a man came over, and welcomed me to the estate. He clearly recognised me as a fellow pupil from Eton. Embarrassingly, I took my usual five minutes to work out who on earth he could be, just about managing to fill the space with old school waffle. By the time I realised that he was Charles Spencer himself, our social engagement had ended.

Launch date was set and publicised for the 10th April 2023. My long to-do list had been shrinking. All those packing, weighing, repacking and shopping tasks were complete, or as complete as they were going to be. Trackers were working and tested, a spare phone purchased, Instagram and Facebook accounts set up with links to YouTube, and all the rest. It was a lot of work pulling everything together, but I felt the bases were sufficiently covered. It was now or never. And after so much preparation and deliberation, I could not bear to delay.

CHAPTER 2

My first guardian angel

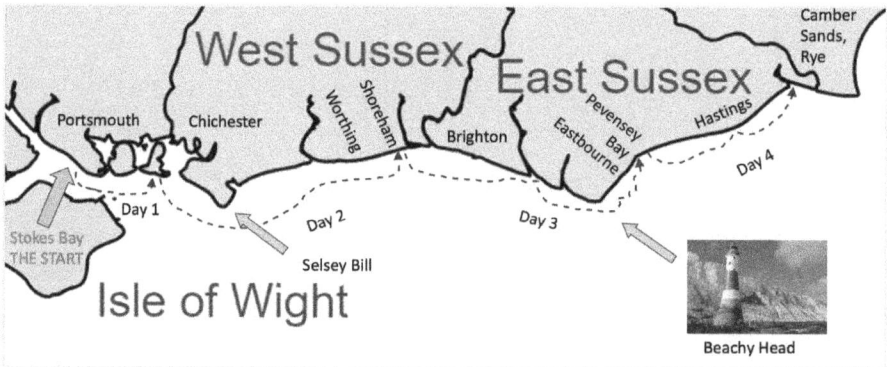

* * *

West Sussex

East Sussex

Camber Sands, Rye

Portsmouth   Chichester   Worthing   Shoreham   Brighton   Pevensey Bay   Eastbourne   Hastings

Day 1   Day 2   Day 3   Day 4

Stokes Bay THE START

Isle of Wight

Selsey Bill

Beachy Head

Day 1, Monday 10th April 2023

To Hayling Island

START	11.00, Stokes Bay
WIND	SW 18–28 (F5–6), rising to 24–35mph (F6–7)
WEATHER	Rain, then clear, 11°C
TIDE	With me till 13.00, max 0.6mph.
SEA STATE	Slight rising to Moderate
HAZARDS	Rain, shipping, too much wind
FINISH	Hayling Island, 12.45
DISTANCE	9 miles
SAILING HOURS	1¾ hours

"You don't have to go," they said as the rain was falling on Stokes Bay. Liz and I both tried out the same positive reframe – "it's a good opportunity to test things out" – but it was me who would look a fool if things went wrong, and I didn't feel I had a large bank of sea sailing competence to draw on. Family and friends said they were coming down to support the launch, so a splash could bring on a confidence crash.

I didn't like letting people down, nor did I like cancelling things at the last minute. I had waited so long for this day, and had prepared as much as I could, meaning there wasn't enough reason to delay. The wind was blowing a healthy 18mph gusting 28, though it didn't look so bad. So, off I went. "It's only nine miles to Hayling Island," I said to anyone who shared a doubt.

Maybe it was my lack of experience at sailing on the sea. Maybe I had not read the forecast properly. Maybe the Met Office wasn't as accurate as I believed them to be. Either way, the sharp increase to 24mph gusting 35mph (some said gusting 40mph) was definitely too much for me. I stopped on the water to ask a windsurfer where I was. And then five capsizes later, I decided to call in to shore for a break, thinking I had further to go.

Mistake #2, or maybe mistake number ten, I dare not count, was to think that because the beach was "just there", I could ease out the main and casually land, like on a lake. A healthy sized shore dump whizzed the boat over, meaning I found myself catapulted to windward (again), and in the process experienced a hard thump on my backside. Whilst scrabbling about in the surf, trying to release the top of my sail from the Hayling Island shingle, a nice young man was watching from the dry, plaintively asking if I needed a hand. "Yes please," I replied.

Then James, who had kindly offered to put me up for the night, turned up. That was good news, since it meant that I had pretty much reached my destination, through good fortune rather than precise planning. Then my wife Liz turned up. Not so good because at this point, I had worked out what had caused the impact on my rear. And by the size of the bruise that grew over the next two weeks, it was a sizeable impact. The centreboard had lost a significant chunk off the bottom corner, and was no longer useable. This was embarrassing. It was my first day and I had suffered a potentially show-stopping accident. What would Liz say? I might have to go home for a day or two, to source a new plate, and would it be safe to leave the boat on the shore, not to mention all the thoughts about this being a silly idea.

The plaintive young man was still hovering about looking helpful. He was wearing an Ineos top so "he could be sailing sensible", I thought. He said he sailed a Laser, so that was good. He said he had heard about my ridiculous challenge via the wonderful 'Yachts and Yachting' magazine publication, of a few days previously. That was even better. He said his name was Craig.

I managed to wrestle the centreboard out of the boat, by pulling the broken corner off its reluctant reinforcement bars –

it's interesting to see the inner workings of one's craft, but a few hours into day one, really was not the time to find out.

Craig then mentioned that he might have a spare centreboard, and asked "would you like it?". I was wet, cold and slightly disorientated, so all I could manage in response to this incredible offer, was "yes please". Craig duly disappeared and came back 20 minutes later with a nice fresh and wholesome replacement, ready to go tomorrow. More than that, Craig refused to take any money for it.

We all parted and I went to warm up and get changed at James's place. I felt I had to contact Craig and thank him again. My upside-down state had meant that I lost some of his surname in our communication. I later worked out that he was not Craig Williams, but none other than Craig Williamson, who was one of the national ILCA trainers at UKLA (UK Laser Association). I didn't dare to go back and ask for some training tips, because when you meet your guardian angel, it feels best to simply soak up the warm glow of reverence. But let me say it again anyway. Thank you so much, Craig.

Day 1, involved a few learning points:

- Top tip to self #1 – don't venture out in an ILCA 7 when it is blowing force 7
- Top tip to self #2 – learn some things about landing in shore break
- Top tip to self # ???? – miraculously, things seem to keep working out

I stayed with James for the night. James captured his thoughts from that first evening.

"Andrew is struggling to finish his spag bol. I am concerned he doesn't like it and is trying to finish it anyway out of politeness, so I tell him not to. It's just that is pretty much all I cook. I remember hoping that's the reason he has gone quiet.

"On the other hand, he has had a properly tough day. Committed to leaving Gosport at a set time, the weather has not been kind, and got steadily worse. I left a couple of kayaks on the East Hayling Beach and told him to aim for them. The wind meant I had to weigh them down with plenty of stones.

"Eventually, the only sailing boat out on the sea draws level and promptly capsizes. It takes some time to right the boat. He turns sharply away from me, heading back from where he had come. I guess he can't see any kayaks through the waves. It looks like turning at all is a challenge, so I set off along the beach to see where he comes in.

"The wind has kicked up the swell, and any landing looks plain nasty. As he comes in, the boat is tipped over. I see his feet flying up in the air as he is thrown backwards, and lands with a splash in the sea. The shrink is now in the drink.

"Fortunately, the waves only maul him for a short while before he is spat out onto the shingle, next to his damaged Laser.

"So, it feels as if the sea has issued its warning. Add to that, the weather forecast is unchanged for the following day, and all his family has withdrawn home. My thoughts turn to the months of sailing ahead, with its large dose of unknown. Can it possibly be this bad all the way? At this point I am completely sure that Andrew's adventure is a daft errand.

"This all leaves me with the feeling that maybe the spag bol isn't the issue. The enormity of the task is now on his shoulders. I ask what he wants to do. An early night makes good sense. He is exhausted."

Day 2, Tuesday 11ᵗʰ April

To Shoreham

START	7.30, Hayling Island
WIND	SW, 15–23, rising to 29mph at midday
WEATHER	Cloudy. 11°C. Dry
TIDE	With me, max 1.3mph till 13.00.
SEA STATE	Slight to moderate, surprisingly
HAZARDS	Selsey Bill. Storm Noa
FINISH	Shoreham Sailing Club, 12.30
DISTANCE	33 miles
SAILING HOURS	5 hours

Storm Noa was due to arrive in the afternoon. I planned to travel north for my brother-in law's-funeral on the Friday, so needed a safe place to leave the boat for a few nights. Paul, who became my self-appointed chief technical advisor, and generally extremely helpful person, suggested Shoreham Sailing Club. That was partly since he was a member at Shoreham, as well as Papercourt, my home club. This would mean an early start.

Liz had found an online forum, discussing the shore break problem so that I might respond to 'top tip to self #2' – about learning how to land in shore break. Reassuringly, it was a well-known mishap with plenty of suggestions, and I figured I had been lucky to avoid a Ron-style broken mast. I was keen to digest the ideas thoroughly, but even better would be to avoid putting them into practice for as long as possible. Shoreham Sailing Club was inside a harbour so a much more sheltered arrival spot, so that should help. After all, there was some recovery needed. Credibility recovery, rather than physical rest.

During the night, wind had effortlessly leapt over the shingle bank of the shore, and tunelessly whistled through the shrubs outside my window. It kept lifting me from slumber until I gave up, and got up before the sun, pretty convinced that I would be unable to make it to Shoreham. The breeze had only calmed down a few hours earlier, which meant that the sea would settle sometime in the afternoon, according to my textbook estimation.

After some breakfast and nervous chatter, James and I went to check out the boat, and the sailing conditions. Much to my disbelieving delight, the sea had flattened a great deal. Without being asked, and with a large dose of early morning enthusiasm, Ptol from next door, came to join the gravelly launch gathering, as the day was lighting up. So, with an additional pair of hands to add to James's kindness, I was off.

I had been past Selsey Bill twice before on practice trips, and had carelessly fallen out as many, if not more times in the area, which offered reassurance of familiarity and apprehension of mishap. Either way, I was very keen to stay in, and on the boat for the day, if nothing other than to rebuild some confidence. The main challenge was figuring out how to do things like have a wee, and (at a separate time please note) to access my lunch box, whilst still on the move. In fact, I didn't dare do the latter for fear of losing my Tupperware, and instead waited for land to arrive.

Guidance into the harbour, a landing ramp, a trolley, a landing party plus a late lunch, all felt incredibly warming, from outside to in, like I had overcome a significant hurdle and survived the start. More importantly, the melee of club members who offered support, both in person and online, felt like a reassuring safety blanket, or extra buoyancy aid, just when it was needed. I was especially grateful to Paul who topped everything off by giving me a lift home. The trip had begun, and what's more, began to feel possible.

＊ ＊ ＊

Wednesday 12th April – Friday 14th April

Travel to Yorkshire and back for Anthony's funeral

A start, albeit a staccato start, felt very different from the previous suggestion state that had hovered over me for a year or two. There was some reality to share and the odd misadventure story, which has the advantage of capturing people's attention. Being with family and relatives, there was plenty to talk about.

Anthony's funeral sat uncomfortably on the other end of the scale, being an unfortunate early stop at the end of a life of struggle. Mercifully, a heart attack was the stated cause of death, rather than anything long and painful. Anthony's teenage onset schizophrenia had placed a significant burden on him, and on his family, especially his late mother, who had passed away close to a year previously. Her death had most likely contributed to his decline and increasingly reclusive lifestyle.

Liz, as his eldest sister, gave a wonderfully well-balanced eulogy, giving light to playful early memories, with his enduring love of farm animals, whilst respectfully acknowledging his illness. At the same time, she gave voice to her brother's silent determination to remain independent and self-reliant to the end.

The occasion felt like a respectful send-off, for a man whose life had ended too early.

Day 3, Saturday 15th April

To Pevensey Bay

START	10.45, Shoreham
WIND	N, 12 – 22mph. 7 – 10 easterly, later
WEATHER	Mixed sun and cloud. 10°C. Dry
TIDE	Tide with me, max 0.8mph, till 1400.
SEA STATE	Slight
HAZARDS	Beachy Head
FINISH	Pevensey Bay SC, 18.15
DISTANCE	30 miles
SAILING HOURS	5½ hours (Seaford, for 2 hours)

My plan was to pass Beachy Head and travel on to Eastbourne. Beachy Head was a significant landmark, and a haunting reminder of my last visit, when going past on a practice trip. I would have to find out whether this day would bring a repeat of events.

Liz kindly drove me down to Shoreham, with my newly sprayed international orange coloured centreboard, all ready for a second start. Gareth and others were waiting at the sailing club, and Pamela came over to present what was considered an essential snack – a marmalade-filled hot cross bun. What kindness from so many people.

After all this attention, I assumed that the man shouting from the harbour wall as I headed out to sea, was wishing me luck. As the hook from his fishing line snagged in the rigging, I realised I had been a bit too eager to be pleased. Then Liz rang me to say that the tracker wasn't working, which required some further fiddling about. Both these events reminded me of the ease with which it is possible to get things wrong. Once I was unhooked from the line, and rehooked online, I was off.

I had a lunch rendezvous with my sister Maisie, at Seaford, and a link with Pevensey Bay Sailing club for landing at the end of the day. Pevensey Bay Sailing Club was the home to both Ron and Neil (Stick), the first and second laser circumnavigators, so for me was an essential stopping point. I was hoping that either Neil or Ron might be free to come down.

Ominously, this day being the 15th April, was the anniversary of the sinking of the Titanic. The date is only memorable since it was the same as Emily's birthday, my favourite (and only) daughter. A moderate northerly, veering to a weakening easterly, were more akin to stalling, rather than sinking conditions, and although it was chilly, there were plainly no icebergs to be seen. I figured the date was not too much of a bad omen.

Having said that, rounding Beachy Head on my practice trip, was one of my more memorable moments from April 2021. Back then, I had spent a comfortable night at Maisie's house in sunny Brighton, and was looking forward to a steady sail to Beachy Head, and then Eastbourne. But things did not go as smoothly as I had hoped.

Shortly after I set off, a thick fog slithered down over Rottingdean, concealing everything around me. The beat to my intended destination was mainly guided by the sound of waves breaking against the cliffs, indicating that I should tack away, back into the mire.

An unwelcome addition to the white silence, were the repeated long hoots of an approaching vessel, probably something to do with Newhaven, I figured. Attempts to call them up on channel 72 (since that was what I could remember from my radio training), went unanswered. I wasn't too sure what to do at that point. The fact the blasts were moving quite slowly in front of me, was mildly reassuring, though sailing in front of a large vessel, is generally a "no-no". The only back up plan I could think of, was to tack away at the last minute, should the ship appear out of the fog. I desperately hoped that would be sufficient.

Luckily, I didn't get to test it out. The tall black harbour wall was also moving quite slowly, when it suddenly stepped into view, but mercifully the unhappy horn was now coming from the other side, meaning I could turn my course to safety. Months later when I met up with Stick for a drink at Newhaven, one of the ferries came into the harbour, standing tall, way above the wall, and I said, "I'm glad I didn't see that up close".

The monotonous zig zag eastwards seemed to progress at a painfully slow pace. The prospect of a turning tide and failing light added to the chilling atmosphere. As the wind was fading, so a brush of blue washed into view up above, and to my delight a huge white cliff, like the face of a glacier, started to emerge from the mist. And then a red and white striped stick of Beachy Head lighthouse, innocently hovered at the murky junction of white and green, completing a portrait fit for a Turner painting.

However, there was a problem. The wind had died. Worse than that, the tide was turning and I wasn't sure where to land. The radio was unlikely to help given that line of sight signal does not work too well next to a cliff. For the second time in the day, I wasn't sure what to do. Maybe it was time to give the paddle a test run. It would definitely be better than bobbing about. The paddle proved invaluable. The prospect of being swept back to the Newhaven ferry path in the dark, was motivation enough to put in some decent strokes. An hour of sploshing, splashing and grunting, brought me to a land-able beach, and a great deal of relief. But my troubles were not over.

Hauling the boat (Lulu on this occasion) a few feet out of the water to safety, I spied prospective helpers on a walkway, gathered at the top of the slope. Crunching my way towards the huddle, it seemed they were engaged in something purposeful, which grew into what looked like practice CPR. Being slightly slow to unwind from the sea, and a little incredulous of the reality, meant that it took a few more steps to work out this was not practice. Oh dear. A poor gentleman who looked no older than 50, had collapsed and was receiving chest compressions.

"Can I help? Would you like me to take over?" I asked, as we had been trained to do.

"You're all wet," was the response, which was at least partly true, "but the ambulance has been called, and there is a code for the AED. It's just along the walkway over there."

With a fellow good Samaritan, we ran off to collect the lifesaving equipment from the wall. When we returned and fumbled our way into the container, we discovered there were no chest pads in the box, so not much use to the poor patient. Tobacco-stained fingers, a graze on his forehead, presumably from a fall, gave some clues as to what might have happened. "A heart attack most likely," I thought.

Fortunately for everyone, an ambulance soon arrived, and took over. Our crescent shaped crowd of impromptu helpers silently stood back in the twilight to digest the terrible scene – things were not looking good. Without saying so, we all hoped we had done our best for him.

Still in my wetsuit, with no concrete plan for eating or sleeping for the night, I figured I could do with some assistance myself. I took the plunge in breaking the silence. I tentatively asked, "Would anyone be able to lend me a hand moving my boat up the beach?" The response was instantaneous and unanimous, fuelled by the relief that some immediate help could be successfully provided to someone in need. All hands round the deck, and Lulu was safely parked up, in just a moment.

Back in April 2023, I was hoping to get a better view of Beachy Head, and an easier run to Eastbourne.

The first part to Seaford was quick, with a stiff offshore northerly giving flat seas, and a fast reach, exceeding eight miles an hour.

I was surprised to find myself getting cold, perhaps due to the speed spray. I noticed that cold can lead to less clear thinking, and poor decisions. "That could be a significant risk," I thought, "because it's really hard to warm up once I start to cool off. Something to keep an eye on."

"Would you like a coffee?" asked my sister Maisie.

"That would be amazing. A cappuccino would be great," I replied, and she went off to find supplies.

Meanwhile, my brother-in-law Pet opened the hamper and started to produce bread, cheese and all sorts, for lunch. We were keen to stay warm, so sheltered behind a low sea wall, out of the wind. The coffee, and family company, certainly helped.

There was chat about Maisie and Pet's upcoming (land-based) world tour. The massively extended holiday was a Maisie inspired 'work separation', having become tired of her engineering employment. Pet was less keen to leave his NHS physiotherapy job, so had taken a bit of persuasion to make the leap, but they were now pretty much ready to go. This travel thing is clearly a family tradition, rooted in my father's restless desire to see the world. He had taken us on many far-flung adventures in our youth, which I remembered very fondly.

My eldest son Sam had taken it upon himself to start producing video content for my embryonic YouTube channel.

"What do you make of Sam's videos?" I asked.

"I liked the one about getting ready, with Liz and Oli down at the club," said Maisie. "It was quite funny."

"Sam is looking for some ideas about engaging the audience even more," I added.

"How about a sweepstake for something? Maybe to guess when you will see your first seal?" suggested Pet.

Lawerence, my nephew, threw in some more ideas: "Or a whale. Or maybe a killer whale."

"Haven't the Orcas been causing some trouble with sailing yachts down at Gibraltar, with a boat even being sunk?" cautioned Maisie.

"Good suggestions. I'll see what Sam thinks. Luckily, I don't think those Orcas will be interested in my little tub. And besides, Gibraltar is a fair distance away."

"Heading to Gibraltar could be something to think about for your next challenge maybe?" taunted Pet.

"I'll think I will focus on getting round this one first, guys. It's still a very long way to go."

The prospect of fading wind turning onto the nose meant that I was keen to get going, and avoid a repeat of the Beachy Head stationary experience from two years previously. I shared my thanks, and we all packed up and parted ways.

Things started out well. Having warmed up with good food, great company, and sunshine, I was enjoying a crisp view of the white virginal looking seven sisters, undulating their way to Beachy Head. It was enough to bring out a burst of song – my very own Laser shanty to the tune of the Wellerman.

There was a man who man who went to sea,
he went to sea in his little dinghy,
to sail around the British Isles,
something like two thousand miles.

And the chorus

Hey Ho, this'll be fun,
especially when on the reach or the run.
One day when the sailing's done
he'll take his laser home.

Beachy Head lighthouse looked much clearer, but also smaller than last time. It is reassuring to make progress that feels better than before, because you think you are doing better. Past Eastbourne, and long past my previous landing spot, the wind was fading. I urged a threatening rain cloud to bring its downdraught closer, and push me along for the last mile or so. Gratifyingly, it worked. However, that too dried up, and the last hundred yards were paddle assisted, making a slightly undignified arrival at the home of circumnavigator Laser sailors. At least the landing was easy.

I had wondered whether the man standing on the shore might be Neil, but it turned out he was away in the US, visiting family. Instead, Ian was there, and then a gentle stream of mostly young club members trickled down the beach to lend a hand. It was great to see young people at a club, and I tried to give inspiration through my story, though I couldn't help feeling slightly overshadowed by my predecessors.

Pevensey Bay hosts national events, so the flat field behind the clubhouse is regularly turned into a camping spot. Ron's unwavering dedication to his tent, and I guess some of Neil's stories of sleeping rough, had meant this patch of green was unquestionably to be my destination, on the pretext that it was some kind of unwritten rule. The first grass cut of the year was lying on damp surfaces, meaning that my possessions would soon be covered in mushy green hair. I wasn't too sure I was liking the feel of this roughing-it guidance. A partly used dry tarpaulin was produced to lessen my discontent, and I was soon pitched up, and reluctantly sorted.

A lift to ASDA for supplies, and then a wander over to Sovereign Harbour Marina, to look for a suitable restaurant, was the food plan. I contacted Ron again to see if he would be able to join me for a chat or some food, but he said he was out for dinner himself.

It didn't seem reasonable to ask Maisie, or indeed another sister to come over from Hampshire, so it was just me and the pasta, suffering each other's company in the restaurant, feeling a little lonely. At least Emily was on the call list for tonight (which I had deliberately set up to help with disconnected feelings), and I knew that her cheery tone would lighten the mood. And it was her birthday.

* * *

Day 4, Sunday 16th April

START	10.00, Pevensey Bay SC
WIND	SE, 7–8mph, stopping then SW 7–10mph
WEATHER	Cloudy 11°C. Dry
TIDE	Against me, max 0.4mph till 13.00.
SEA STATE	Smooth to Slight
HAZARDS	Light wind
FINISH	Camber Sands, 16.50
DISTANCE	21 miles
SAILING HOURS	6 hours

My canvas – or whatever you call the material these days – covered slumber, was as good as could be expected. Having crawled through the zip entrances, and unravelled myself in the morning, I managed to fight off most of the grass cling-ons from my possessions.

Being welcomed so readily felt a major treat, and was a big shift from the practice trips. Back then, I had landed anonymously on strange shores, with a random tale of sailing somewhere – it just doesn't sound so good. At Pevensey, there was already a Sunday morning bustle around the club. I was given a home-made sandwich to help me on my way, which was carefully stowed for later. All packed up and stoked with my porridge cook up from the club kitchen, I was ready to depart. The final donation from the gathering sailors was a parting lift down the shingle, and into the pretty, still waters of Pevensey Bay.

There was just enough wind to keep the paddle in its place, as I edged along the South Coast shores towards Bexhill. Long suffering Liz soon gave me a ring to point out "the tracker isn't working". Such signals of failure can be annoying when unexpectedly pointed out, but I came to realise the importance of the tracker for safety reasons – Liz's primary concern. And as the journey progressed, I learnt of many people who would follow the thin lime-coloured line on their screens for entertainment, or to help with a rendezvous. On this occasion, I can't recall the technical problem, but it was usually something like not turning the tracker on properly, or failing to set off the tack tracker software. Either way, some fumbling around whilst on the water sorted things out.

It was time for another verse of my sea shanty: -

He went to see in his little dinghy
to raise some money for charity.
First there was Place2be,
then ASF and MND.

And the chorus

Hey Ho, this'll be fun,
especially when on the reach or the run.
One day when the sailing's done
he'll take his laser home.

Hastings Sailing Club weren't expecting me since I wasn't expecting them. They were busy with a race in 'not-very-much-wind' conditions. I was half drawn to join the floating procession, though found the temptations of the club café, run by Nicole and family, much more attractive.

It is surprising how effective the simple things in life can be when it comes to rebooting motivation – like rest, a chat, some food and drink. Lunched up and drawn by the allure of what looked like wind on the water, plus a turned tide, I was contemplating a stab at doubling my distance for the day to reach Rye. There was a struggling stream of sailing craft making their way uphill in fits and starts, like salmon heading up a river in breeding season. So, we got chatting.

"I don't really know," was my answer to the question, "where are you staying tonight?" This was true, since I did not know where I would land. "There is always camping."

"We are based at Rye. You could give us a ring if you get there," came the gentle response from Morris and Jan. They were derigging their catamaran. We exchanged numbers and I said I would call, not really believing that it would all fit together. Remarkably, it did.

The wind filled in, the sun came out, gently warming my back, and the laughter of 'The News Quiz' from Radio 4 warmed my soul, as I steadily rolled down to Camber Sands. When coming ashore, I practised the new landing technique that Liz had sourced, not that it was needed. I wanted to enhance my arrival skills, so this was an opportunity to test things out.

Camber Sands was the end point of my first practice trip, which had also ended in sunshine. On that occasion, the journey from Bracklesham had taken five sailing days, whereas a greater distance this time had taken four, which was reassuring. From here on, I was breaking new ground.

However, like last time, the tide was out. And Camber Sands is called Camber Sands for a good reason – because there is a lot of sand. This was going to be an Egyptian style slog of endless fender rolling, and wasted bodies, on the huge journey to the pinnacle of the shore. Surveying the scene, there were plenty of passers-by, who could potentially be captured by the Pharoah of foolish journeys, having just arrived from a foreign land.

I set to work practising my appeals sequence. "Excuse me. Do you think you can give me a hand with moving my boat up the beach?" followed by, "it is quite heavy so we will need more than one person". If necessary, this was backed up with "it would be easier if we get another pair of hands. Shall we ask that person over there?".

To avoid putting people off, I requested help covering 50 yards. I would then release my sore-fingered helpers (it was the weight of the gunwale on their hands that was the worst part). I would thank my helpers profusely, and we would part company. The sailor would set about eyeing up nearby sand roamers, who could be recruited into being my next Betty transport team.

One American family, intrigued by my round-the-UK challenge, finished off their stint with a cheerful quip to camera, "you're the best thing we found on the beach". That made me laugh.

What didn't make me laugh, was to find a square shaped sand furrow, following our trail. "What could that be?" I said. I was troubled to find it was the auto-bailer on the bottom of the boat, whose leading edge had been filled with yellow grit, and then bent back into a near-vertical position. The bailer had no intention of returning to the horizontal – not good for water flow or bailer functioning. Bother, that would need to be replaced somehow.

I rang Morris as had been suggested. To my absolute delight, he came down and whisked me off to his home in no time at all. The arrangements were heavenly. There were handy spots to hang out damp sailing gear, dangling from apple trees in the garden, a put-up in the conservatory, lasagne and salad for dinner plus a beer, charge points and Wi-Fi, plus friendly and welcoming chat. What more could I ask?

Morris and Jan liked to sail a catamaran together, which was a testament to good collaboration. (A spouse in the same boat is a make-or-break pairing. I am afraid the Andrew / Liz combination is better in separate craft.) Their hospitality was overwhelmingly wonderful, especially since we had only met that afternoon. Good sailor Samaritans indeed. The least I could do was to purchase a good bottle of wine, and send a thank you card later, a pattern that became a tradition throughout the trip. Morris and Jan had somehow set the tone in most splendid style.

DOVER

CHAPTER 3

A dash past Dover

North Foreland

Day 7

Margate

Whitstable

Kent

Deal

Dover

Day 6

Hythe

Camber Sands, Rye

Day 5

Hythe military practice area

ssex

Lydd ranges

Dungeness

Dungeness power station ☢

Day 5 to Hythe, Monday 17th April

START	09.45, Camber Sands
WIND	NE, 11–15mph rising to 16–21mph
WEATHER	Cloud/sun, 11°C. Dry
TIDE	With me, max 0.6mph, till 14.00
SEA STATE	Slight to moderate
HAZARDS	Dungeness tide. Military practice areas
LOCATION	Hythe, 15.45.
DISTANCE	21 miles.
SAILING HOURS	5 hours (1 hour at Dungeness)

Morris's departure gift, to add to the many generosities of the evening before, was a large bowl of porridge, plus a lift back to the beach. I was truly grateful.

Fortunately, high tide was approaching, making launching much easier than the long sand slog of yesterday, so the extra time taken to apply duct tape to the protruding auto-bailer, had a double purpose. Dungeness was new territory to me, so I was excited to press on, especially before the tide turned in early afternoon. It is a long, low, gravelly promontory, jutting out to sea like a knuckle, supporting windfarms, an iconic power station and the Lydd Firing Range, which was fortunately at peace.

Dungeness had also been a stopping point for cross-channel migrants, which was very newsworthy given the post-Brexit Conservative government's wish to control the flow of illegal entrants to the country. I wondered if I would see anything. Visions of rescuing a stranded asylum seeker drifted through my mind, though this was rather fanciful given there is barely enough room for me on the boat. Furthermore, I was travelling a few stone's throws from the shore, so would not add much value, if there was a call for action.

I kept going till I was past the power station, in order to set myself a target for the morning. The beat had been surprisingly tiring, and I had only managed nine miles in two and a half hours, so wondered how I would manage to get to Hythe, let alone Folkestone – another fanciful idea of mine.

I went to explore. Scrambling over a stony bank, there was a cluster of single-storey, mostly white dwellings, devoid of the usual trimmings like driveways, gardens and cul-de-sac paraphernalia. They looked as if they had been plonked on the promontory, or maybe just grown up there in some mutant way, deformed by their nuclear neighbour. Sea kale was dotted about the shingle, as if springing from nowhere, appearing equally out of place. Next to one property I found a disused railway sleeper, out of the wind and in the sun, forming a convenient seat for lunch and recuperation. Luckily, no alien fingers leant out of a window and tapped me disapprovingly on the shoulder.

A few stone's throws from me, was the power station. Dungeness B consisted of a series mostly grey boxes, huddled near the water's edge, with a chimney amongst the collection, as if designed by a lazy and unimaginative architect. As I later found out, during maintenance work in 2018, issues with the reactors were detected, which were beyond repair. Hence defuelling commenced immediately. However, the process takes a long time, and the station will continue to produce energy until 2028. Dungeness A ceased production in 2006. There has been regular mention in the news of the fading nuclear reactor stock, and here in front of me was a representation of this stark reality.

Back on the water, I made better progress than expected, with a fetch straight across towards Folkestone, a welcome relief from the endless tacking. The sky gradually closed in around the rectangular structures of Dungeness, as it shrunk into the horizon, as if someone were slowly turning the lights off.

The coastline bends in a long arc passing Lydd, to Great, then Littlestone, to Dymchurch before reaching Hythe, Sandgate and finally Folkestone. On the water, the thin grey coastline in front of me became bluey-green, then darker as I approached. Towns or lighter coloured buildings showed themselves earlier than the landscape details, which are only discernible in the last mile or two.

As I crept closer, thirst for the journey's end grew stronger, and the lure for a hot coffee started swilling around in my mind. Needless to say, goggle-eyed scanning of the thin green line in the distance didn't make me sail any faster, and had the unfortunate side effect of making time run slower. Every wave or lap of the water on the bow felt like it was slowing me down. It was like those long car journeys down to Cornwall, with the oft-repeated calls from the back seats, "are we nearly there yet?" to which replies of "not far now" offer faint, and only temporary reassurance.

On each leg of the journey, there is always the landing hazard to be negotiated. In addition, today, out there somewhere, was a military practice area.

"Was that the sound of a shell passing by? Could it have been a whistle of ordnance?" I wondered.

There was no splash that I could make out. Being shot on day five was certainly not part of my passage plan. Images of a large hole in the sail, or even worse, an end of trip military encounter, passed through my mind. "Sailor lost at sea in military training exercise" would have been a catchy headline, and would do wonders for my profile, but not so good for further progress.

Soon enough, the Hythe coastal pilot craft came out in throbbing pursuit of this misguided dinghy fool. The hull was black, thick, and wide with a rounded edge that looked suitable for a dodgem car, and maybe that was its purpose, though I

THE SHRINK IN THE DRINK

hoped not today. On top of that, sat a white bridge, decorated with orange patches and insect-like antennae, perhaps akin to an albino mutant wasp.

Out of the abdomen came a voice. I figured that was what was happening since the craft was directly behind me and I couldn't sail, and turn my head the required 180 degrees, without causing injury, that would challenge the mending potential of a sexagenarian. The buzz of the situation felt like the wasp had some important message, though I wasn't in the mood for stopping to have a chat.

"Don't blah de blah me," said the voice.

"What?"

"Don't sail de blah me."

"Sorry, I can't hear you. Where do I have to go?" I tried.

That was a mistake since I just got more incomprehensible burble. Anyway, I got the general gist that I was to go the other way, so I had to tack away from the shore. Bother.

This journey was definitely getting longer, and I was sure the boat was going slower, especially when on the tack away from the land – I was back on the beat heading to Dover, not that I could see anything other than grey cloud. So, when the wasp hovered off to the horizon, I thought it had done its duty, and I tacked back to the more enticing green of Kent. In the blink of an eye, the wasp was back. This time I could figure out what was being said.

"Don't go below me."

Ah, that made a bit more sense. On the Navionics chart, I remembered there was a line parallel to the shore, forming the outer edge of the box, marking the map boundary of the practice area, so this must be where I was being taken.

Wanting an end to the journey I ventured, "how far do I have to go?"; perhaps "are we nearly there yet?" would have been better, but I doubt anyone would have found it funny.

The usual "blur de blah, sir, far do la" kind of reply was no good to me.

I did wonder why, oh why, do they not carry a megaphone – £200,000 of boat and no megaphone to communicate to their key audience, seems a bit of an oversight. It's not as if there was anyone else out there to put in a complaint about excessive noise. Anyway, I needed to be grateful for guidance away from danger, and a safe passage so far. Yes, I needed to focus on that. And sure enough, when it finally seemed that the wasp had returned to its water nest, I figured I could head in.

Having not yet mastered landing navigation, I came in to the beach at what I thought was 'any old place', probably in Hythe. The plan would be to figure out where I was, and then move the boat if necessary. There was little shore break, since the wind had dimmed with the day, but the steep shingle beach looked a struggle. Walking uphill is like trudging through fresh snow. Each step you take going upwards involves a lot of painful effort, accompanied by simultaneous slipping back, pointlessly pushing your foothold down to the sea.

However, when I did eventually reach the top of the huge bank, a reconnaissance trip revealed that not only had I landed in Hythe, but I had also landed right next to the Hythe and Saltwood Sailing Club. What a stroke of luck. And many thanks to the guidance of the military pilot boat, for nudging me along the coast, whether intended or not. I even felt a bit guilty for being annoyed earlier.

The beach was abandoned save for a huddle of youths clad in school uniform, some with pulled up skirts, in a defiant attempt to remain cool. No doubt they were having an after-school chillout session. It was the right weather for that anyway. I could ask for their help, but I would need to be careful. One refusal from a group member, and the whole lot would turn away. So having moved the rig, foils and luggage up to a flatter section, I approached a taller standing male, to beg a lift for the hull. With a topping of intro about my sailing journey, we were away. Thank you very much. Then they returned to their chilly chillout grouping. Not one member of the party offered further check-ins or traveller queries, as is the adolescent way.

The next mission was boat storage, and the sailing club seemed the obvious choice. The first person to appear was a dry robe clad male, who looked like he was heading in for a swim. It turned out he was none other than the Rear Commodore of the club. What? I could not believe my luck. James very kindly postponed his unnecessarily refreshing dip, and in no time, boat was in boat park, sailor was through shower, and phone call to friend had taken place.

Despite my lack of notice, Claire very kindly drove over from Deal. She transported me back to domestic luxury, delicious sausage and mash, a glorious catch up, followed by a large comfortable bed. As a fellow medic and Uni mate, she was also on the cusp of retirement from the NHS, so likewise travelling to a new life. I hoped that our shared memories and shared friendships would endure long into the future.

Miraculously, everything seemed to have worked out for the day. An excessive wind forecast for the morrow meant it was to be a no-sailing day, so I could relax. I was tired and soon fell asleep in clean, white, contented comfort.

* * *

Tuesday 18th April

The forecast in the morning hadn't changed my decision to stay on solid ground. I was also meeting Clara for a radio interview at the sailing club, and needed to do a bit of boat maintenance. Claire was heading in a different direction, so a train back towards Hythe and stroll along the seafront to the sailing club, was in order.

Yesterday, James had told me that the beach was in fact closed, which I had unwittingly ignored, perhaps explaining why it was so deserted. Now was my chance to find out what was going on. There were diggers on the beach. Not delicate sandcastle building types, but huge great quarry style trucks, and monster caterpillar diggers, the likes of which would send most prepubertal boys into a spasm of delight. One orange-clad hi-vis workman, who was defending the seashore shuffle from erring promenaders, was happy to take a break for a chat.

"We are moving the shingle back up the beach," was the explanation.

"Is that because it gets washed along by the waves?"

"Yeah. But we weren't here last year so there is more to move this year. It's a big job."

He said it was OK to park my boat temporarily on the launching ramp, for a few Clara-requested photos. Further, the battalion of machines should have moved onto another groyne area by the end of the day, so I would be free to launch in the morning.

Radio interviews are normally churned out in ten minutes, so meeting in person seemed a strange luxury. Clara was not just doing a piece for Radio Kent. She was also at the tail end of her journalistic studies, and wanted to use our edited conversation as part of her final viva. I was touched by this, and wanted to give her all the time and encouragement I could muster. The finished product was broadcast on several stations including Radio Kent, Surrey and Guernsey. More importantly I later learned that Clara had passed. Well done, Clara.

Tides were constantly confusing, to me at least. Somewhere along the Kent coastline, the flood tide changes direction, namely flowing to the east around Dungeness, but flowing to the west around Dover. It is best to refer to someone else for an explanation since I am sure I could do a good job of messing it up. The upshot was that the stonking spring tides past Dover, now ran in my favour. They would be chalking up an impressive four miles per hour tomorrow, if I could make it to the port by around midday. The heavy NE breeze was a downside, but corner #1 had to be rounded at some stage, and those tides looked inviting.

I recall looking at the swim tracks when I was preparing for our relay Channel swim, back in 2017 (with my sister Maisie as part of the team). These tracks had a terrifying huge 'U' shape, dangling down to Cherbourg on the spring tides, and instead, a delicate saucer shaped dip, if it were a neap tide. Terrifying because if you got your timing wrong, you could end up splashing about, further from your destination than from whence you had started, which is not exactly fun when swimming in a cold sea.

Wandering around town was my chosen hotel-finding technique, on this occasion. I must have been at a loose end, since accommodation was usually sourced by a few minutes' search on booking.com, topped up with Airbnb if needed, selecting by location and then price. My choice of the "Swan" did raise an eyebrow or two at the sailing club later. There were stories of street brawls outside the hotel, with tales of furniture being thrown through windows. When I got there though, it didn't look too bad, but I did take the precaution of smiling at folks when I went through the bar in the evening.

I felt surprisingly at home when back at the club for an evening gathering. There were sailors, and a collection of racket ball players, who were stopping over for a meal and beer. Grant, who ran the morning café, providing drinks and snacks to the warming windsurfers and occasional interviewees, was back at the club offering food. Adrian, the Commodore, was about, and gave some helpful advice for my onward travels, notably the Dover port authority phone number. Adrian had also contributed to Clara's interview earlier, kind of like being my friend for the day! I also met Duncan and Pete who had been playing rackets, and then there was Martin from the Netherlands with his impeccable English.

It's interesting to see how different sailing clubs evolve, and create a social presence in the community. Despite being a relatively small club, an embracing approach to other social groups seemed to have created an entity bigger than itself.

Day 6, Wednesday 19ᵗʰ April

To Deal

START	08.20, Hythe
WIND	NE, 17–26mph, rising to 22–32mph
WEATHER	Cloudy, with the sun later. Dry
TIDE	0.5mph against till 10.00. Then Max 4.1mph with me past Dover and 1.7 to Deal.
SEA STATE	Slight to moderate. Rough at times
HAZARDS	Dover Port and sea state off the Western Arm
FINISH	Deal, 14.00
DISTANCE	20 miles
SAILING HOURS	4¼ hours (30 & 45 mins rests)

I muddled through my overnight oats for breakfast in the room. I was feeling apprehensive about corner #1 with its strong tides, stiff winds and port authorities, not to mention all the shipping. There were stories of lumpy seas off the Western Arm of the port, adding to my worries. The White Cliffs of Dover don't provide many stopping points either, should things start to go wrong.

It was early, and especially early for me. The beach was deserted. It was also flatter than it had been, and the diggers had gone, having completed their adjustment work. James suddenly appeared, almost unrecognisable in his work clothes, and gave me a very welcome hand to move things closer to the water. And then I was off.

It was an easy launch, but that was about it for easy. Out of the shelter of the headland near Hythe, the wind became stronger and waves stiffer, meaning that the first hour or so seemed to take an age. It was cold and exhausting. I wasn't even at Folkestone yet.

I decided to take a break on a suitable-looking beach (Lower Leas Coastal Country Park). It was safe enough to land, but the steepness of the shingle meant that I could neither get a foot hold, nor stop the boat from sliding back into the waves. This felt impossible, and wasn't looking like the refreshing stop I had hoped it would be. Good fortune favours the foolish, and two lady dog walkers came over to lend a critical hand on the painter, so that a proper stop could be affected. Thank goodness. I did wonder how I was ever going to make it past Dover, let alone to Deal.

The Port Authority were expecting me to call, 30 minutes before reaching the Western Arm, so they could send out a pilot boat. I was flattered by their potential attentions. But at the rate I had travelled so far, Dover would be hours away, I reckoned. I wasn't going to pack it in after just an hour of sailing, and this did not look like a good spot to stop, so off I went, back into the swelling sea.

Out towards the looming black wall of Folkestone I went, and then off into The Channel, venturing a couple of miles further from shore, into the turning tide. Dirty grey cliffs transformed to gleaming white, as the sun broke through. Even the brown sea began to sparkle with white wave tops. Things were looking up.

To my cautious pleasure, I was definitely moving faster, though still feeling suspicious of the benefits of the tide.

"I better ring the Port Authority," I thought, and happily managed to get through.

"We will send someone over shortly," came the reply.

But no one came. It didn't matter though, since my friendly tide did a fine job of swooshing me past the port, whilst I kept an eagle eyed lookout for those great big ferries, and other large ships that were coming in. I was slightly disappointed not to receive an escort since that would bring a sense of self-importance. "Never mind," I thought. "Better safe, than a celebrity."

I do recall looking behind me at the white topped waves littered all over The Channel, and thinking "I'm not sure I would want to be out in that", and then turning forwards again to realise that I was. You see, it doesn't look so bad when you are staring at the waves being blown towards you, since the light doesn't show so many of them. And the focus is on the next one as it approaches so that you can pick the best course, up and over the rise, trying to make sure the boat keeps moving.

I began to think of it as lazy sailing, or sailing economically. Neil would say, "sail at 70%", and I would say, "I'm not racing". A long period on the beat can cause blisters, and blisters in the soiled sea water of the English coast could bring infections and then more trouble. For me, two hands on the tiller, with the main sheet cleated in, worked quite well. It provided relief from skin pressure, but also meant that different muscles could be used, reducing the risk of fatigue or cramp.

I better get back to the sailing, since St Margarets Bay was approaching really quickly. I was in danger of being washed round the corner, so had to bear away onto a reach, and ended up storming into the shore, exceeding nine miles per hour at times. Whoa, what fun.

St Margarets Bay is a steep sided cove, which looks like a giant has taken a large scoop out of the surrounding cliffs, to help with access to the sea. There was shelter from the wind, a café and clear skies, giving plenty of warming sunshine. I sat down with my coffee and selection of snacks in the sun, to heat up like a lizard, before reluctantly slithering back onto the sea.

Fortunately, Deal didn't take long. The cliffs faded past Kingsdown, as the land flattened out at Walmer. Eagerly looking out for the white sticks of a sailing club, prior to the pier at Deal, I came into the shingle shore to find a waiting party of people.

Evie, Clare, Jim and Martin were all there to lend a hand, having been tipped off by Simon the Commodore, from my email the day before. Simon had replied (unlike Hythe), so I was hoping for something, but this was delightful. It turned out that Martin Styles was father to Harry, not of music and film fame, but of the UKLA – the national Laser sailor organisation – so part of a pedigree.

Downs Sailing Club has a unique system of sledges, to help haul craft over the shingle, an idea I shared with other clubs. Unfortunately, no one else was minded to take it up. It worked a treat, and the boat was soon parked up and safely tied down, ready for more wind tomorrow. What a delightful reception and how wonderfully welcoming. I was so relieved to be around corner #1, and really chuffed at the same time. It felt like I was getting somewhere.

A quick shower, some stuff management and a lift to the station, meant that I was home by 7.30pm. Yes, home. I had decided to take a day off. How lovely it was to see Liz and share a dinner together, relaxing in the glow of home comforts and the day's success.

Thursday 20th April

No-sailing day.

I was doing my best to take my own advice – not to go out in a force 7. Yesterday had been a bit marginal, but I had managed. Today looked worse, and pushing my luck, two days in a row seemed unwise. After all, I was not in a rush, and building confidence, rather than breaking it, felt sensible.

Mowing the lawn, some laundry, some admin and gathering the pre-ordered replacement auto-bailer, filled the morning before heading back down to the far end of Kent.

This time, Graeme picked me up from the station since Claire was away. A top-quality home-made fish pie was on the menu, finished off with dessert, amply satisfying my swollen appetite.

After dinner, Graeme pulled out an old photo album. It was not one of those big coffee table sized things, with six photos to a page held down with sticky plastic, like the ones my mother painstakingly populated. It was a tall, thin book type, the width of a photograph which when opened, displayed the pictures attached to the covers, so you could run your finger down the images, flipping them up to see what was stored on the back. The tactile journey through times gone by, was so evocative, so different from the modern smartphone show and tell. As well as the "who's that?" and "I remember so and so", there was the inevitable commentary about hair styles and outfits, which mark out the fashion of nearly four decades ago.

Smartphones have increased the numbers of photos exponentially, and have massively enhanced the quality. It is not just the number of pixels that has increased, but also people's readiness to be frozen. Those poses from the 1980s were much more random or disengaged. I guess we have simply had more practice, and I think it shows.

One photo of Ed appeared. I was hoping to catch up with him on the other side of the Thames Estuary, despite an absence of contact for several years. I was delighted that a smart snap of the snap, texted over to him, produced a cheery response in no time. Times have changed!!

* * *

Day 7, Friday 21st April

To Whitstable

START	10.00, Deal
WIND	SE/E, 12–18mph
WEATHER	Cloudy, 8–11°C. Light rain
TIDE	Against me, max 1.5mph till 11.00. Again at 14.00.
SEA STATE	Sight to moderate
HAZARDS	Opposing tide most of the way
FINISH	Whitstable Yacht Club, 15.30
DISTANCE	31 miles
SAILING HOURS	5½ hours

Dodging the rain and the puddles, I popped into a local newsagent to collect lunch supplies before heading over to the sailing club. Whilst other sailing clubs might be squeezed into a space like a dent on the line of townscape, Downs Sailing Club sat low, confident and new, largely alone on the beach front. Other dwellings held back on the other side of the road. A neat garden gate gave access to the compound, rather than rusty rickety fences that so often guard a club property. The venue doubles as a bridge club location, and no doubt other non-sailing activities during the week, a testament to good sharing and good caring.

Despite the drippy weather, I was honoured to find Martin and others waiting to provide launch assistance. I was still feeling blown away by people's enthusiasm, for helping with my crazy adventure. After packing up and bidding farewell, I went sliding down to the sea. In fact, so effective were the sledges that I was almost run over by my own boat.

Out past Ramsgate and then on to Broadstairs, the sea went a bit wild. I thought it was meant to be slack tide about that time, but the surface was a mess. The wind strength certainly did not justify the rolling rampage that was tossing me about. Apart from the physical discomfort, there is the uncertainty of what is happening that makes things worse, not knowing what the sea is going to do next. I was mighty glad I was not trying to land at Broadstairs since that looked chaotic, and I wondered how the sailing club usually coped with the waves. And then it all effortlessly smoothed out, when I made it round to Margate. "What was all the fuss about," I wondered? I guess it must have been the tides fighting it out around the north corner of Kent, wondering which way to turn.

A grey view of Margate's ferris wheel whilst I snatched a slow sail sandwich, was not enough to tempt me ashore, so on I went down to Whitstable. At one point in my planning, I had thought about heading straight across to Clacton from Margate, but I could see no need to overdo it just now.

A steady tail wind and rolling seas gave a good opportunity to practise some downwind surfing. I even thought I was beginning to get the hang of it.

I wasn't getting the hang of the landing location thing though. In my rookie way, I was seduced by a row of dinghy masts next to a promontory, thus matching my map description of Whitstable. After I had stopped, I realised I was making an unnecessary acquaintance with Hampton Pier Yacht Club, and not Whitstable

Yacht Club at all. I was three miles short of my destination. It didn't look much like a yacht club either, and it was definitely shut. Urghh! I was getting tired.

I had heard back from Uni mates Jane and Patrick who were at Whitstable, and very kindly offered a place to stay. I had not heard back from Whitstable Yacht Club so did not think anyone would be there. Tankerton Sailing Club also flashed its chandlery at me, enticing me to come over, but I was having none of it this time. I headed on round the back of a harbour entrance to my journey's end, to see what I would find.

Much to my surprise, Amy was shouting and waving from the harbour wall and then ran down to unfold a trolley, ready for my landing on the white shell shore. Andy, the Commodore, then Oli the Vice Commodore, came down with warm smiles and camera-ready head of state style handshakes across the boat, making it feel like an official reception. To add to the surreal atmosphere, I got a call from the security service, whilst I was derigging on the launching ramp in front of the clubhouse. Liz had found the club webcam, so was watching my every move as I was chatting to her on the phone! How cool is that?

Whitstable Yacht Club is smarter than many. There were plenty of dinghies around the launching ramp, separated from the building by a bustling shore trail. An awning provided seated shelter for a path-side café. There were trainers and topper trainees, a big black locked shed where I could store Betty alongside the safety boats, but there were no yachts.

However, there were showers and more welcomes, including a beer in hand at the bar, from Steve. Steve had messaged me on Facebook to acknowledge my destination intention, but I apologised since I had missed it. Being a fellow Laser (or maybe we should say ILCA these days) sailor, he had several focussed questions to ask. Not only that, but Steve had been one of the most persistent followers of the journey so far, and would continue to be throughout the journey. His knowledge of sailing and appreciation of the challenge, coupled with a dry gentle humour, made for a great connection.

Jane and Patrick soon arrived and whisked me off to The Whitstable Oyster Company restaurant to enjoy a delicious dinner, including statutory oysters.

Whitstable is well known for its oysters with the metal rack farms, and shell stacks obviously visible from the shore front. The company claims to be one of the oldest businesses in Europe, with Romans shipping back the slippery delicacy to their home land. In the 1850s the company was transporting up to 80 million oysters to London each year, with the shellfish becoming food for the poor.

The early 20th century saw a significant decline in production following bad weather, pollution, disease and the introduction of the competing prawn cocktail. The company shrunk to only one employee in the mid-1970s. Reinvigoration, reinvestment and the centuries-old freehold of the oyster beds, has seen production increase in the last 20 years, and the Whitstable native oyster becoming the food of the wealthy.

Saturday 22nd April

It was another no-sailing day since there was insufficient wind to cross the Thames Estuary, and I didn't fancy getting stuck in the middle. Little did I know what was to come.

Untroubled by the future, and blessed by pleasant, warm spring weather meant that sitting on the balcony enjoying breakfast and catch-up conversation was a great way to start the day.

A stroll along the shore later was punctuated by a detour up a few steps to the NCI hut. I had heard about the National Coastwatch Institution (NCI) and was curious to find out more. Three older men stood in a small lounge-sized hut in good condition, with windows facing the sea and charts laid out on the table. Binoculars were in plentiful supply.

NCI has a tag line of "Eyes along the coast" and that is exactly what the NCI does. If they spot someone in trouble, they will call the coastguard. Stations are dotted along the coastline but only as far north as Wales and Yorkshire. My guess is that many stations were run by the coastguard before its rationalisation, and staff likewise had evolved across to volunteer for the NCI. The team had seen me come by yesterday, but luckily nothing needed to be done. I planned to keep it that way.

I joined the afternoon race session at the yacht club, which was fun. To give myself half a chance, I emptied out the entire contents of the boat, but then, determined to do badly, I took a wrong turn after the start. In the end I came in fourth, which I thought was respectable. Steve was out. He managed to edge past me using some cunning low wind technique to make use of the waves, which were not much bigger than a ripple. "Impressive," I said. His later explanation sounded simple enough but putting it into practice, as always, was another matter!

I was delighted to introduce Jane and Patrick to the yacht club, for they had not ventured in previously. They were apprehensively excited about the idea of signing up to a level 1 dinghy course, so making it into the building and meeting people felt like a great first step. And meet people we did.

There was an open mic evening on that night. Andrew the commodore from yesterday had now turned into the lead drummer and event organiser. There was Fef who seemed to know everybody. She kindly followed me all the way around the rest of my journey, on Facebook, posting encouraging comments all the way. We met a Jenny and Kerry, and then another Patrick, and later on a Mike and Clodagh. Mike and Clodagh have a place in Salcombe, and I caught up with them in Devon later in the journey, a lovely connection between one end of the journey and another. But no Steve. I hoped he was OK.

There was a nautical chart of the southern part of the Thames Estuary on the bar wall, which inevitably led to pointing assisted advice from local sailors.

"It's a big patch of water with lots of hazards, like sandbanks and shipping lanes," I was warned.

"There are a couple of windfarms which could be useful as waypoints. You are not supposed to go through them though," so I was told.

"Also, there are a few groups of Maunsell Forts to look out for."

I had not heard of those. I was intrigued.

Named after their designer, Guy Maunsell, the forts are army or navy armed towers, built in the Thames and Mersey estuaries during the Second World War, to help defend the United Kingdom. The forts were decommissioned in the late 1950s, but six sets of forts remain in the Thames Estuary, though in a state of disrepair. One of these (at Rough Sands near Harwich) is managed by the unrecognised Principality of Sealand, under the care of the Bates family who have claimed it as their nation state, an inventive use of military detritus!

We also met Christian, who nervously awaited the last open mic slot. He would be singing for the first time. We did our best to settle his nerves with warm words and warm beer, and we were all delighted that it went well. Appropriately the first song was "I'm a believer" by The Monkees. The second was "Love Shack" by the B52s and we sang along, only then realising the tune was incredibly lewd, particularly the way Christian sang it. He did a great job and everyone loved it.

Mike, the Rear Commodore, who was organising the event, produced a collection bucket which filled with donations as the evening progressed, gathering £150 for Motor Neurone Disease.

I was invited to say a few words about fundraising for the trip, holding on to the microphone for a moment, feeling like an imposter. It was amazing to see a different face of a sailing club, metamorphosing at night, made from the same people of the day. Sails and smooth craft transformed into a musical hot house, jiving to the beat of home-made musicians, bursting into song right next to you. What a great evening.

* * *

CHAPTER 4

I love Clacton

∗ ∗ ∗

Day 8, Sunday 23rd April

To Clacton, only just though

START	09.30, Whitstable Yacht Club
WIND	Southerly 15–24 mph. NW 9–15 mph at 16.00
WEATHER	Thick cloud, 11°C. Rain most of the day
TIDE	Flood tide (going W, 1.3mph, till 15.00, then E)
SEA STATE	Slight to moderate
HAZARDS	Tide, shipping, Maunsell forts, sandbanks, getting lost
FINISH	Gunfleet SC, Clacton, 19.30
DISTANCE	30 miles
SAILING HOURS	10 hours

It's not something I thought I would hear myself saying, but its official, "I love Clacton". I have never been there. It was famous to me as the town supporting the first UKIP MP in the form of Douglas Carswell, thus being at the wrong end of my political spectrum. Furthermore, in his book 'Land on my right', my Laser around the UK predecessor Ron, said he had an item stolen from his boat when he landed there, and together these pieces of information, made me wary. But boy, oh boy was I pleased to get to Clacton.

My navigational errors for the day were as follows:

1. Thinking a navy Maunsell Fort looked like an army one
2. Relying on line of sight when the rain clouds obstruct your view
3. Thinking I could see windfarms in the clouds, when it was just rain
4. Thinking the tracker gives real time information and had no delays

5. Not trusting my compass
6. Assuming the forecast would mean that the wind
   would do as instructed

And the list goes on. And on.

Things started well enough. Harry, yesterday's young race leader, came to join me for the first leg, out to the nearest windfarm. I had very much hoped sailors would join me on parts of my journey, so was really pleased to have Harry's company. He was clearly a sailing competent, and reassured me about family approval and radio usage. He even helped fix my compass mounting, since my GoPro Heath Robinson style attachment snapped, just before leaving. Today was a day when I figured I would need a compass. We set off in high spirits under low grey skies, with the warm glow of Whitstable still washing through my limbs.

When we reached the windfarm, I watched and waited to check that Harry was safely on his way back. Instructed not to go through the farm, I turned right to find the Knock John Maunsell Fort which was my next waypoint.

Some two hours into the journey I committed error #1. Coming across a zombie gathering of War of the Worlds type structures eerily parked in the middle of the Thames, was too much excitement for me to appreciate their true identity. They were the Shivering Sands army forts, and looked nothing like the Knock John navy fort, which was the intended object of my desires. Hence, I was about six miles short of where I thought I was.

Sandbars came and went, showing themselves with browner seas and sharper waves. I dutifully followed the compass bearing slightly to the east to compensate for the incoming tide pushing me westwards to Southend and London. Error #2 was to think

I should be able to see where I was, despite the rain. Prompted by impatience and encouraged by error #2, I kept staring ahead, and thought I could see the windfarm near Clacton. But it was just error #3, a figment of my imagination – the rain cloud equivalent of a mirage. Perhaps it should be called a 'Cumulus Fatuus' whereby the shifting grey lumps of humourless vapour, form the blurred grey lines of turbines.

Two hours further on, I was getting a bit tired. The clouds had lifted a little and I could see chimneys and a town.

"Could that be Southend?" I wondered. "It better not be because I'm not meant to be anywhere near there, and if so, I have been washed miles off course."

Just then Patrick and Jayne rang to give a navigational update, as was previously requested. They confirmed that it was most likely to be Southend, according to the tracker, and said that I should turn right to get back on course. Keeping an eye on my live position, the message was "more right", and then a bit more, and a bit more, so right I went. None of us realised error #4 of my ways: namely that the tracker information was delayed in the electronic clouds, so we were being guided by history. This is not so useful if you are about to get lost in the middle of the Thames Estuary.

Liz, the tracker supervisor, rang shortly afterwards. She had snatched a brief break from sailing, as well as running the Laser open event at Papercourt, normally organised by myself. She was ringing to try and answer my "can you help?" messages. She fell straight into the same tracker trap, sealing my fate, repeating the advice "go a bit further right".

The problem was, I had turned so far right, that I was heading back to Whitstable.

The compass was now reading 130 degrees, as opposed to the intended 10, which did not make sense. I was on a fetch heading into the wind as opposed to running with it. According to the forecast, I did not think the wind would shift that much, but I thought it best to follow instructions from my help team.

"Maybe there is something wrong with the compass," I thought. In reality, the gadget was working fine, but I wasn't. I was staring straight at error #5, which was to disbelieve the bearing.

And then the wind died. I had unwisely put faith in the forecast (error #6) and failed to factor in the vagaries of rain clouds when it comes to the wind (error #7). Things were not going well. I was bobbing about in the middle of the estuary, miles from land with little idea as to where I was, at a time when I thought I should have reached my destination.

Now that I was pretty much stationary, it was a lot easier to use the phone. In frustration, I sent a family WhatsApp to say "I am stuck". Then I rang Oli, my middle son, since I thought he might reply. He did.

"The tracker doesn't seem to be moving," he said. "You look like you are in the middle of the sea".

I was. He was worried.

Then error # 8 dawned on me – I had not set the tracker to last for long enough, so it had effectively signed off its duty for the day, courtesy of my overoptimistic short shift allowance. Now I was really alone.

It was time to have a think, so I thoughtfully pulled out a sandwich from my Tupperware box and ate it. That seemed to work. Oh, and at last I applied some good navigational sense by checking my actual location and direction using Navionics, something I should have tried a lot earlier – error #9, if anyone is still counting. So, it was out with the paddle and on with the journey.

Two hours later and still paddling, I was making painfully slow progress, and had resigned myself to camping on the nearest shore. I hadn't realised at the time, but I was looking at Foulness. Foulness is an ex-military practice area and is marshy, as well as supplied with a good dose of unexploded ordnance, so not the best landing spot. That could have been error # BOOM, and game over. Either way, a meet up with Ed and all those home comforts was clearly off the cards. It was now eight hours into the journey. According to information I gathered later, I was in roughly the same place I had been four hours ago, so an unhappy average of zero miles per hour.

Dissatisfied with the day, I thought I would paddle on a bit further before dark, to that 'shore over there' (Dengie Nature Reserve) past 'this river' (River Crouch). There were a few ripples on the water, and a light north-westerly started to fill in, but I was still hardly making any progress despite all the paddling. This didn't make sense either, since I thought the tide should be helping by now, moving us towards Clacton. When consulting with a buoy in the river channel, I was informed that the dratted tide was still flowing against me. Error # 10 was to misunderstand the impact of the myriad red and blue tidal arrows on my app. To be fair to myself, the Thames is pretty complicated with rivers, side channels and sandbanks, running in all manner of directions, washed in and out of the great big funnel that is the estuary. Either way, a change of course was needed, so I tacked around.

In the building breeze, bustled along by the tide (or was it the flow of the river?) I had now accelerated from 1.5mph to a magnificent 7mph over ground, according to my newfound navigational friend. All this because of a simple change of direction. There were nine miles to travel with maybe two hours of daylight remaining, so miraculously Clacton could be possible. With the prospect of avoiding camping, and the possibility of a proper meal, there was only one realistic option, which was to press on.

As Clacton came into view, so did the elusive windfarm, now dressed with a rainbow in the falling light. Chris, one of my squash mates, was my call contact that evening. He rang as scheduled at 7pm, dutifully counting out the groynes that needed to be passed in order to reach Gunfleet Sailing Club. Some last-minute paddling was required as the wind faded with the descending sunlight, but I had made it to land. At last.

A father of family beachgoers gave me a hand to move boat and bits, up to the blue carpet of the club landing strip. "That will have to do for the night," I said.

It mattered not that there was no one there. It mattered little that there had been no reply from the club, the home of Johnno Dunnett, the solo windsurfing circumnavigator. It mattered not that I was tired. It mattered not that the boat was left unprotected on the beach. Because I had made it to Clacton. It's official. I love Clacton.

* * *

Day 9, Monday 24ᵗʰ April

To Felixstowe Ferries

START	11.00, Clacton
WIND	NW, 10–16 mph
WEATHER	9°C, cloudy, dry
TIDE	1.2mph against me till 15.00
SEA STATE	Slight to moderate
HAZARDS	River entrance sandbar. Shipping
FINISH	Felixstowe Ferries SC, 14.45
DISTANCE	17 miles
SAILING HOURS	3½ hours

Ed had picked me up from the empty roadside, in the thick black dark, and drove me back to his house. It could have been a chariot, or heavenly horse drawn coach for all I knew, because I was being rescued from a Clacton bench having escaped from the jaws of a soggy marshland campsite. Warm dry wheels, going to a warm dry white house, was a dream come true.

Camilla joined us as I was indulged in a chicken dinner, whilst we all caught up about families and our three age-matched children, before retiring to a wonderfully spacious bedroom. What an incredible treat. I was sorry I could not stay for longer. It seemed a little discourteous to stop for such a short while.

However, undeterred by my estuary escapade and fuelled by porridge, a good forecast, plus a plan for the evening, I gratefully accepted a lift back to Gunfleet Sailing Club. Noone was at the club (I never did receive a reply), but the boat and all my possessions had remained untouched on the blue carpet, so my fretting was without consequence.

Ed was due to travel to Iceland for some birdwatching, a keen interest of his. Cameras already at the ready, he kindly headed to a Walton-on-the-Naze, a well-known twitcher location, to see if he could spot a lesser numbered white winged Laser fly by. He sent over a great photo of the rare migrating bird in full flight over the water, looking small and vulnerable against a backdrop of a towering wind farm.

It was an easy journey compared to the day before and just as well. No shipping appeared, so none were avoided. Brown waters were smooth enough, making for steady going, and the wind didn't give up until it wasn't needed. The only slight hazard was negotiating the sandbar at the mouth of the River Deben, which had moved since Navionics had marked its location.

I landed on the slipway at Felixstowe Ferries Sailing Club. That nasty crunching sound of fibreglass shifting over gravel-covered concrete, encouraged me to make haste and find a suitable landing vehicle. Apologies to whoever's Laser trolley I borrowed – it was the one furthest to the left on the other side of the path, on a bit of a grass slope – but unfortunately, I had no reply from the club. Thank you very much for the loan, since it was just the ticket.

Although it was Monday, none of the local cafes were open to offer a warm up brew. Instead, I found a glassed porch that wasn't locked, capturing the half-hearted spring sun, just enough to provide bonus heat, whilst I finished changing.

Walking back to the boat I realised my glasses were not on my face. More to the point, they were still in my shoe, the usual stowage location. I must have been cold since, unlike the princess and the pea (reference to the Hans Christian Andersen fairy tale of 1835, in which a prince identifies a princess, because she can feel a pea, even though it is covered by 20 mattresses and 20 featherbeds), I had not noticed the spectacles under my sole. Like the pea, fortunately my glasses were unharmed.

Like the princess, no sooner had I made a phone wish, than all of a sudden, Prince Colin strode out from behind a building. He was accompanied by a dark shiny steed, and a hamper charged with coffee and cake, to rescue me from my delicate state.

"How on earth did you manage that?" I asked in awe.

"I was out for a walk with Willow, and was looking out for you. I thought you might come in at the North beach, but since you didn't, here was the most likely spot. The car is parked just around the corner, so it all worked out nicely."

It was relatively early so there was much more time for conversation. We talked of families and friends, and people we knew through school.

Colin had recovered from a potentially life-threatening illness having been lifted back into health by the NHS, an encouraging story of success which swims against the current tide of relentless public sector gloom. It was also a salutary reminder of the value of our beloved institution, and of the importance of good health, both of which were pertinent unspoken messages to me.

I ended up staying for two nights, because I only made it to Aldeburgh / Thorpeness the following day. Martha created a lovely warm atmosphere, being effortlessly thoughtful and reassuringly validating at every turn, enough to make you feel at home in a moment.

In fact, the second night I was on my own, having been tutored into producing a 'throw it together' oven meal for one. Willow also trusted me to take him for a walk. Willow being a young Labrador was full of energy, the likes of which a middle-aged man can only marvel at. A cool still evening, passing through meadow and wood, across stream, along dry footpath, made for a perfect relaxing backdrop. My evening call was from Sarah at the Hope service who, likewise, has an amazing touch, making everyone feel special with her cheery and interested manner. Thus, everything combined to make a sublime Suffolk evening.

I did have one moment of panic though. Playing the usual game of 'throw the soggy yellow ball for very speedy dog to find', was going fine till I hastily slung the thing into a field of buttercups. I couldn't see the object of Willow's desires and nor could he. Oh dear. After what seemed like an age of both man and dog, zig zagging in some sort of unsystematic wiggle across the yellow dusted field, I began to give up searching, and started to think of excuses, and methods of recompense. It was not a big thing I was sure, but it would spoil the atmosphere at my new home, especially since I already felt so much in debt to kindness. Whilst sinking into my reverie of solace, Willow had continued with his noble toil, and sure enough, came rushing over to catch me in my fall, with one retrieved toy. Phew. "I think I will hang on to that till we get back," I said. Willow seemed to understand. Order was restored and everyone was satisfied.

* * *

Day 10, Tuesday 25th April

To Thorpeness

START	10.30, Felixstowe Ferries
WIND	N/NE, 10–17mph. It stopped with the rain.
WEATHER	Sunny. Sharp rain cloud at midday. 7–9°C
TIDE	Against me, max 1.8mph till 15.00
SEA STATE	Slight to moderate
HAZARDS	Exiting the Deben. Opposing tide. Rain
FINISH	Thorpeness, 15.45
DISTANCE	17 miles
SAILING HOURS	5¼ hours

Returning to the mouth of the Deben included a mini tour. We stopped off at the Woodbridge Tidal Mill Museum, which is the only remaining functioning mill of its kind in the UK. The tall white boarded building, with a Dutch style red tile roof, looked in good shape from the outside, but I learnt that river silt has been causing problems for its inner workings. The exit mill race had become clogged up, meaning that the vertical water drop required to run the mill wheel, was insufficient. Volunteers at the charitable trust were planning to jet wash mud out of the race to allow operations to return to normal, which sounded like a great community effort. Flour to the people perhaps?

I really enjoyed hearing about local issues such as concern about low Suffolk rainfall potentially affecting its breadbasket status. Or windfarm connections to the grid, requiring unnecessary land damage – there are a lot of windfarms along the East coast.

John, the local harbour master, came down for the launch. He had seen 80 or so years in the local area, so had plenty more stories to tell. He knew Colin as well. He was wearing a red jacket and white sailor's cap, which looked good against large brushes of blue sky overhead.

I was keen to get going to avoid the incoming tide of the Deben, so was really pleased with all the excellent help. I was soon away.

A couple of hours into the journey, I had a call from Liz. Whilst I hoped this might be for a chat or general encouragement, instead it was a small dose of bad news. "The tracker isn't working," soon followed by, "I've got a work call in a minute, so I'll leave you to sort it out."

Oh bother. Maybe I had not turned it on. The tracker is tied onto the lower section of the mast. Shuffling forwards on a wobbly Laser is distinctly uncomfortable. The wriggle is made more challenging by trying to see whether a faint flashing green light is on or off, and even worse for fumbling through the waterproof case to identify the on / off button. I thought I had got it working, but truculently decided to leave it for now, and see if Liz called again. I could have checked it via the website – which was a later custom – but I wanted to get on with sailing. It was a worry that tracker errors were still occurring, given their significant consequences from two days ago (error #8), but unfortunately there was only me to blame.

The tide was also annoying me, which seemed to be forever in the wrong direction. I began to realise that the tide times get later through the week, but get earlier as you go north meaning that if I kept going at the same rate, I might be permanently stuck in an opposing tide cycle.

Orford Ness was made famous in my mind, for its longshore drift, as told in Geography lessons, so I was interested to see it in reality. Even though nature had invited me to take a long hard look at the real thing, deliberately creating a pause as I was at the knuckle of this enormous bent finger, I wasn't exactly getting a positive vibe. Knowing that it is the largest vegetated shingle spit in Europe wasn't bringing me joy either. Because, after a short but stiff rain cloud squall, the wind died and I had my first experience of going backwards. Being sloshed about on the disturbed sea, as the waves were breaking on the steep shingle beach, was uncomfortable as well as irritating.

What's more, there were seals on the shore. Big fat grey ones which would bark from their flint hamper in a mocking way, or from time-to-time roll into the water and start to swim over. Being unfamiliar with the creatures I wasn't too sure what their intent might be, but my attempts to get out of the way were in vain. I had seen my first seal at least. And the winner (and only entrant to the seal spotting sweepstake) was James. Well done, James. Sam gave him a special laseraroundtheUK T shirt. (This includes a diagram of a person, presumably me, falling out of a laser. Thanks, Sam.)

Finally, nature threw me some wind, and I beat my way to Thorpeness, which was some comfort after all the frustrations. Being greeted by Martha at the Mere – an inland lake, previously connected to the sea – was even better. On the way back, I was given my second mini tour of the day. We went past the 'house in the clouds', a strange looking repurposed water tower, which was thicker at the top than the bottom. I thought it could have been an extra in the movie "Up". Martha's lilting tour guiding, and soothing reassurances in response to my frustrations of the day, completed the operation of lifting my mood out of the mire. It would be a shame to have to move on.

◦ ◦ ◦

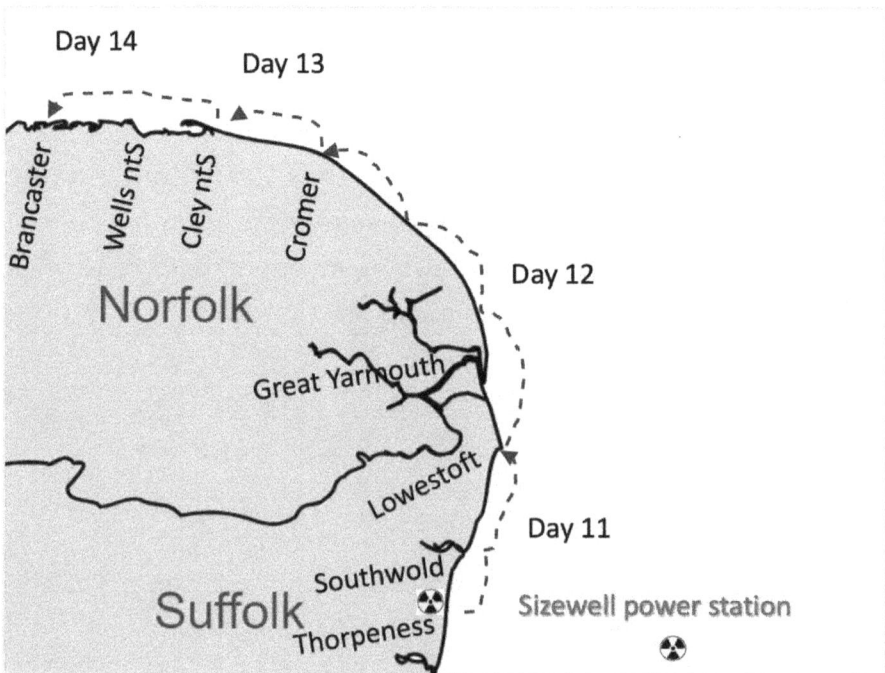

CHAPTER 5

Feeling big and feeling small

Day 11, Wednesday 26th April

To Lowestoft, which is past the 10% mark. Whoopee!

START	11.15, Thorpeness
WIND	SE 9–11mph rising to 10–14mph
WEATHER	Cloudy, 9°C. Dry
TIDE	Against me, max 1.25mph till 16.00
SEA STATE	Slight
HAZARDS	
FINISH	Lowestoft, 17.00
DISTANCE	22 miles
SAILING HOURS	4¾ hours. 1 hour, Southwold

Time on the land can be more interesting than time on the sea, and this was one of those days. Forecast light winds and opposing tides gave me an excuse for a late start. There was also a radio interview to fit in, sharing my newfound Suffolk specific knowledge. The late start also gave me an opportunity to extend my faffing, by doing a time-lapse video of my faffing, namely loading the boat with gear. In line with advice from my content director Sam, I was collecting different types of shot to see if we could scale the dizzying heights of at least 30 YouTube subscribers!

It had been a slow journey past Sizewell B reactor, another on the nuclear power station UK tour (this one is not being decommissioned till 2035, however, and a Sizewell C is yet to be built, in case you were getting confused).

"You must be Andrew," said the young man, just after I landed on Southwold beach.

Strangers, speaking to me as if I were an old friend, was an unfamiliar side effect of putting your life on-the-line, online. The sailing club Commodore had emailed to say that someone might try and meet me, so I soon worked out what was going on.

Josh and I had a nice slow amble into town for a coffee. We shared details of our respective journeys to date. Josh had finished schooling but did not see the need for university, preferring to take up maritime studies and avoid student debt. Having been in the business of looking after young people's mental health, I was always interested in life choices of the young, and Josh was happy to educate me. He loved working at sea and was gaining a maritime qualification alongside employment, hoping to move into in the merchant navy, once studies were complete. It sounded like a really positive option for him, and I bade him well on his travels. He returned the compliment by helping with my relaunch, stepping into the sea in his trainers, to make sure I was safely on my way.

The Royal Norfolk and Suffolk Yacht Club is not in Norfolk and not much in Suffolk, but it does look like a yacht club. It is a large three-storey white-fronted building, keeping a watchful eye over the marina, with spacious meeting rooms, catering and accommodation, standing a little apart from the less prosperous town of Lowestoft. Hence a little bit of a step up from a single storey, creaky sailing club. Having begged my soggy way in, to grab a free shower, I was strongly advised not to leave my boat on the beach where I had parked it, for fear of vandalism. The beach did not seem too bad, and marinas were an anathema to me, so I was sceptical, but in the end persuadable, so round to the marina I went.

Apart from flukey winds at the entrance, I was relieved to find the landing was easy. Having moored up, I discovered one downside of this arrangement, when unloading my stuff from the back of the boat. Leaning over from the pontoon to rummage through a moving luggage hatch, and retrieve my precious belongings, was definitely uncomfortable. I was also being watched. Watched by the ever present cold dark jealous water, who had no intention of returning any dropped items. Hence, unpacking carefully was required.

I seemed to manage OK, till I realised I had lost my earphones. Twenty minutes' panic was enough to find them where they had been deposited, unwisely parked on the pontoon, ready for a nudge into the deep dark sea.

Meeting one person in the yacht club led to another, and soon enough I had a free room on the second floor, overlooking the marina and a clear view of my delicate dinghy lined up next to mighty motor craft. Looking down on the scene, I suddenly felt small, and the self-imposed challenge, even bigger. It was cold, imposing and unfamiliar out there, and warm and welcoming inside, so maybe I was unwise as well.

There was a bar and a bar menu available, together with encouraging chat from the Commodore. Things were getting better. To top it off, overheard conversation led to a meeting with Mark, who turned out to be the boyfriend of Fran. Fran was someone I had contacted as part of my research for the trip. She had completed a wayfarer circumnavigation, which she had called "Fran's big adventure". She had been really helpful and supportive. What a coincidence to meet her partner. Mark was in the area working with wind farms, so was a fair way from his Salcombe home. It was lovely to chat and make the connections. I was looking forward to seeing Mark and Fran in a few months' time in South Devon, and wished him well on his travels.

A quick dash to ASDA for supplies was required before bed, ready for an early rise in the morning. It was getting late so Lorna, who worked at the bar, loaned me a front door key. She cautioned that the bar area was alarmed, and advised me not to disturb the Commodore who would be sleeping in the room next to mine. Simples.

Except it wasn't. The key didn't fit.

"This could be problematic," I thought.

It was a dark night and the wind was getting ready for a chilly blow for tomorrow, seeping its cool fingers through my garments, more suitable for a supermarket dash than a night under the stars. The welcoming glow from the yacht club interior had definitely turned to a rejecting chill. I felt exposed.

The boat was stored in the secure marina so I could not even access my tent, should things get desperate. There was some gravel on the ground, so throwing stones at a window could be an option, though a risky one. It was probably only the Commodore left in the building, and I did not know which window to target, and visions of broken glass scattered over an irate host, put me off the idea. I would have to find a way in.

As I edged around the building I was no longer feeling like a celebrated sailor, and more like an unlikely imposter, or perhaps an amateur burglar. Or maybe a student out beyond curfew, trying to avoid the headmaster's wrath for a late return to his room.

I tried this window and that door until "hooray", the key fitted and I was in. But now what? Stairs led up to a small landing and then another locked door. The metal object in my hand was having nothing to do with going further. It was definitely warmer indoors, and sleeping on the floor could be possible, but not very desirable.

I tried another door which gave to a lobby, and through the glass panels, I could see a large red carpeted dining room with tables made up for a meal. "Could this area be alarmed?" I wondered. "What did Lorna say again?" Putting on my cat burglar persona all ready to steal the silver, I eased the door open, waiting for the calamity of sound. But cacophony came there none. I was safe. And then up the main stairs to my room in a feline flash.

One last thing before bed. "Ah yes, I'm sure that is the sound of the Commodore snoring in the room next door," I purred. I could rest easy.

* * *

Day 12, Thursday 27th April

To Cromer

START	07.30, Lowestoft
WIND	SE, 13–17, increasing to SE 16–24 mph
WEATHER	Cloudy 9–11°C
TIDE	1.7mph with me till 10.00, then 1.6mph
SEA STATE	Moderate
HAZARDS	Tide. Not many towns. Cold
FINISH	Cromer, 16.30
DISTANCE	40 miles
SAILING HOURS	7 hours, with 2 hours of rest

Having tasted the delights of a following tide on the previous afternoon, with a near doubling of speed, I was keen to catch the early flow. Hence, a twilight start was needed. There was a decent tail wind so a chance to put in some miles.

Overnight oats in my water bottle was not very solid in the morning, so heating it up would be useful. However, schoolboy sailor tried to warm it in the kettle, forgetting that the milk burns, and porridge sticks to the pan if heated too fast. The bad smell coming from my makeshift cooking pot, hinted at a problem. A good ten minutes of scraping and prodding managed to remove the worst of the brown mess on the flat element. The porridge wasn't cooked either, so it was a general cooking failure. I hoped no one would notice. Either way, "I won't be doing that again", I thought.

Setting off at 07.30, the usual thirty minutes later than planned, I headed out onto a comfortable run with following wind and following tide. I made it to Great Yarmouth in about an hour, travelling at seven or so mph over ground, which was really encouraging.

I was now in Norfolk with the coast offering mostly low-lying dunes or sandy beach, meaning I could stop more or less anywhere. Knowing that the tide would turn at ten o'clock, I was keen to press on. I sailed past Caister-on-Sea, Hemsby and then just past Winterton-on-Sea, where I stopped for a rest. I had travelled more than 18 miles, more than my previous day's distance, completed before yesterday's launch time! What a difference the conditions can make.

Sailing dead downwind is a bit warmer than other tacks, since the relative wind speed is lower, but it is uncomfortable. It is the most unstable point of sail, meaning you have to sit in the middle of the boat in a crouched but ready position, to keep balance. The boat tips and rolls as it goes over a wave, creating even more of an unsettled feeling. At times I would try to practise downwind surfing technique, but that exacerbates the imbalance, meaning that I did not put up with it for long. Besides, I was not sure I was adding much speed, and it definitely increases the risk of falling out, so an early return to a steadier state was the norm.

It is also possible to bury the nose in the back of the upcoming wave, making the Laser 'submarine'. It pops up again provided you are not going too fast (in which case a pitch pole is possible – like tumbling over the handlebars of a bicycle, if something jams in the front wheel, though with a softer landing). Burying the nose does mean that the cockpit gets filled with water. I liked to avoid that, because the boat goes slower with its extra

15 kilograms of load. What's more, with cockpit full, the not-so-dry-bag tends to fill up with water, potentially soaking my possessions. Either way, you have to keep concentrating, which makes the sailing quite tiring.

I found a peaceful landing spot with a gap in the dunes which served as a windbreak. A happy hour was spent enjoying the solitude and bursts of sunshine, as I warmed up and fuelled up. The empty green of the flat Norfolk farmland spread on as far as the eye could see, as did the thin yellow strip of sandy beach, marking a line between one green and another. Sometimes it is great to be alone with the world.

The wind was picking up as the forecast predicted. The tide had turned against me, so the next section was likely to be slower and rougher, so I thought I would try putting in a Ron style reef for the sail. It didn't work too well since it unwound from the mast after about 20 minutes. The launch was also a bit messy, probably because I thought it was going to be straightforward. "Something I need to work on," I thought. The cockpit was awash with water and would not drain very well, which I learned later, was because of gravel in the mechanism. All of this meant that the next couple of hours were even more tiring and uncomfortable. Quite exhausted and wondering whether I would make it to Cromer, I stopped at Cart Gap, short of Happisburgh.

On the shore, I met Dave and Anna who were out for a windy beach walk. Noticing the MNDA logo on my sail led to inquiries about the journey and fund-raising efforts. Dave had lost a niece to Motor Neurone Disease at what must have been a very young age, so he was particularly keen to offer support. Not only did he make a generous donation, he also put me in touch with a 'Jock Gordon' from Skye, and with a name like that, I was dying to meet him. It never ceases to amaze me, how generous people can be, even after a fleeting meeting.

More warming up was needed. The sun had been covered by cloud, and Norfolk green had turned to flat and desolate grey, so a building was needed. The only one about was a RNLI shop, which luckily has inside space, and supplies for provisioning. The shop was manned by Julia who kindly allowed me to drip indoors and chat, whilst tucking into one hot drink after another, plus a pile of filling snacks.

That was just enough to see me on my way again. I was not feeling very enthusiastic about setting sail. Apologies to Cart Gap, but it is not exactly a commercial centre, or key crossroads, so not a great place to stay. The thought "don't waste the wind", together with a tide that would soon turn in my favour, meant that there was not enough reason to stop, so onwards I needed to go.

It was another two hours before the pier at Cromer came into view. The good progress from the morning had been restored with the tide, and the wind had dropped a little, making the final hour more comfortable. The final thirty minutes can sometimes drag on interminably, but although it was dull and overcast, the pier did not seem to take too long to welcome me to a suitable landing spot. I had definitely had enough for the day.

The shore was a mix of beach and pebbles, and I picked the least wavy spot behind a groyne, to make landfall. The tired struggle to manoeuvre the boat up above the high tide line, came with a helping hand from a fisherman. Dry clothing reluctantly passed over cold clammy skin, whilst I sat with my back to the wind. I was definitely more interested in capturing some warmth, or avoiding a pebble in the pants scenario, rather than worrying about exposing indecency to an occasional disinterested passer-by. At last, everything was done. Forty miles was my greatest daily distance travelled so far. I was knackered, and a lot more focussed on meeting up with Guy, than any form of celebration. Guy, my brother-in-law, had been keeping an eye on progress, and we had been messaging.

Cromer is on a hill, a rare divergence from the flat tradition of Norfolk. Steps from the beach were laid out a bit like a grand staircase in the entrance to a country home. Although requiring more effort, at least it involved different muscles, my feet were on the dry ground and the vertical toil would help with warming up.

The town had some energy about it, and I was sure would look good in the sunshine. I was amused by a pub audaciously advertising its food with the notice "Fat people are harder to kidnap. Stay safe, eat lots here", thus crashing a whole collection of offences into a few short words.

Guy was driving over to find me. We agreed on a rendezvous opposite the Co-op, where I had stopped for a mini shop, including 'thank you in advance' gifts. I was really pleased to see him. We headed over to Holt for my first fish and chip dinner. And then on to Guy and Jacqui's nest for a rest. I was tired.

Day 13, Friday 28ᵗʰ April

To Cley next the Sea

START	14.40, Cromer
WIND	NW, 14–22 mph
WEATHER	Cloudy and fog. 10°C
TIDE	Against me 1.4mph till 17.00.
SEA STATE	Slight
HAZARDS	Fog, and few landing landmarks
FINISH	Cley next the Sea, 17.30
DISTANCE	11 miles
SAILING HOURS	3 hours

The key sailing question over the next couple of days, was "What to do about the Wash?". It is not as far as the Thames Estuary, there are fewer sandbanks and less tide, but I dearly wanted to avoid a repeat of my legion of estuary errors. And yet, there was a temptation to try and dash across from the top of Norfolk to Skegness, if the conditions were right.

For Friday, conditions definitely weren't right. A north-westerly breeze would make the crossing an impossibly long beat, and the now traditionally opposing tide would make it even harder. And as it turned out, there was fog. Thick gooey fog.

There was also the problem of where to land. There were plenty of spots I could come ashore safely. However, they were often on a long beach, or miles from an accessible road, both of which could involve many hours of trudge at the beginning and end of the day, to get nowhere.

Wells-next-the-Sea was an example of this, because it is not next to the sea. Instead, it is a long way inland up a tidal inlet. There is a Wells Sailing Club which is still further inland. A sailing club is usually an indicator of a good place to stop, but the website shows boats with motors on the back, and no sign of any sails, so perhaps not the best spot.

With the help of Guy and Jacqui's local knowledge, we pored over Ordnance Survey maps, spread out amongst the breakfast toast and tea cups, to work out the most viable options. I was contemplating having a rest day, but in the end, we figured that some miles were better than none, when it comes to the chess game of crossing The Wash. So back to Cromer we went.

Local fishermen Ryan and Dan were pleased to have their photo taken, as official members of the boat launching team, and I was pleased to have their help.

When the fog descended, I hugged the shoreline, and was just about able to see and hear land when I came close, which was sufficient for navigation. The sailing itself was not complicated, but my first taste of serious fog put me off going to Wells, and it did make landing more complicated.

Approaching what I thought might be Cley, there was no pier landmark, or in fact any distinctive features at all. It was like Orford Ness with a long homogenous shingle bank, stretching as far as the eye could not see, bordered by a fog bank. By now the tide had turned and I was scooting along the straight stony shore, thinking that if I missed my stop, it would be a long sail back to somewhere. So, I rang Liz. Astonishingly she picked up. And even better, Liz was able to look up my location, and, the tracker was showing real time information.

"I think you have just passed it," she said.

"Cripes," I exclaimed, and "er, thanks very much," closely followed by a quick gybe around. I could just make out a red roof above the shingle ridge. The roof belonged to the Cley Beach car park toilets. When viewing them from above on Google Maps, the building looked like it has been randomly plonked on an empty seafront. It was the only construction for miles. Either way, it was where I needed to be, thank goodness, and thanks to my impromptu navigator, Liz.

Walking inland to my rendezvous spot involved going down a few feet off the banks by the road, marking the edge of reclaimed land from the 17th century. Like Wells-next-the-Sea, Cley (pronounced Cleye from Anglo-Saxon times because of the abundance of Clay) was once one of the busiest sea ports in the country, trading grain, fish and malt with the Netherlands. It was hard to imagine its former life, looking at the quiet flint stoned village and fine church. Siltation of the tidal channels got the better of both ports over a century ago, and now Cley has only a tentative connection to the sea.

This is probably just as well, given climate change and rising sea levels. Some quayside properties in Wells were damaged when existing sea defences from the 1970s were overwhelmed by a storm surge in 2013. In fact, large areas of Norfolk and neighbouring Lincolnshire are considered at risk over the next 20 years, including Great Yarmouth and land surrounding the Wash, all the way to Cambridge. It's quite a worry.

I ended up staying three nights with Guy and Jacqui. My stops were in an arc, with their property forming the centre of the long side of an ellipse, so hopefully not too burdensome on the transport front. Guy was married to my eldest sister Fiona, but they divorced and Guy had remarried some 20 years previously. They moved to Norfolk near to where Jacqui grew up. It was lovely to catch up with family news, and hear stories I had not learnt about before.

Having a base, and the luxury of a top floor room with ensuite bathroom, was an absolute delight. Waiting for conditions to ripen for the day also meant a couple of late starts and a chance to enjoy the daytime, which all felt like a holiday.

I did my best to help with catering, but it was difficult, such was the hospitality. Much to my culinary delight, there was chicken for dinner, and then tofu the following night, with porridge AND toast for breakfast, all of which added up to a feel of a top-class hotel, without the bills.

Despite my induction into Norfolk life, I was being a lousy local, struggling to pronounce Cley correctly, repeatedly falling back into the 'Clay' version. Luckily, I was guided back on to an appropriate phonetic path, on a regular basis. (Speaking of which, how on earth did anyone manage to turn the letters Happisburgh, which I had passed the day before, into the sound Haysborough?) I did my best to add to the local news with a further radio interview. Red tulips were out, marking the spring season, and the sun was gaining more strength, which I was hoping might add more warmth to my travels.

In the sporting news, the Red Roses managed to win the women's Six Nations rugby tournament for the record-breaking fifth time. The men's team had not been quite so successful, and Eddie Jones came to the end of his coaching tenure!

* * *

Day 14, Saturday 29th April

To Brancaster

START	13.45, Cley next the Sea
WIND	E, 10–14mph
WEATHER	Sunny!!! And warmish, 13°C
TIDE	Against me 1.4mph till 16.00
SEA STATE	Slight
HAZARDS	No significant hazards
FINISH	Brancaster, 17.30
DISTANCE	18 miles
SAILING HOURS	3¾ hours

Sam came up to Norfolk for the weekend with friends Sophie and Mills. They joined Jacqui and Guy in supporting the launch at (or near) Cley. The sun had come out, transforming the beach from its grey grind of the day before, to a mighty freckled arm, marshalling the sea along its line, preventing its advance over the land.

The boat was being guarded by an elderly couple. Not quite protected I suppose, since Rob and Sarah were using the upturned hull as a handy back rest, whilst they soaked up a few recharging rays, on a break from their walk. They were very understanding about the prospect of having their newfound seat thrown into the sea, and stopped for a chat and photo shoot before travelling onwards.

Having had a surfer's education, Sophie gave me a hand, counting the waves, looking out for a suitable gap. With her help, I managed to slide straight off the shingle onto the sea without getting my feet wet – very satisfying.

That kind of set the tone for the day. I had a pleasant meander along the Norfolk coast, past Wells-next-the-Sea (which I couldn't see), the sand dunes of Scolt Head Nature Reserve, and then on to Brancaster.

I did see some overcrowded clinker style boats hovering about near the beaches at Scolt Head. For a while I thought these must be refugees trying to land. However, a moment's reflection made me realise that a) the next land mass was a LONG way away, b) the boats were staying a distance from the shore, rather than getting closer, and c) when I came near, the occupants carried on staring inland, paying no attention to my good self. The collections of mostly black sausage shapes on the sand gave the answer. The boaters were seal watching. Slightly affronted by my lack of celebrity status, I sailed on, turning the boat's nose, and mine, away from the tourists.

This time, the diggers on the beach were children, and not monster shingle shufflers like at Hythe. The kids were enjoying the afternoon sun whilst engaging in the essential happy developmental stage of excavating pointless holes in the sand, free from the guiding gaze of a parent. Meanwhile, I was very pleased to have the assistance of Sam and friends to help move my boat up the beach, so that I could continue with my very own, and more grown-up, pointless activity the following day.

Then off to the Jolly Sailor we all went, for a beer or two, in the afternoon sun. In search of more video content, Sam insisted on taking embarrassing photos of his dad in front of the pub sign, no doubt as on-going payback for all that dad discomfort handed out over the years. No one else seemed bothered, and indeed no one else seemed to notice that I was sitting in the pub wearing full sailing gear and buoyancy aid. This is obviously normal in the UK. It was a fun afternoon and felt like a mini party. What an enjoyable day.

CHAPTER 6

Pursued by seals

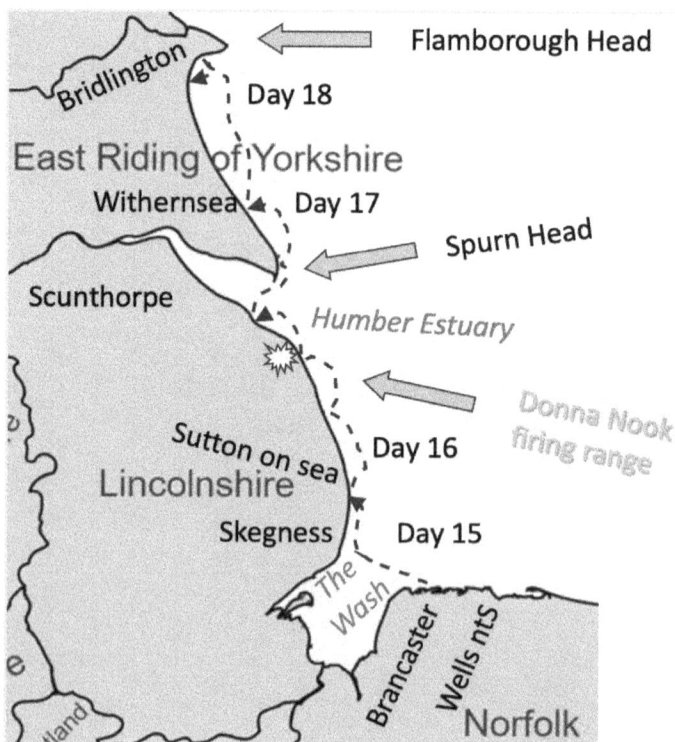

Flamborough Head

Bridlington

Day 18

East Riding of Yorkshire

Withernsea   Day 17

Spurn Head

Scunthorpe

Humber Estuary

Donna Nook
firing range

Sutton on sea   Day 16

Lincolnshire

Skegness   Day 15

The Wash

Brancaster

Wells ntS

Norfolk

CHAPTER 6

Day 15, Sunday 30th April

To Sutton on Sea

START	10.50, Brancaster
WIND	S/SE, 11–18mph
WEATHER	Sun and cloud, rising to 16°C. Dry
TIDE	N from 16.00, but mostly E – W
SEA STATE	Slight
HAZARDS	Wind dying. Stuck in the Wash
FINISH	Sutton on Sea, 17.30
DISTANCE	27 miles
SAILING HOURS	5¾ hours (45 min stop)

Looking out across the waters of the Wash, I felt trepidation with the spectre of the Thames hanging over me. Stepping out into the unknown with no sight of 'Skeggy' felt foolhardy once more. The forecast was for a similar but lighter wind direction compared to Day 8, and getting stuck in the middle again was not an attractive prospect. "Would the wind hold up?" I wondered. At least there was less chance of rain, so the risk of pressure disruption (as happened on the way to Clacton), was lower. However, I had come to realise that feelings pass when out on the sea. The task in hand takes over, with fears and worries quickly fading into the distance. It's best to keep moving. So, I did.

It was a wrench leaving Jacqui and Guy motherland. I had been so well looked after in an interested and unfussy way, which I really appreciated. It was a joy to be part of their household for a while, to feel part of their world, to be part of Norfolk, and to give them the pleasure of being part of my journey. Parting is such sweet sorrow.

With a following wind, and slight seas, the sailing was comfortable and I started out making nearly 6mph, a respectable cruising speed in a laser. The yellow line of Brancaster beach grew smaller, and with the miles, lost its colour, then turned into a hazy blue grey slither, before finally disappearing. Low lying Lincolnshire wasn't going to rear its hazy head any time soon, so out in the middle I could see nothing but blue, and bluey grey all around me. I was completely alone.

This time, I stuck to my compass bearing. This time Guy and Jacqui rang, and the tracker was up to date and properly set. This time navigational advice fitted with my own estimation, and no U-turns were instigated. This time, when the wind softened, it didn't die and although speed dropped, I was still moving. This time there was no need to paddle.

It was time for another verse of my sea shanty: -

The boat he sailed was made for a lake.
He began to think it was a mistake.
And then one day a wave did come
and tried to wash him off by gum

And the chorus

Hey Ho, this'll be fun,
especially when on the reach or the run.
One day when the sailing's done
he'll take his laser home.

Skegness was soon to be voted the worst seaside place to stay in the UK, which sounds pretty harsh. I had also heard a radio programme about seafront hotels being dedicated to temporary housing for refugees. The situation meant that the seafront was populated by listless men, agonizingly waiting for their place to shuffle forwards, on a faceless list. Not a happy scene. The town looked OK from the sea (and so did Clacton). Either way, I wasn't stopping there since there were more wind miles in the day, and the tide was due to turn in my favour.

My anticlockwise route round the UK was chosen, partly since I could stop more or less anywhere for a break, which was useful given my novice status. Grasping this opportunity, I stopped at Seathorne, next to Ingoldmells Beach, for a Wash-crossing celebratory coffee. The beach front was fairly full despite the spring season, with families tucking into plenty of anti-slimming devices.

My son Sam is a fan of holiday parks and told me later that many of the leading companies are based in the area, much to his excitement.

Skegness Butlins was just up the road as well, and soon came into view as I sailed on up the coast. It provided plenty of beach-based kid screamers, possibly aiming their voice in my direction as I passed by, but definitely letting off steam before returning to school. "Good for them," I thought.

Sutton on Sea was quieter all round, and was a satisfying 27 miles on from Brancaster, without incurring too much sailor pain. My list of local friends and suitable sailing clubs had run dry, so I was back to searching for local hotels. I found Dave's Airbnb. It was about 20 minutes' walk from the shore. It was a smartly appointed property in a cul-de sac, decorated in bright white, with a cosy bedroom and shared bathroom. Just the ticket and not too expensive.

Heading back to the High Street, bollards were decorated with coronation-themed knitted attire, such as crowns and flowers, reminding us of the upcoming regal event.

I was still in good spirits but getting peckish. Being Sunday most of the restaurants had closed except for a Chinese, whose menu had whetted my appetite. Unfortunately, they only took cash and I didn't have any. With dipping energy levels and rising hunger, I could feel a sense of humour failure coming on. There were plenty of cash machines, but none that would give notes without a card, and I didn't fancy the thirty-minute round trip to collect one. Someone suggested the Spar would do cashback and they did, so I picked up some purchases and went to the till to pay with my phone.

"Sorry, we can't do cashback without a card" was the reply.

"Really?" was all I could muster, and just as well, since anything else would have been unfair and unfriendly.

Slumping in despair, I grumbled out of the shop, wondering what to do. Things were not going well.

Remembering the maxim 'Everything is better after one beer', it seemed sensible to try my luck in the Bacchus Hotel nearby. A young and enthusiastic barman served my drink. Much to my surprise, he agreed to provide cashback, which delivered sufficient change to see me through the evening. I was delighted and told him so, thanking him profusely. At last, I could find some food, and restore a sense of physiological balance. It was off to the Chinese for some chop suey, and then on to a seafront park bench in the dark, to quietly munch through my reward, keeping out of the cooling wind. I was happy and content.

I resolved to keep some bank notes to hand, to avoid getting caught out again.

※ ※ ※

Day 16, Monday 1st May 2023

To the Humber

START	09.30, Sutton on Sea
WIND	NW, veering NE 9–14 mph. Then nothing
WEATHER	Cloudy, 13°C. Rain around midday
TIDE	Mostly into the Humber
SEA STATE	Smooth
HAZARDS	No wind. The Humber. Firing range surprise
FINISH	Humbermouth YC, 17.30
DISTANCE	20 miles
SAILING HOURS	8 hours

1st May was the start of my second calendar month. April had been fairly staccato, with several breaks, allowing me to ease my way into things, and learn from mistakes. Sixteen per cent of the journey was now complete, which maybe doesn't sound much, but to me it was a lot. I usually think 10% feels like a significant landmark on a long cycle ride, with 20% ticking excitement too, but then miles bring less emotional pleasure till you get to 50%. After that, everything changes again.

In my Southerner mind, places like East Anglia, then Grimsby and Hull sounded far away. The Humber also featured as a significant geographical landmark with strong tides, and shipping to worry about, and yet I was nearly there. I was making progress.

Dave from the Airbnb kindly drove me down to the beach and helped with launching which was much appreciated, given it was low tide. Every bit of help speeds up the process.

There were diggers on the beach. This was becoming something of a seaside habit, I figured. They did not get in the way, or delay my exit, but it was mesmerising to see another out-of-place collection of machines squeak past, in order to attend to a miscellaneous stuff-moving project.

A north-westerly breeze would be pretty much on the nose, given that England was leaning slightly to the left as I went north. This would give a net speed of about three miles per hour over land, given beating conditions. The wind strength looked comfortable and persistent, maybe even becoming more favourable, veering to the north-east later. I reckoned five hours should take me the 17 miles to the Humber. I was very wrong.

The first hour went as predicted, making progress past Maplethorpe and some other 'Thorpes', but then the wind died. And guess what, there was opposing tide as well. I really wanted to get to a suitable Humber crossing point that day, and even better would be to take up Darron's kind offer of landing support, if I were to make it to the Humbermouth Yacht Club. Darron had responded to my email of the previous day, which was a great sign. However, it might take forever to get there.

Recalling my road map plans (these were AA road maps which I had cut up and annotated with stopping points), confirmed by my unfulfilled staring at the shoreline, I realised that there really weren't any other 'Thorpes' along the way. (Thorpe is a middle English word for a hamlet, by the way.) Hence, I was short of a backup plan, other than a tent.

In frustration, I got out of the boat and started to tow her along the beach. Walking through knee-deep water is hard work, as you know from your summer holidays. Towing the boat is a manageable extra, but only until your arm gets pulled backwards as the Laser sticks on the sand, when the waves go out. It was five steps forward, and 15 seconds waiting whilst jostling with the waves, making the whole process quite uncomfortable.

Furthermore, I noticed some pieces of plastic in the water, that I thought looked alarmingly familiar. On closer inspection,

I could see that the Camber Sands problem had reoccurred. The auto-bailer had bailed from the boat. This time it had been completely ripped off from the underside by the sand snagging and dragging, with only a stump remaining. What's more, the holding screw was bent. The worry here was that I might have caused a leak. If you take the screw out, the subsequent hole provides an unobstructed route into the hull. Hence, if the structures around the screw were damaged, I could be at risk of sinking. I would have to make repairs that evening.

Donna Nook is a well-known site for seal colonies, so I was told, but it was not listed on my hazards for the day (nor was the wind dying). At one point I landed just past one herd, only to realise there was another plump a little further along. I was still unsure whether seals may be friend or foe, but wanted to avoid them in the interests of preserving their peace, and mine.

Despite having to paddle an extra distance, I tried to give them a wide birth when I set off, but that didn't work. It seemed like the whole colony got into the water to follow me, playing a marine version of Grandma's footsteps. They created a hubbub of ripples dotted with grey noses on the glassy sea behind me. On occasions there was a loud splash a few feet short of the rudder, when some wily whiskered watcher got in a flap and made a dash back to the comfort of the group. Clearly, they had learnt the rules of the game.

I picked up a message from Neil that evening, kindly warning me about the Donna Nook firing range. I hadn't listed that on my hazards schedule either. I had wondered what those super large archery style targets were doing on the beach, but chose to ignore them since I had other irritants to worry about, clearly more important than a nearby missile.

It does amaze me that the military make it so difficult for civilians to figure out how to avoid being shot by friendly fire. On the gov.uk website, military practice areas are listed by name with land and sea sites jumbled up in one alphabetic order. Then there are firing ranges which are reached via a separate site. When I got round to Wales, I realised there are also privately run ranges, which you can't find unless you look somewhere completely different, and Airforce ranges on top of that. You would have thought that something like a colour coded map of the UK with links to the relevant websites would be a useful home page, but...

I was rescued from my painful paddling, by a bit of breeze. Later on, Darron's incredibly patient guidance into the muddy channel of Waithe Beck – I was really struggling to see the club amongst the greenery and sandbanks – pulled me along to the desired destination.

When I finally landed on a squelchy muddy shore, Darron turned up with a tractor asking whether I had a trolley. "Er, sorry no, I haven't," was my puzzled reply. It was gone 17.30, and the shadows were starting to lengthen. It had been eight hours of travelling and I was tired and fed up. I was struggling to see how we might make it over the sticky surface to the estuary edge. But sure enough, Darron returned a little later towing a rib sized trailer, big enough to escort my fully rigged boat, back to the clubhouse.

Other folk were waiting. In a stroke, my needs were attended to. Next to the clubhouse, there was an area of hard standing creating a space so that I could focus on repairs. I was handed a hot cup of tea. I was advised that there was flat grass around the other side of the clubhouse suitable for camping. However, I had no intention of using that, because I had already spied the changing room – warmish, flat and dry with no need for constraining canvas. And finally, I was given a lift to the local carvery where I tucked into a chicken tikka masala, just before the kitchen closed. Many thanks to all those wonderful helping Humber hands.

Ken Fowler was my caller for the evening, which was a very welcome accompaniment to the curry. As ever, he shared good advice, on this occasion giving a summary of the pros and cons of different weather forecast, suggesting the addition of Windfinder, since it shows wave height. I really appreciated his wise and well-chosen words.

It had been a long, slow day. I was tired, but also worried about the Humber crossing for the next day. Determined cargo ships, and strong tides were a big escalation on the hazard scale, compared to snooping seals. What's more, the forecast wasn't looking too lively, and the prospect of being becalmed in the middle of that melee, was troubling me.

* * *

Day 17, Tuesday 2nd May

To Withernsea

START	09.30, Humbermouth Yacht Club
WIND	NE veering SE, 8–9mph, then 12–15mph
WEATHER	Cloudy, 10–12°C. Dry
TIDE	Out of the Humber till 11.00
SEA STATE	Slight
HAZARDS	Shipping, wind dying, Spurn Head swells
FINISH	Withernsea, 16.00
DISTANCE	19 miles
SAILING HOURS	5 hours (30 mins at Spurn Head)

I woke early from a restless sleep. My throat was a little sore, and my voice sounded different, though I did not think much of it, since I had the Humber to worry about.

Darron very kindly came to the club before his work, to tow the boat down to the sinking sea. He also gave tips about the appropriate radio communication. I was to use channel 14 which was for Vessel Traffic Services (VTS), which sounded grand and mysterious. He also cautioned about 'The Binks', an area close to Spurn Head which can be rough.

Half a mile off the shore was Hill Sand Fort. Built in the 1900s it was another decaying estuary structure, though not as dramatic as the Maunsell Forts. The yacht club was previously the radar station for the fort, which perhaps explains its imperfect location, and adds to the wide variety of club histories along the coast.

Past the fort and out into the muddy Humber, I was looking and listening out for ships. I could hear chat on the VTS channel about shipping manoeuvres, and radioed to let whoever know about my intended crossing. There was no reply. I tried again and again, with the same lack of response. "What am I doing wrong?" I wondered, speculating that I was too insignificant to receive a response (amongst other persecutory thoughts).

The key question was whether the ships I could see in the distance were moving, or anchored like the one that was just in front of me. I could not be sure. In another attempt to rouse a response, I tried to contact a vessel on channel 16, as I passed by its stern. Yet again, answer came there none.

The wind was fairly light, and on the nose, meaning that progress was slow. I was desperate to reach Spurn Head (that long spit of land, dangling into the estuary, like a Uvula hanging down into an opened mouth). If the tide turned before I crossed to the north shore of the Humber, I was sure to be washed back towards Hull to the west. Paddle sailing needed to be introduced to my repertoire. It was uncomfortable, but felt necessary in my frantic state to make it to the far shore. Leaning out of the boat on the beat, I would add a bit of speed by paddling as well as sailing. I needed to adjust my body position regularly, in order to avoid too much back strain. I couldn't be sure it was adding much speed, but at least I felt I was doing everything possible to avert a disaster.

I was still trying to call on the VTS channel, but just could not raise a response. After a while, I figured the best thing to do was to make a dash for it, and skip this radio nonsense. Across the Humber I went. Paddle, sail, tack. Paddle, sail, tack. Paddle, sail, tack, for what seemed like an age. Every so often I would look over my shoulder to check whether a ship was now bearing down on me.

I was very pleased to make it to the shelter of Spurn Head. What a relief. I stopped for a celebratory break, and left a final radio message, thanking my would-be listener for their patience, and reassuring them that I was safely across. Still there was no reply. How strange.

I also noticed that I had scraped a sizeable chunk of skin off a finger knuckle, whilst paddling, leaving a glaring pink hole. In my agitated state, I had not noticed. Or maybe the crinkled white tissue had sloughed off all too easily, in the cold and sodden conditions, without causing any discomfort. I would need to keep an eye on that sore, since it could take a while to heal, and might become infected.

The rest of the journey became easier as land bent round to the west, and the wind veered to the east. The beat transformed into a reach.

I was surprised by the size of the swell, however. Metre-high rolling waves were ambling in from the north-east, presumably formed by a faraway storm the day before. There were also much smaller waves, crossing from the east, formed by the current breeze. I guessed this was primary and secondary swell – the north-east being primary, and the east secondary. This is all very interesting you might say, except that it meant there was a large shore dump, where I intended to land at Withernsea.

Having learned a lesson or two from day #1, I assessed the situation carefully, wanting to avoid a repeat performance. However, I could not figure out an alternative. Despite my trepidation, and not for the first time that day, I decided to make a dash for it.

After taking a while to pick out a smaller set of waves, I hurtled in as fast as I could, and met the shoreline with a crunch. Feeling pleased for a moment, I failed to account for the rip. The boat was dragged back out to sea, and tipped over. I fell out, and lost control of my precious craft. The sail became trapped under the ebb and flow of the sea, and I feared a Ron-style mast breakage or similar. It caused a few minutes of panic, struggling to release the sail cloth from its watery snare, similar to Hayling Island. A brief and undignified struggle in the froth restored order, however. Luckily nothing was damaged. Thank goodness. I did wonder how I would launch in the morning, with swell like that. At least I was on dry land and the sailing day was over.

Unfortunately, whilst I was on the water, the Airbnb accommodation I had booked the previous night, had been cancelled with no explanation. How frustrating. I would need to find a replacement plan.

What followed, grew into a learning tip for the day – 'if you are feeling out of luck, hang out by the RNLI building'. Propped up by the smart red bricked building, I sat out of the wind, warming up in the afternoon sunshine. Sitting hunched up and staring at my phone, I must have looked like a morose adolescent. A concerned-sounding rescuer approached and invited me into the lifesaving haven for a coffee. The adolescent was perking up. Even better, was an offer to park the boat in the neighbouring boat park. And better than that was a suggestion of the Alexander Hotel in town, which after a quick fingered adolescent phone assessment, turned out to have vacant rooms. The day was practically sorted.

Then Jonathon rang. He was a friend from school. "Where are you, Andrew?" he said. "We are looking at your boat on the beach right now."

Wow, that was a big surprise. We had previously been in contact since I had hoped to stay with him, but it had not worked out. Instead, he had tracked me down and made the two-hour journey with his wife Sarah, to pay a visit. How incredibly kind.

The three of us went to a local curry house (Prawn Khari and Lassi for me) to catch up.

I had spent many happy days visiting Jonathon at his parents' farm in Romford, during adolescent years. Every boy loves a tractor and I was no exception, relishing the opportunity to hear about the big machines, and maybe even take to the wheel. The challenges of farming were also refreshingly different from the bookish, office-based world of medicine.

One time Jonathon and I thought it smart to test our recent chemistry knowledge, so mixed a balloon with a 50/50 acetylene and oxygen mix. From memory that seemed to be the right ratios for a hearty explosion. Hiding behind a tractor, we found a long stick, and lit a candle to set off our experiment.

It worked a treat.

Jonathon's poor parents came screaming out of the house, running at full tilt towards the nearby barn, when they heard the enormous bang. We, in contrast, physically unscathed by the blast, crept sheepishly out from behind the tractor to show our sorry faces to his relieved parents. There was no need to repeat that experiment we thought.

Keeping up the family tradition, Jonathon moved to Lincolnshire to press on with farming, hence the visit. He usually had a number of new ideas on the go. In the past it was combine harvester sharing, or baby monitors so that tractor drivers could adjust the height of a delivery chute, to minimise potato bruising. These days it was wind farms, or a proposal to make a barrier across the Wash to help generate electricity (and presumably protect from flooding). It was fun and exciting to hear of Jonathon's new ideas, several of which have turned into reality.

Family innovation was not restricted to the land. Jonathon was a key player in producing the first foiling catamaran called Icarus, which held the world sailing record on the sea, for many years. Very impressive.

One of their sons had picked up on his father's inventiveness. He had been selling T-shirts whilst at university. In the process he had chalked up nearly half a million views on TikTok. I had managed about 400 views on my YouTube channel, so I was feeling a bit jealous. "How do they do it?" I wondered, feeling firmly part of an older generation.

That reminded me of social media use for some young people I worked with. A 15-year-old had managed to reach one million views on TikTok. Her profile was not secretive and was easily and openly viewable by professionals. The posted content was often nothing more complicated than crying to the camera, but had attracted a huge following. An irony from a professional point of view, was that face-to-face conversations were very unproductive, with only a few drops of exchange, during an awkward interview. Risk levels were high, so the need for communication was considerable. I half jested with colleagues, that the best way of finding out this young person's mental state, was to see the latest updates online. Over time, my hesitant comment proved more accurate than I had predicted – video content proved to be the most accurate method of gaining an update, both good and bad. Thus, online communication had all but replaced offline dialogue.

Happily, things improved over time, and a more level balance was restored, over several months.

Another enterprising young lady managed to gather a substantial following online. Not content with views, likes, or affirmative comments, she had supplied purchasing suggestions, linked to an Amazon account. Followers obliged, and sent her gifts. She posted more content, and they posted more gifts. Simples.

When things deteriorated clinically, she was admitted to psychiatric hospital for a couple of months. Her online posting continued and so did the parcels. Staff not only had to deal with providing care and treatment for the young person, but were also obliged to find a storeroom to accommodate the boxes and boxes of donations, from anonymous sympathetic followers. 'Sickness is marketable', I learnt. I had never imagined that such things might be possible.

On leaving hospital, the young person did well. I later asked her what she had done with the accounts. On feeling better, she deleted them, and hence her shopping lists too. "I didn't need it anymore," she said. I was delighted for her.

Back to the realities of Withernsea, the meal was drawing to a close. What a fantastic and uncomplicated evening it had been. Feeling refreshed, we parted company and returned to our respective journeys.

Having a spacious chalet room all to myself, I settled down to a much-needed sleep.

Day 18, Wednesday 3rd May

To Bridlington

START	10.30, Withernsea, (1 hour late)
WIND	SE 12–20mph
WEATHER	Sun/cloud 12°C. Dry
TIDE	Against me from 12.00, up to 1mph
SEA STATE	Slight
HAZARDS	A deceased whale at Bridlington
FINISH	Bridlington, 15.30
DISTANCE	26 miles
SAILING HOURS	5 hours

Several people turned up for the launch including John, Tracey and Melanie from a mix of the RNLI, and the Withernsea Residents' Community Group, who had heard about the trip via Facebook. I was flattered by people's interest, and amazed that folks would make the effort to come down to the beach, all of which made a charming start to the day.

The swell had eased and the tide was out, so the waves were much smaller than I had feared. The sun was coming out and the south-easterly breeze provided a steady following wind. What a difference a new day makes.

My chest was hurting though, and coughing was painful. Was this a bruise or a type of cold? I wasn't sure? My voice was still sounding different as well, so it was probably a virus. I would need to keep an eye on things. I didn't want to make myself ill.

With a steady following wind, the sailing was pretty comfortable. I did manage to fall out, however, which was the first time since day one. "I think I'm getting better at getting back into the boat," I said to myself afterwards.

On this occasion, I was practising some downwind wave surfing and managed to fall into windward – a classic Laser mishap. When I was back in the boat, despite a full turtle, and momentary inspection of the scratched international orange paint on my replacement centre board, I was surprised to find that my top half was completely dry. Not only that, but none of my cockpit luggage had washed away. My valued blue Co-op 3-for-1 sponge, was still under the lunch box, alongside the not-so dry bag. To top it all off, the unplanned roll had given the cleats and pulleys a cunning rinse, washing away the inevitable blocking sand, from my last beach landing. Consequently, all rigging was now running smoothly. Success!

Luckily no one was watching.

I was sorely tempted to sail round Flamborough Head, because it would have taken me on a perfect broad reach, but I remembered the words of Ken, who cautioned against overdoing it. Furthermore, Ron had broken his mast in the waves on Filey beach, and Neil didn't have a great time of the place either, so I thought it was better to bank the miles and stop at Bridlington. Besides, it was going to be windy the next day and I was feeling below par. There was also the temptation of a coronation party near home at the weekend, so going south for a few days was a possibility.

The sun had gone in, but the wind hadn't, and now that I was no longer travelling downwind, it was blowing harder and colder. It was cold, like seven degrees Celsius, and I was cold. My chest was hurting when I coughed, and so were my ribs. It felt like I was coming down with something. Could this be pleurisy or something similar?

I needed to find a place to store my boat. After the statutory beachside coffee, I went to hang out at the local RNLI building, where else, to see if I could find some help. After about ten minutes of hobo style loitering, I was hustled inside the large spick and span building. Another hot drink was soon provided (thank you very much) and I was instructed to wait until Bob turned up.

Captain Bob, they called him, and you could see why. A sturdy man with a Captain Bird's Eye type beard (from the 90s adverts) and plenty of chat to go with it. He seemed to be at the centre of everything, knowing everything, and helping guide everything, through his effervescent phone and matching presence.

I was directed to sail back over to the nearby Blythe Boat Park, of the Royal Yorkshire Yacht Club. "Not the first white building which is the Bridlington Bay Boat Storage facility, but three pylons further on to the second building," or so he said. But at that distance from familiarity, without my glasses and all the 'B' words involved, it was all a bit of a blur. Very grateful for the help, and not wanting to ask too many repeat questions, I was sure I could find it. But I ended up going to the wrong place.

My journey would take me past the dead whale on the beach. At 17 metres long and an estimated 70 tonnes, it was a mighty beast and had deservedly made it to the papers, but would have been better off swimming around with its mates. The poor fin Whale had beached itself and, crushed by its own weight, sadly was beyond the expertise even of Captain Bob and his yellow booted life savers. There was chat as I waited, about what to do with the carcass, such as towing it back out to sea, but in my hurried state, I missed the conclusion to the discussion.

As I was preparing to relaunch, I noticed a man walking towards me with purpose. Not a young man but an older gentleman with a stiff and slightly stooped gait. He was wearing a red top that I did not recognise. I carried on re-rigging the boat, but looked up to find that he continued to aim straight for me, with focus like an Arctic explorer close to reaching the North

Pole. "Perhaps an interested local coming to chat," I thought.

However, his walking looked familiar. In fact, he looked quite like my father-in-law, Peter, but it couldn't be. Peter does not have a mobile phone, and he didn't know where I was, so how could he be here, on this precise part of a large beach? It didn't make any sense. With each step closer, those well-known features restamped themselves on a reluctant mind, and the blur of incredulity was finally broken to reveal that it was indeed Peter.

"How on earth did you find me?" I asked incredulously.

"I drove over to Filey, thinking you might be there, but couldn't find you. Then I asked someone where you were, because I could remember the website. And they looked it up on their phone and it said you were heading to Bridlington. So, I came over here and waited round for a while. I was sitting over there chatting to a nice lady for a bit, then saw your sail, and came over."

Captain Bob came over, so a more extended chat with Peter would have to wait. He gave Peter some directions to a local car park that neither of us fully understood, and we parted in opposite directions, hoping that a reunion that day might be possible despite a mobile-free back up plan. (How on earth did we manage in the olden days?)

Captain Bob had found me at the wrong boat park. Not only that, he found Rear Commodore Steve to help with the boat moving enterprise. We all went to find a trolley from the cadet compound, which involved clambering over the perimeter, and then manhandling of said trolley back over the fence. Teamwork was definitely needed to move the boat back up to the park, since the soft sand was putting up a decent resistance. I did wonder how I might get it back to the sea on my own, when it came to relaunching, but I thought it best to leave that worry to another day. And then Captain Bob, who really is a very useful captain, sped off to go and run a training session.

I was left to quietly rummage in the hold of my boat, to retrieve and then file items. I was preparing for a potential few days away, loading take-away luggage into rubble sacks. These were handy collapsible bags which were very convenient, but gave more of a 'lost on land' look, than a well-prepared circumnavigator appearance, which I might have preferred.

When exiting the compound, I was approached by a local sailor and we got chatting. He offered to take me back to the most likely car park, so we could participate in the game of "Where's Peter?", and of course I accepted.

In the very short journey, I learnt quite a number of things. I learnt that he had been sailing in the bay in his yacht, as I had come in to land on the beach. He had lived in the area for a while, and had seen three of the four fin whales that have beached themselves, in the last 50 years. I also learnt that Tony was father to Jim Saltonstill, who is a sailing coach of international standing. Jim had helped many youths to Olympic fame over the years, including Ben Ainslie. What a connection!

No longer in the youth bracket myself, and well out of the Olympic zone, I was very happy with a few Saltonstill pointers about rounding Flamborough Head. These were concise and easy to follow, obviously a family trait. "Yes, the sea can be quite lively round the headland and it is best to get the tide timing right," he said. That affirmed my decision not to press on today.

In a moment, we found Peter, so I hopped from one car to another, bidding farewell and thank you, to my impromptu coach.

We headed back to town and I was treated to chicken and bamboo shoots at a nearby Chinese restaurant, and a few repeats of the "How on earth did you find me?" story, which still had not quite sunk in. Health worries had restricted Peter's movements over the last few months. However, he had decided to throw caution to the wind and go in search of a crazy sailor, without the guiding compass of a smartphone. For Peter, it was his own adventure. Hence, our meeting was a pot of gold for both of us, but in very different ways.

I did have one more favour to ask. "Can I come and stay with you tonight?" does not quite sound right, even from a son-in-law. A little bit of shuffling round the subject was required to land the request safely, but I got there, happily without spoiling the camaraderie of shared adventuring. The super slow drive back to West Yorkshire, did provide a late tester to our bond, but the reward of rescue from the chilly wind, and the knowledge of a warm bed at the end of the road, was enough to prevent good humour from nodding off. Thank you so much, Peter.

* * *

Thursday 4th May – Sunday 7th May

The forecast for Thursday was looking too windy to make a pleasant day, so after only a mere moment of deliberation, I figured it would be a no-sailing day. My chest was still hurting and it seemed smart to take a rest, rather than push on and risk making it worse. The prospect of a Saturday party sealed the deal, so I figured that some days off were in order, including a trip back home.

I spent Thursday catching up with some laundry, outstanding admin including completing an article for Hull Live, before heading over to Otley for a walk with Peter.

Peter's enthusiasm and enterprise of the day before were still echoing round in my head. I wanted to reciprocate in some way, so spending time together felt like the best thing to do. As a widower of 18 months, company was at a premium, and mine was freely available so it was the least I could do.

Previously reliant on our spouses for catering, we decided to break with tradition and ventured out to shop for, and prepare, a manly spaghetti bolognaise for the evening – a wholesome communion to top off the day. It was delicious.

It was local election day and the Tories lost a lot of seats.

My chest was starting to feel better, though coughing was still painful. I was thinking this was a form of viral tracheitis, which I had not had before. Holding respectfully to the maxim of "physician heal thyself" I thought that outside advice was not needed, and instead time, and the great assets of this wonderfully designed body, would restore good health. It felt wise to have taken a break from sailing.

I had another great sleep

Friday 5th May

Armed with dry clean clothes and my Senior railcard, I was kindly dropped off by Peter at the local station so that I could make the five-hour train journey back home. Five hours seems like a long way by train, and it is. But as I sped past the green hills of England, I reflected on previous journeys to Yorkshire from the south. They had felt like major expeditions over great distances. Indeed, they were, and yet I had somehow made it all the way to Yorkshire on my tiny dinghy. It was a little hard to believe.

At home, I was on my own since Liz had taken a walking holiday in Spain with friends. Our neglected garden was calling. I had been trying to save my box hedges from the invasive caterpillars. The warming weather had been encouraging the pests to start their cycle from larvae, to leaf munching caterpillars, and on to be breeding moths. So now was the time to take action to tackle the invasion. Last year I had pulled about 1000 caterpillars from mine and my elderly neighbour's hedges. There wasn't time to pick the wriggly squidgy sneaky things from the bushes, so spraying was the way.

Saturday 6th May

Investing in some more warmth seemed like a good idea. Getting cold is a significant risk if you are out at sea with no way of warming up, making a vicious cycle of declining temperature, compounded by poor decision making as you cool. I had wondered about acquiring a dry suit, having never used one. Jonno Dunnet sailed around the UK on his windsurfer, and used a dry suit the whole way, so maybe I should do the same. Neil and Ron had gone down the wetsuit route. I asked Paul about this, when I went up to Papercourt Sailing Club for the morning. He suggested a dry suit is large and cumbersome for sailing, as well as uncomfortable around the neck if used for long periods, so cautioned against it. Besides, the weather should be warming up.

Paul also gave a brilliant piece of sailing advice. I had tried 'hove to' in a double hander so was familiar with the term, but had not tried it in a Laser, believing that two sails were needed. But the manoeuvre works just as well in a Laser – pushing the tiller and mainsail to leeward, when the boat has stopped.

Paul's tip proved to be a game changer. After trying this out, I found I was able to do more or less anything out on the water, in more or less any conditions, except for go to sleep. So, I could look at my phone to check on navigation, change clothing or adjust rigging or the tracker. I could have lunch, have a rest or have a wee, all without worrying about falling out. I felt a bit foolish that

I had arrived late to the knowledge of this essential trick. I only partly managed to reassure myself by recalling my amateur status, and something about this trip being a learning journey. Anyway, thanks, Paul, for this massively important piece of advice.

I had checked out a dry top online but that looked similar to my existing aqua fleece. Something like fifteen percent of heat is lost through your head, so maybe a better hat would help, whilst attending to the weight and comfort down sides of a dry suit. So, I went down to Cotswold Outdoor in Guildford, fuelled by the prospect of the visceral comfort that you get when shopping, which so often heals a range of semi-conscious anxieties. I found a suitably expensive option with ear flaps for extra warmth, and a retaining chin elastic to prevent wind theft, so plumped for that. And in the process of browsing, I had a shopping accident. I found a ridiculously expensive air mat. It was really compact and super light, and blew up to be a thick and sizeable piece of portable comfort – an essential item for every achy, and reluctant ancient camper.

The long-awaited party was a grand black-tie affair, which was well worth the journey, slightly muted by Liz's absence and my need to head North the next day. It certainly had the effect of providing a social top up.

* * *

Sunday 7th May

One of the joys of the journey was to feel like there was time; to throw off the shackles of schedules and ticking arrangements. However, trains, when they are excused from the ongoing litter of strikes, don't tend to wait. Being late is a special skill of mine, and despite having all morning to get ready, I ended up running down to the station, making my freshly laundered T shirt all sweaty.

Will I ever learn? And to answer my own question, probably not.

I was sorry to be leaving the comforts of home and sorry to miss our street party that afternoon, in honour of King Charles' coronation. I love a community gathering and had helped organise the last one.

But the journey had to go on. Bridlington beckoned. At least I had my two replacement auto bailers with me – one was clearly not going to be enough – and a new waterproof hat, plus large air mat to provide small comfort. And we all had a new King.

CHAPTER 7

North Yorkshire and beyond

Day 19, Monday 8th May

To Scarborough

START	09.15, Bridlington
WIND	S/SSW, 11–22 mph. Becalmed off Filey Brigg
WEATHER	13°C and rain at times
TIDE	With me from 9.00, 0.5 mph, (looked 2mph)
SEA STATE	Moderate notably at Flamborough
HAZARDS	Sea state at Flamborough Head. Filey
FINISH	Scarborough harbour, 12.45
DISTANCE	23 miles
SAILING HOURS	3½ hours

Having squeezed into, and squeezed out of, my guesthouse for the night, filled with statutory porridge for the day, I stepped into a taxi to find my way back to the correct boat yard. Betty was waiting patiently to see me. Despite the 8am hour, on a bank holiday Monday, locals came out to help with moving us to the beach, and returning the trolley to its rightful place. People are so incredibly helpful at whatever time of day, it seems.

Back on the road after a few days off, so to speak, I was reinvigorated, ready to go and able to cough without pain. However, time on shore makes the ties of the land grow stronger, and the tides of sea feel more ominous. I was worried about scare stories I had heard from Stick about Flamborough Head. There were cautions from Tony from a few days previously. Ron, laser circumnavigator #1, had broken his mast at Filey, and been stuck there for a few days. All of this added salt to my wounds of anxiety – but I needn't have worried.

Having taken a few days off, the tide had caught up with my schedule, so was now running in my favour all morning. In fact, it was more like a sprint than a run, when I passed a buoy near Filey Brigg, all the more obvious given that I was strangely becalmed at the time.

Perhaps nature had cast a short spell over the wind, inviting me to reminisce about happy holidays at Filey over the years. As I sat stationary on the water, looking towards the huge sweep of shore from Flamborough Head, along to Filey Brigg, I remembered happy times.

Walks on the beach or crabbing with the kids in the Brigg rock pools. Boogie boarding in the waves. Making a sand sculpture of my father-in-law Peter, asleep after a picnic lunch. Or sandcastle competitions in which my eldest made a model toilet complete with sand poo – he didn't win. Or Liz's mum supplying endless sandwiches and cups of tea, to the shivering assembly huddled behind a rickety windbreak.

Ah enough of that, since the wind came in again. In the end, I made it to Scarborough in three and a half hours as opposed to the expected five, breaking 8mph of speed at times, all in good time for an afternoon beer at the Scarborough Yacht Club.

My new hat was doing a good job at providing rain protection. It all became a bit irrelevant, however, when boat speed picked up on a reach. The spray from Betty's bow provided a much more effective downpour, cunningly splashing out to the sides, and then being blown with precision by the oncoming wind, right into my face.

I was pleased to get a reply on the radio when coming into the harbour – this was the first time I had used it in these circumstances. I felt like an excited kid finally getting his walkie talkie to work, and then being able to have a conversation. It was also reassuring to know that not everyone sticks rigidly to marine radio speak. I found the effort to remember page 25 or whatever, of the VHF manual, somewhat inhibiting when trying to open a social exchange.

The only problem with this newfound success, was that I was called straight over to the office to pay the harbour fees. Straight over is not the right phrase, since it involved a long walk all the way round the perimeter to the other side of the entrance.

Passing a warehouse-type shed, I stopped to watch a seagull, who was tucking into a fish meal, presumably a discarded piece of commercial catch. Not quite your standard knife and fork human eating operation, or even the peck it and pull it approach. No, this particular eager eater was doing his or her best, to swallow it whole. The head of the fish that is. Which was no smaller than the seagull's own skull, so was proving quite a challenge. Picking it up and getting the meal the right way round was no problem for my handless friend, but getting the damn thing to go down was really too much. In it went, followed by some unmistakable retching, and out it would come again, relaunched onto the dirty floor. Round two was no different.

"You need to chop that up a bit, don't you think?" was my paternalistic advice, which was duly ignored. At least the forager was unperturbed by my voyeuristic presence. The gull seemed hell bent on the same failed approach. Stuff it and retch it, stuff it and retch it, stuff it and retch it, went the cycle. Until, at last, the 'peck it and pull it' refinement was introduced. I think we were both relieved by the change of tactic. I went off to settle my own stomach with a beer!!

Stepping off their own craft, parked a few berths further up the pontoon, Jim and Karen introduced themselves as I was mooring up. They had worked out who I must be, since there weren't any other Lasers moored up in the harbour. Tom, the Vice Commodore, had mentioned in an email that a couple of members would get in touch, so here before me, must be my delightful mystery hosts. Not wanting to be outdone, Peter had travelled over again from West Yorkshire, to offer support, and further exercise his own navigational skills.

We all gathered in the yacht club. It was a white rectangular building, perched on the seaward arm of the harbour wall, topped off with a lighthouse. The building and lighthouse were matched in architectural design, finished with fresh white paint, meaning that club and operational entity merged into one. In fact, this was the history of the building, because until 1952, the yacht club had been the harbourmaster, and lightkeeper's accommodation.

Entering the yacht club, sailors clambered up steep and narrow stairs, reminiscent of a hazardous gangway. The steps led to the first-floor bar, where they were afforded great views of the town on one side, and the sea on the other, as if on the bridge of their very own ship. I am sure a boisterous evening session, awash with stories of sailing adventures, could add alcohol-inspired swaying, to supplement the virtual reality experience.

Scarborough had its share of waterside attractions, rather quiet in the chilly May weather despite being a bank holiday. Quiet in terms of visitor numbers but noisy from pinging, ringing and flashing attractions, which were doing their best to draw in reluctant tourists.

Alongside Filey, Scarborough had been a regular holiday destination for Liz and her family. I was pleased to be able to add a tour of the marina, to Peter's album of memories, since it was not on his usual trail. I took Peter out for an Italian meal to repay his kindness from Bridlington, whilst holding my appetite for the offered meal up the hill later on. Unlike our last meeting, this occasion had less focus and Peter decided he would head back home before dark. Peter kindly took some unwanted items with him, so that they could make their way back home, including the replaced air mat. Then we bade each other farewell. It was the last time we would meet for the duration of the trip, but we kept in touch by phone.

The view from the top floor of Karen and Jim's house complemented that from the yacht club. Steep paths fed locals between houses and across intersecting roads, onwards and upwards. With each step away from the bustle of the harbour front, climbing ever higher, one could capture vistas over rooftops, beyond the lighthouse and across the sea to cliffs of the Yorkshire coast. How serene. All this was freely available to me from my bedroom window for the evening, yet again a generosity that felt hard to fathom.

Karen, who worked for the ambulance service, had sadly lost her husband two years previously. Jim was a local boat builder of many years, and their recent partnership meant that they now had a small fleet of no less than four yachts which, it soon transpired, was a measure of a unifying love of the sea, rather than burnt funds or a desire to show off wealth.

I had lost a pulley in my derigging process and wondered if by chance there might be a spare, assuming the answer would be 'sorry, no'. But the house was well stocked, and Karen so helpfully found a replacement pulley (and a spare) amongst the boat bits. I was delighted with yet more good fortune and generosity. I considered it my duty to lighten the chandlery load for the property, in exchange for a well-deserved tenner.

Over a delicious home-made spaghetti bolognaise and a beer, we shared stories of sailing trips, boat building and health service frustrations, before graciously retiring.

* * *

Day 20, Tuesday 9th May

To Whitby

START	09.50, Scarborough
WIND	NW/NE. 7–11mph. Then nothing
WEATHER	Mostly cloudy, sun later, some rain
TIDE	With me, Max 1.2mph, till 15.00
SEA STATE	Smooth
HAZARDS	No wind. Rocks at Robin Hood's Bay
FINISH	Whitby, 16.00
DISTANCE	19 miles
SAILING HOURS	6 hours

Quick one day and slow the next, was definitely the way to spoil the fun. The wind dying after an hour was a bad omen, and unfortunately set the tone for the whole day, despite the forecast showing something. I was keen to make as much use of the favourable tide whilst it lasted, so had been paddling all day. I could have stopped at Robin Hood's Bay, I guess, but I had an offer of a whole house to myself at Whitby, which was quite an incentive for continuing.

My head was throbbing ever louder as I was leaning over the deck to paddle Betty past the elusive harbour arms at a pitiful 1mph.

Poor Liz rang, only to be greeted with a super snappy response of "why do you only ring when the wind has died?"!

"I saw that you seem to have stopped, and I was just ringing to check that you are OK," she plaintively replied.

"I'm in a really bad mood, I'm afraid, and I'm struggling to get past the harbour entrance now that the tide has turned," I grumbled. In fact, I was in such a bad mood that I could not bring myself to be civil, and thought it best to focus on the last mile, rather than subject Liz to any more snarling.

Stepping onto the sand was a relief. I needed to go and find some mood improving sustenance and figure out where I could leave Betty for the night. Such was the lack of wind that I simply left Betty fully rigged, to be gently caressed by the cool fingers of the sea, carefully guiding her towards the access ramp on the incoming tide. My casual briefing to a nearby mother on the beach about my whereabouts, would most likely suffice, should any attention be needed. Or so I thought.

The gentle burble of unhurried seasiders, going about their meanderings in the warming, still spring air, provided a soothing backdrop. I found a comfortable bench where I could suck in the good humour of my own portion of comfort coffee and cake, and for a change, I was not cold. Sam rang offering gentle chatter, meaning that I could blur into the verbal background. Thus, the transformation from grumpy sailor, albeit still inconspicuously dressed in full sailing gear, into happy Whitby seaside holidaymaker, was completed.

But then the coastguard rang.

"We have a report of an incident at Whitby with a boat being found abandoned. We are ringing to check whether you have landed safely somewhere."

"Ah, yes. I'm at Whitby and have landed safely a while ago. I'm sorry I had not rung you to let you know," I replied. Walking down the slipway I could see the tide was almost touching the cobbled ramp, and more troubling was a burly looking gentleman dragging Betty across the sand, making me wince.

"Is this your boat?" was the slightly gruff enquiry from one of the blur of assembled officials.

I was thinking of something like "I was all of 50 yards away, dressed in full sailing gear, so couldn't you have worked it out, and saved yourselves some trouble?" but luckily civil responses were more readily to hand than earlier in the day. We walked through the usual niceties of 'Sorry to have troubled you', and 'Thank you so much', and 'Yes I'm fine'. And 'Yes, I will move the boat round into the harbour for tonight'. After all, they were just doing their job.

Someone had called the coastguard to report an abandoned boat on the beach. They had presumed that the sailor was lost at sea, and the boat washed ashore. I hadn't even considered such a scenario since, to a sailor's mind, the scene was nothing like the imagined calamity. The moral of the tale for me, however, was that not everyone has a sailor's mind. And the easy solution to avoid a repeat scenario, was to write a note on the centre board saying:

> **Gone for coffee**
> **Please call**
> **[my mobile]**
> **If concerned**

That way I could take it out of its casing and place it on the deck, message side up, when I had landed. Simples.

One other thing before I go on up the hill to my luxury house for the night. When checking through the cockpit luggage, I realised the Tupperware lid was missing. How strange, I thought. I guessed that the box had been opened in search of the missing sailor, and then the lid put down elsewhere. No lid meant no lunch, kind of thing, until I could find a replacement. In the unlikely event of success, I thought I might as well put out a search party, just in case. I did ask one or two beachcombers at the sea edge, who responded sympathetically, but to no avail.

Happily, I found my precious piece of plastic, half submerged in the water, about 30 metres away, and almost jumped for joy at our heartwarming reunion!! (It is mysterious how such trivial successes can be so gratifying. And, it was not the last time my lunch box would have a lucky escape.)

Ruth and Simon had so kindly lent me their entire property, for not one, but two nights. Light, bright, clean, well located, well equipped and well stocked, with a comfortable warm bed, what more could I have hoped for? Nothing. I was in heaven.

A vegetarian sweet potato dish at a local restaurant, together with orange juice and lemonade, married with a restorative conversation with Liz, were finishing touches. I then headed to heaven, for a celestial sleep.

Oh, and I had passed the 20% mark!

* * *

Day 21, Wednesday 10th May

To Redcar

START	10.30, Whitby
WIND	W/SW, 9–19mph
WEATHER	Sun, cloud, rain. 14–15°C
TIDE	With me, 0.9mph, till 16.00
SEA STATE	Slight
HAZARDS	Secret rocks at Redcar. Iffy wind
FINISH	Redcar, 17.30
DISTANCE	21 miles
SAILING HOURS	6 hours (1 hour at Saltburn)

Whitby is a pretty town, all the better for some sunshine. Settled along the banks of the River Esk, the town makes its way gracefully down to the sea, untroubled by industry, amusement arcades or through traffic.

Betty was parked on the Tate Hill Sands on the south bank of the river. Given there was no wind when I greeted her in the morning, I figured it would be opportune to redraw some of the map on her underside, since it was almost completely rubbed off. Cornwall was badly affected. In my haste, I gave it a bit more of an extension than it was due. I am sure the good people of the South-west would be pleased to know that their homeland had been expanded towards America, albeit by some careless cartographer.

The next few days were a bit samey on the sailing front. Light or variable winds, grey, sometimes rainy skies and occasional sun, with modest distance gained each day, and a smattering of paddling. Wednesday was no exception.

My plan was to travel up to Saltburn-by-the-Sea and catch the bus back to Whitby, where I could repeat my luxury stay. Saltburn, as it is usually called, provided a pleasant stop and statutory hot drink (hot chocolate this time). However, it wasn't so good as a landing spot since there was a long sandy beach, and no obvious place to park. The wind had turned up by surprise for an afternoon outing, so it encouraged me to venture onwards to Redcar. It was only five miles further but took ages because I ran into some rocks.

As I was approaching my destination, I could see a long straight strip of waves breaking over an object which I assumed was an out-flow pipe. However, there were no markers as would be expected. I approached the obstruction very slowly, hoping I could slide over it. I was puzzled to find another shelf just before it. Stepping out from my stationary boat to investigate, I found I was standing on rocks. "Hmm, this is strange," I thought. And looking round I could see more rocks under water. I had landed in the middle of an underwater minefield.

I needed to return to the shore to work out what to do, since barging into submerged objects at full speed, would not be good for Betty. Returning from whence I had come, I threaded my way through more rocks, eventually getting out of the boat, so that I could walk her by hand, to the safety of sand.

I asked a passerby, and took a closer look at local terrain on my phone. I learnt that there were a number of rock shelves (which were becoming ever larger with the falling tide), called things like 'Salt Scar', or less imaginatively 'High Stone', which crept out under the sea like treacherous fingers, ready to add another unsuspecting ship to its catalogue of wrecks. I would have to go round them, which was a nuisance, since I had had about enough for the day, but needs must.

Heading back out on a speedy broad reach, I was really hoping I had calculated my route accurately, since an error would surely have led to another replacement centre board, or worse. I sailed round the outer limit of the hazards, as far as I could tell, and then returned to land on a long tiring beat, past a wind farm.

Luckily, I made it to Redcar beach all in one piece. I had landed slightly to the north of the main town to reduce the risk of interference from any over interested locals. It was a barren and wind-swept stretch of sand next to a car park, used by townsfolk to take an afternoon stroll, so not the safest spot. In hindsight I was perhaps lucky to get away with a trouble-free night for Betty, given my experiences of other locations later on in the trip.

It was a dash to catch some emergency fish and chips, before boarding my £2 bus back to Whitby. Whilst being welcome instant grub, the food was a mixed blessing. The first few bites were reassuringly filling, but as the fat and batter started to make its way through the digestive system, the whole effect was less enjoyable. I sensed the globules of oil and grease, oozing through my vessels into hapless tissues. Rather than a satisfied customer, I ended up feeling like a blubbery seal, half incapable of movement. I resolved to keep that menu choice in reserve!!

* * *

Day 22, Thursday 11th May

To Sunderland

START	11.30, Redcar
WIND	E/NE, 7–11mph. Very variable
WEATHER	Sun/Cloud, 12–13°C. Dry
TIDE	With me till 17.00. Max 0.5mph
SEA STATE	Slight
HAZARDS	Running out of wind
FINISH	Sunderland, 16.30
DISTANCE	23 miles
SAILING HOURS	5 hours

It was a lovely ambling bus journey, dipping in and out of valleys as it wound its way back up the coast, tempting the passengers with views of the sea, before plunging back inland. Green, resplendent and lush were the hills, uncluttered by development or traffic.

Approaching Saltburn-by-the-Sea, there were a number of hairpin bends on the way up to the main town, quite a contrast from the gently winding route the road had taken so far. It is in the town that the funicular railway reaches its summit, before clanking back down to the seafront, and the pier.

Saltburn has the honour of hosting the only pleasure pier in the North-east. Not only that, but the funicular is the second oldest water-powered tramway in the world, the oldest being found in Portugal. It was originally built in 1884, and was renovated in 1998 (for those who would like some reassurance about safety), with new water pumps and upgraded brakes. Water powered means that the underneath of the upper car is filled with water until it counterbalances the weight of its lower partner. When it reaches the bottom of the track, it is emptied, since gravity has done its work. The procedure is then repeated for the new round of passengers. How neat is that?

My sailing journey was unremarkable. After several comfortable hours, I found my meandering way into Sunderland harbour, a large expanse of still water sprinkled with sunshine on this May afternoon, embraced by two sturdy arms keeping guard over the mouth of the River Wear. Sunderland Yacht Club was my destination on the northern shore, peacefully located up a short beach, sheltered from the main channel by a breakwater. There was a section of grass between club and beach, making it a fantastic landing spot. But despite its proud modern structure and bold location, there was no one about, and no reply to my email. Some investigation was required.

Following the sound of voices, I made my way to a half-opened gate, where I spied a group gathered round a pile of equipment. On closer inspection this did not look like sailing stuff, but more like diving gear, which was not quite what I was looking for. I wasn't expected either, since my enquiries about emails, sailing round the UK, or a place to park my boat, were met with blank faces.

However, Brian, who was mostly covered in weighty gear, said that he was about to carry out a test dive with a student. He said, "I should be able to contact someone who might be able to help." I was suitably grateful.

Sure enough, things, worked out. Alison soon appeared. She was chatty, kind and incredibly helpful, pulling in the assistance of her recently betrothed spouse Christine, who had access to some handy extras, like gate keys. In no time at all, Betty was installed behind a sturdy metal fence, on lush green grass, all safe and sound for the night. The timing worked out just right so that I could congratulate the divers as they emerged from the murky North Sea.

My evening rendezvous was with Ian, whom I met on a Kilimanjaro ascent a few years back, and we had stayed in touch via Facebook.

Kilimanjaro, for those who have not tried it, is an incredible journey, taking you through several different worlds in a few days. You witness a topographical transformation as you ascend, moving from tropical rainforest, to alpine scrub, up to a craggy crater, pockmarked by shrinking glacial lumps. There is also your personal journey through a range of physiological stages, brought on by increasing hypoxia from the altitude. The volcano is nearly six thousand metres in height, so way more than Mont Blanc. As you ascend beyond the clouds to a dizzying summit, breathlessness grips you ever more tightly, until you reach the top, full of smiles and, if you are not so lucky, vomit. The moral of that particular physical tale, is to take it slow, respect the elements and know your own limitations, some advice I have continued to give myself on a regular basis.

Ian was a town planner, who had been part of the redevelopment of the seafront at Seaburn, on the northern side of Sunderland. I congratulated him on his contribution, since the area had an atmosphere of purposeful calm, with open pedestrian spaces, smart shops and amenities, whose occupants all seemed engaged in contented recreation. We joined in, going along to a bar and then to 'The Shack' for a Katsu Curry and catch up. It was lovely to see Ian again and I was really touched by his kindness in meeting up.

I walked back down towards the harbour to find my cosy room at the Roker Hotel on the seafront. I wrapped up warm in anticipation of the next day's sailing.

* * *

CHAPTER 8

Northumbrian pipes

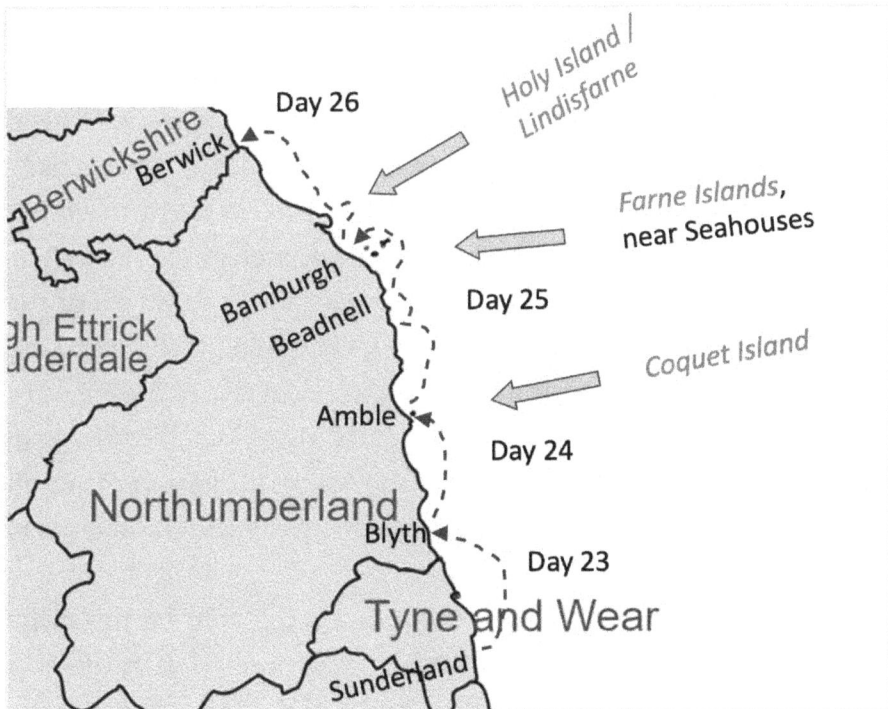

Day 23, Friday 12th May

To Blyth

START	11.00, Sunderland
WIND	N, 13–19mph
WEATHER	Thick low cloud and drizzle. 8–10°C
TIDE	With me, max 0.6mph till 16.00
SEA STATE	Slight
HAZARDS	Cold
FINISH	RNYC Blyth, 15.15
DISTANCE	16 miles
SAILING HOURS	4 hours (15 mins lunch on the water)

It was one of the coldest days for the whole circumnavigation with a chill northerly breeze blowing in my face all the way. Low cloud reduced definition, made worse by the drizzle incessantly blotching my glasses, creating a uniquely blurring film in front of me, for the full four hours on the water. Fortunately, I found some substitute windscreen wipers in the form of the back side of my glove, which sufficiently cleared the rain with a single swipe, without adding a smear of unwelcome grease. The forecast of eight degrees Celsius meant that I put on all of my clothing, neck and head heating layers included, before setting off. I also had the benefit of a dressing room, since Alison very kindly let me change in the yacht club, away from the icy grip of the wind. Thus, I managed to stay warm all day, very much helping with my enjoyment, and assisting my cough on its way into history.

Brian came over for the launch, and suggested he might be able to do a drawing of me, as a token of appreciation of the trip. At the time, I wasn't sure what to make of this hugely generous offer, and thought nothing of it for a while. But sure enough, a few weeks later, a fantastic coloured pencil drawing appeared at my home, captured faithfully from the photograph that was taken on the morning. So now I sit amongst other drawings on Brian's website as the pretender, nestled in amongst a collection of well-known celebrities, like Elvis Presley and Marilyn Monroe. Brian, how incredibly kind, and forever remembered.

Friday night was folk night at Blyth Yacht Club also known as the Royal Northumberland Yacht Club. Mike, the Commodore, had already replied to say that I would be welcome to join the occasion, but he was not sure there would be any seats available. "Surely, you must have heard of Kathryn Tickell?" he declared. Trying not to sound too ignorant or ungrateful, I confessed that unfortunately I had not.

My first attempt to find the yacht club left me puzzled. I could see its location on Google Maps, but on the ground, there was nothing but large industrial looking hangars scattered around a marina. There was no sign of a clubhouse building, however large or small. Following the route on my phone, I came to a gate in a fence, which looked like it could be relevant, but didn't seem to go anywhere. As I was hanging about the barrier, a man called Dave approached the entrance with confidence whilst eyeing me suspiciously. I asked him whether this was the way to the club, which he confirmed, and said, "It's over there," pointing towards the marina. I wasn't sure that helped a great deal, since his finger was aiming precisely in the direction from which I had just come. But there was nothing for it, so I followed his lead. Sure enough, a few steps down the path revealed what I had been looking at all along. The club was a ship. And not just any old ship, but a light ship, still fitted with its central lantern.

Light Vessel 50, or LV 50 was originally built in 1879 and moored on Seven Stones reef, about halfway between Lands' End and the Isles of Scilly. The ship was run by a noble crew of seven men who stayed on board for two months at a time, manually operating the oil powered warning lamp, in all the foul conditions that the Atlantic could throw at them. The ship was rescued from the breakers yard in 1952 for the princely sum of £600, and towed to Blyth where it was renovated ready for club use. It is one of the last remaining floating wooden light ships in the UK, perhaps not surprising since they were only intended to last for 30-50 years.

There was just time to find my booking for the night at The Tavern in town, before I dashed back to the ship, to see if I could squeeze in for the concert. Approaching the magic gate, there was a small group gathered around a man sitting on the floor, with a graze to his head. It looked like others were attending to his needs sufficiently, so my interference was unwarranted, and needless to say I was late. Clattering down the steps into the hull, I almost bumped into the reception desk, only to be told that the concert had been sold out. "Oh dear, that's a shame", and "is there any way of squeezing in one more person?" I appealed.

"It's a small space and we have tight fire regulations as you can imagine" came the sympathetic sounding reply. "But wait a second."

There was chat about someone called Jeff who had fallen over. And he was being taken to hospital for a check-up. And that meant that his ticket would be available. And would I like it?

I am not sure that is exactly what schadenfreude is supposed to mean, but I certainly had a fantastic evening, benefiting from the misfortune of poor Jeff. A front row seat, listening to the exquisite sounds of Kathryn Tickell and Amy Thatcher, making music divine enough to float you away to another dimension. Their music was born of Northumbrian pipes, fiddle, accordion, and even dancing on a spare ship plank, acting as an impromptu clog board. Kathryn was brought up in Northumberland so had decided to provide a concert at this intimate venue, much to the amazement of the organiser Frank.

And such was the local welcome, that I was invited to say a couple of words about my laseraroundtheuk journey during the interval, slightly embarrassing given my august company, but hard to refuse.

Dave, from my earlier gate opening meeting, was kind enough to offer a lift back to the hotel. In the short journey, we touched on some of the town's history. Decline in coal mining and shipbuilding industries had left working men a bit lost. Redevelopment in the 1990s had seen buildings refreshed, and investment brought in. Dave was still finding it hard to harness a regenerative mood amongst locals, when trying to launch local projects, tending to feel the weight of 'what had been' holding back the conversation. It felt like the past was more important than the future.

I thanked Dave as I stepped out of his car near my hotel, before moving on myself. I ducked into the local takeaway, with cash in hand this time, for a late-night Chinese. I felt thoroughly and joyously doused with local culture, all in a few short hours.

I slept well.

Day 24, Saturday 13th May

To Amble

START	12.00, Blyth
WIND	E, 8–13mph
WEATHER	Cloudy, then sunshine, 10°C. Dry
TIDE	With me 0.3mph from 13.00
SEA STATE	Slight
HAZARDS	Light wind
FINISH	Coquet SC at Amble, 16.30
DISTANCE	17 miles
SAILING HOURS	4½ hours

Light morning wind and an opposing tide weren't rushing me back to the shore, but at least there was some sunshine on my walking route back to the boat. I was pleased with my landing on South Beach since it was a steadily sloping short stretch, sheltered by harbour arms, and a bit out of town so relatively safe from peaky beachcombers.

So I was not pleased when I stepped over the dunes to see Betty all roughed up on the sand. That shot of tension gripped my being, as I frowned, and fretted my way over to my righted hull, trying not to panic, or shout. I wanted to scream "who has done that?" – sand was scattered all over the hull surface, no doubt clogging up pulleys and cleats, with the sail half unravelled. The lock, still intact, was stretched between secured items. Examining the hatches, I thought maybe they had been undone and then closed, but nothing was missing. This was puzzling and disturbing. Having the harbour master drag the boat across the sand at Whitby in broad daylight was mildly annoying, but some mysterious and purposeless person tampering with my precious

Betty during the dark of night, left me feeling quite vulnerable.

Bob, whom I hadn't met before, came over for a chat, so I needed to recover my happy face. He talked of his long association with the yacht club. Although he had not been at the concert, he surprised me with his connection to the wonderful Kathryn, whom he knew because he lived next to her father Mike, so had met her many times. My tales of adventure prompted many of his own sailing trip memories, stories which softly lapped at Betty's sides as she was prepared for the next leg. We were journeying northwards, getting ever closer to Scotland.

I am not quite sure it is an appropriate term for sailing, but if it is, then I ambled my way up to the happy town of Amble. I took a peaceful and contented stroll past green hills, undulating coastline, and onto Coquet Island, stationed at the entrance to its namesake river. The sun even came out for a while.

Such was the smoothness of the journey, that I managed to fix a cord back into the neck of my sandwich box holding bag (if you follow that?). One of those tricky jobs, like reinserting the drawstring into your swimming trunks, having pulled too hard at the wrong end. A job that requires patience, dexterity and more than one hand, so not easy when steering a boat. I am pleased to report, that I was pleased with my significant achievement for the day.

I also tried out some standing up sailing, grabbing extra balance by holding onto the painter in one hand, and the tiller in the other, a stance that provides useful back stretching exercise and a different perspective on the surroundings.

On days like this, the radio helped while the time away. I quite often started with the Today programme via BBC Sounds, though hopefully getting myself to move on to something else before the news came round for the third time. On this day, yet more rail strikes were being announced, and yet more interest rate rises were upon us. The good news, you might argue, was that recession had been narrowly avoided. Offering some glimmers of hope in the ghastly internecine war in Ukraine, those dastardly Russians had withdrawn from Bakhmut. "We could all do with a bit more of that," I thought.

The weather said it was going to be cloudy and ten degrees, but it was much warmer because the clouds left early, and there was sunshine all day. The easterly, blowing straight into the mouth of the river, made for a gorgeous spring sail up to Coquet Yacht Club, where there were, to my surprise, some yachts.

Less gorgeous was the mud on landing, which made for a messy and gooey squelch about, before Kevin came down to my rescue with a trolley (and shortly afterwards, a hose). In front of the club was a good patch of grass, so I could spread out and dry clothing in the sunshine on a bench, so a perfect spot. It was ideal for camping as well, but you know what I think about that. Kevin and his wife very kindly bought me a steak and kidney pie at the bar, which was gratefully received. However, I did think to myself afterwards that a pie might be sliding towards the emergency food category.

As I was pushing peas around my plate and scooping up the last of the gravy-soaked pastry, the coastguard rang.

"Is that Andrew Hill-Smith?"

"Yes, it is," I replied, wondering what could have prompted this call.

"Do you have a white dinghy on South Beach at Blyth?"

"Well, I did go there yesterday and I parked it there overnight, but left this morning. I'm now at Amble," I offered, still puzzled about where this was going.

Then came the explanation that filled in a few pieces from the earlier puzzle. "The police were contacted this morning, since someone found the boat on the beach, and thought maybe someone was in trouble. And they then contacted the coastguard, so we are contacting you. Can you confirm that you are safe and on land?"

"I am indeed," I confirmed. "But it's now 6pm, and the incident was reported this morning. It seems like a long time between now and then if safety was a worry," I tried, fishing for some kind of procedural clarification. Unfortunately, no new information was forthcoming.

Therefore, I had gained an explanation of what had happened that morning, and at the same time, lost an explanation as to how the coastguard might operate, in order to prevent my drowning. Given that I was more interested in being rescued, should the need arise, the conversation did not feel like a very profitable exchange.

Still, it is best to do something in face of adversity, so it was out with the black marker pen again. I copied the message from the centre board, onto the hull - **Please call [my mobile] if concerned** 😊. That might help.

A guy called Dave was pottering about when I landed. His trimaran was parked outside the entrance to the clubhouse, with the two hull wings folded up like a swan, so as to avoid taking up too much space. A ladder was propped against the vessel, to allow access to the central hull.

We ended up chatting over our respective pie and peas. He told me about his ten-year project to build his trimaran, and tomorrow was indeed the culmination of all that effort. At the handsome age of 78, he was planning to launch his fine construction on the rising tide, so that the swan could spread her wings and test her buoyancy. I was excited for him as were others, but Dave, who declared that he was not very sociable, was holding back. He preferred to focus his attention on flotation anxiety.

There wasn't much holding back when it came to recounting his wife's disinterest in his grand project. She did not care much for sailing, and had no intention of joining him on future voyages. But it didn't sound like he had been showing a lot of interest in her interests either. A relationship described as 'ships passing in the night' came to mind. Presumably to get in some relationship practice for the months to come, he was planning to sleep on board his craft for the night.

I half considered begging a berth on the fresh trimaran, but thought better of it. Instead, I ended up at the Amble Inn on the other side of town, regretting my decision to reject the camping option, as my destination seemed to get further and further away with each step along the way.

I stopped at a garage for a coffee and snack to top up dinner fuel. With my hand on a chocolate muffin, a member of staff said I could have it for free, rather than pay the reduced price. I was simultaneously grateful for the freebie, and at the same time insulted. "Do I look like some kind of impoverished tramp?" I wondered. Maybe the dishevelled hair, rubbish bags draped over each sagging shoulder, and journeyed demeanour, were too much of a downtrodden look? "I might have to smarten up," I thought. However, the muffin was worth every mouthful.

Though the Amble Inn was quite expensive, I had an enormous room, so settled down to watch the tail end of Eurovision. Liverpool was hosting the show on behalf of Ukraine, who had won the previous year. The UK had come in a miraculous second, thanks to Sam Ryder and a great following on TikTok. It was back down to the bottom in 2024, with poor Mae Muller doing her best, whilst excitedly holding onto the poisoned chalice of a UK ticket. Sweden won again.

Part of the fun of the event was to eye up all the costumes, which were becoming more and more outrageous, but a sign of the times. I was wondering whether I was losing a sense of proportion or something, but "isn't everyone dressed in a gender fluid way?"

I wondered. Even the usually leather clad dark skinned, well-toned and tanned Italian biker bloke, who was strutting his stuff, appeared in a sequin covered sleeveless top. So, it was the second time that day that I thought I might need to revisit the contents of my wardrobe.

Day 25, Sunday 14th May

To Bamburgh

START	10.30, Amble
WIND	SW/S, 6–11 mph
WEATHER	17°C, dropping to 13°C with rain
TIDE	Max 0.5mph against. 1.6mph with at 1400
SEA STATE	Slight to moderate
HAZARDS	Low wind, rain, tide at Seahouses
FINISH	Bamburgh, 17.30
DISTANCE	22 miles
SAILING HOURS	5½ hours. Beadnell SC for 1½ hours

It was a warm morning for a change, with a pleasant wind blowing out to sea, so just was what was needed.

Dave was already on the pontoon, having manoeuvred his beloved craft down the slipway, and wings were gracefully spread out in its white shining splendour. A couple of others were mingling about, half watching the moment, but there was no sign of Dave's wife. I managed to persuade the reluctant Dave to pose for a photograph, to capture my excitement. His boat had not sunk, so he was looking sort of happy-ish, maybe.

His plans were to test the craft locally, then sail up to the Orkneys, before continuing his solo journey down to warmer Spain for a few months. The sails would be added another day, so we would not be sailing out to sea together, as I had half imagined. Instead, I wished him luck and went on my own sweet way.

My plan was to stop at Beadnell Sailing Club. A guy called Peter, whom I had met at Blyth, had talked highly of its splendid views. It was also a potential waiting spot, should I need to hang about till the tide changed – there were some stiff flows as the water is squeezed between Seahouses and the Farne Islands.

Feeling confident that I had the correct bay, I went in to land, cautiously weaving my way between rocks to the safety of sand. The bay was the right shape, and about the right distance. Everything looked right. But I couldn't see a sailing club.

Pointing to a property on a nearby hill, I asked a passing couple, with baby on a parent's back, "Is that Beadnell Sailing club?"

"No, I'm afraid it's the next bay" was the reply.

"Oh, thanks," I said. "How foolish of me."

It was foolish, since I had my location completely wrong, and was out by a couple of miles. It was not too much of a problem on this occasion, but it was not the first time I had made a similar mistake.

So, I set off again, wiggling my way out through the rocks. My top tip to myself for the day was, 'in future double check your location on Navionics before landing'. I figured it would be better to assume I was heading to the wrong place, and then check, rather than assuming I was in the right spot, to then discover it was wrong. Either way, Beadnell Sailing Club was indeed in the next similar-shaped bay, this time without any rocks.

Bilge keeled yachts were parked on the sand, whilst men prepared their boats for the season ahead, and kindly pointed the way to the sailing club. I displayed my 'gone for coffee' sign on the centre board, fearing a repeat of the Whiby incident, and trudged off over the smelly shoreline seaweed. My attempt to make contact with the club had failed, because completing the 'contact us' form had led to a nil response. The clubhouse is in a great location, as Peter had said, with an area of decking looking out across the bay. I was sure it would be wonderful on a summer's evening, but on this day was frankly chilly, since the sun had disappeared.

I was half hoping for some offers of help, but even my not-so-subtle hints like, "do you have any suggestions about accommodation round here" were not getting any traction. There was little point in stopping at Beadnell.

With a free instant coffee and a place to safely drip without causing too much consternation, I set about searching for a place to stay, and form a plan for the next day. Bamburgh was a good place to land, being past the worst of the tide, though hosting super pricey accommodation. Berwick had an ample supply of beds, but would be a twice taxi ride away. I had a contact in Berwick, the father of a fellow sailor from London, but I would not want to prey on his hospitality, so thought it best to book for two nights. I could then engage in the 'Whitby shuffle', making use of public transport to and from Berwick.

I had been wondering about sailing between Holy Island and the mainland, since I knew there was a causeway which flooded at high tide. I liked the idea of sailing over a road. Fast talking knowledgeable James came into the clubhouse and chipped in with his advice. He had engaged in the round the [Holy] island race a few times, and said that the tidal window was pretty small, so suggested I go round the outside, unless I wanted to risk a lot of walking. I didn't.

James also remembered meeting Ron from something like 20 years previously. James had provided Ron with a meal after he had landed at Beadnell, and before Ron retired to his tent for the night. It felt eerie to be walking in virtually the same footsteps as my predecessor, but it also felt like a glowing connection, made through the stories of others, preserved for nearly two decades.

On the way up to Beadnell, I managed to lose my sun hat. Vanity and slight discomfort meant that I had been wearing the hat strap on my head, and not under it. The dressing folly proved ineffectual when a burst of wind arrived unexpectedly, and whisked it like a frisbee into the sea. Grey hat, on grey sea, under grey cloud does not provide the best visual clues. I could see it well enough to start with, though lost sight of the thing after completing part of my hat overboard procedure. A bit of weaving back and forth was to no avail, and I guessed my worthy sun protector was no longer on top, but submerged under the waves. It was only worth £12 from Mountain Warehouse, but I was surprisingly upset by this misfortune. I felt the weight of my own error that could not be undone, and a loss that would be hard to replace (because of my sea-based status). "The feelings will pass and the hat will be replaced," I said to myself.

I passed Farne Islands Nature Reserve. It was closed to visitors because of bird flu. Another wave of the dreaded virus had been devastating wild bird populations up the East Coast for a couple of years, with the added risk of affecting domestic poultry production. The spectre of COVID was still floating in the air, so there was also the worry of another zoonotic jump to humans. I was not tempted to visit, even if it were possible.

The tide was at its lowest ebb when I landed in the drizzle, next to the imposing black block of Bamburgh castle.

Bamburgh castle was originally constructed in the 5th and 6th centuries, on a volcanic outcrop and was possibly the capital of the kingdom of Bernicia. It was later destroyed by the Vikings in the 10th century, along with most of the historical records.

Norman reconstruction remains at the core of the current castle, which then changed ownership over the centuries, including coming under control of the Crown for a period. Deterioration of the building led to the eventual purchase and careful restoration by Lord Armstrong at the end of the 19th century, whose family still own the Grade 1 listed property today.

The castle is open to visitors, but it was not the time or occasion for such touristic frivolity for me. It was going to be a long slog up the beach to the distant dunes and it was already getting late.

Julie and Steph mercifully came over to see if I needed a hand. They had come up from Newcastle for a girl's weekend and were bemoaning the reluctance of other party members to embrace the drippy outdoors.

"Who is supporting you?" I was asked. I gave the now standard reply of "you're my support team", which brought on a giggle, and a good dose of extra Geordie chat. And with that we collectively huffed, puffed and laughed our way up the beach. Getting understandably tired, Julie and Steph were looking for extra boat carrying recruits, and spied Terry who was putting his dog in the car. Despite being hailed, he disappeared at a critical moment, pursued by good natured tuts. When the boat was finally parked on a grassy patch of dune, Steph finished off with the charming line to camera, "when Julie said we were going on a boat trip, I didn't think we would have to carry it". Julie concluded, "We wish you all the best for the rest of the trip and don't forget to sponsor Andrew." I was quite tempted to go and join them in a local pub.

Dogless Terry then turned up with a trump card, presenting the ace of hearts in the form of a lift to Berwick. It was not only miles and miles, but also miles and miles in the wrong direction for him. Terry was a youngish looking, tall but gentle man, who had retired early from his trade. He let me sit in the front seat on a plastic bag, rather than trouble me to get changed. It is strange how people meeting for the first and last time, can dip straight into personal stories, and for whatever reason this is what happened here.

The prompt for retirement and a change of life direction came about because Terry's partner had suffered a frightening assault from Leukaemia. In my medical student eyes, Leukaemia for adults was very bad news, and almost always terminal, so the account of stem cell transplantation and a curative intervention was a joy to hear. Input had been very gratefully received at the hands of the local NHS, and the good news still sounded fresh. This was the second time I had heard of life saving intervention for Leukaemia within the last month. With all the bad health service sentiment around, it was wonderful to hear of quietly spoken, and yet profound stories of success in the face of extreme adversity. Life for Terry and partner could begin again.

And so, we arrived at the Rose and Thistle Hotel and our lives parted, both feeling better, having exchanged metaphorical cards of goodwill.

Decorum and a desire to give a good first impression, meant that I felt obliged to get changed before going into the hotel. Being dressed in full sailing gear in the middle of Berwick might also appear odd. However, the only suitable space nearby was a glass sided bus stop, suitable because it provided protection from the continued rainfall.

The process was straightforward to begin with. Removing a hat or buoyancy aid and placing it on growing piles on the floor, was decent enough. Getting down to the business end of things, did risk embarrassment, exposure, or perhaps a charge of indecent exposure, should there be an awkward slip down, or an inopportune gust of wind. Worse still would be an arriving bus, disgorging its passengers onto the street in front of me. I imagined a Mr Bean moment of sitting uncomfortably on a cold damp seat, furtively maintaining privacy with random scraps of wet clothing, whilst departing locals cast disparaging looks over their shoulder, as they strode off round the corner. That would be bad.

Luckily the lack of road, or pedestrian, traffic saved me.

Unluckily, all my courteous preparation before entering the hotel, was for nought.

There was no one to open the door at the hotel. Worse still, I had missed a couple of key words on the Airbnb email receipt, and if you too should happen to see these few, then be afraid. Be very afraid.

'Self check-in' sounds innocent enough, but it can lead you down many dark avenues into endless barriers, ghosted phone calls and frustrations, like trying to type your name onto a a blank electronic key pad. The self-check in arrangement demanded extra security clearance like evidence of my passport, which I did not have. Other personal details were required, even though they were already shared with Airbnb. Then all those details had to be verified by a non-responding person somewhere in the ether. An automated email offered reassurance that my information would receive a response within eight hours. This was not reassuring. At all.

Problems were compounded by the fact that it was now seven o'clock on a Sunday night, and I was having to stand outside in the rain, getting increasingly short tempered. How a good mood can be so easily spoilt. Such is the rollercoaster of life.

After a forty-minute stomp around town, I came back to the hotel to find someone coming out. He explained how things worked, in ways that even I could understand. And at the same time, the precious codes pinged through, so everything was suddenly sorted. What a relief.

And finally, to the Chinese to grab some food, which was happily only a few doors up from the hotel. But oh no, they only take cash and I had run out again.

When I was struggling to locate the nearby note dispensing machine, a fellow pedestrian offered to help. Fortunately, he used gesture to aid communication, since not only was he very drunk, but also his Scottish accent was so thick to render his rambling instructions all but incomprehensible. The good news was this meant I was VERY CLOSE TO SCOTLAND.

* * *

Day 26, Monday 15th May

To Berwick-upon-Tweed

START	11.30, Bamburgh
WIND	NW/N, 15–20mph, then 8–12mph
WEATHER	Sun/cloud, 10–12°C, dry
TIDE	Against me max 0.8mph till 15.00
SEA STATE	Slight
HAZARDS	Long beach. Tide against me
FINISH	Berwick, 17.45
DISTANCE	15 miles
SAILING HOURS	4¾ hours (90 mins at Holy Island)

The taxi back to Bamburgh took longer than I remembered, and more expensive than I had thought, adding my appreciation to Terry's spontaneous kindness of yesterday. My cheerful driver had returned to work for want of more things to do, and made me think about my post-retirement plans. Yes, keeping busy would be key.

A stopover on Holy Island felt like a must. After all, I was on holiday. What's more, it was a bright sunny day making the distinctive island spectacle, shine like an apparition.

My first port of call was Pilgrims café in the unimaginatively named town of Holy Island. In the warm sheltered sunshine, I was enjoying my treat of a cappuccino and carrot cake. When the distraction of a phone call ended, I realised I was not the only one enjoying a Holy Island treat. Three overfriendly sparrows, boldly balancing on the edge of my plate, were pecking at the lush sugary and expensive topping with impunity. "Good for them," I thought. I ate what was left.

And then on to Lindisfarne Castle for a visit. I figured I was a bit short of time so ran off over the lush green grass up to the castle. Fully dressed in sailing gear, which had now become the fashion, I made a half-hearted attempt to blag a free pass to the ancient monument. After all, like a Viking, I had taken the trouble to sail there. The staff were having none of it.

Lindisfarne Castle, like Bamburgh, is located on volcanic rock, lifting it to its iconic position. It was first constructed in the 16th century as a defensive fort, given its proximity to the Scottish / English border. Sir Edwin Lutyens extensively redeveloped the castle in 1901, with Gertrude Jekyll contributing to nearby garden design, and the National Trust providing more recent renovation in 2018.

The history of the island, interchangeably named as Holy Island or Lindisfarne, goes back much further to 6th century AD, which you may recall from your school history lessons. At its founding, the monastery was a key centre for Celtic Christianity, under Saint Cuthbert amongst others, whose contributions were recorded by the venerable Bede. The influence of the island was said to have spread across the world.

Similar to Bamburgh, the Vikings invaded and destroyed the monastery. The Normans reinstated the building and its functions in the 11th century. Finally, the stone from the monastery was used to build the castle as part of Henry VIII's monastic dissolution programme. Now it is in excellent condition having been fully restored, so is well worth a visit. Make sure you get the causeway tides right though.

Back on the water and out past the island, the wind died for about 40 minutes for some mysterious reason, but then filled in nicely, making for a pleasant fetch into the mouth of the Tweed.

A bit of phone guidance from Andrew helped me make my way to the invisible Berwick Sailing Club, invisible since it had not shown up on my pre-trip Google Maps tour. Andrew's instructions helped me pick my route round sandbanks and S bends, as I struggled to make ground going upstream. Delightfully, Andrew was waiting with a laser trolley on the shore, when I reached the club.

Like so many of the people who assisted me on the journey, I had never met Andrew before. Andrew was the father of a sailing companion on the Thames Valley Circuit called John. John had the grace to allow me to beat him on occasions, and sailed with a kind and considerate nature, both on water and on land.

Keeping characteristics in the family, Andrew was kind and considerate too, and also highly efficient. Hardly had a thought, or a possible need passed my lips, before it was attended to, quick as a flash. A towel for the shower in the clubhouse, back to the house to say hi and drop some items for washing, return to the club for boat repairs to the transom, and fitting the long-awaited auto bailer (which I had brought up from Bridlington), spare gorilla tape for my supplies, back to the house for a delicious vegetarian chilli, dried clothes, and to top it off, Andrew gave me a replacement sun hat that he no longer needed. There was great company as well, including his wife, stepdaughter and her child. Goodness. 'I better keep my random talking out loud thoughts to myself for a few hours,' I thought, or I might feel overwhelmed with kindness.

The house was beautifully located with a peaceful view over the fields down to the river Tweed, dressed by the grand sweep of a railway viaduct, rhythmically clacking in even Victorian arched steps over the valley to the town beyond.

When crossing the road bridge heading north to my accommodation, Andrew provided a snippet of local history to add depth to my journey. As a border town, there was a long history of tension between the English and Scottish nations. Although it has been in English hands since 1482, the population still feel hesitant about loyalties, with a recent survey giving testament – 25% consider themselves English, 25% Scottish, and most sensible of all, 50% consider themselves Berwickers first and foremost. 'A neat way of preventing unnecessary divisions,' I thought.

CHAPTER 9

Scotland and the Firth of Forth

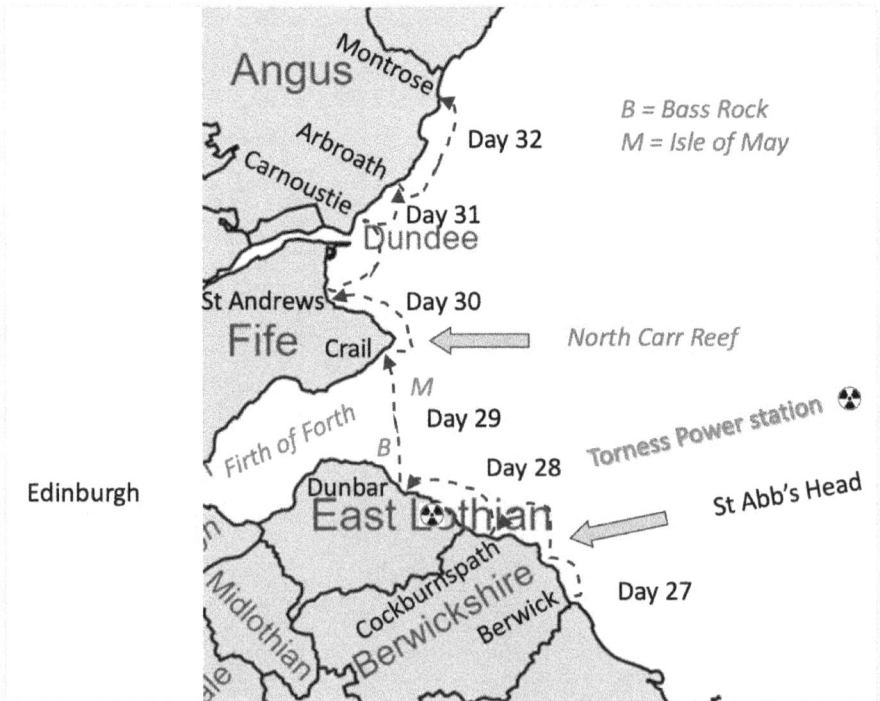

Day 27, Tuesday 16th May

To Cockburnspath, or thereabouts

START	10.10, Berwick
WIND	NW 15–25mph, dropping to NE 9–12mph
WEATHER	Sun and cloud 15°C, then 11°C with rain
TIDE	0.5mph (looks like 1.0mph) till 15.00
SEA STATE	Slight to moderate at times
HAZARDS	Variable wind. Not reaching destination
FINISH	Pease Bay leisure park, 18.00
DISTANCE	21 miles
SAILING HOURS	6½ hours. (75 mins at Eyemouth)

Yesterday's intermittent northerly had meant a slow 3mph over ground, mostly tacking into the wind, and I was hoping for something quicker. I was going to be disappointed.

After two hours of tiring beat, I was coming up to a collection of white buildings huddled in a valley, the first sign of human habitation in a long line of inhospitable cliffs. "That must be Eyemouth," I thought. I wanted it to be Eyemouth since I was feeling tired. On checking, I was disappointed to find I was only at lowly Burnmouth, a mere five miles into the first leg. Hence, I had been making a pathetic 2½ miles an hour, despite what I felt was a decent amount of wind, and a lot of effort.

Some places around the coast are spared the honour of tidal arrows on Navionics, so on this occasion I was left to deduce what the speed of flow might be. A passing buoy, local knowledge, and I was horrified to see a current of at least 1mph heading south. That kind of explained the problem. However, it didn't tell me what to do.

Stopping places were in short supply up this part of the coast, and if I were to make Cockburnspath, I could be in for another Thames Estuary length of day. What's more, I might miss dinner. After a bit of contemplation, I came up with a new approach to my passage planning problem – namely to swop my meals around. If I landed at Eyemouth, I could go and grab a hot meal, and then save my sandwiches for dinner. It would also eat up some time till the tide turned. That cheered me up.

Having implemented my plan and stepped onto the shore, I also realised I was IN SCOTLAND. I couldn't quite believe it. It had sounded such a remote, fearsome and impossible place to reach, and yet there I was, with two feet and a dinghy, standing solid on the beach.

After my motivation-restoring pub lunch of leek and potato soup, followed by chicken and chips, I came back to find a young man called Jamie, standing next to Betty. I sometimes tip her on her side when landing, so that the sail rests on the land out of the wind, meaning that the bottom of the boat is available to read. To my delight, this is what Jamie had been doing, ready with lots of questions when I returned. He asked where I was going today, how I was finding the journey, and he had even looked up some of the online videos. His dad was out sailing in the bay, but Jamie had lost confidence on the water, so I was doing my best to encourage him to have another go. He thought the round the UK sailing stories might well be enough to inspire him to brave the seas once again. I very much hoped they would.

The wind was on the move, swinging round to the north-east and picking up as I was rounding St Abbs Head. It was a large lump of looming cliff, home to a mass of swirling birds, delightfully swooping around the boat. For a while I was on a screaming reach making speedy progress, trying to keep pace with my aerial friends. I was having fun, compared to the painful grind of the morning.

Unfortunately, I fell out when I missed the size of an incoming gust. Still anxious to keep the tumble count down and maintain sailing esteem, I was doing my best to minimise the significance of these events. A hop back in, and on my way again was the usual form, followed by reassurance to myself saying, "it was nay bother".

Sadly, that was it for the wind. It completely disappeared after some rain, and didn't come back. The last six miles were a now all-too-familiar, paddle-assisted plod.

One last thing about the lunch spot. A few days later, I discovered I had been there before. When rummaging through photos to check my trip notes, I typed in Eyemouth. To my surprise, up popped a photo of my good self, with foot on the harbour wall and a fishing boat backdrop. The photo was from 1985, so nearly 40 years previously. There I was as a 20-something young man, staring comfortably at the camera, wearing one of those dark blue neatly knitted Jersey jumpers.

The photo had appeared because my siblings and I have been digitising my mother's huge pile of neatly ordered albums, after she died. The thing is, I had absolutely no recollection of being in Eyemouth previously. I used to joke that my mother could recount my own life better than I, and so here she was again, taking me back to times I had forgotten, even when she was no longer with us. That made two endearing lives warmly remembered, all in one shot.

Day 28, Wednesday 17th May

To Dunbar

START	12.10, Pease Bay Leisure Park
WIND	E, NE, then W, 5–10 mph, more later
WEATHER	Cloudy, up to 17°C. Dry
TIDE	Against me max 0.5mph till 18.00
SEA STATE	Slight
HAZARDS	Little wind. Landing at Dunbar
FINISH	Bellhaven Beach at Dunbar, 18.00
DISTANCE	9 miles
SAILING HOURS	3¾ hours

A key planning objective was to safely cross the Firth of Forth, and it looked like a decent westerly was coming in for Thursday, the next day. Given that I thought I could tackle the 20 miles, straight across from Dunbar, there would be no need to stop at North Berwick Sailing Club. This was a slight disappointment since the club included an enthusiastic group of laser sailors, whom I would have enjoyed meeting.

For the present, however, there was no need to go further than Dunbar. The upshot of this, together with the late tide and lack of wind, meant that a slow start was in order for today.

Rob, my Airbnb host for the night, had given me a lift up the long steep hill from Pease Bay, to his home at Cockburnspath, for which I was hugely grateful.

Refreshed by a good sleep, filled with porridge and a topping of kindness, I was equally grateful for a morning stroll, back to Pease Bay. The route was all downhill. I sauntered along quiet green paths, dotted with buttercups and cowslip, dressed with the warmth of sunshine, and still Scottish air, all the way down to the bay. There was no rush, and nothing to worry about for the day, so it was a gorgeous peaceful immersion in the countryside.

There was even time for a jacket potato lunch and some Wi-Fi in the leisure park Smuggler's Arms, before setting off – that was the one and only time I had lunch before launch.

Surfers were out in the sea, which struck me as surprising since there was absolutely no wind. The tide was coming in, and there was some swell, making a trip into the water worthwhile for those carrying their board. I thought the bay exit would be straightforward, but it was harder than I realised, receiving several good dowsings as I paddled my way out through the waves.

Then it was a radio assisted crawl along the coast to Dunbar, past brooding cliffs, which then levelled out when approaching Torness Power Station – another rectangular block of building, perched on a promontory. Here, we must pause for a moment, to take in the essential sights of our next location on the nuclear power plant tour.

Torness was built in 1988 after much consultation, and indeed protest. It is a highly visible landmark from the A1, and was the last of the second-generation nuclear reactors, being of an advanced gas cooled design, for those who might be interested. Torness was owned by Scottish Energy, but has now passed to EDF. It was due to end operation in 2030, but cracks have been appearing, so the decommissioning date had been brought forward to 2028, thus being part of our ailing stock of energy generating plants.

I had envisaged a nice easy landing at Dunbar, heading straight into East Beach near the town. I was planning to meet up with Ian, a university medic friend, who was hoping to get away from work and come to meet up. However, edging closer into East Beach, all I could see was rocks, so I couldn't land there. This is not how things looked on Google Maps. On closer inspection from the land later, the sand had indeed departed, presumably washed away in a winter storm. Google Maps was clearly out of date.

The next option was the harbour. The Google Maps view from above made it look quite a challenge, and the perspective from sea level didn't trouble that impression, not least because I couldn't find the entrance. Surrounded by stacks of sandstone on all sides, and more rocks out to sea, there is a narrow gap forming an entry point. From there, you are fed into a slender inner harbour, then under a bridge to another drying section, all with steep and moderately unmountable walls. Ian said he had sailed into the place, in a topper many years ago. That was all very well if you know what you are doing. I didn't.

So, I rejected Dunbar Harbour and went on to Belhaven Beach round the corner, landing next to a bunch of kids having surf lessons. There was a lot of sand. Maybe it's where the East Beach grit had gone to.

After I landed, I met Paul and Zeita. They came over to help with the boat problem. Paul was tall, German and on holiday, with impeccable English, and a demeanour to match his nationality. My fatuous comment of "you're tall", luckily not topped off with the full monty blurt out, of 'you're tall, Paul', was swatted away with a sarcastic expressionless reply. What I was trying to say was 'I'm a bit stuck here, and being tall, I hope you will be able to help', which I did manage to explain when I had recovered a degree of dignity. The problem was, I could not open the back hatch on the boat. This was potentially catastrophic.

All my worldly goods were stored within the boat, and I couldn't get them out. I had images of wandering the streets of Dunbar in sailing gear, being kindly guided to a rescue shelter for homeless people. Or of food festering in the hull, creating a stink that would repel helpers in the future. Or having to break open the hatch, thus leaving Betty and me vulnerable to sinking. Even super-long-armed Paul would not be able to reach from the front hatch to the back, not unless he had picked up a Spiderman-like arm stretching talent, on his way over from Germany.

My fingers were hurting from all the pushing and shoving, in my earlier failed attempts to unscrew the plastic cover. My nails were showing splintering lines, where a slip had started to pull them from their beds. I figured I needed all hands on deck. That is, tall Paul and I, since there wasn't room for Zeita.

Trying to turn this way and then the other, there was a lot of grunting, followed by pausing and standing up to discuss what to do next. The hatch moved a little one way, then stopped, stuck firm. It moved the other way and refused to budge further. We were wondering what was the matter, and couldn't figure out what to do.

Then all of a sudden, with one more wrench, it released, and we were free. "Hooray," I said. "What a relief." Paul didn't say anything. I felt like giving Paul a big hug, but thought it might not have been appreciated. Also, I was probably the wrong height to do the gesture justice, so stuck with the traditional "thank you very much". Paul and Zeita continued on their Scottish holiday, no doubt pleased with their rescue efforts, but keeping it firmly to themselves.

Inspection of the obstruction revealed nothing untoward – no grit in a groove, no distortion, no thread damage on either surface. I concluded I had merely misaligned the lid, when closing it that morning.

One other thing I noted, was that water had come in through the hatch, presumably when I had been washed through the waves at Pease Bay. And my second folly of the day, believing that there was little risk of ingress, was to casually leave the dry bag open inside the hull, just enough to capture incoming drips and feed them neatly down to my no longer dry luggage. "Bother."

However, it was just water. A major calamity had been averted. I had learnt my lesson, and I would be very careful when packing up in future.

Then Ian arrived. I was delighted to see him and was really looking forward to catching up. Since university, we had remained in touch over the decades, meeting up intermittently as our paths crossed. He had driven over from Edinburgh after work, estimating that it would be simpler to return us both to his own house (as opposed to staying at his mum's place in Dunbar), despite the significant journey. It was all the better for me, since I could catch up with his wife Emma as well, thus completing the home away from home feel, that comes when reconnecting with old friends.

We collected belongings and clambered over the 'Bridge to Nowhere', which crosses a small stream. The 'Bridge to Nowhere' is named as such because at high tide, it is stranded in the sea, with no land connection. At those times, it looks purposeless, other than to form an iconic photographic centrepiece, amongst a rippled sea, reflecting a twilight sky.

Back in Edinburgh, Emma was home from work. Around the kitchen island, we chatted about family, friends, work and oh, yes, the occasional sailing story. Together, Ian and Emma rustled up a delicious salmon dinner and homemade cake, sufficiently moreish to mean that my stomach needed to give me a stern telling off, before I would utter the words "thank you very much, but I think I have had enough".

* * *

CHAPTER 9

Day 29, Thursday 18th May

To Crail

START	12.45, Dunbar
WIND	W, 10–17mph, most of the day
WEATHER	Cloudy but dry, 15°C
TIDE	Flowing W, 0.5mph turning at 15.00
SEA STATE	Slight to moderate
HAZARDS	Getting stuck in the middle
FINISH	Crail, 16.00
DISTANCE	18 miles
SAILING HOURS	3¼ hours

Ian and Emma were up and out before me, being part of the honourable working population. I was left to my porridge devices, and a trip to the bus stop. It was such a filling stopover that it was sad to move on. I was left with a feeling of warmth and a strong desire to meet again. I was sure we would.

Forever thoughtful, Ian had put me in touch with other (semi-retired) Scottish doctors from Fife (once I had crossed the Firth of Forth), who might be able to help with a place to stay. How wonderful. Yet more unfathomable generosity was slightly overwhelming.

I did have a small problem, however, in that I was really keen to take a day off, so wanted to stay for two nights. There was nothing for it but to ask, and so I did. Peter, my potential host, paused for a moment on the phone to make a mental calculation on bed spaces - they had a group of four visitors staying the following night. Once computations were complete, like so many remarkably munificent people I met along the way, Peter welcomed me with open arms.

Public transport was needed to return to my boat. Bus #5 and then an X7, all for the lowly cost of £8 took me all the way into Edinburgh, and then back out to Belhaven Beach.

Stepping off the bus, a brief conversation sprung up with a fellow pedestrian, exchanging pleasantries about the day ahead. She soon declared that "I can't go sailing because I have PTSD", a forceful conversation stopper, I felt, and a form of explanation that is more common these days.

There are so many stories, experiences, understandings, misunderstandings, relationships, expectations, perceptions and so much more, all contained in such a short phrase, and a phrase that commands sympathy. It is remarkable how much leverage one can load into a few words, if it is fired up with a medical term or two. In my past clinical work, I have had the privilege of being able to listen through many of the accompanying threads, attached to a self-declaration of this sort, but today provided neither the time nor the place.

I was left feeling it was both a bit strange, and unnecessary, to dangle one's life history in front of a stranger, in a casual encounter. Wouldn't it have been easier to simply say something like "sailing is not my thing". The worry, I felt, was that a disorder can start to define a person, and I was unsure about the helpfulness of that. Furthermore, it is an increasingly common way of introducing oneself. As someone who has made many diagnoses over time, I worried that some of my practice could have been causing harm – through diagnostic misuse. I would need to think about that some more.

Back on the beach, the surfers were out again. From my elevated position on the 'Bridge to Nowhere', I could see a group gathered round Betty, and I thought I could see her being lifted and turned over. I hurried over to take a closer look, and to protect my precious sail mate, if necessary. What transpired was a little misunderstanding.

The group had indeed taken an interest, and were reading messages written on the hull, but were still puzzled. When I arrived, they were curious to find out more from the alleged owner. This wasn't for the intended purpose of looking up the website, following on YouTube, or donating to charity. Instead, like so many others before, they had thought the craft had been abandoned, and were trying to figure out what to do with the debris.

One wave rider piped up when I asked what he made of the writing on the boat. He didn't think the message 'please give to a chosen charity', meant, 'please give some of your money to one of the charities listed on the website, that you can see on the side of the boat in front of you, and you can use the QR code if that makes things easier'. Instead, he thought the reader was being asked to give the boat away to a charity of his very own choosing! I simply had not considered that as a possible interpretation. I would have to try and add some more words to make it clearer, but I doubted I would succeed in attending to all audiences.

The sail was a quick and easy reach, with the wind holding up for the whole journey, a combination that had not really occurred before. The only downside was that I found myself getting a bit cold, probably because of the speed, the spray and the cool air. Maybe it was a sign that I needed a break. Maybe my irrational rage at the unopening cockpit drainage bung was another sign. Maybe it was I, rather than the cockpit, that was getting drained. I needed a rest.

Bass Rock and the appropriately named Isle of May provided useful landmarks, helped by good visibility. I was getting better at using Navionics to check my landing point whilst on the water, so I found Crail on the distant shore without any difficulty.

The sheltered and relatively empty sloping beach, next to an attractive town, formed the ideal arrival spot, only slightly tempered by the sight of a dead gannet. The general advice at the time was to avoid touching a deceased bird, but I learnt that there was no need to report a solitary carcass – a group of three or more met the threshold.

Once I was confident about boat security sufficient for two nights, and that the back hatch was working properly, I set off up the hill.

The first statutory stop was a delightful café. Entering a low doorway, customers were guided out to an uneven surfaced, but sheltered terrace. It looked like it was hewn out of the cliff, sloping gently down towards the sea and an uninterrupted view across the Firth of Forth. Another fantastic spot to enjoy cappuccino and cake, and a place to warm up.

Charged with double supplies of gifts for my hosts, I enjoyed a top deck front seat view as the #56 wobbled its way down the coast. I enjoyed the vista and the meandering journey, whilst chatting to Shereen from my call list, a doctor colleague from Surrey. Soaking in the prospect of a day away from the sea, I was drifting into a happy reverie, and nearly missed the Upper Largo bus stop. I scrambled down the steps just in time, to find Peter waiting.

Peter was slender and energetic, tending to whiz about in person and in conversation, being interested in all things interesting. He was also motivated by kindness, and a desire to be helpful, characteristics that I recognised in myself, and in many medical colleagues. The energetic productivity was therefore both familiar and strangely comforting, more so perhaps, since I had found myself in something of a medic fest over the last few days.

However, the phrase "Would lentil soup be OK?" did fill me with panic, thinking that might be my lot on the food front for the evening. Having just arrived, I did not feel in a position to present my bowl and plaintively ask, like Oliver, "Please, sir, can I have some more?". But bread was reassuringly offered, then more soup, then cheese. With each new arrival of sustenance, my gaze could relax its grip on potential morsels of carbohydrate.

I could allow myself to look away from food items, and focus more generously on the general conversation, before darting back to search the room for extra nourishment. Hunger does funny things to your brain.

Mercifully, I ended the evening well fed, and relaxed.

Friday 19th May

What luxury to have a day off. What's more, I had the house to myself for the morning, so could potter around at my own speed, writing thank you cards, thanking donors, editing video material, and planning the days ahead.

And how incredibly trusting of Peter and Rachel. I moved about carefully making sure I did not break anything, or put items back in the wrong place for fear of reprimand, or embarrassment.

Hence it was with some nervousness that I hung out my laundry on the Hills Hoist in the garden. The stem had a significant rusty bend in it, so looked liable to break at any moment. This required careful risk assessment.

The first consideration was the wind strength. There was none in the morning and no forecasted breeze, so I considered there was a low risk of sudden gusts, which might overwhelm the delicate structure. Next, some load testing. Positioning lighter items gingerly on one side, I carefully rotated the frame, looking for excess lean, or unexpected deviation from its crooked state, before adding the next item on an opposing side. And finally, to the weightier items. A bit like a game of Jenga, I was worried that placing the last item on top, would destabilise the whole thing. Items were carefully spread out across the drying wires, and I nervously watched as it rotated round under the power of gravity. Then it stopped and stood still. Nothing broke. Phew. All seemed to be going well.

Having completed the risk assessment and carried out an action plan, it was time to conclude the job with finishing touches – namely to cross my fingers, and then head off to the bus stop, hoping for the best.

A stunningly beautiful, windless blue-sky day beckoned me down to the harbour at Anstruther. I was to be a tourist for the afternoon. It was blue, blue everywhere, crisp and clear, so solid a colour that you felt you could almost taste it. There was hardly so much as a ripple on the water. Photograph-ready craft floated patiently in the harbour, lined by a strip of white seafront buildings, dressed with red roofs, punctuated by a grey spire from the local church. Everyone looked content and relaxed. Well, almost everyone.

After a haircut, I sat on a chair opposite a sandwich shop, waiting for my lunch to be prepared. A man on a mobility scooter stopped for a chat with my seated neighbour, passing conversation in front of me, whilst I obligingly stared at my phone. The exchange, I assumed after listening for a while, was a local equivalent of "hello, how are you?" and "isn't the weather wonderful?" or "how is Jimmy etc?". But to the innocent bystander (or by sitter for that matter), it sounded more like a heated row, ready to boil over into fisticuffs. Every other word was 'F'ing this' and 'F ing that', cursing the world, the NHS, society and everything else, for I don't know what, maybe just being there, all delivered in thick loud Scottish accents. I knew better than to do anything foolish like look up. Then all of a sudden, he scooted off. And then my sandwich arrived. So, I too, well, err... ~~f ed off as well~~, ~~no~~ left.

After a soothing stroll about town, and quiet coffee on the waterfront, it was time to catch the bus. When getting ready to board, a red-faced man started to argue about his place in the queue. An older man, whom I assume was his father, gave short tense furtive looks and admonishing comments, trying to temper the temper that was emerging. I was not sure his attempt to soothe the situation was working too well. Wise or not, I don't know, but

I chirped up with "the bus won't go till the last person has got on".

Fortunately, no busted nose, broken jaw or general slagging off followed, which was just as well because I would have been late for dinner. We all shuffled forward in a quiet and orderly queue, and the bus left. This to me was all part of the immersive experience of being a tourist.

It was a wonderful dinner with guests from Bristol and Canada, with rich conversations about North America, travel, politics, Putin and medical student teaching amongst other things. And on the news, there was talk of the spring offensive in Ukraine, aiming to push the Russians eastwards. We wished them luck.

Day 30, Saturday 20th May

To St Andrews

START	12.00, Crail
WIND	S, 6–10 mph
WEATHER	Cloudy, 12°C. Dry
TIDE	With me till 12.00, then against, 0.9mph
SEA STATE	Slight
HAZARDS	North Carr rocks. Opposing tide
FINISH	St Andrews, 16.45
DISTANCE	12 miles
SAILING HOURS	4¾ hours

Having heartily thanked Peter and Rachel for looking after me so well, I caught the bus back to Crail to make tracks to St Andrews.

One of the main worries, given the lack of wind and turning tide, was getting around Fife Ness, the bit of land sticking out at the end of the Firth of Forth, before it retreats westwards towards St Andrews. What's more, there were hazardous rocks to be negotiated. Peter had told me about North Carr, a reef of sandstone extending a mile and a half off the mainland, completely covered at high tide, and therefore ideally designed for shipwrecking.

Robert Stevenson, a well-known Scottish lighthouse engineer, was tasked with building a warning, so in 1813 set about the task. However, his stone construction was largely destroyed in winter storms before it was completed, so a metal structure replaced the stone in 1821, and the finished product still stands today.

You might think you have heard of Robert Stevenson, but unless you are focussed on 19th century lighthouse construction, the name is probably new to you. However, Robert Louis Stevenson, of 'The strange case of Dr Jekyll and Mr Hyde' will ring a resounding bell, both to you, and to the modern generation of school pupils, since it is required reading. The Stevensons are indeed related, the former being the grandfather to the latter. Hence, they have both left lasting legacies for our nations, but of very different forms, one in writing, and the other in lighting.

On Crail beach, it was all action on this quiet Saturday morning. A group of ladies were neatly organised around a leader for a yoga class.

And then a couple came over to talk to me. Sandy and Thomasina had worked out the connection between boat writing and sailor, so I could not possibly refuse their request for a chat, given their inestimable initiative. Crail, I learnt, was a popular second homer town, being not too far from Edinburgh, but far enough and nice enough, along with other towns in Fife, to qualify (I was less sure whether Anstruther would pass the necessary tests). Anyway, it turned out that I had met Sandy's third cousin, some time ago, who lived on the other side of

Scotland – what an amazing coincidence. Sandy and Thomasina kindly made a donation to charity later, showing appreciation for my adventure.

Equipped with wellies, Sandy also gave me a hand in launching through the seaweed, which had become exposed by the low tide.

But first, I needed to join the Yoga class. I would have had to move Betty right through the middle of the group, so it felt rude to be disruptive, and rude to decline an offer to join in. Besides, it was a novelty to me, looked fun, and why on earth refuse a free taster session in a once in a lifetime location? So, I stretched, and sighed, and smiled my way into a new relaxed state, being elevated to a higher plane, free of wind or rock worries. We all felt better after our brief union, and I thanked Laura the leader for her patience.

Having launched, there was precious little breeze. Beyond the harbour wall, there was just enough wind to make progress towards the North Carr beacon, before the tide was scheduled to turn. The wind had all but died, so every mile of progress had become critical.

Stories of waves crashing on rocks were still ringing in my mind, but I was keen to avoid a two-mile detour out to the ancient navigational mark. I was more than happy to read about the landmark later, rather than make an in-person inspection. A combination of standing up to gain a better view down into the water, and intermittently checking hazard locations on my phone, meant that I safely weaved my way northwards, through the rocky reef.

Mercifully I have forgotten much of the rest of the sailing day because it was strolling-pace slow.

There were dinghies out in St Andrews Bay, so I went to ask safety boat drivers which way to go. Jill's excellent radio communication strung all the necessary pieces together. Before I knew it, I was in the clubhouse, with tea and cake provided, Betty safely parked up on a trolley in the compound, with relevant access codes for the morning, and some navigational advice from Mark. Sailors know how to look after each other.

A St Andrews Bay story I heard recently is worthy of retelling at this juncture. A few years back, some loose safety procedures led to a couple of incidents. The first was placement of a marker buoy too close to a wall, leading to several craft crashing into the obstruction, as they gybed around.

Soon afterwards a dinghy went out without the bung properly inserted. The 420 sank lower and lower into the water, before disappearing under the waves. Crew were safely rescued, but the submerged craft was nowhere to be seen.

The supervising Scottish sailing authorities were alerted, and raised questions about local procedures, ready to issue a reprimand. A couple of weeks later, the club had a reprieve when there was a call from North Berwick Sailing Club. A trawler had picked up an unexpected catch, which on closer inspection proved to be none other than the missing sailing dinghy. It was retrieved from the sea, unscathed other than a few scratches. Hence it had been washed south, safely swimming at seaweed speed round the North Carr Reef, and then across the Firth of Forth, past Bass rock, to North Berwick, some 25 miles in total. How extraordinary.

Back on land at St Andrews, Rob picked me up from Morrisons. Colin, who you may recall from the River Deben in Suffolk, had put me in touch, since Colin and Rob's children knew each other. They had remained friends. Luckily, my arrival timing coincided with a convenient gap, so we were able to meet up.

Tall and charming, Rob identified me without hesitation, and sped me away to his wonderful abode, and his wonderful wife Heidi. Warm and welcoming, I was reminded of her name's sake, from the 1974 TV series whose adventures in the Swiss alpine mountains brought feelings of freedom and joy. Once again, I was ushered along in a soothing stream of comfort, and hospitality. Dinner consisted of ham with roast potatoes, and strawberries to finish. Then on to conversation in the drawing room, and finally retiring to my room for the night.

The bed was a luxury I had not imagined possible. This was something else. Expansive, white, and supremely soft, lying down felt like floating, suspended in the sky as part of a cloud, meaning that all the usual aches and pains of the night, slept quietly in their own sweet slumber, making room for a night filled with busy dreams.

* * *

Day 31, Sunday 21st May

To Arbroath

START	12.00, St Andrews
WIND	Mainly NE 12–18mph
WEATHER	Cloud and rain, 13–14°C
TIDE	Against, max 1.2mph till 17.00
SEA STATE	Slight to moderate
HAZARDS	River Tay tide
FINISH	Arbroath, 18.15
DISTANCE	17 miles
SAILING HOURS	5 hours, (80 mins at Carnoustie)

Before launching in the morning, Heidi offered a tour of the town, whilst its occupants were still hiding under a grey blanket of cloud, not yet awakened for Sunday routines.

St Andrews is a relatively wealthy town supported by the traditions of golf and university. It is said to include one of the most expensive streets in Scotland. The Royal and Ancient Golf Club of St Andrews was founded in 1754, and incredibly, exercised legislative authority over the game of golf worldwide (except in the United States and Mexico), until 2004. In addition, the 'Old course' is the most frequent venue for the Open Championships, which is the oldest of the major golfing championships. It goes to show that getting there first is important. The town has managed to hang on to its balls, so to speak, since the high street was littered with golf related shops, and the odd tartan store, designed to lighten the load of any passing tourist wallet.

We went past St Leonards school, shielded by a perimeter of ancient stone walls. It is based in the old grounds of St Leonards college of the university, and therefore boasts a number of fine buildings, as well as holding a prime position in town. With some foresight, it was established in 1877 as a girl's school, only becoming co-ed in 1999. The school continues to strike out on its own, being the only school in Scotland to offer the International Baccalaureate throughout its curriculum years.

The University is said to be the oldest in Scotland, and the third oldest in the English-speaking world. In line with local traditions, the university is not happy to rest on ancient laurels, and still attracts applause, being ranked the best in the UK in the 2022 'Good university guide'. After the drive around town, I felt encouraged to come back and take a longer visit one day, perhaps without the hazards of a game of golf.

At least there was some wind blowing, but it was from the north-east giving me another long hard day on the beat. Furthermore, the tide was against me for much of the way. The tidal direction also meant there was a strong current in the river Tay, pressing me to visit Dundee. I declined the offer.

But first, I needed to cross the Tay itself. As I approached a sandbank on the south side of the river, I was alarmed by a long line of breaking waves, presumably produced by wind and tide ruffling up the surface. Being new to disturbance of this kind, I was not sure what to do. The white water extended some way out to sea, and having been hanging out of the boat for a couple of hours already, I wasn't keen to add any unnecessary extras by going round. After a bit of deliberation, heading straight through the surf looked like the best option. Obstacles usually feel less challenging after they have been overcome. To cement my achievement on this occasion, like a boy scout, I awarded myself another sea sailing competence badge.

I really wanted a break at Carnoustie. Unfortunately, the beach was bordered by underwater rocks, scattered along the shoreline. Unfamiliar with the scenario, I wasn't sure what to do. Mandy and Alan had been watching from the beach at shouting distance, trying to advise against my approach, but the prospect of feet on the ground, and maybe a coffee, was too enticing. For the second time that day, I threw caution to the wind, so to speak, and simply stepped into the sea.

Treading carefully over the slippery underwater surfaces with Betty in tow, I carefully edged my way to the sand. I made it unscathed, ignoring any considerations about how I might launch again later. I doubt I would have been able to manage, if there had been an onshore breeze and / or breakers.

Mandy and Alan were local sailors and kindly offered to help in whatever way they could. At the time, the nearest coffee stop was highest on my agenda, but I accepted the offer of number exchanges should anything else be needed later. It was.

After a restorative drink in the Station Hotel, still wearing my drippy sailing gear, I retraced my steps over the railway line. A party of holidaymaking men, full of chatter and clatter, had just left the train. Lugging golf bags over shoulders, they sounded keen to reach their hotel, so as to indulge in what seemed to be an essential local pastime. I was feeling like I was missing out.

I too was keen to reach my destination, though had unwisely selected a solitary and unpopular mode of transport on this grey wet day. But journey onwards, I must.

At last, to Arbroath, and into the marina I sailed, mooring up on the pontoon and pleased to be standing up again. Then the lock gates closed. Ah, I had not clocked that. Sure enough, on closer inspection of the Navionics map, there was a thin V-shape, marked across the inner entrance. There was also text to explain the symbol on the description detail, but it had not occurred to me to look for this. So, I was stuck. At least until midday the next day, when the tide would rise sufficiently for the gates to open again. I lay on the pontoon for a few minutes to contemplate what to do. There was nothing for it, but to have a lie in. How unfortunate!

Definitely unfortunate was to drop my top sail baton in the water when derigging. Unaware of the buoyancy of this piece of plastic, I learnt that there is effectively none, as evidenced by the wiggling and determined course it took when disappearing into the grey green water, like an eel looking for prey. Not only that, I must have knocked the flag off the top of my burgee, when lying the boat over at Carnoustie. I would need to find some replacements.

It was time to call Alan. I waited till I had secured a place to stay and dinner, at the one-stop Townhouse Hotel. I then rang him to ask if he might be able to help in any way. He thought he could. Having rummaged in the dinghy park, Alan came over and we met in the marina. A hacksaw came with Alan's bundle of sticks, so we shortened a disused windsurf baton to the appropriate length.

To finish the repair, I applied Sugru to the ends, so as to protect the sail pocket from any sharp edges. If you haven't tried it before, Sugru is a neat product that describes itself as mouldable glue, and sets like a firm rubber. It was perfect for the job. How fortunate to have taken Alan's number, and how incredibly kind of him to travel over to find a fix, a mend that lasted for the remainder of the journey. Thank you so much, Alan.

* * *

Day 32, Monday 22nd May

To Montrose

START	13.00, Arbroath
WIND	SE 6–9 mph, but variable
WEATHER	Cloudy, 12°C. Dry
TIDE	Tide against, max 1.1mph till 18.00
SEA STATE	Calm
HAZARDS	No wind. Going backwards
FINISH	Montrose, 19.30
DISTANCE	13 miles
SAILING HOURS	6½ hours

Arbroath is well known for its ties with the fishing industry. However, since the heyday of the 1980s, there has been a shift from landing, to processing fish. Arbroath is proud to be the home of the Smokie, very much in evidence on a short wander around the town. Having achieved PGI status (Protected Geographical Indication), the Arbroath Smokie sits alongside Parma Ham and Champagne in terms of brand stature, and can only be produced within five miles of the town centre ('fit of the toon' in local dialect).

To make a Smokie, first catch your fish. Typically, a Scottish Haddock is used, which is prepared with gutting, head removal and overnight salting. The salting cures the fish and helps it stand up to the heat of the smoking process. A fire of hardwood is prepared in a pit or brick barrel. The fish are then hung in pairs on sticks, about a metre above the flame under a closed lid, for about 40 minutes. The hardwood gives the fish a darkened colour, and the process produces a "creamy firm flesh with a slightly smoky, almost sweet flavour, which has to be tasted to be believed", so the adverts say.

My compulsory sampling of a Smokie, unlike the advertising, was a slightly rushed second breakfast, leaving me over full, and perhaps noticing more of the bones than the delicious texture. I thought it was just as well that I was not a food writer.

The previous afternoon I had met Neil and Sean on their yacht Waikare. They too were circumnavigating the UK on their modest yacht. They were raising money for the British Heart Foundation, after Neil had experienced a heart attack.

"Are you guys getting on OK?" I asked, posing the standard question to any pair of travellers, committed to a long and confined journey. An open and jovial response from Sean, with a twinkling smile to match, made for an instantly likeable connection. They had set off from Ipswich in April so were travelling more slowly than I, but since we were heading round in the same direction, we were sure we would meet again. We exchanged contact details.

One of their fundraising approaches was to ask the harbourmaster to waive fees in lieu of a contribution to their charity. This sounded like a cunning move which had worked very well to date, and an approach that I thought was worth trying myself.

However, Arbroath had not been so enthusiastic. After landing their request, there was deliberation from the listener, but a disappointing outcome. Different from the usual "I'm very happy to support that", or "what a great cause", instead the reply came back "I'll knock off a fiver". Sean was a bit taken aback.

My own interaction with the harbourmaster was more one sided. Having made a few failed attempts to find the recipient, I decided to flee without paying, and instead followed Sean's advice by gifting the full £25 to charity.

Maybe it was payback. On this day, I was travelling at the speed of a tortoise, or perhaps a sloth, or maybe a snail. Or even at the speed of a submerged dinghy? It had to be the slowest day of the journey so far, and slowest for the whole trip, thank goodness. I was very close to turning back, and may have done so earlier in the circumnavigation, if my tolerance of such stasis had not increased to its current level.

What counselled me to carry on was a buoy, those well-known therapists. Smooth, even headed, steady and reliable, they can give excellent non-judgemental advice. On this occasion, I was advised that things were not as bad as they first seemed, and circumstances may be about to change – just the encouragement that was needed. Thank you, buoy. I carried on.

Nearing Montrose, fed up with the arduous paddling slog, I headed for the nearest landable spot, next to Scurdie Ness lighthouse. This was just as well since Montrose is a largely commercial port, unfriendly to dinghies. The sailing club is even further inland on a tidal muddy basin called 'The Basin' on the South Esk River, which dries at low water, so not good for me. However, I was glad to hear it is a popular spot for sea birds and a designated nature reserve, and I thought it was best to leave them to it.

The flat water had meant that I could keep in contact with Montrose Sailing Club during the day. Rory, the Commodore, had roped in Roger to come and assist, and the tracker provided final location details. After landing, I was struggling to manoeuvre Betty over large round stones on the sea edge, but miraculously help suddenly appeared. Like marines disguised in civvy uniform, Rory and Roger stepped out of their special forces vehicle, and swooped onto the beach to complete their well-timed and expertly delivered mission. I was saved again.

Rory told me a bit about the town as we drove down its wide High Street. Red-stoned imperial-looking buildings added both a touch of grandeur, and unusual Scottish colour to the vista. It was indeed one of the most spacious high streets in Scotland. The town had built prosperity from its port, originally trading in skins and hides in the 16th century, and then moving with the times, to more modern commodities, but still with international connections. Today, its trade is linked to Aberdeen with fluctuations in prosperity with varying supplies of oil.

It was quite late by the time we sat down for a bowl of spaghetti bolognaise. Rory and Jill were both working, as a production engineer and a vet respectively, so had very kindly squeezed me into their schedule, alongside looking after their three children. Thank you very much to Rory and Jill.

After dinner we managed to assemble a Scottish burgee onto my flag-free stick. Some hollow strimmer flex proved to be just the right dimension to slide onto the metal rod, either side of the flag frame (provided by Roger). This secured the precious emblem whilst allowing it to wave freely in the wind. It is really satisfying when some low-tech problem-solving works so well. Appropriate national order had been restored, and I was soon to be the proud wearer of a Scottish flag. I felt confident it would guide me on my travels around the top of this fine country. Our make do and mend approach lasted till the finish.

CHAPTER 10

They catch a lot of fish at Peterhead

Day 33, Tuesday 23rd May

To Stonehaven

START	10.15, Montrose
WIND	SW/S, 8–15mph. None from 14.00
WEATHER	Sun, then cloud, max 15°C. Dry
TIDE	With me 1.1mph till 14.00
SEA STATE	Slight to smooth
HAZARDS	Wind dying. Cliffs. No stopping places
FINISH	Stonehaven, 16.30
DISTANCE	21 miles
SAILING HOURS	6¼ hours

Rory and Roger came down for the launch before heading off to work, which was very good of them, given their busy schedules.

The road to the lighthouse was a private drive. Unfortunately, we got into trouble with the owner. She came down to berate the partial road blocking behaviour, fearing a delivery of hers would be delayed. Rory moved the van.

Roger gave me a hand with launching. But before I had left, the lady returned. We thought she would bring more complaints. Instead, she came down towards us, offering a small bottle of gin to compensate for her admonishment. Slightly puzzled, we gratefully accepted the gift, and said we would pass it on to Rory, since we thought he deserved it most.

Maybe this kind of approach should be encouraged – getting a reward for being told off? It would certainly make the experience of a reprimand more enjoyable. I think I might suggest it in future.

The day started well enough with sunshine, a timely launch and favourable wind, waving my new Scottish burgee in a northerly direction. Two large dolphins swam by, and later a lone seal popped up to say, 'Hi'.

The first ten miles were gobbled up in 90 minutes, duping me into thinking I would be at Stonehaven in no time. As the morning turned to afternoon, clouds came over and the wind faded to a familiar stop, with the tide putting the boot in by turning against me. I was not amused.

I sat sulking below the vertical grey cliffs of RSPB Fowlsheugh, which were dotted with white blotches making them look like barnacled rocks. For a few minutes, I admired the Kittiwakes and Guillemots circling overhead. Humans gazed back down from their viewing platform, through the swirling flock, at the marooned sailor, perhaps wondering what he was doing down there.

My estimation was that there were only three miles to go, which would normally be within paddling distance. But with the tide in furious flow, and the occasional pause, I was making maybe half a mile an hour over ground. That meant that Stonehaven could be six hours away.

I needed an alternative plan. As I was heading over to a possible pausing spot on the shore, a couple of older kayakers appeared, and very kindly offered to give me a tow.

"Of course," I said to their generous offer. The female of the couple tied a line to my boat. This was great, but I was not sure how long it could last, given my weight and her age. With us both paddling, we were just about making progress against the shoreline. That was something at least.

After maybe 20 minutes, we were all beginning to tire. Then a rib came into view, effortlessly scooting over the still water, below the brooding ruins of Dunnottar Castle. My propulsion buddy shouted despairingly at the approaching craft, wanting to rid herself of this onerous drag on her relaxing outing. She needn't have worried. It was Ditta.

Ditta, as I came to learn over the next couple of days, was a force of nature, tirelessly organising, and giving to others around her. She was a real credit to her sailing club and community.

I had emailed the club and Ditta had responded. Having seen the doleful progress of my little green electronic boat via the tracker, she had taken it upon herself to come and offer some motorised support. We gratefully accepted.

I was tied onto Ditta's craft and thanked my departing kayaker acquaintances, as they gently slid off over the still waters. I did feel I needed to remain on board Betty whilst we were buzzed along, feeling that a separation would somehow make the final circumnavigation incomplete. I was mighty relieved to have been spared the sweat of the last couple of miles.

Ditta's generosity was not reserved for just the one Laser circumnavigator. Stick had been there before, and he too, together with his partner, had been entertained at Ditta-ville. What a delightful surprise and how interesting to hear another's perspective of his journey. Listening to those stories, I felt a visceral connection to his history, having sailed through the same harbour entrance, stepped into the same house, talked to the same people, and sat around the same table. It was like we were on the same team.

After a lovely vegetarian dinner and chocolate for dessert, I suddenly felt tired. I was set up in the rather elegantly named "room of requirements". It was kind of a spare room, but as the name suggested, was designed to cater for much more, like reading, sleeping, listening to music, or simply gazing out of the bright full-length window, across the garden and into the fields beyond. I was worried the sofa bed might be uncomfortable, perhaps still spoilt by the memories of my cloud-like affair at St Andrews, but I needn't have fretted, and was soon fast asleep.

Day 34, Wednesday 24th May

To Aberdeen

START	09.15, Stonehaven
WIND	S, 10–16mph
WEATHER	Sun and cloud, 13°–15°C. Dry
TIDE	With me, max 1.1mph, all the way!
SEA STATE	Slight to moderate
HAZARDS	Rocks. Boat safety near Aberdeen
FINISH	Aberdeen, 12.00. Final landing, 12.30
DISTANCE	15 miles
SAILING HOURS	2¾ hours

I wanted to see Aberdeen as part of my East Coast tour. Ditta and Phil had very kindly offered to allow me to stay for a second night. There was a train between Aberdeen and Stonehaven, so the plan was to head off to Aberdeen, and then return to happy Stonehaven for the evening. What a delight.

Pushed along by a healthy tide and more southerly wind than was predicted, I reached Aberdeen in under three hours.

Passing the breakwater of the commercial port, I was puzzled by an oil rig, parked up within the perimeter, which seemed to be missing a leg. Still ruminating about the three-legged structure, I took an unwise dash in front of an incoming windfarm supply ship, which came closer than I would have liked. I soon landed at the mouth of the River Don, and could relax on the safety of sand.

In line with Ditta's earlier suggestion, I needed to park further upstream on the northern bank of the river. This was to move away from housing estates, thus improving the security situation. Rivers exiting via the beach can make for complicated launching sites, since there is an extra set of forces from the 'wee brown burn' running out to sea. Failing to factor in the flows properly, I messed up the launch and fell out, more or less tumbling back on to the beach.

When I arrived at my parking spot, I realised that my precious Tupperware, containing homemade rye bread sandwiches, lovingly prepared in Ditta's kitchen, had not joined me when I reboarded the boat. Annoyed by my mistake, I walked the mile back to the sea, engaging in the futile exercise of trying to find my lunch.

I thought that it might still be afloat since the lid seals had worked well to date. But there was no sign of it in the river. There was no sign of it by the sea, and the occasional walker had not spotted anything either. The stream was going out, and the wind blowing onto the shore so I hoped it would be deposited further along the water's edge. I weaved this way and that, across sand and water pools, to no avail. It was time to give up, but just one last look, a little further into the unlikely distance, maybe, just maybe.

And then, there it was, bobbing about in the shallow surf, proud, upright and untarnished, waiting to be collected, like a fresh message in a bottle. I was overjoyed. My happiness was fuelled not by the rescue of a piece of plastic, but by the repair of a mishap of my own making. What's more, the sandwiches were still dry, giving a double layered dose of healthy delight. The message, I sensed as I swallowed, is that 'if you persist, things may just keep working out'.

I wanted to spend the afternoon in Aberdeen. The name means 'Mouth of the River Don'. Aber is a Celtic word for 'mouth of the river', and 'deen' being, well, a Scottish pronunciation of Don, perhaps? In truth, the town was originally Aberdon in 1172, then Aberden, and finally Aberdeen, so not quite the phonetic stretch that you might imagine.

Incidentally, the prefix 'Aber' is also used for many Welsh coastal towns – Abersoch, Aberystwyth, Aberdovey, Abercastle to name but a few – thus heralding an ancient linguistic connection.

In Aberdeen centre, the sun was out, making the grey granite gothic style buildings look splendid against the blue sky. Aberdeen Art Gallery was recommended to me by a fellow traveller, as we were dismounting a bus so I went to check it out.

On the second floor was an exhibit of photographs of artists at work. Hence, like peering through a kaleidoscope, I was viewing portraits, captured on film by a photographer, viewing an artist, who in turn was viewing the world, so that he or she could capture their own impressions for us to gaze at, on some later occasion. A picture by Philippe Halsman of Salvator Dali, at work in his bed, was necessarily whacky. Another room-high, black and white photograph, showed Pablo Picasso staring out of his studio window into the sunlight, an image that was arrestingly serene.

In the gallery, bright light was shining onto white walls, and a complete absence of human sound meant that I was deliciously alone in the present, whilst being delicately soaked in the past. What a divine half-hour. I guess that is what galleries are for. Long live galleries.

I love the comfort and containment of a train journey. However, this relatively brief trip, came with an unwelcome jolt.

I learnt that my friend Rob had sadly passed away. I knew that he had been ill with bowel cancer for several years, and signals from his wife were that things were going downhill. I had tried to call over the previous couple of weeks, but had been unsuccessful, presumably because day-to-day care needs were more pressing. In one's state of ignorance, it is easier to imagine that life will carry on as it has done before, despite its difficulties, so the finality of a death comes as a real shock. And a real sadness.

We had known each other for 30 or more years, and our families had holidayed together on many occasions. My train window view added one more memory to the Rob collection. Beautiful cliff tops, peaceful fields and blue sky were trundling past, just as the news arrived, so reminiscent of walks, fresh air and conversation that we had shared, and Rob had so loved. It felt like he was with me. One way or another I felt I must return south for the funeral, to pay my respects.

Back in Stonehaven I watched the evening's dinghy racing, from the comfort of the club committee boat, and then joined in with fish and chips for afters. It was lovely to be included amongst a happy gathering of sailors, both out on the water and in the clubhouse, with young and old rubbing shoulders in a shared passion for sailing. Ditta was particularly encouraging of the young topper sailors, which was a joy to see.

I heard accounts of winter storms in Stonehaven. Sometimes it wasn't just the water that would come crashing over the breakwater. The occasional boulder might be heaved into the air and thrown across onto the seafront, like Neptune launching weapons at a sinful shore. There was a time a few years back when a water-propelled missile crashed into a storage shed, causing considerable damage. It was hard to believe such stories, when the sea lay so sweet and innocent next to the clubhouse, just as the tale was being told. However, it was a necessary reminder that things can change dramatically, and the force of the wind and waves should not be underestimated.

When conditions were unsavoury, the club would use inland water at Loch Skene for sailing, which was several miles to the north-west. However, there were times last year when the Loch was out of action as well, not because of bad weather, but because of dead birds. The dreaded avian flu had laid waste to migrating geese, taking advantage of their innate desire to gather, and spread its wicked RNA throughout the flock. I was told that the shores were littered with white carcasses. A depressing vista indeed.

And finally, back to the house for some more conversation. Ditta and her husband Philip were geologists by training, and had moved in and out of the oil industry, such was the way in this area of Scotland. Their inside knowledge helped me rectify my earlier confusion when passing the port of Aberdeen. That three-legged rig just didn't look right. Maybe it was half complete and was waiting to be finished? Maybe it had lost a limb in a tragic accident and was in for repairs? Philip solved my puzzle in a simple stroke. What I had seen was entirely normal. The structure was as a jack rig, ideal for exploration, since like an adjustable stool, three legs make an easily balanced platform when on an uneven surface. Simples. I could rest easy in this newfound knowledge.

In the rest of the UK, the sun was out, at the start of a long early summer heatwave. Inflation had come down to 8%, which was still lagging behind the rest of Europe, and interest rates had gone up, leaving the country with the bitter taste of consistently troubling economic news.

In my own head, as I settled down to sleep, I was worried about Peterhead. The land protrudes a long way out into the Noth Sea, meaning that the tide rips round the corner in its rush to keep up its twice daily schedule. Strong winds may combine to make the sea really rough, so I was told. Fran, whom I had spoken to before departure, was storm-bound at Peterhead for five days. I didn't fancy that. Hence Peterhead loomed large in my imagination as a significant landmark, to be respected and tackled carefully.

Day 35, Thursday 25th May

To Cruden Bay

START	10.20, Bridge of Don, Aberdeen
WIND	SE 8–12mph, but variable then dying
WEATHER	Sun and cloud, 11–13°C. Dry
TIDE	With me, max 1.3mph till 13.30
SEA STATE	Slight to Smooth
HAZARDS	Wind dying and tide against
FINISH	Cruden Bay, 14.40, and 17.30
DISTANCE	20 miles
SAILING HOURS	4¼ hours, (+1¾ hours later)

Despite mine and Philip's protestations, Ditta very kindly drove back to the Bridge of Don. We bade a fond farewell and I thanked her profusely, for all the incredible kindnesses.

Being well refreshed, I was looking forward to being with Betty, and anticipated a contented meeting in her snug spot amongst the dunes. It was not to be. From the relaxed happiness of Ditta's company, I was rapidly thrust under a dark cloud, by the sign of Betty's righted hull and scattered possessions, strewn across the beach. Or so it seemed. Ditta had been right to worry about this location. I suspiciously eyed up the blocks of flats across the water, wondering whom I could fix with a steely vengeful stare. But there was no one.

Turning back to Betty and the bits, as ever, it was not so bad once I had calmed down a fraction. Similar to the occasion at Blyth, my lock remained intact, and items were merely stretched to their furthest extension, rather more forcefully distributed. The hatches had been opened and closed, but once again, nothing was missing. Even the windex, with its little orange plastic flag, was recovered from the grass, unharmed and unbent.

Was this idle curiosity? Was it teenage tampering with a vulnerable object, liable to be ruffled up, since her friends were not there to defend her? Was this a concerned passer-by, who was so dumbstruck by Betty's awesome presence, that they suddenly lost their ability to read text, or dial my phone number, either of which would have settled their strife? Who knows? I never did find out, and this shall remain one of the small mysteries of the world, forever.

Out on the water, it was a pleasant day of mostly hands-free sailing, swooshed along by the increasing north-going tide, and a steady southerly breeze.

I don't think I have explained hands-free sailing before, so will take a moment to share a few details. The sailors amongst you, may remember rudderless sailing from your RYA level 2 course. The rudder would be lifted out of the water to make it ineffectual, so that you needed to use your body weight to steer the boat (in the opposite direction to the way it is tipped). It was the same idea for me, but instead of raising the rudder, I would tie down the tiller, using the foot strap elastic. This was a thick piece of cord, knotted loosely so it was easy to undo should the need arise.

The arrangement worked best on lighter wind days, and when on a downwind course, so the sail would be out of the way, and the main sheet secured in a cleat. The set up meant that I was more or less free to do what I wanted in the boat, like stand up, look around, use my phone, eat lunch, change clothes, everything short of having a cup of tea (though I could have done that as well, if I had had a suitable kettle). With some sun out and dry weather, this was very pleasant, almost Mediterranean, perhaps even better than that since it was not too hot.

Cruden Bay which is about eight miles south of Peterhead, was a peaceful white sandy beach, backed by a small town, hence ideal for a coffee stop. Sometimes when in the boat, I would take off my boots and wetsuit socks, to dry them out. On this occasion, I decided to leave them off. So, on landing, like Robinson Crusoe, I stepped straight out onto the warming sand, and walked barefoot up the dry beach, wondering what I might find in this strange and foreign land.

In my exploration, I found a sign. Nothing terribly metaphysical, but a fitting storyboard of adventure – Cruden Bay was the site of the first successful flight across the North Sea.

In 1914, one Tryggve Gran from Norway, at the age of 26, set out to fly back home. He was no stranger to adventure, since he had already taken part in Captain Scott's South Pole expedition. On his first attempt, he took off from a field above the Bay, but flew into a bank of fog, so he wisely turned back. When landing on the beach, he had to divert his path away from some rocks and in so doing, drove into the sea.

His second attempt nearly ended in disaster as well. This time, when halfway across, lack of fuel pressure meant that the engines cut out when changing tanks. His plane plummeted towards the surface. Luckily, the downdraft on the propellers restarted the engines, and the plane flattened out, no more than 30 metres above the waves. He landed safely in a field near Stavanger, Norway, thus completing the 510km journey in four hours and ten minutes.

One final note of optimism to all would-be adventurers, is that these kinds of challenge must be good for you. Tryggve died in 1980 at the age of 92, which, if translated into modern life expectancy, must be equivalent to living well into the hundreds. I am feeling hopeful.

Back on my own adventure trail, I was wondering whether to head on to Peterhead. Both the wind and the tide had swung round by 180 degrees, so it was going to be difficult. At least the feared storms were nowhere in evidence, so it might be worth a try. Ambition got the better of me and I headed off. The gentle afternoon sun made for a gorgeous setting as I beat my way round the corner, past the ruins of Slain Castle where tourists were out for a stroll. I could sail right up to the guano-covered cliffs, where red rocks plunged into clear water, and bird life squawked overhead. Further on, a small inlet made a space for me to shelter from the full tidal stream for a moment. Finally, after a slow mile or two, good sense took over, and for the first and only time in the trip, I knowingly turned back.

Booking.com said the three-star St Olaf Hotel was full. A call to the venue offered a gruff but alternative view, saying there was a bed, but I would need to get there by 7pm if I wanted any dinner.

When I arrived, I guessed that the man in reception was the owner of the growly voice. Having received my key and dumped my luggage, I came down to the dining room to find the same elder gentleman serving as a waiter. He looked an unlikely character to be in this role, since he had a stick in his hand, and a pronounced kyphosis of the spine, meaning that he walked with a significant limp. A smart new waistcoat added a touch of colour to his outfit, but that was it. A thick Scottish accent delivered in staccato blasts was a tough translation task, and when coupled with an apparent visual fascination with the floor, rather than his customers, service had a definitely frosty feel. Watching food and drink being transported on a tray, balanced on his upturned hand, whilst the rest of his person negotiated a wobbly route past tables and chairs, aided by his valiant stick, was a nerve-racking sight.

I am sure Fawlty Towers would have been impressed by the terrible service, but I did end up feeling sorry for him. It was easy to imagine that he had run the hotel for years and felt unable to let go, maybe through lack of staff, shortage of money, or perhaps pride and a simple determination to carry on. I thanked him on my way out, but as you can imagine, a reciprocal smile was off the menu.

It was a glorious still evening with views from the hotel over the silent and ripple-free North Sea, past the flowering yellow broom scattered in the fields, arranged around an orderly smooth green golf course. The vista led onto a soft blue sky, that reached up and out, seemingly going on forever.

* * *

Day 36, Friday 26th May

To Peterhead

START	10.45, Cruden Bay
WIND	S/SE 8–15mph
WEATHER	Some sun, 14–16°C. Dry
TIDE	Tide with me, 1.5mph
SEA STATE	Slight
HAZARDS	Strong flow at harbour entrance
FINISH	Peterhead harbour, 12.15
DISTANCE	8 miles
SAILING HOURS	1½ hours

Down on the sand, I was pleased to see that Betty had had an undisturbed night. On closer inspection, however, it may have been peaceful, but it was also pees-full. A dog had done its wicked deed, and the liquid had collected in the gunwale of the upturned boat, forming an unpleasant yellow moat. Yuck. No further explanation was needed on this occasion.

For all the trepidation and anticipation that came with the name of Peterhead, the sail was remarkably straightforward. A steady following breeze, and a vigorous tide, had me there in no less than 80 minutes. It hardly felt like sufficient use of the conditions for the day, but I really wanted to see Peterhead. In through the entrance between the great outer arms, I sailed away from the restless seas of the rushing tide, on to flatter waters, then into the marina, and on to the sands in front of the sailing club.

People were about, arranging boats and getting ready for training. Meren kindly helped with finding a trolley and a place to park the boat. And she helped me find a tap. Poor Betty had not had a wash in weeks, and was appreciative of the desalination. I also met brothers Jack and Harry, who went out racing later. I gave Jack a hand with his Laser rigging, as a gesture of encouragement. They all looked like they were having fun, which was great to see.

There had been sunshine in the morning, so for a grey afternoon, it was not that grey. But the town was grey. Remarkably uniform stonework gave a remarkably uniform palette, undecorated by any unnecessary flourishes of advertising or plant life. Maybe it was a sign of social deprivation, since Peterhead does languish at the bottom to the county's table.

In my wanderings, I met a hapless victim of a range of social misfortunes, or so I guessed. I saw a slender lady in front of me, making very slow and slightly awkward progress along the pavement, with a paper coffee cup pressed onto her hip, by her elbow. I thought she must be trying to do things that required three hands, so as I came level, I offered to help. "Do you need a hand?" I asked. She looked up in reply, exposing a more or less tooth-free expression, and I am sorry to say, the remaining pegs looked in urgent need of dental work. Further, on second sight, slender was something of an understatement. She looked very thin. Her reply took me by surprise. "Are you looking for business?"

Thoughts of, "that's not quite what I was thinking" and, "what kind of business are you suggesting?" hopped into my head, before being unceremoniously dumped into the North Sea. Instead, a slightly shaken "no thank you," was issued before making haste to my destination.

Feeling hungry for experience, I had earlier opted for the economically priced Waverley Inn. I did wonder what I was letting myself in for, since reviews mentioned people drinking beer at breakfast time, though on arriving, the place was pleasant and comfortable. I was expecting worse. A delicious afternoon snooze, compensated for a noisy street outside my room at night, but the stay was good value overall, I thought.

On the following morning, the more genteel rooms were closed, and so the included breakfast was served in the pub section of the hotel. A full Scottish offering was a nicely prepared heart-stopping affair. It was accompanied, as the reviews had predicted, by a large handful of men with full pints dotted around the bar, meaningfully engaged in drink staring, whilst a screen scrolled through 1980s pop videos. The bar lady looked like she was someone who would not be taking any trouble, nor was she pitching for any tips for that matter. Sensing I was a little out of place, I felt it was my duty to eat up, not say anything in English more than was absolutely necessary, and skedaddle.

Peterhead, in my head, was a big fishing port. After Brexit, I saw a map of the UK showing the volume of catch, graphically illustrated by the size of a dot. There were many cute pink pockmarks scattered around the coastline, but for Peterhead there was a great big blob obscuring the town and most of Aberdeenshire. Increases in quotas had been part of the EU trade deal so slavishly negotiated, but they had a disproportionate effect, depending on the species of fish covered in the new arrangement. An example was Western Mackerel which was caught in the North Sea off Peterhead. It had seen a significant increase in quota, so the town had benefited from Brexit, netting the majority of the UK's extra tonnage.

I heard from the club sailors that despite the increase in catch, the fishing quotas are reached within a few months of the year, leaving many of the workers to languish without gainful activity for much of the remaining calendar, sadly followed by a listless drift into pubs. I had been tempted to ask my bar mates if this was a motivation in selecting their beer breakfast, but I was feeling short of Louis Theroux etiquette, and devoid of an attendant camera crew, so thought it best to keep my questions to myself.

* * *

Day 37, Saturday 27th May

To Fraserburgh

START	10.10, Peterhead
WIND	W, 10–18mph, rising to 18–24mph
WEATHER	Cloud and sun. 13–15°C. Dry
TIDE	With me, max 1.2mph till 16.00
SEA STATE	Slight
HAZARDS	Increasing wind later
FINISH	Fraserburgh, 14.30
DISTANCE	18 miles
SAILING HOURS	4¼ hours

The increasing wind forecast meant that I was feeling apprehensive when leaving the comfort of Peterhead's harbour walls. Given the lack of wind in the last couple of weeks, I should have been delighted, but maybe the spectre of the cold North Sea, or the aura of the name Peterhead itself, was still looming large, or maybe I was just a bit out of practice!!

The section to Rattray Head was a pretty speedy reach, exceeding seven miles per hour at points, but as I bent round the corner, the westerly turned into a fetch, then a beat, making the journey quick, then slower then slow. The forecasted stronger winds did not arrive till after I had landed.

Rattray Head includes a fine lighthouse built in 1895 by David and Alan Stevenson, members of the highly industrious family of the same name. These two were grandchildren to the previously mentioned Robert, so between the three generations, they must have had a hand in the construction of a large majority of Scottish beacons.

Fraserburgh has an amazing labyrinth of harbours within harbours, protecting small fishing boats, then bigger ones and finally great big vessels, but not quite on the scale of Peterhead. I was radioed into the smaller section to park up.

As I was derigging, I noticed a smart red craft, parked up near a light crane, and stopped to watch what was going on. The fisherman was using a winch to haul his crab baskets onto the wall, whilst his missus looked on, jigging the 'wee bairn' in her chest sling. Meanwhile, in the water, a grey nose popped up, eyeing the scene, no doubt looking for any scraps that might be coming his way. Thus in a few short moments, the sea and the land had come together turning many cycles of life in one go – the sea feeding the fisherman, the fisherman feeding his family, the mother feeding her child and the fishermen feeding the seal. How beautiful to watch. In the warm afternoon sun, standing on the pontoon amongst orderly craft in their bobbing rows, for a moment, I felt part of the fishing community.

The town was more compact and more upbeat than Peterhead. In fact, there are plans for major infrastructure developments at the harbour, adding even more layers. This is in order to cater for larger ships, with the intent of expanding business opportunities to cruise ships, ship maintenance, and windfarms. The Moray East wind farm is situated just off the coast from Fraserburgh, and is to be one of the largest in Scotland, when it is finished.

I found a nice place to stay called The Café Bar and Tavern, which summed up what it did in a no-nonsense way. I managed to persuade a local to have a couple of games of pool which he kindly let me win. And then off to Wetherspoon's for a veg curry and beer. Despite all of that, the lonelys were creeping back, and thoughts of home were tugging at my heart strings.

Day 38, Sunday 28th May

To Banff

START	10.00, Fraserburgh
WIND	W/NW, 12–18mph, dropping later
WEATHER	Some sun, then cloud, 10–13°C. Dry
TIDE	With me, max 0.4mph, till 18.00
SEA STATE	Slight
HAZARDS	A long beat
FINISH	Banff, 16.00
DISTANCE	20 miles
SAILING HOURS	5¾ hours

It was a long slog to Banff. Six hours on the beat is a serious grind, both physically and mentally. Heading out to sea on port tack, it looks like you are going nowhere since the view behind you does not change. And sailing back in on starboard, feels the same. It is only when you head out again that you realise progress has been made, because shoreline vista has changed a little, which feels like a meagre reward for all that effort.

I was delighted to receive not one, but two calls on the water for a chat. And just as delighted that the reception and sound quality held up despite a reasonable amount of wind noise. As ever it is affirming to exchange our day-to-day happenings with another human. Graeme, whom I stayed with in Kent, was watering his garden as we chatted, marking the weather difference induced by our separation of several hundred miles.

The second caller was Rob from my sailing club. Being a fellow dinghy helm, he was more inclined to discuss minutiae of my day, which I was happy to share in abundant detail. He asked about physical well-being.

"My backside is absolutely fine, thank you, Rob," was my response to the standard bottom question, "but my back has been hurting a bit," I added. I was thinking I needed to stretch it up some more, to make sure it didn't get worse, which Rob thought was sensible.

Rob finished by saying that he had a contact further along the coast at Findhorn, who might be able to help with a stopover, to which the answer was "yes please". The suggestion was very much appreciated. Rob would get in touch and see if the arrangement might be agreeable to Neil.

Nearing Banff, a dolphin leapt out of the sea, a short distance in front of me, making an aquarium style arch in the air. How amazing to see, I thought. But maybe dolphins can only count to two, for there does seems to be a reluctance to offer a third splash of gymnastics. Instead, the crestfallen spectator is left limply pointing his camera at the still scene, having failed to unload and fire up his gadget in time. It looked like my friendly flipping neighbour had been having fun, nevertheless.

Banff harbour had reopened two weeks previously, after the completion of £2 million sea wall repairs, so was looking fairly empty. The virtual absence of trawlers meant much less seagull mess on the pontoons, a welcome relief, and a good opportunity to dry some of my neoprene on the decking. Sunshine and a clear blue sky added to a crisp clean feel all round.

I went to ask my yachtie neighbours where I might find the harbourmaster, and discovered that I was speaking to him. Alastair and his sailor mate Alan welcomed me on board for a cup of tea. Together we made the triple A team! They were preparing their boat for a holiday later in the season, and we hoped we might meet round the top of Scotland.

I was also given some navigational advice. Alastair suggested using Antares charts which link to Ordnance Survey maps, all accessible on a phone. He said these could provide helpful extra detail about landing spots (and anchoring locations for yachts) on the West Coast of Scotland. This proved to be an invaluable extra tool in the navigational armoury, for more remote sections of the journey. How helpful a specific technical piece of advice can be, and what joy to be supported by fellow sailors.

My evening's accommodation at the Trinity Manse Guest House (Manse, by the way, is a Scottish Presbyterian equivalent of a rectory) in the high street, also had a crisp clean feel. However, there were a few anxious minutes hanging around the front door, waiting for an email response from the host, Berwick-style, just long enough to make me nervous, but not long enough to spoil the beautiful evening. And then for a drink in the Market Arms and a sit-down meal at a local Indian, to top off a very pleasant few hours before bed.

Day 39, Monday 29th May

To Buckie

START	10.15, Banff
WIND	NW, 12–14mph, veering NE, 6–9mph
WEATHER	12–15°C, sunny all day
TIDE	With me from 12.00, max 0.4mph
SEA STATE	Slight
HAZARDS	Light wind
FINISH	Buckie, 17.00
DISTANCE	17 miles
SAILING HOURS	6¾ hours

It was another slow day, on the beat. However, it felt less painful since the sun was out all day, and the wind a bit lighter, meaning it was less effort per mile. I had a nice lunch stop on the water off West Sands, bobbing about in the warmth. Then the wind died, but soon came back, having swung around through 180 degrees. I had a sublime run down to Buckie for the last five miles, with no care in the world other than to watch the coast trickle by. It slowly transformed from cliff, to town, to beach, then cliff to town to beach again, as I passed Portknockie, Findochty and Portessie, all good Scottish sounding towns.

Peter, my father-in-law, rang for a catch up, adding to a summer seaside feel.

I was pleased to get through to the harbourmaster on the radio. Once I had managed to explain that I was sailing a dinghy and not a ship, he directed me down to pier 4. Edging past the sizeable vessels, loaded with logs, malt, and other cargo, I was hoping that the fourth section of Buckie would buck the trend (sorry) and produce a neat set of pontoons dotted with other sensibly sized craft like the night before. Instead, there was a small finger of platform, and just enough space to squeeze in between a couple of well used and very smelly trawlers, whose fishing gear was scattered over the landing space. There was no neat ramp with side supports, leading to a gated entrance and fob security. There was no luggage trolley to wheel cases or possessions to one's hotel. No, Buckie was a commercial harbour.

Instead of all the finery, there was a 20-foot-high iron ladder, dug into the slimy green wall. This was awkward.

I decided to leave the mast standing vertically in the boat, with the batten-free sail wrapped around it, to avoid my sail being dunked in fish detritus, a stowage practice I regularly adopted henceforward. Going up the ladder, I was very keen not to drop one of my bags, or even myself, since it would have been a significant fall, most likely followed by broken bits, a splash, and a serious sense of humour failure. Success. I made it to the top.

Stretching up to dump my bags on the concrete surface, there were vans passing and large lorries carrying goods, only a few yards from my nose. This was quite different from most twee harbour fronts. Buckie was definitely a commercial port. I was pleased to be in with the action.

I went to go and find the harbourmaster to settle the matter of fees. He was busy because a ship was leaving, and reminiscent of my boy style fascination with the diggers at Hythe, I could not help but stand and watch the vessel depart.

This big bed floating bucket had precious little room to manoeuvre out of the port, needing to complete two parts of a three-point turn, without hitting any of the walls on the way. There were no more than a few feet to spare at either end. Hi-vis clad men stood in a small cluster at the bow, clutching radios, occasionally leaning over the edge, as the craft inched backwards at jellyfish speed. There were no options of pulling out a paddle to provide some special directionality, or leaning out to push off from the wall, luxuries afforded to dinghy sailors, like me. Very careful touches on the propeller and occasional bow thruster squirts were the things to hand. It was delicate work, and eventually they made it, out to sea past West Muck (Muck being a Scottish name for a rock) and on to the next port of call.

The conveniently located and reasonably priced Marine Hotel was in need of some maintenance. The lift wasn't working, the Wi-Fi was out of order, the décor was tired, and the room windows wouldn't open, but I didn't mind. After a meal up the hill at the Brig and Barrel, of veg curry, sticky toffee pudding, and a healthy topping of Wi-Fi, I returned to my digs. My non-closing curtains provided an uninterrupted view of a gorgeous 9.30pm sunset as the sun sank gracefully into the sea.

I slept well.

* * *

CHAPTER 11

Limping along the east coast

* * *

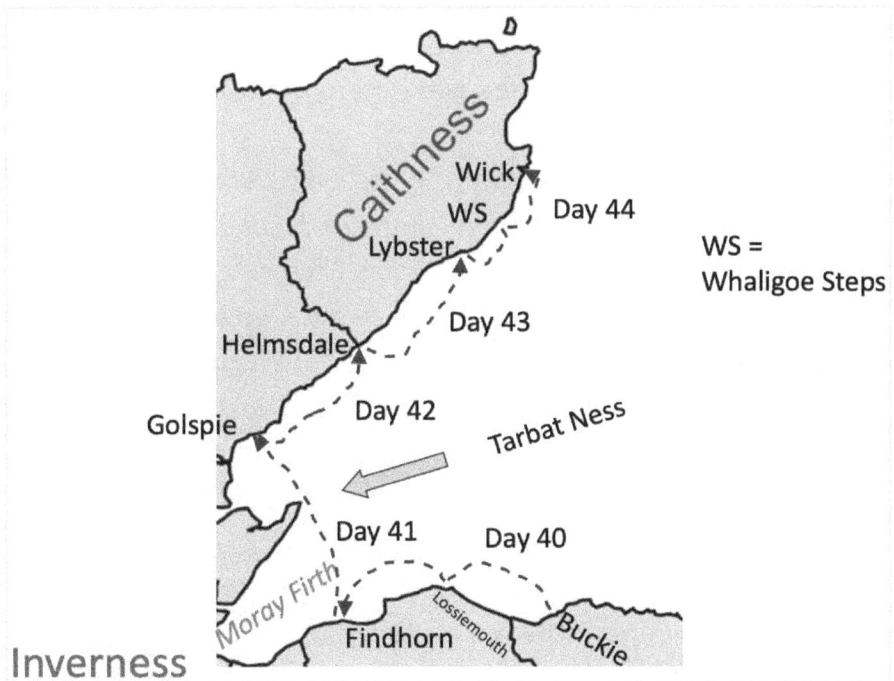

Day 40, Tuesday 30th May

To Findhorn

START	10.30, Buckie
WIND	NE, 7–11mph
WEATHER	Sunny, 12–14°C
TIDE	Not much
SEA STATE	Slight
HAZARDS	Light wind Rocks on launching. The river channel on landing
FINISH	Findhorn, 16.45
DISTANCE	26 miles
SAILING HOURS	6¼ hours (I hour at Lossiemouth)

On returning to my iron access ladder, I was relieved to find that no one had nicked my prized Scottish burgee. It was still waving at shoulder height from the harbour wall, convenient grabbing distance – I had meant to pluck it from the top of the mast myself, before I left the night before, and had woken in the night worrying about its fate.

It was a lovely sunny morning, matched by a rather limp wind forecast, beautifully purposed for a no wind day, but it turned out to be almost idyllic. Once I manged to slither free from the slime covered walls of the harbour, I was away. A steady breeze blew me on a broad reach down to Lossiemouth in a couple of hours. I had hoped to catch up with the local club sailors when I landed, but unfortunately the timings did not work out.

Instead, I did speak to Sean and Neil, whom I'd met at Arbroath. They were heading out on their yacht, as I was heading in. This I discovered when I switched on to the harbour radio channel. I interrupted the usual stayed maritime conversation with a shout out for Waikare (their yacht) to "hang on for a bit", which the harbourmaster politely interpreted as "interference on the line". Feeling appropriately reprimanded, I rang Sean on the phone later. They were sailing over to Helmsdale on an overnight passage, thereby cutting straight across the Moray Firth, an option not available to me. Hence, they had overtaken me and I wondered whether our paths would cross again. It was a shame to miss their familiar faces, but I bade them a safe journey and fair winds.

Unlike Buckie, Lossiemouth was a bustling tourist town, with a coffee shop overflowing towards the water. I did my best to lower the tone in my sailing gear, but people were simply having too much of a sunny lunchtime, to bother with boating types. There was nothing to keep me at Lossiemouth, and I did not want to waste the wind, so headed on down to Findhorn.

When finishing the journey for the day, my main challenge was to find my way to the sailing club, which was up the river towards Findhorn Bay (which was an inland tidal lake). At low tide, there was plenty of sand exposed. Looking along the yellow shoreline, I could not see a break where the river might be emerging. It was the same problem with the Scottish islands on the West Coast. The islands look the same as the mainland, so at dinghy level, you cannot see where one starts and the other ends. Here it was simply a line of endless sand, stretching away into the distance. I paused to ask some bathers, who had come out to enjoy the surf in the crystal-clear waters, and was pointed in the general direction down the coast, so on I went.

At last, the river and up the channel I went, spotting a marker buoy not far ahead. Feeling more confident and seeing darkness below me, corner cutting was warranted to hasten my arrival. But alas, this was not a good move.

I came to a sudden stop, and was thrown forward in the boat, accompanied by a nasty grinding noise. I had run aground, and what was worse, it sounded like a rock. That was bad. Looking around, I could see nothing but sand so "where had that wicked rigid thing come from?" I wondered.

Having released myself from this unwanted obstruction I sailed on to the club, still sailing over deep dark water.

On approaching the pontoon, I managed to run aground again! "This is ridiculous," I said.

When I got out of the boat onto the platform, I realised my error. Unlike the glassy clear water at the beach, I was looking down into dark brown brine. I could only just make out a rock, a foot below the surface, so my usual view through the water was mostly blotted out. I had thought that dark meant deep, but instead it meant Scottish peat, washed down in the river. Bother. No wonder I hadn't spotted the hazards. The centreboard had a decent dent in its leading edge but was otherwise intact, and to my relief, no emergency repairs were needed.

Neil was there to meet me, having come down on his bicycle. Rob, from my sailing club, had made the introduction a couple of days previously.

Neil and Rob had met when doing an MBA together and stayed in touch. Neil had been living in the Surrey area, but had taken a few taster holiday trips to Scotland with his wife and daughter, and then they had decided to make the move permanent. Both Neil and his wife Lorna were still working and were very much valuing their decision, and so was I.

The house was a delightful light, single storey dwelling, walking distance from the sea, in more than one direction, but sheltered from the wind. I had only managed to rustle up a chocolate gift on this occasion, since I was not close to shops, but was pleased to see that it was appreciated after our vegetarian dinner.

It was hard to communicate my gratitude for the kindnesses offered to a strange traveller, welcomed into a home for the night. A small nibble, or tipple seemed inadequate, and an endless supply of thankyous, too much. I could only hope that our altruistic nature as humans, was satisfied by this most simple of offerings. In time honoured tradition, I later wrote a card to thank Neil and Lorna.

* * *

Day 41, Wednesday 31st May

To Golspie

START	10.00, Findhorn
WIND	NE 7–11mph. Reality is N/NW, finally E
WEATHER	Cloudy, then sunny, 12–14°C, dry
TIDE	Eastwards max 0.4mph till 16.00
SEA STATE	Slight to smooth
HAZARDS	Running out of wind
FINISH	Golspie, 17.30
DISTANCE	26 miles
SAILING HOURS	7½ hours

I ended up with a double breakfast by mistake, since Lorna invited me to help myself before she sped off to teach, which I duly did. Then Neil came back from an early meeting and made porridge, something we had discussed the night before. I didn't need to worry about overeating. Neil very kindly came back down to the pontoon to bid farewell before pedalling off to work again.

I heard on the news that Tina Turner had died age 83. What an icon she was, fighting her way to musical success, out of an abusive and controlling relationship. She went on to set trends for performance, and an example to women around the world. Her album 'Private Dancer' was one of my treasured LPs in student days, whose songs would burst out of my record player in a passionate embrace, rescuing me from some dreary textbook.

We did go and see her perform live a few years back, when she was 70 or so. It was a fun evening and fantastic to see Tina the person, in the flesh. I did reflect afterwards that it was probably best to remember people in their heyday. It sounded more or less the same, but some of the vigour was lost. Long live the memories of Tina Turner at her best.

As I was getting ready to depart, a charming couple came down the walkway towards me and we got talking. They were going to place a new yacht mooring in the river. One conversation led to another, and I eventually worked out that they were the parents of a person called Scott, whom I had met at Stonehaven. Scott had said he learnt to sail at Findhorn, which had helped make the connection. What a coincidence.

Derek and Ann had been members of the Findhorn Yacht Club for years, but it had slightly lost its way recently. A tussle between dinghy sailors and yacht's folk, meant that some of the social activities had been neglected. As the dinghy sailors had moved on, as they so often do, the heart had fallen out of the club somewhat. This tale was a reminder to me of the incredible importance of bringing people together on a regular basis, to make organisations work.

The plan for the day was to head straight across the Moray Firth to Golspie, a decent stretch, not far off the Thames Estuary mileage. However, it didn't feel as daunting, because I had learnt a few things along the way (thank goodness), the hazards were fewer, and importantly, I could see where I was going. There was also a handy halfway point in the form of Tarbat Ness with lighthouse included.

Turning left at this point would have meant heading in towards Inverness and the entrance to the Caledonian Canal. This was a route choice that many had suggested in order to avoid the dreaded Duncansby Head / Pentland Firth combination at the north-east corner of Scotland. For me, it was onwards and upwards, blocking my eyes and ears from the frightening stories. Besides, the Scottish Canal Authority manage the Caledonian Canal, and as I later learnt to my cost, they were not too keen on small boats.

A nervous exit over the sandbar near Findhorn saved some time, but that was it for journey efficiency, but I got there in the end.

I have told many people that I saw an Orca off Tarbat Ness, so it must be true. A big black fin shape, stuck on top of a big black body, appeared out of the water in the middle distance, and slowly arched its way out of view, taking at least double dolphin time for a breath. It wasn't a male though. They have a large pyramidal dorsal fin that looks like it has been drawn on by a kid. Instead, it was a more delicate feature, curved at the front and the back, altogether more ladylike. Like the dolphins, this Orca could not count to three, breaking the surface only twice, so I didn't catch the sighting on camera.

There had been several reports of Orcas attacking sailing vessels in the Gibraltar area, with an unhappy female teaching others how to ply her aggressive trade. The assault often involved biting a rudder and sometimes disabling it. On one occasion, the rudder was pulled off, which then led to the yacht sinking. A friend at Papercourt said that his yacht rudder had been attacked, so the threat was both real and present.

At the time, I thought that I was pretty safe since Scotland was a long way from Gibraltar. However, I understood there has been a recent report of an attack in Scotland as well. Maybe I was in more danger than I realised. Whatever the truth, I was convinced I saw one, and it showed no interest in causing me any trouble. I can also say with certainty, that the only species to assault Betty throughout the whole four and a half months of travel, was, yes, you guessed it, Homo Sapiens.

Approaching Golspie I could see hills rising majestically up into the distance, as the landscape ascended to the Highlands of Scotland. Being the largest county by area in the UK, the Highlands extend all the way round to Tobermory on the West coast, day 56 in my world, or the best part of a month away.

On top of one of the hills was a statue, which I later learnt was the infamous Duke of Sutherland. For me, it was a convenient landmark because I could not see the town. I knew it was there, but there were no white shapes on the shore, and instead nothing but green. I could see the town of Brora to the north, but no Golspie. When I arrived, I realised it was not some illusion, or a cunning town trick to avoid being spotted. It was simply that buildings were set back from the sea, and were on level ground surrounded by trees, so from four miles out, all I could see was vegetation.

The Golspie reception went on and on, in a delicious stream of welcoming locals and friends. First there was Jennifer who came down to the beach with her five young children. A nurse friend of mine had met Jennifer's sister Louise via drumming events in the south of England, and had connected to Jennifer at Golspie. Then Jennifer's mother Christine joined the party on the beach. Jennifer and Christine live next door to each other in the town. Christine had very kindly offered to accommodate the shrink in the drink for the night.

Next there were rowers from the Gig Club. They were preparing to head out for a spell on the water, but came over to offer assistance and suggestions about boat storage, since their clubhouse was only one hundred metres away. I later learnt that some of the rowers were world champions in the over 50s age group, which sounded very impressive.

Finally, to round things off, Rupert and his partner Lucy arrived. Rupert was a work colleague with whom I had remained in touch after our paths had parted, someone whom I very much respected in terms of working and therapeutic practice. He had also been very supportive about the trip, having a sailing background. Rupert and Lucy had been staying at Loch Lomond, so had driven for two hours to greet me. What a treat, and what a wonderful compliment that they should take the time out of their holiday to come and say hello.

Rupert, Lucy, Christine and I went off to the Golspie Arms for a drink, leaving Jennifer to tend to her children, and rowers to pull on their oars. We spent a delightful warm hour or so, catching up, blessed by a still clear evening, with Christine comfortably blending into the conversation, as if she too were an old friend. Ah, the joys of excellent company. Sadly, Rupert and Lucy needed to head south to their accommodation for the evening, but they had left a glow of comfort with me and memories to savour.

Back at Christine's house, over a gammon and vegetable dinner, topped off with some Merlot, she gave me a potted family history. Christine's husband had died a few years previously. As a surveyor, he had organised the construction of the property we were in, as well as the home next door, where Jennifer lived with her husband and young children. The properties were spacious, as well as being separated from each other, and both had good views over the sea. Hence, they were comfortable, close, and yet not on top of each other – perfect for harmonious relationships. The unescorted kids popped round in the morning to say 'hi' to Grandma before heading off to school. Jennifer's husband had also dropped round to meet me, so it felt like a thriving and welcoming community, within a thriving and welcoming community of Golspie. Christine kept in touch as I travelled round the country sending the occasional encouraging text, adding persistence and authenticity to her open house. How incredible, especially so, at a later and more vulnerable time in life.

Feeling full with goodness, I went for a snooze at ten past ten, but didn't wake till morning. I must have been tired.

* * *

Day 42, Thursday 1st June 2023

To Helmsdale

START	11.30, Golspie
WIND	E, 12–16mph
WEATHER	Cloudy. Sunny evening, 12–10°C. Dry
TIDE	With me from 12.00, max 0.4mph
SEA STATE	Slight
HAZARDS	Rocks on the shore at Golspie
FINISH	Helmsdale, 16.30
DISTANCE	16 miles
SAILING HOURS	5 hours

I overslept.

Over breakfast, Christine confirmed that the statue on the hill was the Duke of Sutherland, who had been involved in the "clearances".

Filling in more details later, I learnt that he had been a major landowner in the Highlands during the 19th century. A business opportunity arose to move farming from smallholding and cattle, to the more profitable sheep industry. That meant moving existing tenants out of the way, hence the term the "clearances". Areas were progressively cleared during the first 20 years of the 1800s with varying degrees of incentive, or at times force. Once people left, housing was typically burned down to prevent a return of the residents. Many settled on the coast, but many others emigrated to Canada or Australasia, seeking a better life.

I had not heard about this before, and was quite alarmed to think of the forced eviction of the poor at the behest of a wealthy landlord. There had been much news coverage of the felling of Edward Colston's statue in Bristol because of his slave trader background. His egregious crimes were against other nations, so felt further away. To have harms recorded on a large scale against people on our own land, felt like it was breaching a barrier. Maybe I was just being naïve or simply ill informed, but either way, I was troubled.

"Has anyone considered taking his statue down?" I asked Christine.

"There has been talk," she said, from which I surmised that there had not been enough feeling to follow through.

At the top of a steep hill (as opposed to Edward Colston's brazen location on the main Bristol waterfront) the duke was more likely to be approached by breathless hikers, rather than listless university students. One would imagine that it would be students rather than hikers, who would be minded to create a corral of objection. Maybe that was why it still stands. The statue was simply too much out of the way, to generate sufficient protest for it to be removed from its pedestal.

In line with Golspie tradition, helpers were ready at the beach to assist with my launch. Rob, John and Will from the rowing club, had come down unprompted. I was slightly taken aback at this show of generosity and wondered how it had happened. The answer was Facebook. Similar to the process at Withernsea, a post or two on a community group had led to a collection of real physical responses. We hear so much about overreactions and divisive opinions online, but here was an example of a unifying benefit. The community had come together in simple and unflustered ways to lend a gracious hand. How lovely is that, and what a great community?

The tide was in, so it was easier to make my way past the strange line of rocks bordering the beach, which had proved troublesome the evening before. After that it was a trudge up to Helmsdale on a chilly but steady beat.

The radio was working OK. I enjoyed a programme about mitochondria and the fascinating symbiotic relationship between bacteria and these essential energy producing cells, a relationship that must have been formed millions of years ago. OK, ok, I found it interesting. And then a drama starring Bill Nighy. I was looking forward to listening to further episodes on subsequent days.

The sun had come out by the time I arrived at Helmsdale. It was a quiet and contented harbour, similar to Banff, with an easy clean pontoon landing and no harbour master. What a nice spot.

The hills around the town meant that I would need to rely on my wit rather than phone signal, to find somewhere to stay. Asking around, there was a suggestion of a harbourside house run by a lady called Ann, who was 81 years old. I was told she was still going strong, but selective in her guest selection. I wondered if I would qualify. Rather than wait and hope, I headed into town and found a café, and then the Kindale Guest House. The guest house was up to the challenge, and I secured my booking.

Back down by the harbour a little later, an elderly lady, cleverly guessing who I was, asked me whether I was still looking for a room. She was kindly, a little stooped but encouraging. Ann introduced herself and was keen to report on her longevity, and her ongoing commitment to travellers despite the absence of financial need. I thought 'good for you', and 'how brave to keep running a guest house as an octogenarian'.

Then Joe Biden popped into my head. He had recently tripped over on the way onto a stage. The column inches dedicated to his minor stumble felt an overblown drama at the time, but now I was not so sure. Aged 81 and running a guest house is one thing, but 81 and running the United States, was quite a different matter. Like one of those head swopping apps, I was imagining Joe Biden's features on Ann's torso, and apologies to Ann, but I was feeling a little disturbed.

Heading into the Belgrave Arms, I approached the barman to order some food.

"Could I have the sweet potato curry, and a chocolate Brownie to follow."

"Would you like anything else?" he asked.

"Oh, yes, a beer would be great," I added.

"Anything else?"

The pub was fairly quiet and looking around I could not spot anyone who might be easily offended, so cautiously asked an extra question.

"I don't know if it's OK to ask, but I was told about the clearances recently. I hadn't heard much about that before. Is that something that is quite familiar to locals?"

"Oh yes," he replied without hesitation. "Quite a few families left for other countries. That was quite a long time ago though." And after a short pause, "Is there anything else?"

So, it really was true. I was still feeling quite shocked by the morning's conversation. To think that brutal eviction of landowners in the interests of sheep, could be acceptable as recently as 200 years ago, felt alarming. Being new to the history, I was feeling a little outraged, but fortunately had not triggered a matching sentiment. Almost the opposite – what seemed to be a casual acceptance perhaps.

And then dinner arrived. The barman had transformed into the waiter, having seamlessly taken a role as the cook in the meantime. I was propped up on an elbow like a Roman emperor, lounging on the grass outside the pub. The turf was dry enough to avoid a soggy bottom, and we were not too far into the summer, which might have resulted in an ant invasion. Perfect. And dinner was accompanied by the excellent phone company of Pippa, a doctor friend, who was part of my evening call rota.

In my local news, I had missed Nick Ray. He had a large Instagram following under the handle "life_afloat". That says it all, since he spends a lot of time afloat on the sea. Nick was from Tobermory on the West Coast, and described himself as a writer, mental health advocate and sea kayaker. I knew he was travelling round Scotland in a clockwise direction, so our paths would soon cross. Despite my best efforts of emailing and trying to call, he had sneaked past on the inside track – or so he said when he replied a few days later. He reckoned he might have seen me out at sea. I had really wanted to meet him in person and hear about his motivation and travels. He also took some amazing pictures such as a puffin in mid-flight, or a seal asleep on the sea, so I had wanted to learn about his set up. Sadly, it was not to be.

In the international news, 'Big C' had sunk. Andrew Bedwell was attempting to sail across the Atlantic in his one-metre length craft, thereby setting a world record for the smallest sailing dinghy to do so. It looked a very uncomfortable boat, and a crazy adventure indeed. Fortunately, he had gone for a test sail when heading off from Newfoundland, and unfortunately the vehicle had sprung a leak. Even worse, when it was then hoisted onto the dock, its extra weight meant that it collapsed and was beyond repair.

A tearful Andrew posted a long message on Facebook, thanking his supporters and mourning the sudden end to his major life work. Feeling connected to another insane solo sailor, I was really sorry that so much of his effort had come to a juddering halt. I was also relieved, since a leak in the Atlantic, and his likely demise, would have been much worse, and a bad omen for me.

Instead, I was into a new month. I was also ahead of my pre-ordained six-month schedule, so feeling pleased with progress. It was upwards and onwards from here.

* * *

Day 43, Friday 2nd June

To Lybster

START	11.15, Helmsdale
WIND	SE, 6–10mph. In reality E, very little
WEATHER	10–11°C, sun and lots of it
TIDE	Against me till 13.00, max 0.3mph
SEA STATE	Calm to Smooth
HAZARDS	No wind and no landing
FINISH	Lybster, 16.00
DISTANCE	18 miles
SAILING HOURS	4¾ hours

I had a restless night, worrying about Duncansby Head, corner #2, and one of the feared tidal race locations. The water can run at eight miles per hour, or so they say. Stick had told me about his struggles to round the headland, saying he had to wait for a few days, needing to time his rounding to perfection. The next stretch beyond the head is the equally treacherous race, inappropriately named 'The Merry Men of Mey'. Further, there were very few places to stop safely, should things go wrong. It sounded difficult.

In Helmsdale, it was a gorgeous morning. Picture postcard blue skies made the yellow heather look effervescent on peaty green hills, hills which strode up into the cool fresh Highland air behind the town, where buildings bristled white in the early summer sun. Such was the delight of this Scottish morning that everything became joyful. The stroll down to the harbour past quiet houses; the trip to the Co-op for supplies; and even the retrieval of cash from a wall overlooking the Helmsdale River, where it trickled its way down the valley, brought a smile to my face.

The harbourmaster, when I found him in his office, had been taken by the mood as well. He gave a helpful description of the partly concealed entrance to Lybster harbour, details to aid my afternoon arrival, and then waived the harbour fees which I duly donated to charity.

Clearly this weather thing had gone to my head, because I was becalmed again, but simply not bothered. The Guillemots gathered on the glassy surface around me, jiggling and chattering in their groups, though unusually staying put, despite the presence of Betty the swan, drifting slowly by. Sunlight shone into the depths of crystal-clear water below me, making it feel like it was possible to reach down to infinity. Even the cliffs smiled majestically across the reflecting blue, with their fine colours and brushed indentations, spread out in a steady sweep, a backdrop fit for a painting.

Occasionally, just occasionally, I would wonder where I might land that night, only lightly troubled by the necessities of food, land and sleep. I sauntered onwards, warmed by the rays of the sun, solitary, silent, at one with nature, and content.

Sadly, all good things must come to an end. Some wind wrestled me from my trance and thrust me forward, onwards to Lybster and its half-hidden harbour, buried into a break in the cliffs.

There was no one about when I arrived. An absence of pontoons meant that I tied up to a yacht, so that Betty would be spared the indignity of being dragged up and down the harbour walls with the overnight tides. A note on the boat was added, in case of an irate sailor finding their exit obstructed in the morning, but I needn't have worried.

It was a bit of trek up the hill to Lybster town, but a gorgeous evening again. Luckily, I was offered a lift by James who was passing in his truck. He also drove me to the Portland Hotel, suggesting it was about the only place in town that might offer accommodation. I thought I would settle with his advice, rather than risk wandering round town for a cheaper alternative.

There was a room for me, I was pleased to discover. It was a close-run thing, however. The hotel, being located on the A99, had been full the night before with a North Coast 500 party taking up all the spaces. This was a bit of a worry for the next few weeks since the summer season had arrived, and I would be following the famous touring route round the coast.

Dinner was a five-bean stew, cheesecake for afters, and a beer.

In my room, I noticed that my nose was a little red from too much sun. The extra rouge made my face creep closer to crustacean colouring, so a fortunate accompaniment to a ditty I received from Guy – my brother-in-law, with whom I stayed when in Norfolk. He had been keeping an eye on my progress. Ever astute on the phonetic pronunciation of places, he knew that Lybster was pronounced 'Liebster' and not 'Libster' as I had imagined, thus making the lines scan better. Whether he was referring to me, the 'at one with nature, dreaming sea sailor' or a proper marine animal we need not know. Either way, his rhyming efforts needed to be applauded.

Lybster lobster
where are you?
Gone for coffee
Back at two

I gave him a ring to congratulate him on his new appointment as poet laureate.

⚬ ⚬ ⚬

Day 44, Saturday 3rd June

To Wick

START	11.00, Lybster
WIND	N, 6–11mph, but stronger in reality
WEATHER	Sun/cloud, 10–12°C. Quite chilly. Dry
TIDE	Heading N from 13.00. Max 1.8mph
SEA STATE	Slight
HAZARDS	Variable wind. No landing spots
FINISH	Wick, 14.45
DISTANCE	14 miles
SAILING HOURS	3¾ hours

The weather had turned grey, transforming the rather dull Lybster high street into something even less vibrant. Straight, flat and wide, it had little to say for itself, other than something along the lines of "there is plenty of room to park". Pebbledash was a popular form of building dressing, not reserved to Lybster I might add. I hoped that this bobble wrap external feature did provide some building protection, because I am not too sure it added much in the way of an aesthetic uplift. I began to wonder who might live at Lybster and what informed their livelihood, but then my mind unashamedly strode off down the hill, to tidal races and the days ahead.

I liked the idea of stopping at the Whaligoe steps, a halfway point on the day's passage. Cliff staircases usually come with a dramatic view, and a serving of history, especially if they have been afforded a specific name. The hotel receptionist mentioned that a member of staff had recently slipped and fallen, causing significant injury, adding an extra measure of intrigue to the landmark. For me, there was the prospect of a coffee shop at the top of the climb as a reward.

The steps were carved out of the cliff face, some 200 years previously, to serve a port of sorts. Sailing in, I was not too sure what the folks of old had been thinking, since this was more like an amphitheatre of doom. Stark black precipitous cliffs encircled a tiny inlet and micro beachette, strewn with more lumps of rock, perfectly sized to puncture a hull. Rocks to my left, rocks to my right, rocks in front of me, rocks below me, rocks above me. Apparently, fishing craft would moor up to a wall-type feature. The area had been disused since the 1950s, so when I arrived, there was nothing for me to grab onto. Wind swirled around in all directions, but never quite ceased, in this sun deprived hole, making every move of mine a hazard. Fortunately, there was little to no swell on my approach, but I was sure that if there had been, the inlet would have made an excellent death trap.

History says that the steps were forged to aid fishing. Small wooden craft would tie up and offload their catch. Herring, cod or haddock would then be gutted and salted, making use of a flat area called 'the bink', and then lugged up the hill on the back of some hapless local. Given that Wick was only eight miles to the North, there must have been sound economic reason for making use of this inhospitable spot, but I was struggling to imagine the details.

Trying to land looked unnecessarily risky. I waved at tourists who had descended the steps, but didn't think they could help either. I concluded I would need to forgo my midday coffee indulgence, and instead, headed back out to the open water and on to Wick.

Happily, there was more wind than forecast. In addition, the tide suddenly picked up the pace, having been fairly sedate hitherto, a taste of things to come no doubt.

Unlike Whaligoe, Wick was a vibrant and bustling port where it was safe to land. Geoff was my contact and like so many before and after him, was waiting on the pontoon to greet me.

I was introduced to Geoff by David, whom I had met in Stonehaven. And I was introduced to David by Ditta when I was there. Ditta, as you may recall, had come out to rescue me from paddling ignominy, having picked up my email to Stonehaven Sailing Club. In case that feels like an incredible series of links, indeed it is – yet another testament to human generosity, and a tribute to the desire of sailors to support each other.

Geoff, like David, was a Solo sailor (which is a type of dinghy, slightly bigger than a Laser, but not so beach-worthy). I learnt that Geoff had sailed from his youth, competing locally and nationally, coming second at one national event, a ranking that earned significant respect in my eyes. He used to work on the rigs, ensuring that support vessels maintained their position alongside a drilling platform or other object. It sounded like a job where a great deal of effort is required to make it appear that nothing is happening. My own Laser experience of holding position on a start line had taught me that it is challenging task, let alone having to deal with huge waves and the enormous bulk of a ship.

Having retired, Geoff was putting more time into fishing, both on land and sea. He worked as a part time Gillie in the Scottish salmon rivers, but also had his own trawler. Not a large one, but a refined vessel with a wheelhouse and open deck, plus line holding reels and metal trays to catch the captured fish. He gave me a tour of his boat. I very much enjoyed the look around, and peppered him with questions about the mechanics of the craft, and the life of a small boat fisherman.

My education included information about 'purser' ships, or ships using the purse - seine method. These, Geoff explained, were enormous commercial trawlers, fitted with radar and huge nets that would locate shoals, then scoop up all but a few of the identified swimmers, and funnel them into a frozen hold for onward processing. "They don't stand a chance," said Geoff. It was not like the refined art of line fishing from the back of his boat, or the skilled whip of fly casting, to lure a single hunter to a hooked line. The description of industrialisation of fishing helped explain the situation at Peterhead, and indeed internationally. With such force being meted out on our fish folk, the need for effective regulation seemed most urgent, to avoid destruction of what remains.

Geoff knew many of the locals, had an extensive knowledge of tides and local conditions, which made him an excellent counsel for one apprehensive newcomer. He introduced me to others, and kindly interpreted when an accent became too thick for me to make sense of the gurgle of Scottish noise. I heard stories of pot buoys being thrust down to the sea floor with the force of the tide. There were tales of experienced fishermen who mistimed their return to port, and were cruelly caught in the teeth of tide and storm - and such was the ferocity of the sea, that neither ship nor soul were ever seen again.

Finally relieved from the stream of disturbing tales, we returned to Geoff's home. Alison was both welcoming and accommodating, supplying food, laundry, interest, and a casual disinterest in fish related matters, other than when they made it into the fridge. Their three children had moved away from home but one remained nearby.

As ever, I was royally entertained. Food, a comfy bed, laundry, a space to spread out and dry things, were all generously provided. I was invited to stay for not one, but two nights. This was hugely appreciated, not least because I could discuss the passage past the Merry men of Mey for as long as necessary, or at least until some of us were no longer pleased to listen.

As the evening progressed, I realised that fish were perhaps more important than DIY in the house. I was advised that a bathroom shuffle might be needed, to achieve desirable washing conditions, since the cold tap was working in one room, and only the hot in another.

Fortunately, Alison and Geoff were amused to hear about my maintenance mishap during the night, and even suggested "you'll have to add that to your book", when I told them about it in the morning.

Here goes.

Waking up at 5am as I often do, for a toilet trip, I stumbled out of bed and headed for the door. It was an uncomplicated journey downstairs to the bathroom, and I was confident about leaving my hosts undisturbed. I gripped the door handle and carefully turned it to prevent too much creaking, and then pulled. The door handle moved smoothly into the room. Unfortunately, the handle was no longer attached to the door.

All of a sudden, I was wide awake. Equally sudden, my bladder gave a sharp squeeze, reminding me of my urgent predicament. The square spindle was still located in the mechanism, though as all who have tried it know well, fingers are just not sufficient to produce the required rotation. I tried. And failed.

Looking round, I was searching for options, either to open the door, or to provide some wee relief till the morning. I was not keen on the idea of using a water bottle, and soon realised that it was downstairs, which was at least some small hygienic respite. There was no sink. The window perhaps? But it was a ceiling Velux arrangement and .... I need go no further to illustrate the problem.

If really desperate, I could try calling Geoff or Alison on the phone, but I wanted to avoid doing that. Not just yet anyway.

Back to the door spindle. I needed something to assist with grip. Clothing made no difference. What about the handle of my toothbrush? No good. Or the side of my multitool which could be stronger. No good either. What about two of them?

Ah, how foolish of me. In my morning haze I had forgotten that I had a mini pair of pliers on the second multitool, something I had added to my 'everything' box at a late stage of packing. Holding it carefully like James Bond, on a mission to stop an evil dictator's bomb going off, I turned slowly hoping nothing calamitous would happen. The mechanism turned, and I was out. Hooray! And "Phew".

Having been relieved, I quietly returned to my room. With my newfound confidence I decided to reattach the handle and close the door, before heading back to bed. Risky, you might say, but it worked. And I got back to sleep.

CHAPTER 12

When you are the top,
you are the top

Orkney

K = Kirkwall
S = Stromness

M = Merry Men
of Mey

Dounreay Power Station

Dunnet Head

Day 47

Day 46

Pentland Firth

Hoy

S

K

Stroma

Duncansby Head

Cape Wrath

Day 50

Day 49

Day 48

Day 45

Day 51

Durness

Talmine

Betty Hill

Strathy

Scrabster

Thurso

John O'Groats

Wick

Kinlochbervie

Caithness

Scourie

Sutherland

Day 45, Sunday 4th June

To John O'Groats

START	12.10, Wick
WIND	SE, 7–11 mph
WEATHER	Cloudy, 10–12°C. Dry
TIDE	With me from 13.00, max 2mph
SEA STATE	Slight to smooth
HAZARDS	Nowhere to land
FINISH	John O'Groats, 16.00
DISTANCE	16 miles
SAILING HOURS	4 hours

In the news, there were more train strikes in the UK.

In India a major train crash in Mumbai had resulted in many tragic deaths, and many more injuries.

Manchester City had won the FA Cup, so were in line to win an historic treble. Would they be able to manage I wondered. I hoped they might?

For me, it was "D Day". Duncansby Head day. I felt as prepared as I could be, with plans, back out plans, and support plans. The thing is, you can never quite tell what is going to happen. The sea and the weather are answerable to no one, and have a habit of behaving just as they please when you least expect it. The land, oh yes, we love the land, because it is so much more reliable. Tiny me would look pathetic up against the mighty dark cliffs of the north-east corner of Great Britain. Corner number two. What a landmark.

After rounding the headland, there would be no more travelling north. It did not bear thinking about just yet. I needed to stay focussed on my destination and the day ahead. If the wind died, I would be mere flotsam on the tide, drifting to wherever I might be taken, with no escape on the wing, or into the depths as my sea fellows might do. I would have to take my chances.

Geoff came down to help with the launch, so my usual pedestrian plod was transformed into a preparation jog. To catch the tides just right, we figured that a midday departure would be needed. "You'll be smoking along, when you get to the corner," he said.

Looking back, I realise I was very fortunate with the timing – I had anticipated a wait at Wick for a few days, to allow conditions to align in a necessary combination to make for a safe rounding. But here we were, with a light south-easterly wind and an afternoon spring tide to take me onwards, without delay. Hopefully. Thank you, luck. Thank you, Neptune, or perhaps thank you, Janus, the Roman god of beginnings, endings and time (hence January).

It was a cold day with thick cloud pressing down on the coast of Scotland, creating an ominous shroud over land and sea, blinding me from my view of the future and the past. A thin sliver of brown was visible at the junction of smudgy greys, giving me just enough sight of safety.

There was sufficient wind to make progress out of Wick Bay and on past Noss Head, but as I crossed Sinclair's Bay towards Skirza, the wind thinned to almost nothing, and then stopped.

A Fulmer seagull swam close to the boat, and even took a casual tour around my craft as I floated towards the headland, thus circumnavigating a circumnavigator.

I had been worried that I would not make it to Duncansby given the light winds, but the tide accelerated as I came closer, touching eight miles per hour. Yes, eight miles per hour. I hadn't believed the accounts other people had given. However, my stated speed must have been a true reading, since it came from the tracker, whilst I was stationary on the water.

In awe I watched the swirling waters lurch and wrestle their way past the lighthouse. I listened in wonder as the sea rushed past silent rocks, gazing down with disdain at this daily pointless hustle, the sea sounding more like a swollen Scottish winter burn than a becalmed headland. And then I was past it.

I need not have worried about making it to Duncansby, given the tidal pace. However, in my admiration of the forces of nature, I had forgotten to think where the sea might flow beyond the head. It was not going round the corner as I foolishly imagined, and instead was taking me straight on to the Orkneys at some pace.

It was time to panic and get the paddle out again. Frantically flapping away on each side of the boat, looking like a Guillemot in take-off mode, I made a bit of progress. Remembering my O Level physics, I headed straight across the line of the stream in order to make fast my escape from this relentless conveyor. Then, just as I was beginning to tire, I was assisted into calmer waters by a welcome puff of wind.

What a relief. And then after some more paddle sailing, what joy to make it into the tiny harbour of John O'Groats.

I had imagined grabbing hold of the harbour wall as I was swept past. In reality, it was a pleasant squeeze into a sheltered spot, keeping out of the way of the ferry as it came and went. I moored up to a trawler in Lybster fashion, adding my paper explanatory note.

And then up the grassy slope to the pole of celebration, hovering around the journey men and women, who had made it on their wheeled machines to the end of their cycling road. I was having a wonderful time soaking up the atmosphere in the calm evening air. I couldn't quite believe it. I had to say it to myself over and over - "I have reached John O'Groats."

I chatted to a cyclist called Philip who had just completed his ride. "Really well done. That's amazing," I offered.

I couldn't help myself and added, "I have just arrived as well. I have sailed up from the Isle of Wight in a Laser."

He wasn't sure what I was talking about till I showed him Betty parked up in the harbour. Philip was sufficiently impressed to make a £100 donation to charity. How incredibly benevolent. I hope my excitement did not temper his own enjoyment, and monumental achievement.

My own cycling memories were swirling around in my pleasure-soaked mind. Back in 2011, Henry, a school parent of our parallel children, and I, had guided our respective sons (and an extra), on an unsupported cycle, finishing on the day that GCSE results were published. More or less as we were pulling up at the finish point, the grades came through with no child, and no parent, feeling disappointed. It was a remarkable clean sweep, especially gratifying since we had just reached the pinnacle of our journey. What a celebration that was.

What a buzz. I was so pleased and so relieved all at the same time.

Geoff had kindly agreed to pick me up, but I had time to kill before his arrival. An inevitable café sit down was accompanied by some phone time. There was travel planning to be done. Robin's funeral was coming up and I really wanted to be there. Trains, flights, a place to leave the boat etc, all needed to be organised.

I also had spares shopping to do. This included a pair of gloves, since the current ones were getting worn; Teflon discs for the bottom of the mast, because the existing circles had been chewed to mush by all the sand and grit; and finally, a replacement waterproof phone case.

Stick had struggled with his phone, saying there was no way you could get around without a replacement. Ron had a Nokia brick which was mainly used for calls. (I wondered how he managed at all, since he relied on laminated road maps stuck to the deck, which were his main navigation aid!) I had a spare phone in the hold, though preferred the idea of preservation. Because you only find out there is a leak when a case fills up with water, it seemed like a good idea to upgrade the protection before it was too late. This proved a smart move, since I was able to hang on to my original throughout the trip.

On the way back to Wick with Geoff, we took a detour to Skirza to see what the potential landing spot looked like in reality. The alleged harbour was one up from Whaligoe, but only just. A wall protruding out into the bay, surrounded by beach, carpeted in kelp and rocks, was best described as interesting. Perhaps this was a taste of things to come.

Stick sent me a congratulatory message about arriving at John O'Groats. I was really touched that he had been following my travels, and had taken the time to send a message. The gloss of the day continued to glow.

Day 46, Monday 5th June

To Scrabster

START	11.45, John O'Groats
WIND	NW, 8–11mph
WEATHER	Cloud and some sun, 10–13°C. Dry
TIDE	Heading west from 14.00, max 3mph
SEA STATE	Slight
HAZARDS	No wind. Strong tides. Wind vs tide?
FINISH	Scrabster, Pentland Bay, 17.00
DISTANCE	19 miles
SAILING HOURS	5¼ hours

The plan was to reach Pentland Firth Sailing Club, and park the boat so I could head south. I had had an email reply which was great. There was just the matter of getting there, past the Merry Men of Mey, the last section of the Pentland Firth. The main worries were lack of wind, and being washed somewhere I didn't want to go, like into rocks. Geoff reminded me, however, that the sea goes around obstructions, so I should be escorted on the long route, rather than straight into the hard stuff. And wind against tide? I wasn't sure whether I needed to worry.

Geoff was heading off to perform his gillie duties, so conveniently hurried me along in the morning. I bade a warm farewell to Alison.

At John O'Groats harbour, we chatted to a local fisherman to check on conditions, with Geoff once again decoding local dialect when needed. Kevin the fisherman had worked these shores for many years, and pointed out hazards we had largely captured already, which was reassuring. Kevin was a well-built man whose son had been competing in "world's strongest man" events so likewise was with a substantial frame. He was invited to take a look at Betty.

"Och, you need a bigger booat," he scoffed. To which I replied, "It's fine. And you are welcome to join me."

We laughed about that. The imagined sight of Kevin and I, squeezed on board poor Betty, brought on a few chuckles. I pictured the scene in my head – feet, knees and luggage all tangled in the cockpit, and water sloshing over the gunwale as we tried to make progress in a confused state, somewhere between dinghy and submarine.

There was a reasonable distance to travel to Scrabster, especially if there was no wind. It was certainly too far to paddle, but hopefully the tide would help. I had an hour or so before the tide turned, so out on the water I hugged the rocky coast as closely as possible, beating along the shoreline. I then headed out towards St John's Point and into the path of the Merry Men of Mey, leaving the island of Stroma on my right. It was slow going, but the surface was calm and the pace was quickening to six miles an hour with the increasing tide.

Just as I thought I had passed the worst, the sea started to heave below me. I looked around for a passing ship that might explain the sudden swell, but there were none. Could this be a wind against tide effect I wondered? There was only a light breeze so that seemed unlikely. I could not figure out what was going on. Up and down I rolled, like passing across huge ripples. It was as if the ocean had turned into a giant serpent, awakened from the deep, stretching its mighty back as it stirred from slumber. I did not know this beast. I did not know how to talk to it, or to tame it. Was I in serious danger? I really could not be sure. The undulations grew larger and swirls added to the turbulence. I could only imagine what might happen from here. Those ugly fishermen's stories, so vividly refreshed from a day ago, were wreaking havoc with my imagination. A plaintive look to my left at the royal residence of the Castle of Mey was reciprocated with a stern stare. I was on my own again.

As rapidly as this eerie monster had appeared, so too it faded back into still water, resting its weary soul on the sea floor. "What on earth was that all about?" I asked out loud to the settling sea. I had no idea. I guess it was something to do with those Merry Men, but who knows what they were up to. It was gone but not forgotten. Thank goodness the winds were light, for I dared not imagine what would have risen from the deep if there had been a storm.

Dunnet Head was next, the most northern point on the UK mainland. It was accompanied by more upwellings, and swirls, but no swells this time. Then the wind faded and more or less gave up, so it was out with the paddle. I did not need to provide the urgency of Duncansby Head. However, there was a risk of missing Scrabster altogether, if I should fall into a puddle of complacency.

A puffin was waiting for me as I approached my end point. Untroubled by my slow pace, I was able to sneak fairly close, before this famously shy bird took flight. It was my best picture to date, but still nothing compared to Nick Ray's superb wildlife photography.

I had another wonderful reception at the sailing club. Kate sailed out to meet me in her dinghy, which was fortunate since the club was not quite where I imagined.

Ian found a trolley and helped pull Betty to the compound, where Vicki was ready with a key. Then into the clubhouse for some tea and chat. I met Kyle and Bella. Bella very kindly gave me a spare chicken dinner and tatties, to help with refuelling. And then there was a birthday celebration and cake to follow, for a fellow sailor. The club members were mostly young, which was a refreshing change from the usual population of middle aged men. There was a vibrancy and strong community spirit amongst the group, which was both welcoming and energetic, and was wonderful to witness.

With Betty safe in the boat park and future access arranged, it occurred to me that there was time and opportunity to make a touristic detour to the Orkneys. After all, the ferry was a mere half mile away, and I was certain I would be welcomed as a last-minute foot passenger for the final sailing of the day at seven o'clock. I had never been to the Orkneys and it seemed wasteful to miss out on the final hop to the islands.

Ian gave me a lift most of the way to the terminal, which was just as well. Instead of the anticipated welcome, I was reprimanded for my tardiness, and strongly advised to be punctual when returning via Stromness terminal, because "they are much stricter than we are. If you miss the 30-minute deadline, they won't let you on".

I took the ticket, and the advice, and went to sit down.

Heading out over the calm seas, I could trace my itinerary back past Dunnet Head, but could not see all the way to John O'Groats. I could hear Kevin's voice in the distance, and was pleased to let him know that I had listened to his counsel, and I was indeed on a bigger boat.

Liz rang as I was sitting down on the aft deck, which was perfect timing. Then Sam called to talk about YouTube videos. There had been nearly 2000 views for the latest offering, which was so much more than our own expectations. "What great work, Sam," I said.

I smiled many happy smiles as we slid past the Old Man of Hoy, and into the peaceful port of Stromness. Like the evening before, I was flush with the joy of making it this far, and thrilled by the rush of a hasty escape to a surprise destination. I had seamlessly transformed from fearless sailor to fervent tourist, and I was loving all of it. I felt free and happy and full in every way.

* * *

Tuesday 6th June to Sunday 11th June

The next few days were a mix of tourism, travel, a funeral and a party.

Having had a comfortable stay at the Orca Guest House, and Wi-Fi fuelled breakfast, I took a bus over to Kirkwall. Stromness had quiet ambling streets which undulated up and down, then left and right along the hillside, as if it had not a care in the world, perfect for a meander. Kirkwall, however, was heaving with mostly German middle-aged tourists, who had poured off a cruise ship or two, and were combing the streets looking for items of interest. I couldn't complain since I was adding to the throng.

I was interested in buying some "SKIN so SOFT". I had been told that it was a fantastic anti-midge spray, something I was bound to need in the coming weeks. I found some in a chemist, but the bottle blurb made no mention of insects, and instead gave a modest eulogy to moisturising, making me feel suspicious that I had brought the wrong product. I nearly took it back, but instead also bought some Jungle Formula anti-mosquito spray as a backup.

In my wanderings, I learnt that the Orkneys has been, and continues to be, a thriving and proud community in its own right. There have been recent finds of Neolithic settlements at the Ness of Brodan, suggesting habitation from thousands of years BC. In more recent centuries, farming and fishing have been significant industries because of fertile soil, temperate climate, and of course plenty of sea.

In the 18th and early 19th century, Kelp production added to trade. As well as being a type of seaweed, Kelp refers to a glassy oily substance used in industrial processes, important in the production of soap and glass. Seaweed washed up on the shores was dried and then burnt in the summer months, to make Kelp, which could then be exported south. However, with European embargos being lifted and changes in markets, trade faded and the industry collapsed, resulting in great hardships. The hardships contributed to emigration and indeed the clearances. To an uneducated tourist like me, it seemed like it was a smart use of a natural resource.

The islands were ruled by Norsemen for centuries, wanting to make use of the territory as way points on their westward journey to Greenland and beyond. In the early part of the 12th century, Earl Rongvald Kolsson from Norway instigated the building of a cathedral, in honour of St Magnus, revered by the locals. Reportedly this was an attempt to win the hearts of local dignitaries, in a tussle over territory. Whatever the motivations, the finished product, still standing in glorious red and yellow sandstone, was a marvel to visit, some nine centuries later.

Unusually, the cathedral has never been owned by the Church of Scotland or England. Instead, it has remained the property of the city and Burgh of Kirkwall, no doubt adding to a sense of local ownership, both literally and metaphorically. The cathedral was free to visitors, and the environment was beautifully maintained, with many plaques pointing eager tourists to interesting detail around the building. One such item was a modern tapestry given by the King of Norway, to the Queen Mother to celebrate her birthday, a symbol of the enduring connection between the nations.

I really liked the blending of grand antiquity and local pride. Outside the main gate there were red sandstone pillars, which in their original state would have been smooth and cylindrical, straight from a mason's chisel. Now, some were hollowed out, to make cup-like shapes, worn away by wind and rain. Others were half intact. The actions of the elements had exposed uneven layers, feathered away by time, to make a wooden grain-like surface, exposing thousands, if not millions, of years of geological history, all within two steps of the entrance doorway.

I spoke to one of the cathedral volunteers on my way out.

"Thank you so much. It has been a really lovely visit to the cathedral."

She was young and enthusiastic and said, "We are really proud of the cathedral. And really proud of being Orcadian, since it is such a great place. I'm glad you enjoyed your visit."

I certainly did.

That evening, having successfully caught my ferry back to the mainland, I returned to the Pentland Firth Sailing Club to carry out some boat maintenance - gel coat repair, epoxy filler to the centre plate housing, and replacing a telltale. It was a training evening so I chatted to fellow sailors as they drifted past. Betty seemed to attract more attention from onlookers when she was showing her bottom. Smooth plain fibreglass is not normally of much interest, but on this occasion, each scratch told a tale, each piece of duct tape, each point on the underside map spoke of a story, so there was plenty to talk about.

I offered a helping hand to those venturing onto the water, with rigging and a scattering of technical tips. I felt pleased to be of some small assistance to this great community.

*　 ＊　 ＊*

7th June

I really liked the communal nature of the dining room at Sandra's Backpackers. The hostel was down to earth, down on price, and close to the train station, so suited my needs just fine. For breakfast, most people were staring at their toast, or sheepishly asking a "where can I find the bowls?" type question. However, Jan and Martin were in chatting mode, and so was I. They had been to the Orkneys and were heading south. We got as far as our breakfasts would allow, and then headed off.

On the Thurso station platform, there were Jan and Martin. Hence, we carried on where we had left off, whiling away many slow train stops on the way to Wick. We shared stories of our travels to the Orkneys. I shamelessly added a few of my own sailing adventures, keen to distribute my excitement at reaching the summit, to eager listening ears.

They had their own adventure story to tell.

"Our grandson fell whilst climbing in Skye a few years back," Jan said.

"Oh no. Was he OK?" I asked.

"He was really lucky because the fall was 90 metres so he could have died. But he was saved by his backpack, which helped break the fall. He managed to escape with cuts and bruises mainly. We were so worried when we heard about it," Jan added.

"Wow. That sounds an incredible escape."

Martin finished the story. "Yes. The rescue workers were so surprised that he survived that they asked him whether they could display his backpack as a memento, so it is now on show in the museum in Portree!"

Jan and Martin were in their 70s and had worked as a play therapist and a youth worker respectively, so we talked about mental health, and changes we had noticed over the last few decades. That kept us going all the way to Wick, where they needed to disembark. What a great connection, and how lovely to share stories with them.

Failing to make the transition from dinghy to aeroplane passenger, I had forgotten to leave my multitools behind in Thurso. This was necessary, because I thought the super sharp knives would be confiscated by airport security. I was reminded of a moment, many years ago, when I had watched with horror as a precious childhood penknife was thrown mercilessly into a bin at Gatwick. I wanted to avoid a repeat. When I reached Inverness train station, I thought I better make a plan.

Objecting to the £15 left luggage fee, to store envelope-sized goods, I contemplated leaving them on top of the lockers. Thinking things through, I calculated that, if they were missing when I returned, the cost of inconvenience and accompanying bad mood would outweigh the fee. Hence, I grumbled my way to paying for a secure space, enormous for the job in hand.

A few days later, I realised that I had not read the airline restrictions properly - knives shorter than six inches in length can be carried onboard EasyJet flights. I thought, "that is good to know". Then again, I wasn't so sure. Surely a five-inch super sharp knife is a lot more dangerous than 200ml of water? The logic of safety restrictions was starting to evaporate. Either way, my essential equipment was safe for now.

I scuttled out of Inverness train station before my connection to the airport. I wanted to grab a glimpse of the city, basking in June warmth.

Glistening sunshine reflected off shop fronts, as contented pedestrians strolled along the High Street. A busker was singing into a microphone. He started on the classic 'Ave Maria' by Schubert.

Some tunes just catch you and this was one of mine. The tenor's rendition was superb, beautifully crafted and perfectly paced. I paused to watch. Tears started to form, and I found myself looking away, to mollify the emotion, but it would not pass. I would have wept great sobs if circumstances had allowed, falling into a hopeless haze of oblivion, floating in a dreamless mist of notes, rendered with mystical powers that take over all senses, and all sense of control.

It felt like a time at the end of our Land's End to John O'Groats cycle trip when I was travelling back on a train. I was on my own, looking out of the window across the sea, which was smiling back at me with a brilliant blue. The feelings were so intense despite everything around me being peaceful, and radiantly beautiful. It took me ages to untangle the puzzle of emotions. Eventually I realised it was released tension, wrapped up in raw happiness, that had taken over. Here it was again, somehow descending, to fill me with the same painful jubilation.

Thursday 8th June

It was lovely to see Liz again after all this time, and she was relieved to find me in one piece. The comfort of relationship familiarity is so affirming, and domestic routine so reassuring.

It was the day of Robin's funeral, a couple of hours' drive away, not the most joyous of occasions, but wonderful to have Liz's company for all those hours.

The day itself was a glorious classic English summer's day, with bright blue skies and still air, with the land still lush, before it is scorched to crisp yellow in the July heat. Rachael, a friend from university and Robin's widow, was calm, and graceful, softly guiding well-wishers to appropriate places. Then a traditional Wiltshire church with a flint exterior, packed with friends and family, to share in the celebration of Robin's too-short life. He was the same age as me when he died.

Robin was a thoughtful, considerate and well organised man, with Swiss origins, and it showed in his offspring. His children, who matched ours in age, shared the honour of the eulogy, and did so with great dignity and prowess. The innocence of youth somehow softened the gravity of the situation. We all wished them well, as their words stepped through their father's life, so elegantly, so lightly, so lovingly.

The final sentence of the service was of Robin's last WhatsApp message, shortly before he died. I will not attempt to recall the exact phrases, but the lines were almost poetic, imploring the virtues of love, and its enduring value for all those who have lived around him. It was beautifully written and bravely orated. Those words took our breath away.

What stuck with me, was that these were his last words before he died. He wrote them, right on the cusp of passing away. He knew the time was coming. Then it came.

I was struggling to imagine what it would have been like. I could not put myself in Robin's shoes, when he wrote that message.

So much of what we hear and see is relatable, since we have shared similar experiences – being in love, being alone, being destitute, being joyful. Like you, I have not been at the point of death before. I was struggling to imagine the scene, the physical sensations, the thoughts. I was struggling to be with Robin's heart, with its poignant thoughtfulness and relationship vigour, and yet being within the final few beats. It seemed impossible to be so full of life, and so full of death, all at the same time. As if it were the beginning and the end, all at the same time.

In my professional career, I have seen many people die and it was not like this. I watched my mother take her last breath. She was so pleased to be going, but I can't say I enjoyed it. I still can't work out whether it was better to miss the very last moment, as I did with my father, or to be there, as it was for Mum. It all felt bad.

I guess I was not sure I could bring myself to do such a thing. To speak to the world in one's dying moment, would take a huge act of courage and selflessness. To speak of love to the world with one's last breath, seemed extraordinary, almost improbable. Maybe those were the last words he felt he needed to say, and then he could slip away. But why not say them earlier if he knew what was coming? Maybe he had been thinking about it for some time, and the words finally came. Maybe, something else. I will never know. I could not ask him, so I was left with my imagination, which was where I was getting stuck.

To be in the last moment of life is, well, unimaginable. To be in the last moments of life, to know it, and yet be so full of life and love, and to be able to speak, seems impossible. It was if life, love and death had all become merged into one, in that moment, encapsulated in a single message. How incredibly brave. How agonisingly beautiful.

Thank you, Robin. Our memories of you will live on, forever.

* * *

Thursday 9th – Saturday 10th June

Back in Godalming, the garden was pleased to see me. Liz's reluctant attention to the lawn had kept it under control, but the rest had been left to its growing devices. The peonies had come out, and the mock orange was in bloom, releasing puffs of its exquisite sweet scent on the gentle air. In Scotland, tulips were showing off their brightly coloured petals, marking the contrast in season between the two ends of our mainland.

My box hedges seemed to be doing OK, whereas my elderly neighbour's equivalent were looking wrecked, despite my efforts to save them from caterpillars the previous year. Maybe my hedge husbandry was making a difference, to some of us at least.

Of significance in the news was the resignation "for now" of Boris Johnson as an MP, after the Partygate investigation by the privileges committee. And Ukraine started its much-awaited counter offensive. We were all hoping that they would make significant gains, and bring that ugly war to an early end.

In my local news, I had a lovely time catching up with relatives at Phil's 40th party. The evening was fanned by a gentle soft breeze of a summer's evening. I was still glowing in a flush of fame, having reached the top of Scotland, and was happy to lap up any appreciative comments, wherever they might fall.

Then after that, it was back to business. The sailing journey must go on.

* * *

Sunday 11th June

It was definitely cooler in the north. Refreshingly so, since the south was hot and stuffy.

I had time to explore Inverness in more depth in my day-long trail from bottom to top of our mainland. Inverness means "mouth of the river Ness" in Scottish Gaelic (as opposed to Aber which is 'mouth of the river' in Celtic, as you may recall). The river Ness flows from Loch Ness, and then out through the middle of the conurbation, providing a fine natural feature. Inverness was only granted city status in 2000, and has a relatively small population, though has been blessed with strong economic growth this century, giving it the highest 'quality of life' ranking municipality in Scotland.

I crossed the river a few times, checking out the occasional shop, and the not so occasional church – there are a lot of churches. I didn't have time to visit the castle, which gazes reproachfully down on the city, from its imperious position atop a hill. Red sandstone gave colour to the streetscape, which glowed in the warm summer sunshine – such a relief from the usual Scottish grey.

My last stop before the 1754 train to Thurso was to grab a coffee in a bar, only to be distracted by Eurosports on the TV. Novak Djokovic was playing in the French Open final against Casper Ruud. Novak made the enterprise look easy, winning in straight sets. Although he's perhaps less likeable than some others, I could not help but admire his athleticism and tennis craftsmanship. To see him succeed for a record breaking 23rd time, I marvelled at his mental strength, to keep disciplined through the years, and to keep motivated through many, many hours of painful struggle. What an incredible achievement, and wonderful to witness. Well done, Novak. Could this have been the last? He said he was not done yet!! Let's watch, and gaze on in wonder.

The whole return journey from Thurso to home and back, had cost me no more than £100, which I thought was an incredible bargain. This was thanks in part to my Senior railcard, low-cost air fares, but also the four-hour trundle train from Inverness to Thurso, courtesy of Scotrail, coming in at £4 per hour of travel. It was like a holiday on wheels.

Refreshed and reinvigorated, I was ready for the next phase of the adventure.

* * *

Day 47, Monday 12th June

To Strathy Hill

START	10.00, Scrabster
WIND	N, 5–12mph
WEATHER	Cloud then sun, 16–17°C. Dry
TIDE	With me, max 0.3mph till 14.00
SEA STATE	Smooth
HAZARDS	Wind dying
FINISH	Strathy Beach, 16.30
DISTANCE	19 miles
SAILING HOURS	6½ hours

The next few days were slow going.

Beautiful clear skies and summer heat, that was even making the locals sweat, was doing nothing for the wind. I had imagined the occasional sea breeze swooshing me along, but my enduring impression is that they just don't seem to happen in the UK. It should have been ideal conditions, with warm land and cool seas, but there was nothing. According to the textbooks, a sea breeze in the Northern Hemisphere will blow to the right, which was one of the reasons for choosing to go anticlockwise. However, the wind, as I had already learnt to my cost, sticks to its own opaque rules.

Stick had said that he traversed the top of Scotland in one day. He may well have done, but not even Stick the magnificent could have managed in these conditions. It is tempting to make comparisons and feel inadequate, but I reminded myself that I was ahead of my own schedule and in that case, I was doing just fine.

After a slightly less pleasant dormitory night at Sandra's Backpackers, I hailed a taxi back to the sailing club. In my haste to get going, I forgot to return the hostel key, but fortunately remembered before we had travelled too far, so returned to deal with the excess luggage.

At the club, Donald very kindly came down before work, to give me a hand with launching, which was hugely appreciated. What a great club. So many people had gone out of their way to be supportive over several days. Thank you, Pentland Firth Sailing Club.

I said my farewells, and beat my way to Holborn Head, and then bore away onto a pleasant reach (pleasant enough to allow some shirtless sunbathing), to my planned destination of Bettyhill.

Of course, I had to go to Bettyhill. Betty Hill-Smith wouldn't have sounded quite right at the top of Scotland. The shortened version was, to me, naming confectionery.

Despite my hunger for making some miles, plenty of daylight, and refreshed determination, the wind packed up and went home at about four o'clock. So, I decided to bail – reassuringly sensible, I thought. Bettyhill would have to wait.

Before I land, I must give you an update about Dounreay Power Station. "Thank goodness," I hear you cry, worrying that I might have omitted this key spot on our nuclear tour.

It was one of the early reactors built in the UK, first commissioned in 1955, eventually covering three sites, and producing power from 1962 until 1994, when the last reactor was decommissioned.

As well as producing energy, the site was a research facility to test material's response to intense irradiation, for instance fuel cladding. It was later used as a nuclear fuel processing plant. Initially under the control of the UK Atomic Energy Authority, the site has been transferred to the Nuclear Decommissioning Authority in 2005, and spent fuel is being transferred to Sellafield for reprocessing. The site therefore still employs a large workforce.

However, the decommissioning process is due to last for several years to come. Waste fuel removal is to be completed by the late 2070s, and the decommissioning process to end in the 2300s, with restoration as a brownfield site by 2336. Yes, 2336!!

I vaguely remember political discussions from the noughties, about the cost of disposal of nuclear waste, and it was likely that learnings from Dounreay were part of the debate. I don't remember anything about 300+ years to decommission a reactor. The figure is staggering, being both alarming and reassuring at the same time. Alarming that so much time and effort is required to restore safety, and reassuring that long-term planning is in place to ensure the job is to be done properly. No wonder there is so much agonised discussion about building nuclear plants, despite climate change pressures.

Back to the journey.

I set foot on a miscellaneous beach, in the middle of nowhere with no facilities, no road access, and no food. The surroundings were empty, pristine and beautiful, with smooth soft untouched sand, stretching into the distance. The sun was out, the skies clear and the wind absent – a wild camper's paradise.

I managed to fender roll Betty above the tide line, and then went to explore camping spots. Over the dunes and down to a grassy dip I went, to find a flat and wind protected spot to park my camping stuff. "That should do," I thought. The centre plate came with me to act as a mini table. With the tent erected and my position secured, the next challenge was to find water and food. Up the steep grassy bank I clambered, noticing a small collection of campers in an adjacent dip as I went. I was not alone after all. Would that be a security risk, I wondered?

Nearing the top, a man started walking down towards me, and thinking nothing of it, I carried on.

He approached me and said, "You must be Andrew."

That stopped me in my tracks. "How did you know that?" I asked.

"We have a mutual friend called Paul who mentioned your trip."

"Do you mean the Paul who is a child psychiatrist in Doncaster? I trained with him years ago."

"Yes, that's the one. We know each other through our local sailing club," Phil added, who had by now introduced himself.

He went on to explain some more. "When I saw your boat coming into the bay, I thought there can't be too many other Lasers round here, so looked up your location on the tracker, and put two and two together."

Still tethered to the spot, I was trying to overcome my surprise. "That's incredible." Then added: "But what brings you here? Have you come on your own?"

Phil gestured to the top of the hill behind him. "I'm here with some friends. We are doing a North Coast 500 tour on motorbikes, and I persuaded them to stop here for some camping. There is a free shower and toilet block by the car park, which looks really nice. It's run by volunteers."

I went to meet Phil's biker friends who were setting up camp for the first time, possibly in the windiest spot in the local area. They seemed to be having a good time and were very welcoming. I went to check out the toilet block. It was made like a log cabin and was well maintained, but had no electricity other than to power its lights. The water was tepid at best, heated from a roof panel. It was certainly a welcome surprise addition to the wild camping experience. Perhaps it wasn't as wild as I first thought.

However, I would need to get to Bettyhill if I were to find some food. I was hoping for a biker lift. There was a shortage for suitable pillion spaces and helmet, till the fourth party member came back, so I thought I would try my luck with hitching a ride.

It didn't take long. I was picked up by a local fisherman in his truck who had an English accent.

"Have you lived here for long?" I asked, striking up conversation.

"Oh aye," he said. "For about 30 years."

And then he carried on. "But they are all racists round here."

"What do you mean?" I said.

"It doesn't matter how long you have lived here; they still treat you as a foreigner," he complained.

I kind of knew what he meant, but I did think it was a novel extension of the term racist.

I was dropped off at the hill, and gratefully followed the fisherman's advice, heading over to the appropriately named 'The Store, Bistro and Bar' – it provided what it said on the sign. I tucked into chicken burger and chips, with a beer, but didn't need any supplies.

I was thinking that I would sail past Bettyhill the next day, so was keen to explore the area. Out of the bar window I could see a hill on a promontory, which I thought must be Bettyhill. It reminded me of the Rumps in Cornwall, or maybe the Mumbles in Wales. I wanted to go there, to catch the evening views.

I went scampering down the road and up the heathered hill, like an excited lamb in springtime, flushed with freedom and the joy of standing on energetic new legs. The skies had completely cleared, so were set for a beautiful still evening, bathed in the softening yellow light. The views were fantastic. There were inlets on both sides and uninterrupted views to the west, showing the beginnings of the Highlands. I guessed that one of the lumps in the distance could be Cape Wrath. There was no one about and no one to be seen, just me, the hilltop cairn, the smooth sea and lands of North Scotland. It was idyllic.

Unfortunately, I needed to get back to Strathy. More unfortunate was the fact that my thumb had stopped working. There was less and less traffic, and more and more midges, so I took cover in the Bettyhill Hotel. There were no taxis available and it was too far to walk. Things were starting to look desperate. As luck would have it, the barman kindly agreed to give me a lift, at the end of his shift. Whilst waiting, I had a sort of wash in the toilets. I was hoping the lift might be free, in line with the generosity I had become used to, but I was asked for a tenner. "Fair enough really," I thought. "I would have had to pay a lot more to stay in the hotel."

Day 48, Tuesday 13th June

To Farr Bay, Bettyhill

START	10.45, Strathy Hill
WIND	NE, 13–17mph. Reality, none
WEATHER	Sun/cloud, 18–23°C. Dry
TIDE	With me, max 0.4mph, till 16.00
SEA STATE	Slight then smooth
HAZARDS	No wind and nowhere to stop
FINISH	Farr Beach, Bettyhill, 17.00
DISTANCE	13 miles
SAILING HOURS	6¼ hours

I had a cosy and comfortable night in my tent, I was pleased to say. You tend to wake earlier in a tent, but most activities are slower, like washing, toileting and making breakfast. Then there is packing up and loading up, so departure often ends at the same time as staying in a bed and breakfast, despite the extra journey.

I went back up the slope to the shower block, to find some water and make porridge. It was also a good opportunity to mend my centre board. I had brought some metallic epoxy from home, so set about filling in the Findhorn dents on the leading edge. The epoxy was really meant for cars, but was being adapted for use on a boat. I was delighted it worked so well, holding up and holding on, throughout the rest of the trip. Some modern products are amazingly strong and incredibly easy to use - I was impressed.

I chatted to Phil as I pottered about. He had been working in a cardiac catheter lab as a nurse practitioner / manager, so we had some health service discussions in common.

Roland came down with Phil to help with moving Betty to the sea line. It was just as well, since the tide was out. It was a long beach and we had to stop several times. It would have taken me ages on my own.

Despite the clear skies of the night before, a Haar (also called a sea fret, or a sea fog) had come in for the morning. I thought I might have run into one of these on the East Coast, but I had escaped till now.

I thanked Phil and Roland and wished them a safe journey. I turned away and set off into the fog.

There is a long finger of land stretching north past the bay, like a pointing left hand, meaning that I needed to travel over two miles out to Strathy Point, before making any progress to the west. After more than two hours of paddle beating through the gloom, I finally made it past the point, which was incredibly slow going. To add to the misery, the sea was really disturbed for some reason, despite the lack of wind. No wind and a disturbed sea produces a really uncomfortable bobbing about experience, like being in a cramped dodgem car, with no power, surrounded by aggressive adolescents.

Despite the promising forecast, there was really no wind, and I eventually gave up at Farr Beach, below my beloved hill from the evening before. Another inlet, so to speak, but close to an official campsite, and the Bettyhill Hotel, once again.

Liz rang not long after I had landed, too soon for me to recover from the frustrations of my single-figure mileage day. Poor long-suffering Liz. I rang her later when I had topped up with food, and some more sumptuous views at the hotel restaurant. That was better.

As I was settling down to sleep in my tent, I noticed some determined midges had followed me in, before I closed the flap. This called for action. Full blast effort to slay the little nippers was required. Out came the jungle formula and a strong squirt around my raided confines, should do the trick. This was a bad idea. I am not too sure what happened to the midges, but I estimated that too much more of the DEET in my airless tomb, might do me in. Coughing and spluttering I grabbed at the zips. After much tugging and snagging, they eventually opened enough for me to scramble out into the fresh air. Relieved to be inhaling chemical-free, clean Scottish air, I said to myself, "I don't think I will try that one again."

◈ ◈ ◈

Day 49, Wednesday 14th June

To Archininver Beach

START	09.45, Farr Beach, Bettyhill
WIND	N, 5–11, but less in reality
WEATHER	Sun 14–22°C. Dry
TIDE	With me max 0.4mph till 13.00
SEA STATE	Smooth
HAZARDS	No wind again
FINISH	Archininver beach, 14.30
DISTANCE	9 miles
SAILING HOURS	4½ hours

Down on the shore I found a note, concealed under the centre board. Not an angry one, but a nice kind message. It said, "Many congratulations on making it to the halfway point (and getting through the Pentland Firth). What an incredible journey."

There was no name or number included, so I was left to imagine who had taken the trouble to offer encouragement in this way. The writer had clearly followed the link on the side of the boat, and understood my route, which counted as a high level of interest. Then under the paper I found £20 in cash. I was really touched. How thoughtful and what a wonderful gesture.

Even the virtually wind-free day did not spoil my mood. This was comparable to the special Arbroath section, at a miserable two miles per hour, but I was getting used to my plight. At least I could head in a straight line. In contrast, those land-locked wheeled folk, were having to twist and turn their way, up and down and round the hills, at times discovering that their great efforts had progressed their journey, no more than crossing a stream!

There were occasional puffs of breeze, and then a scattering of beautiful peaceful islands to admire as I cruised past, which helped while away the time. Some wind made a fleeting appearance in the early afternoon, tempting me to think I could possibly make it to Durness, but then in line with tradition, it faded. I turned back to land at Achininver Beach, another deserted, sun-soaked, sublime sandy location.

A man was digging on the beach. His skin looked like it had seen a lot of the outdoors. I asked him what he was doing.

"I'm looking for bait for fishing," he said.

His name was Ian, a local sheep farmer with his land tumbling down to the shore a few yards away. We discussed where to park Betty to make sure she would be safe. I wanted a spot that wouldn't require too much manoeuvring in the morning, and somewhere that would still be accessible at high tide. With Ian's help, we found a suitable place. We settled Betty amongst the rocks, which were poking up through the sand, like sultanas on the surface of a bun.

"Is it far to Talmine campsite?" I asked.

"Would you like a lift?" he offered.

"That would be amazing, thank you very much, but I don't want to put you out."

"I would need to go and get my Land Rover," he said.

"Are you sure? That's no bother since I need to store the boat, get changed and sort some luggage, which takes a good 40 minutes," I replied.

Sure enough, just as I was finishing off, Ian came bumping and twisting his way over rocks, soggy sand, and round streams, in his rusty four-wheel drive machine, to make it to my self-styled dinghy parking lot. I was really flattered that he had put in so much effort to come and greet me.

It sounded like it was a tough life being a farmer. He philosophically described his lambs being regularly taken by foxes, and eagles as well. Eagles taking lambs sounded great for tourists, but dismal for the farmer. Fortunately, he seemed contented enough, and wished me luck when we parted.

At the Talmine campsite, Christine was doing her best to tell me that there were no spaces, but a bit of explanation about my predicament and the size of my tent, meant that I was allowed to squeeze in. I was also allowed to use the charging point in the staff area, which was a blessing given my desperation for power. I wasn't feeling love for the campsite oozing off our host for the day, since the place looked a bit tired. Furthermore, I wasn't too sure that Christine had a great love for people either. I was ticking off a few Autistic Spectrum Disorder diagnostic boxes in my head, as we talked. But who was I to complain? I had what I needed at a fair price, and it was another gorgeous evening.

To top it off, Ryan and Jo from the next-door pitch kindly offered some pasta when I came back from the local shop, which spared me the trouble of cooking up a meal myself. I was very happy to contribute grapes and yoghurts for afters.

They were travelling round the NC 500 in their Mini, for a summer break. Ryan was a plasterer, who had changed his product to a Venetian-style finish, since it was more lucrative. I had not heard of it before, though roughly understood after an explanation.

He told a few stories about customers not paying their bill. This sounded particularly galling if he had put in a lot of work, in good faith. One customer was being especially difficult. The man did finally pay what was due, but only after Ryan went round. He threatened to take all the plastering down again, a day or two before the anticipated celebration, for which the work was commissioned. It must have been really stressful for Ryan, a side of life that I had been spared in my salaried profession.

Like clockwork, the midges suddenly appeared as the sun went down. Jo recommended trying the 'SKIN so SOFT', saying that it worked for her. Still feeling sceptical, I sprayed a bit on, to see if it kept the insects at bay. It seemed to do the trick. Then I started to spray it everywhere – hands, back of the neck, ear, face and even hair. I learnt that if there was so much as a slither of unsprayed skin exposed, it would be attacked, so a proper dousing was needed. Once completed I could then watch the fuzzy haze hover around me, tracking my movements as I moved about, but not quite coming in to nipping contact with their target. That was so much more comfortable. It was necessary to keep the product to hand though, since you could only relax for a moment, at your peril.

Day 50, Thursday 15th June

To Durness, at last

START	09.30, Achininver Beach, (Talmine)
WIND	N, 7–11mph
WEATHER	Sunny, 19–21°C. Dry
TIDE	With me max 0.4mph from 11.00
SEA STATE	Smooth
HAZARDS	No wind
FINISH	Durness, 14.00
DISTANCE	11 miles
SAILING HOURS	4½ hours

At last, I would make it to Durness, the stepping off point for Cape Wrath, and corner #3. Bill and Maggie who were parked a few vans away, kindly gave me a lift back to Achininver, but they needed to be away by 07.30, which was a convenient hurry me up.

A slow but steady sail brought me to my destination with only a limited requirement for paddling, which was a welcome change. Brilliant blue skies and mighty grey black cliffs topped with green, plunged into the sea, providing a dramatic backdrop for the day's travel.

I landed at Durness Beach on a warm and sunny afternoon. When I had more or less packed up, ready to climb the steep path to Sango Sands campsite, a man approached me.

"Hi there. Have you come far," he asked.

"I've sailed over from Talmine today, but I'm sailing round the UK," I replied. I was anticipating the typical follow-on questions of things like 'are you on your own?' or 'where is your support boat?', or 'where did you start?'.

Instead, the next question, delivered with a quizzical look and angled glance, was, "are there many more of you coming round?".

Slightly taken aback, I asked him what he meant.

"A couple of years ago, there was another guy in a Laser who landed in the next-door bay."

Now excitedly interested in the conversation, I had to ask, "Really. Was that a guy called Stick, by any chance?"

Indeed, it was. Alan had continued as the groundsman for the campsite. He had helped out when Stick had arrived, and remembered him well.

Alan continued with his story. "It was a breezy day. When Stick arrived, it was quite late, and he came rushing up the hill desperate to find a pub. I was in the office. So, I pointed him over to the Oasis Bar. I heard he went in and found some fishermen to have a drink with, and didn't come out till closing. And when he went back to find his boat, he couldn't find it, cos he was looking in the wrong bay. He did find it eventually but by then it was getting really late and he was pretty drunk. He couldn't be bothered to put up his tent, so he just went to sleep in the changing rooms in his wetsuit."

What a ridiculous and hilarious scenario. With his energetic zest for life and derrring-do, one can't help but smile at Stick's antics.

"You wouldn't catch me doing that," I concluded. "Besides, I would have felt wrecked in the morning, and not much good for anything."

Back to the serious business of getting round Cape Wrath, I had some planning to do. It was nearly 30 miles to the next town. I was told there were no stopping points but to my reckoning, there were a couple of possible beaches at Kearvaig and Sandwood Bay, each being about a leg of nine miles. Given my hopeless progress over the last few days, and paltry forecast for the next, I estimated I would need to stop at both of those places.

I would need some additional supplies. Water was number one. I found a two-litre container and washed it out, and filled it with water. That was not a huge amount but better than nothing. I did not want to overladen the boat, and I might be able to boil some water as I went around.

The local store had a good range of supplies, and I purchased a gas cylinder to back up my stove. And then a bar of cheddar cheese, couscous, raisins and pesto sauce, following the advice of my mountain climbing nephew. Plus, the usuals of apples and bananas, and some bread and salami for lunches. That should do. You can cook up or expand couscous in cold water so I was told. Therefore, a congealed dinner of sticky yellow cheese, on polenta like couscous, with a slimy green topping, and a peppering of sweet black swollen grapes, would be something short of delicious, but would do the job.

The next problem was what to do with the tides. For Duncansby Head, the moon and the tides were well aligned to my personal clock, meaning that I could set off normal time, and catch the spring flow at the headland. I could not rely on Cape Wrath obliging in the same way.

Having learnt from corner number two, I could not rely on the current to turn a nice bend along the track of my passage plan. Equally, I really did not want to get past the cape and end up being thrown back again. I needed a time window for reaching Kearvaig, so that I could decide whether to land on the remote beach for the night, or carry on.

Liz, who is really good at these kinds of calculations, kindly gave me a hand to work it out. It was wonderfully reassuring to hear her putting together the tidal times, estimated speeds at different spots, patiently and meticulously looking up the information as she went. We came up with a time window – I needed to reach Kearvaig before half past one, in order to be able to carry on. If I was late, I would need to stop. That was so much easier to hold in mind when on the water, compared to all the other jumbled metrics. That meant I had all the bases covered.

Except for one thing. It was another military practice area. I can't quite remember the details, but it must have been a no-firing day, or maybe I got fed up and just went to the pub.

Ryan and Jo were there so I bought a round of beer. It was lovely to see them again, both with an easy welcoming manner, it felt like catching up with old friends on a holiday together. They were heading on down to Ullapool. Although I had kept up with them in their winding route to Durness, the road headed due south, whereas the coast did not, so they would surely stream ahead of me. Our paths would probably not cross again.

Jo had been a paramedic for the ambulance service, but had taken a break to turn her hand to other things. She felt that patients had become too entitled. I knew exactly what she meant. In my working life, I had been shrouded in compassionate responses to any form of distress, so I had not heard patients described in that way. Jo, however, was out of it, and forthright to boot.

Several years ago, a father of a young person I was helping, talked about a shift in culture which he described as 'compassionate narcissism' as the new normal. I thought that neatly summed things up, and chimed with Jo's, and my, experience of relationships. But then again, we need to move with the times, and times will always bring change, and if I were to return to practice as I planned, I would need to adjust my own expectations and practices. But not tomorrow. For tomorrow I had something else on my mind.

Day 51, Friday 16th June

To Cape Wrath and beyond

START	09.30, Durness
WIND	NE 4–7mph, backing N 9–13mph
WEATHER	Sun, 18–23°C. Dry
TIDE	With me from 12.00, max 1.5mph
SEA STATE	Smooth to slight
HAZARDS	No wind, military practice area
FINISH	Scourie Bay campsite, 18.30
DISTANCE	32 miles
SAILING HOURS	9 hours

Down on the beach, it was another beautiful day as I was rigging up.

"Good morning, Alan," I said, surprised to see his unannounced but cheery face. "It's really good of you to come down."

"I thought I'd come and see you off."

"I'm hoping to get round Cape Wrath but it's not looking too likely with the lack of wind."

"Hmm. Yeah". He paused. "I have a new drone, and wondered if I could test it out, and maybe take some footage."

"That would be great. I had thought about bringing my own drone, but I realised it would too difficult to operate from the boat, so some aerial shots would be amazing."

"OK."

"I loved your story about Stick, by the way. I got in touch with him. He remembers you well, and sends his regards."

"And do send him mine."

I did.

I was disappointed that the video was of yet more paddling, having had a fantasy of triumphant views of Betty and me, conquering the oceans. I was reassured when others saw the clips later – they were untroubled by the muscle powered progress, and instead really loved the sense of isolation and aloneness, as our small white blip edged slowly across the expanse of blue green sea. It remains an iconic section of video.

And yes, it did mean that I was paddling again. It took nearly an hour and a half to reach Faraid Head, the end of an irregular finger of land sticking out past Durness, past which, I was hoping to catch some tidal assistance. It was a meagre two and a half miles out of the target nine, so I was increasingly convinced I was heading for a Kearvaig camp. I estimated I was likely to reach my decision point, an hour or two late. I was resigned to the situation and instead soaked up more of the wall-to-wall blue that surrounded us.

What's more, I could not see any tidal flow, an impression that was confirmed as I pushed past a buoy – there seemed to be no movement in either direction, despite a scheduled turn. It didn't make sense, but then again, lots of things didn't. I could see the majestic Wrath cliffs in the distance, tinged with a reddish hue and topped with a speck of white lighthouse. They are reportedly the tallest cliffs on the mainland, which bring awe and fear to seafarers who pass nearby, but in these conditions the scene looked welcoming, rather than irascible or tempestuous.

About an hour further on, near a rock called An Garbh-Eilean, I could hear a sound like a river tumbling over rapids, and as I approached, a band of ruffled surface explained the noise. At least that meant some flow had started, though I knew not why this patch of sea was so affected. As I write, I realise the rock stood on an underwater ledge and the sea was indeed flowing over it, just as the sound had suggested. However, the scale and dimensions were all very different, making the overall effect appear mysterious, even though the mechanics were the same.

I will try to explain that a bit better.

For a river, there are two banks. If the river is deep and wide, the water flows slowly, and the surface is smooth. If the river becomes shallow, such as over rapids, the water flows quicker. Also, there is less depth, so the water pushes and shoves to get past, creating turbulence within the stream. An uneven riverbed does yet more pushing and shoving, to create more turbulence. All swirling and tumbling in the water appears on the surface.

On the sea, there is only one bank – the shore. The tide is like a river, though on a much bigger scale, like a river that is miles and miles wide. The fact that you cannot see the other bank somehow makes it seem like the water should act differently. But water is still water, even if it has salt in it. And the mechanics of water don't change if it is in the sea.

Tidal currents are like enormous rivers (except that they change direction every six hours, and don't go downhill). The tidal flow is affected by the surface underneath, and on the edge of the sea, in the same way as a river. The sea looks big and flat, so it is easy to assume that the sea floor is big and flat as well, but it isn't.

The sea will form eddies around obstructions like headlands, or will create turbulence like upwellings, or maybe overfalls if it is flowing fast. The headlands of both Duncansby Head and Cape Wrath, create pinch points, so the flow increases a lot round the corners, and accelerates considerably as one approaches the bend.

Usually, the flow is slower in shore, because it is shallower, thus creating resistance.

However, if the underwater level changes suddenly, such as when going over a ledge, the water can't change direction and is forced over it, speeding up and becoming roughed up, as if it were in a rapid. So that is what happened at An Garbh-Eilean. The sea was accelerating as it was approaching the corner. Then suddenly it was forced over a ledge that I could not see, thus creating the rapid in the middle of the ocean, that looked bizarre and completely out of place. But now I understand, and hopefully you do as well.

Maybe there was something similar at the Merry Men of Mey – fast flowing water, going over an underwater obstruction. The obstruction must have been larger, smoother, wider and deeper, than at An Garbh-Eilean, hence a different result. It was still creepy though.

On the water, some wind appeared, coming from astern which was unexpected. Then Kearvaig Bay, marked by a sharp rock at its entrance. I checked my watch which said twelve-thirty, so unbelievably, I was well on time. That meant I was going round the Wrath. How incredibly exciting.

There was one more hazard. Duslic Rock was a small outcrop, half a mile from the lighthouse. According to reports, it is used for target practice, so a potential spot to find more unexploded ordnance. I needed to avoid it, but equally was not sure how the current would respond.

Heading in shore of the obstruction, it felt like the speed of progress significantly slowed. Once I was confident that I have avoided an impact, I headed back out, away from the mainland, into the waters where swirls and upwellings were more obvious. I was hoping to catch more flow. It worked. I was now doing six or seven miles an hour, and the land at last looked like it was moving as I sailed along.

I would like you to take a moment to sit on board Betty, if that is alright? Don't worry, it's not scary. It's quite safe.

You are sitting comfortably on Betty's deck. Your feet are planted safely in the cockpit with room to shuffle about if you need to. You can hold onto the toe strap if you feel a bit uncertain.

This is champagne sailing. The air is warm and you are dressed in a light splash top only, to protect your skin, with a sun hat and glasses to dampen the glare from the glistening sea. Betty bristles white in the sunshine. The sail with its bold '3' and charity logos is stretched out in front of you, a proud sign for all to see. There is no one around. Nobody at all. No yachts, no people on the shore. Nothing. Nothing but bright blue and the line of the land.

The wind blows steadily behind you meaning there is no danger of falling in, or being becalmed, so you can stand up and stretch out if you need to. The main sheet is cleated in, so only needs one arm to sail. The tiller sits lightly in your left hand, feeling the effortless flow over the rudder. Water burbles round Betty's prow as you gently push through delicate waves, looking around at the coastline, slowly easing by, with not a care in the world. Ahead, you can see something.

"Oh, that looks like Sandwood Bay," you say out loud.

"We were thinking about stopping there weren't we?"

After a few minutes of contemplation, you add, "I don't think that is going to be necessary now."

"Let's just carry on till the light begins to fade, or the wind maybe. There is nothing to lose."

You lean down and open the sandwich box for a bite of lunch and then some water. Nothing is a rush.

"How about an apple?" you ask. "Yes, that would be lovely."

You are heading south. South towards home. You smile a long and contented smile, at nobody, at nothing, and at everything. The smile fills your being, from warm head to dry fingers, through your chest, freshened by the clear clean air, all the way down to your comfortable little toes. South is a new direction, a new chapter. Despite this splendid isolation, where only the most intrepid trekkers make it to those edges of the far North-west of Scotland, it feels safe and full of happiness. You are a real adventurer. You are at one with the world.

Wow. Take a deep breath. What a day.

Thank you for joining me.

On and on Betty and I went. Kinlochbervie, could be a stopping point, but that was some way inland, and there was still wind to be cherished. I passed Loch Inchard, Loch Dughaill, then Loch Laxford. Goodness there are lot of lochs.

Squeezing between islands, I was wondering whether to stop at a hamlet called Tarbet which I had noted on the map, but it looked nothing more than a house. Handa island stood tall in front of me. I could see a beach and sloping grass, so that might do for wild camping.

The wind had swung round through 180 degrees during the day so I was now on a beat, and the swirling waters around me meant tidal trouble, so if I were to make further distance, I would have to fight my way forward.

I had a vague memory of a campsite up ahead which spurred me onwards, but progress was becoming ever more difficult in the dying evening breeze. On the tracker, the Zs of my path were becoming more compressed, making progress feel perilously slow. Cormorants stood watching imperiously from a ledge, but sped off in disgust as I approached within a few feet of their rocky outpost, such was the precipitous nature of the land.

One last spec of cliff needed to be overcome before I could step out of the increasing tide, and into bay safety. Furious paddling was needed. After nearly nine hours in the boat, I needed a break.

And then the stream was gone. I could drift peacefully into Scourie Bay, and find a landing spot. Across the still waters I could clearly see a campsite with gathered tents, vehicles and amenities. All was calm again. What a relief. What an incredible day.

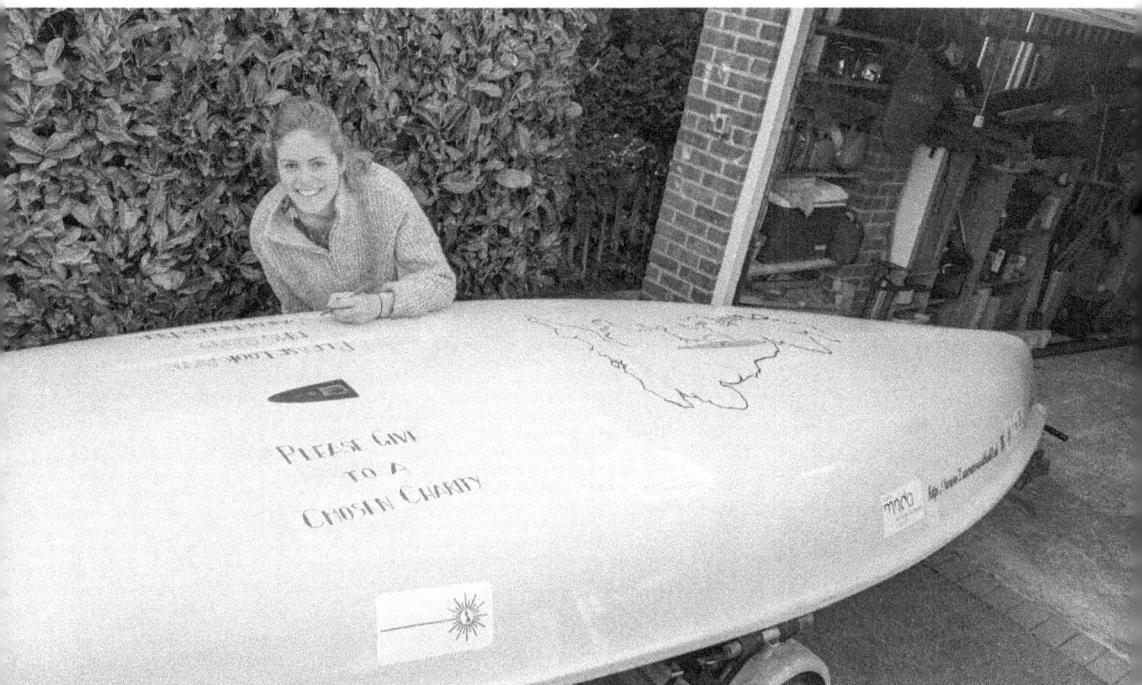

Boat preparation, courtesy of Emily

Day 1. The replacement centre board, with James and Craig, angel #1

View from my room at Royal Norfolk and Suffolk YC

A park beach bench perhaps, at Cley Beach, Norfolk

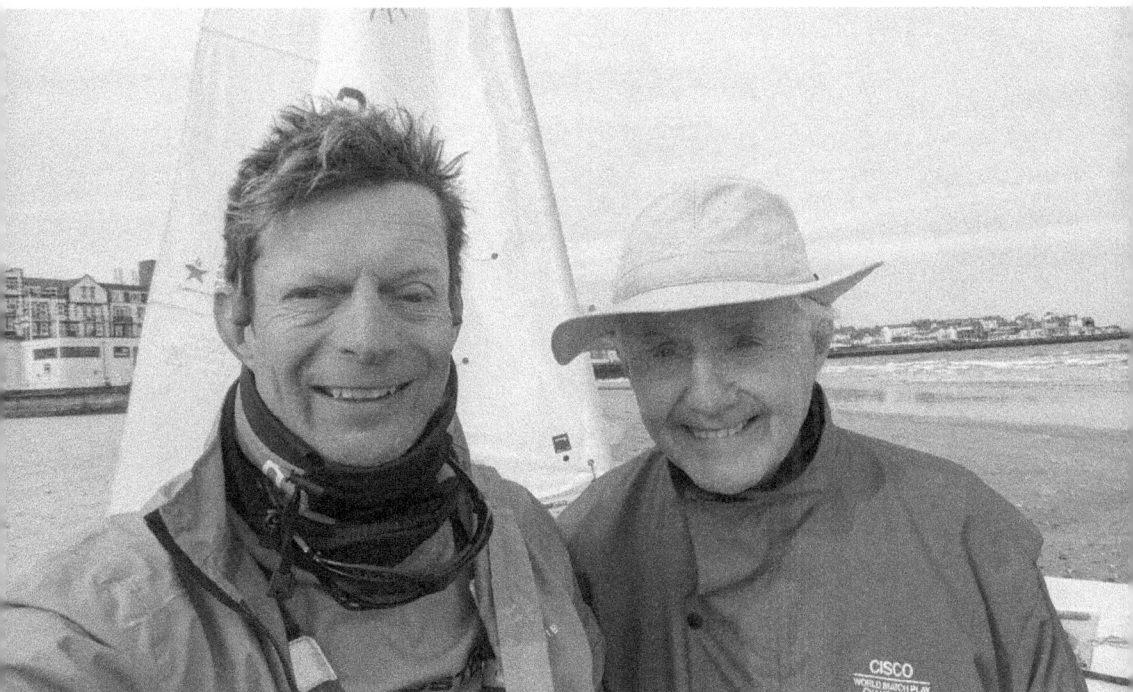

Bridlington beach with Peter the intrepid explorer

Harbour at Banff, E. Scotland

Gift from Brian Tinmouth, Sunderland. Coloured pencil drawing

John O'Groats, of course

Camping spot by Strathy Beach, N. Scotland

Jen and Pete at Mallaig, Scotland

Alternative transport past the Crinan Canal!

Heading to the Isle of Arran, Scotland

My family visiting at Ardrossan, with Oli, me, Liz, Sam and Emily

View from Burrow Head towards Kirkcudbright, Scotland

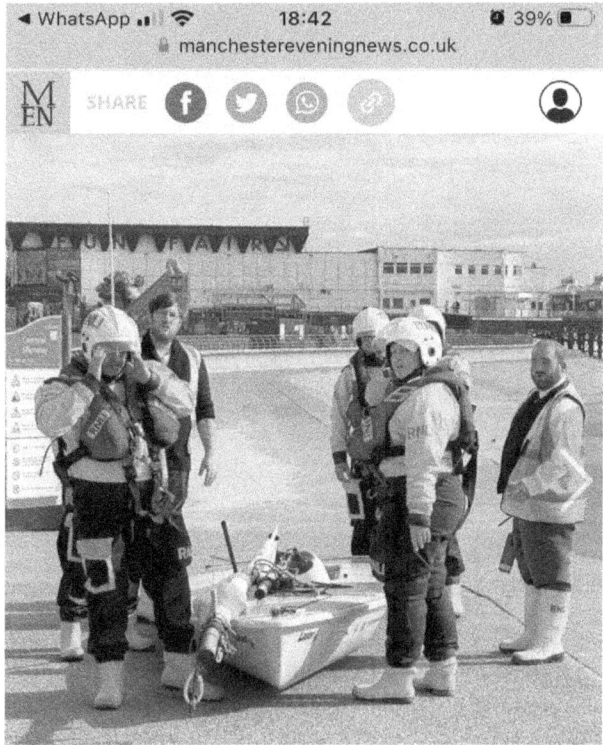

I made it to the shore, and the Manchester Evening News, at Blackpool

Ron's funeral, with Hillary, Ron's second partner, Neil Peters and Eric

View from Gwennap Head, near Land's End

Liz, Andrew, Guy and Penny for the Salcombe launch

Dolphins off Mumbles, Wales

Day 101. Last day landing at Stokes Bay

Map of stops on the journey

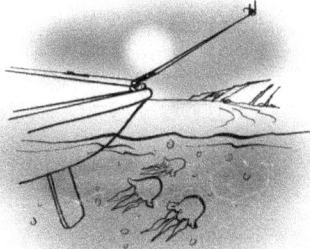

CHAPTER 13

The wilds of the west coast of Scotland

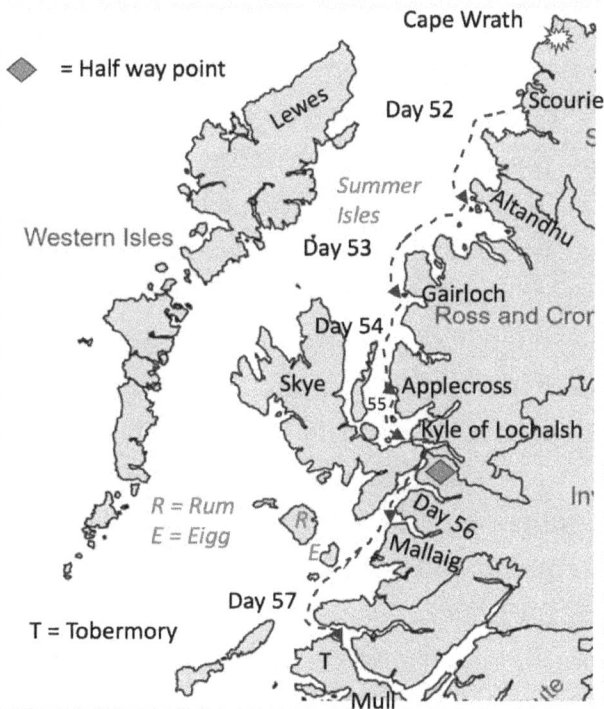

- ◆ = Half way point
- Cape Wrath
- Scourie
- Lewes
- Day 52
- Summer Isles
- Altandhu
- Western Isles
- Day 53
- Gairloch
- Ross and Cror
- Day 54
- Skye
- Applecross
- 55
- Kyle of Lochalsh
- R = Rum
- E = Eigg
- Day 56
- Mallaig
- In'
- Day 57
- T = Tobermory
- T
- Mull

Day 52, Saturday 17th June

To Althandhu / Isle of Ristol

START	Scourie Bay, 12.00
WIND	NW, 10–15mph
WEATHER	Cloudy, 15–18°C. Some rain later
TIDE	With me max 0.4mph, till 18.00
SEA STATE	Slight
HAZARDS	Few landing spots
FINISH	Port a Baigh campsite, 19.30
DISTANCE	27 miles
SAILING HOURS	7½ hours

I loved Scourie Bay campsite. It was a great spot with friendly, helpful staff, who came back to sort me out with a pitch, despite my late arrival. It was really well organised, with simple printed messages about the site, kindly guiding quests to act in harmonious concert to care for their camping. There was a kitchen area with free kettle, microwave and cookware, and power supply. There were pay as you go laundrette facilities, with a dryer. A bar was busy in the evening and served food for those who were not too late, and was filled with happy campers. The showers and toilets were clean and well maintained.

A final exciting feature was the toilet brushes. I hadn't seen ones like that before. Usually there is black or grey plastic fuzz on a stick, polluted with brown and white particles, dripping in a dish puddle, which spills when you try and take it out. Consequently, many people don't, making an altogether unpleasant experience.

At Scourie Bay, there was a much better set up. Firstly, the holder was attached to the wall in a double skinned container so that the brush, when removed was dry. Next, instead of long clogging filaments, there were protrusions on the surface which would have a cleaning, but not catching function. The material was rubbery silicone rather than hard plastic, so moulded to the shape of the bowl as needed. And finally, instead of being cylindrical in cross section, it was lozenge shaped, providing good contact with the required surface, but also meant that the storage site was flush to the wall, so to speak, and off the ground. So much neater and more elegant, and just right for a public facility.

Unfortunately, I needed to leave. The wind started kinder than yesterday morning, with a moderate north-westerly driving me along on a broad reach. I traversed two large patches of water of over ten miles each, the first to Stoerhead lighthouse and the second past Rubha Mor. The challenge was to make for a destination, more or less on the end of a finger, rather than heading in towards the palm of a hand, so to speak, which would necessitate doubling the sailing distance.

With this in mind, I nearly overstretched myself again. In the last seven miles, the wind swung round to the south, came and went, like air from an exhausted set of bellows, sometimes with spits of rain thrown in. It was cold, the tide had turned, and I could see nowhere to land. I felt a rising panic well up within me, fearing the night falling and being adrift on the sea. Spying a buoy near to a settlement called Reiff, I paddled with exhausted vigour to reach my prize of bobbing security.

A few minutes of rest, attached to my floating friend, my nerves began to settle. In line with tradition, I had a chat with my white counsel, who said that I had already escaped the worst of the tide, and now that I had had a bit of rest, the best thing to do would be to press on for the next few miles to the campsite. And so, it was.

Tired after another long day, I left Betty to her own devices, waving gently on the beachy shore, and headed off to find the camp owners and some food.

* * *

Day 53, Sunday 18th June

To Gairloch

START	Althandhu, 10.45
WIND	NW, 8–12 mph. More later
WEATHER	Sun and cloud, 14–19°C. Dry
TIDE	With me max 0.4mph from 12.00
SEA STATE	Slight
HAZARDS	No wind and nowhere to land
FINISH	Gairloch, 18.15
DISTANCE	34 miles
SAILING HOURS	7½ hours

In the Fuaran Bar the night before, an oddly upmarket restaurant despite its remote setting, I got talking to a family. Alistair and Cat were with their daughter Laura. Cat was a GP and Laura was studying medicine, so we had plenty in common, adding great company to good quality food. Laser around the UK stories inevitably entered the conversation. I did not think more of it when I returned to my tent. Little did I know at the time, but I would stay with Cat and Alistair, in Dumfries, all arising from this chance encounter.

Given my late arrival the night before, I was in no mood for dashing off. Besides, the wind had not woken up. However, in order to avoid an hour-long detour, I needed to cross the short causeway to the Isle of Ristol, before the tide went out, so I needed to keep an eye on time.

There was time enough to chat to my fellow travellers, nevertheless. Many of the campers had come to explore the shores, or splash around inlets in their kayaks. I could see the attraction of this remote venue. The Summer Isles themselves form an archipelago of uninhabited and roadless stops within tempting paddling distance, scattered around the mouth of Loch Broom, making perfect treasure troves for those in search of an undisturbed nature gold mine.

Along the grassy edge of the campsite, there were: one person; two person; and then full-scale camping kayaks. Talking to the owners, I learnt that you could carry great loads on board, like 60 or more kilogrammes of equipment, much more than I had imagined, and much more than I had on board Betty. Packing a set of wheels to help roll the vehicle up the shore was another common practice, which added to convenience. This looked like a great pastime.

James, with whom I had stayed on the first night, was on holiday at the Isle of Mull, engaged in precisely this activity. He had been raving by text, about the joys of the experience and beckoned me to come and join him. I had hoped to catch up with him in person, but I didn't think I would make up the miles before he had to return to the south.

I met Pat who proudly showed me his much-loved petrol stove, which formed part of his camping gear. A neat design, it included a pipe passing through the base of the flame to help vaporise fuel, before it reaches the air. The design makes the stove cook hot and hard. It certainly made a speedy morning cup of tea, and gave my helper a pat on the back (sorry about that).

As I was coming out of the communal area, with microwave porridge in my collapsible dog bowl (which fortunately did not melt in the machine), I met a Chinaman. At least I think he was from China, because English vocabulary was a bit limited. He indicated that he wanted a hand with the WiFi code, having located a sign on the wall.

I felt sympathetic, remembering a trip to China a few years back, when, despite being on a standard tourist trail, virtually no one spoke English, and all signage was incomprehensible, rendering the non-native tourist completely helpless. Between us, pointing was more or less the only form of communication.

I was impressed that my fellow camper had managed to find the piece of paper in the first place. In addition, he had entered the code correctly, as far as I could see. However, he had misunderstood the subsequent characters in the stream, so despite his dutiful copying, he was being repeatedly rejected by the security system. He had added '(lowercase)' after the correctly typed password. I foolishly tried to explain what lowercase meant, but quickly gave up. Instead, I took over and corrected the error on his phone, so that we could each be on our way without a major international gesture convention.

Down on the beach, James came over to see what I was doing whilst I was loading the boat. My role as a child psychiatrist came up early in the conversation, and James was off, outlining his own consultation needs, occasionally checking whether he was oversharing.

"It's fine. Do carry on," I reassured him.

He had set up a new business, organising Amazon deliveries amongst other things, and was going really well. He was employing several people as the business expanded, but inevitably this was time consuming. His worry was about his stepson, whom he felt was drifting away and increasingly sullen. In between stuffing sleeping bags into the hold, I provided a listening ear, and a few pieces of advice – about relationships, plus how to access services, should that be needed.

Given that James did not scoff, or drift off to attend to a sudden camping related duty, I had the impression that my comments were appreciated. He said it was helpful, and felt better. I felt better too. It was a pleasure to freely give to someone else. I was also reassured that I could string together sensible sounding sentences, despite being at sea for months.

And finally, as I was launching, Ross and Helen came over. We had met the day before at Scourie, and I recognised them easily, not least because Ross was missing part of his arm. They were keen to lend a launching hand by keeping the boat steady whilst standing on erratic kelp-coated rocks. Ross slipped me a tenner as I was about to head off, a beautifully timed and heartfelt contribution, to help me on my charitable journey.

I made it past the causeway, just in time, and then drifted on towards the first of the Summer Isles, acquainting myself with the increasingly populous jellyfish. I was familiar with the clear blueish round things that wash up on a summer's beach. You can pick them up if you feel brave, and throw the squelchy slippery circles at your sister, if you are that way inclined. Here, there were huge great cream monsters, with dalek shaped cones sticking out of their base, ready to zap you, or announce, "I AM A JELLYFISH," in electronic tones. They looked scary, but I was not sure if they were the dreaded Lion's Mane species. Anyway, I wasn't planning on sticking my hand in to find out.

There was really no prospect of making the 34 miles to Gairloch, given the lack of wind, though I hoped to reach one of my back-up destinations, maybe 15 miles onwards. As I was approaching one of the islands, the wind started to fill, at first appearing like an aberration, but then holding, providing just enough propulsion, to make me think I should keep going.

Across the expanse of Loch Broom, I could see a bluey grey collection of hills, not jagged like the Alps, and not rounded like the inland south, but somewhere in between. Perhaps like coloured mounds of sand from a sand art picture, all bunched up in a huddle but spreading right across the picture. Some of the hills might have been Munros, but I understand they prefer to gather further south near Loch Ness. Oh, and a yacht appeared, smoothly traversing the scene, like an added feature in a puppet show.

After five hours, I had reached Rua Reidh lighthouse so had passed from one headland onto another, and had crossed the halfway mark. Then, you guessed it, yes, the wind died. I was still some 12 miles from Gairloch, and probably eight to my nearest back-up stop, too far to paddle at that time of day. Once again, I thought I had overstretched myself. There was only one thing for it, which was to do nothing.

Luck favours those who wait around to catch it, and indeed good fortune arrived in a double dose. Firstly, the wind turned up to provide a handsome run at 4-5mph down towards Loch Gairloch. And secondly, less to do with patience and more from planning, I called ahead to book accommodation from the water. The good news was that the signal was much better out at sea, making the whole process so much more effective. And it meant that I grabbed the last room. My gambles of the day had paid off.

I had a Golspie problem on landing, in that I could not see the town for the trees. I spied a grand looking building, so headed for the beach below that. It was populated by a few listless folks who had trickled down across the sand. Beachgoers seemed fairly uninterested in my arrival, which felt odd. On approaching a person or two for local knowledge, I was getting blank looks and broken sentences in reply. I soon realised, they too were tourists, who no doubt had just rolled off a bus. The building I had been looking at was the Gairloch Hotel, and was where they were staying.

It was strange being amongst tourists, since the last town I had visited was Wick, nearly three weeks previously. However, I had journeyed to Gairloch since it was a town, and I really wanted the respite of a bed. In fact, two beds, since the weather looked wet and windy for the following day, and I fancied a break.

For now, though, I needed to figure out where I was going. A bit of signal pointed me in the right direction – further south to Charlestown, which really was well hidden in the trees. A relaunch, a re-land on South Beach this time, a scrambled pack up in the dunes and then a run over the hill to the Old Inn for dinner, desperate to make it before last food orders at eight o'clock. I arrived all sweaty at 1957, only to discover that I had an hour to spare. Never mind. I had arrived.

Given that I had now crossed the 1000-mile Rubicon, it was time for another verse for my shanty. To the tune of the Wellerman, if you recall.

After a while the doc did smile
when he'd passed one thousand mile.
The folks he met were ever so kind
helping through the daily grind.

and the chorus

Hey, Ho, this'll be fun
Especially when on the reach or the run.
One day when the sailing's done
he'll take his laser home.

Monday 19th June

A rest day

I slept well, having rediscovered the pleasures of a bed.

After breakfast, I returned to my room to do some planning. This meant spreading the AA road maps I had annotated before the trip, across the expensive floor. Working out where to land was complicated round here. Combined with some Wi-Fi, and the online OS maps which I had purchased following advice at Banff, I could select possible places to stop, and then mark them on Navionics on my phone. Somewhere around Wick, or marker 0028 on the app, I realised you could name the blue pins. That saved a lot of confusion, since selecting the wrong numbered blob to 'boat to' when out on the water was frustrating, to say the least. The Navionics coastline on my phone was now littered with these blotches, looking a bit like a badly decorated Christmas tree.

Because of pressures on accommodation, I needed to move from the Gairloch Highland Lodge down to the Old Inn (where I had had dinner the night before) during the day. I was allowed to hang out in the lounge, like a student in between room availabilities, staring longingly at my phone. Needless to say, I was being productive, with video and photo editing, posting and the like, if you believe that. It was good to be indoors and out of the rain, resting and recovering.

Outside, there were Rhododendron trees which were still flowering. That felt very strange, since they were blooming at least a month later than their counterparts in the south.

I managed to bag a lift into town from some folk, who were hanging about in a car park. After Morrisons for supplies, I walked back along the shore to the Gairloch Hotel where I stopped for a coke, and sat down near friendly, German-sounding tourists, who were moving into a whisky-tasting session.

Gairloch (which means short loch in Scottish Gaelic. So, Loch Gairloch means 'Loch short Loch'. Someone was clearly running out of naming suggestions. However, it is not quite as bad as 'Loch Lochy', which is a real place!), seemed like a nice place for a stopover, even in the rain. Indeed, it was, since it was one of the principal villages on the north coast 500 route (sorry, I thought it was a town, but it seems not).

At the Old Inn I had roasted tofu followed by Eton mess. Dessert was appropriate since in the news, the parliamentary privileges committee had reported on Boris Johnson's behaviour. It sounded like parliament were supporting the damning findings of the report, thank goodness.

And interest rates went up again.

* * *

Day 54, Tuesday 20th June

To Applecross

START	10.45, Gairloch
WIND	S, 8–15mph
WEATHER	Cloudy. Some sun, 16–17°C. Dry
TIDE	Not much tide
SEA STATE	Slight
HAZARDS	A long beat. Few places to stop
FINISH	Applecross, 19.30
DISTANCE	24 miles
SAILING HOURS	8¾ hours

Refreshed after a day off, I was ready to step back on board. Retracing the route back to South Beach over rocky paths, amongst shrubs and trees, felt like a cleansing, but short hill walk. It was easier to appreciate, since I was strolling with purpose this time, rather than sprinting, as was the case when I'd arrived a couple of days before.

I was, however, worried about the ominous prospect of eight hours on the beat, which I thought would be needed to complete the 24 miles. (That is 24 / 3, since it is max 4mph, upwind, and less 40% for beating, makes 3mph roughly). I had back-up stops in mind, but as ever, I would need to see how things went.

Phil and Cameron came down to the beach to see us off. Having found a Laser in the dinghy park at Charlestown, I had tried to link up with sailing club members the evening before, but the timing didn't work out. Instead, they kindly came down in the morning to bid me farewell. Thankfully, no one had touched Betty despite two nights on her own. The tide was nearly in, so with their help, it did not take long to get away.

It was a long day as I had predicted, but warm and not too windy. After exiting Loch Gairloch, I went past Loch Torridon. I then headed in between the mainland and the Isle of Rona, and then Raasay. Having land all around gave a sense of comfort.

A motor craft spoiled the atmosphere when it came towards me in mid-channel, giving not an inch of leeway, despite a prospective collision. I thought that was rude, at best. It was not as if the place was crowded.

As is familiar, the wind packed up early, and the last few miles were super slow, though blessed with a beautiful evening, and gorgeous still surroundings. Jellyfish were dotted about in the bay, some moribund on the surface like fizzy clear lilies, but most were busy fanning themselves along in a purposeful way. I think I had now figured out which were the Lion's Mane type. They were medium size, with a clear propulsion dish, like the common moon jellies. Below that there were brown splodges, followed by long trailing white tentacles, the overall effect being one you could just about imagine into the shape of a lion's mane, if you tried hard.

I was a bit confused about where to land. I think that was because Google Maps shows the land line at low water, which at the right time extends a long way out to where the gently shelving beach comes to an end. Whereas at high tide, the alleged terrain was submerged, so the territory in front of me looked quite different from the map.

As when arriving at Gairloch, I thought it best to land early and ask, so headed for a few houses at Milton. I stepped off the boat and went to explore. Soon, I approached a couple who were walking along the shoreline. They told me about a campsite up a lane, "behind the trees over there". And then added, "they also do food from a burger van, but I think they are closing soon".

That called for some urgent action. John and Helen were happy to lend a hand in parking the boat.

I had initially stopped on sharpish gravel stones. Now the tide had come further in, so Betty could easily be lifted onto the grass verge. Grass verge is a phrase usually reserved for a roadside, but I can't think of a better phrase, because it was like that. The sea stopped, and then a foot high ledge, and then grass. Admittedly the edge was nowhere near straight, and instead, a wobbling natural line, roughly contouring the high-water mark. The grass (if it was grass, since internet searching has not provided clarification) was smooth and soft and short and green, like a mown lawn. "How strange," I thought. Except the grass had big holes in it, which went back down to the level of the shingle. Treading carefully, we were able to slide Betty up the lush surface, tentatively treading on manicured vegetation, avoiding the now waterfilled dips in between. This was not something I had seen before, but proved to be an excellent landing surface.

With John and Helen's wizened guidance, we hurried up the lane and along a secret path, to arrive at the campsite check-in, and burger van, just before total shutdown. Smothered in 'SKIN so SOFT', and the parental affections of John and Helen, I was able to enjoy the luxury of a camping chair, and some more conversation. I was delighted.

John and Helen had driven up from Woking in their campervan, which had just about made it over the Applecross pass behind us, a regular challenge for a heavily loaded vehicle. John was a retired town planner. Coincidentally, I had met their daughter Rachel via professional meetings, a couple of years previously. She worked in the SEN department (Special Educational Needs) in Surrey, so organisationally alongside me on a few cases.

As part of the royal welcome, I was hosted to a cup of tea in the midge-free van, and then treated to some milk for the morning. I felt blessed by the wonderful kindness of strangers.

Relieved and physiologically restored, I thought I should attend to the outside world. The only WiFi was from the steps of the site building, so leaning against the locked doors I eked out a meagre signal, whilst waving away the midges. Yvonne, my call contact for the evening, had been trying to ring, and was on the point of approaching the coastguard to declare that I was lost at sea. I confessed that I had not rung them either. After apologising for my tardiness, I reassured her that all was well, and would do my duty of calling the not-so-coast-guardian-angels later.

Yvonne and I shared an office years ago, and she used to refer to me as her work spouse, a title I echoed in return. As a nurse, I could see that Yvonne was better at connecting with others than me. She was endlessly practical and helpful, qualities that I very much admired, and ones which complemented my own.

We have stayed in touch over the years, and it was great to catch up. Yvonne finished by mentioning a friend who lived near Oban, who might be able to help with support, to which I gave the invariant "Yes, please" in response.

It was going to be a windier day tomorrow, with strong tides around the Skye causeway, so I needed to do some planning. The poor signal made this tricky. What's more, there were no power sockets in this campsite, and no kitchenette. It was not a patch on Scourie, even though it was the same price. I was not impressed.

Then at last to bed.

Unfortunately I didn't sleep that well.

* * *

Day 55, Wednesday 21st June

To Kyle of Lochalsh or Kyleakin

START	09.30, Applecross
WIND	W, 15–25mph
WEATHER	Cloudy, 12–15°C. Rain showers
TIDE	With me, max 1.5mph at causeway
SEA STATE	Moderate
HAZARDS	Tide at causeway. Pontoon landing
FINISH	Kyle of Lochalsh, 11.30
DISTANCE	13 miles
SAILING HOURS	2 hours

Stick (or Neil) had sent a video of his landing spot on Skye, and recommended it to me. "Just head under the causeway and there is a little harbour there," he wrote. "Look right and you see a pylon, and on the shore, look for Leopard Man's hovel. Lovely and isolated."

And then later, "It's worth a visit. You may need to rebuild the roof though. It's only a sheet of metal held on with rocks, and the midges are bad so take some spray."

The video was of Neil and his boat, parked up on the heathered shore, talking about making it down to Tobermory the next day, some 50 miles.

I wrote back, "Thanks, Neil. I'm loving the video. I totally get the feel. Will look out for the bothy. I'm angling for someone's house in Kyle, being a bit of a softy on the comfort front. No sleeping in the shower block for me."

Romantic though it might sound, I could not see the point of sleeping in a broken roofless midge-infested shed, when there was a suitable house next door. I mentally filed that in a section entitled "Neil's bad advice", which was to be politely ignored.

My hoped-for accommodation on Skye did not work out in the end, but I found something else, under the category of 'house'.

At Applecross, luckily the rain held off whilst packing up the tent. John and Helen kindly came down to help me launch, and we huddled under nearby eaves, whilst a stiff shower passed by. The tide had come back in, so the launch involved literally slipping off the grassy surface into the sea. It felt quite majestic. I waved goodbye to my surrogate parents, and wished them well for the remainder of their journey.

The wind had stiffened soon after I set off. I crossed Inner Sound and went past Loch Carron. I reckoned the wind was being accelerated as it was funnelled between islands. The outcome was a screaming broad reach, during which I touched ten miles per hour, probably with a bit of tidal assistance. Either way, it had me on the edge, clearly remembering day one. On this occasion, I experimented with playing the main when going over waves, sheeting in and out as the surface level changed, which helped keep the boat flat, and in control.

"That is a technique worth repeating," I thought.

It's exhilarating going at speed, especially when your backside is no more than a foot from the water. But I was still new to the pace, and I was grateful that the wind calmed down before I reached my destination.

There was a pay-as-you-go pontoon, sticking out into the strait at Kyle of Lochalsh. It was a slightly hazardous arrangement given the ample wind and tide, but it was a convenient novelty. I paid my online pontoon parking fee, and went into town for an early lunch of jacket potato and haggis, followed by a Co-op stop for supplies.

This really was a town. A slice of tooth had sheared off one of my molars a few days earlier, so I was hoping to find a dentist, thinking that a quick lump of cement would fill the hole. Ringing up a couple of potential fixers, I soon got the message that this was not going to happen. I was told that you needed to be registered with a practice, including private dentists, which involved a four-year wait, and then many more months for an appointment after that. I was not in an urgent predicament, but I did spare a thought for someone who might be in a worse state than I. It seemed an impossible situation.

My brother-in-law, who is a Scottish dentist in the south, tells me the access problem is a lot to do with the government contract, that was set up in April 2006. The fee structure lumped many procedures together and costed them as simple, therefore attracting a lower fee. Therefore, fees were pegged at the bottom of a broad range, meaning that delivering a public sector service became financially perilous. Given that fees were governed under the Dentists Act of 1984, finding sufficient parliamentary time to mend the decaying system was caught up in a major Westminster logjam, what with Brexit and the rest. The consequence was that we have nations full of broken teeth.

Back down on the pontoon, it was time for my tongue to do something other than examine the unfamiliar space in my mouth. Instead, I got chatting to a couple on their yacht.

"Would you like to come on board?" Philippa asked.

Being in no rush, I couldn't refuse. Once on board, I tucked into a second lunch, which was quickly spread out on the table, in the warm and sheltered galley.

We got talking about Kyle Rhea.

"We came through that yesterday," said Richard.

Kyle Rhea (Kyle, by the way means 'narrow, or strait', in Scottish Gaelic) is a renowned channel with whirlpools and ferocious tides, that can run at up to eight miles per hour. Attempting to go at the wrong time would be a no go. Loch Alsh sits between the Straits of Kyle (which is where I was having lunch) to the west, and Kyle Rhea to the south. Loch Alsh is a bit like a bagpiper's pipe bag, with the Straits of Kyle as the mouthpiece, and Kyle Rhea as the chanter. When the tide flows out, it is like the piper squeezing with their elbow to accelerate matter down the narrow channel, creating speed enough for a tune.

"We were humming along yesterday," said Richard. "You could see the land whiz by."

"My goodness. I better check my tide times carefully for tomorrow, by the sound of things."

Richard and Philippa needed to resume their journey to a night time stop, as did I, so we bade farewell. I sailed across the strait to the island of Skye, having selected the Backpackers Hostel for my night.

Traversing the strait would have been paralleled by a ferry in times gone by, but they were replaced by the Skye Bridge in 1995. The bridge was constructed under one of the first private finance initiatives, set up by the government. The project was backed by an American bank who negotiated a toll fee to recoup costs. The toll proved highly controversial since it was the most expensive (per metre of bridge) in Europe. The excessive cost led to protests, and a campaign of deliberate non-payment. Regrettably, those who refused to pay had to return to court, located on the island of Skye. This would have been a substantial round trip, and additional crossings of the bridge, which would have rubbed more salt into already raw wounds.

The Scottish Executive, in its newfound form, made it a priority to end the tolls. In December 2004, it purchased the bridge for £27 million, more or less the same cost as the original construction, from ten years earlier. In those intervening years, the tolls had raised £33 million, set against maintenance costs of £3.5 million, so disappointing value for money. No wonder the Scots were aggrieved.

Having found a respectable landing spot, I set about making a few more centre board repairs. I sat amongst dry waving grass, in the afternoon warmth, overlooking the bridge, whilst pedestrians chattered by.

When satisfied with my handiwork, I went to a local restaurant, no more than a stone's throw from my seaside seat. The hostel was another stone's throw away, so all very convenient.

For the evening meal, it was to be another haggis, neaps and taties, and some phone calls. The meal wasn't as good as Liz's version, I am sorry to say, but the chocolate brownie for afters was scrumptious.

It looked like it was going to be a tough day tomorrow.

I was quite tired since I hadn't slept so well the night before. But I was delighted to be sharing a bunk in a dormitory, rather than putting up with a bed of heather in a bothy.

Day 56, Thursday 22nd June

To Mallaig

START	09.20, Kyleakin
WIND	S, SW 10–18mph
WEATHER	Cloudy then sunny, 14–19°C. Dry
TIDE	With me, max 0.5mph only
SEA STATE	Slight
HAZARDS	Kyle of Rhea
FINISH	Mallaig, 16.30
DISTANCE	23 miles
SAILING HOURS	7 hours

This was a special day because it was the longest of the year, with the sun finally disappearing at 10.30pm at night, having risen long before I did. It was therefore the mid-point in the annual cycle, and from here on, the days would be getting shorter. Secondly, in tune with nature, I would pass my own journey watershed.

According to the official measurer, the halfway mark was at Glenelg, just south of Kyle Rhea. Given that I was already below Inverness, it seemed strange to be at the lowly 50% mark, but it's things like Wales and Cornwall that were getting in the way of my homecoming. Whilst I would have liked to hear that I was much further on, soothing words would not have magicked miles into thin air, so soldier on I must.

I was hoping to meet a friend before launching, but urgent parish council business had delayed her morning departure, and funnily enough, delayed mine as well – I am not used to waiting since I am usually last.

I wanted to catch up with Jock Gordon who had been in touch from the east coast. He lived in Portree on Skye which I felt was too much of a detour. And he had suggested several other folk to meet, but sadly none of those connections came off. But thank you, Jock, for being so kind, and such a great connector. Hence Skye was the location of many missed meetings.

I set off at a steady and comfortable reach, on nearly flat water, propelled by a south-westerly, blowing over the Isle of Skye and tumbling down hills onto the water. Up ahead, the land loomed large in spectacular shapes, leaping out of the Loch to reach into the air and beyond, building an amphitheatre of greenery around me. The scene created a sense of awe and wonder, flavoured with trepidation about the infamous Kyle Rhea.

Going round the corner, into the piper's chanter, I was hoping for a stiff stream to propel me southwards. However, it looked to me as if the musician had taken their elbow off the metaphorical bag, since I could see little to no action. I was too early, and it was still high water. I was deflated. Sadly, I was going to miss the whirlpools and wild streams.

Instead, it was to be a long beat.

A fair and steady wind made the journey manageable. A couple of yachts were tacking the same course. I was doing my best to match their progress, looking out for subtle wind shifts to make extra ground, being helped by the nimble turning ability of my craft, and guided by my deck compass. I didn't let them get away all day, and had a congratulatory conversation with a group of Frenchmen, when they had yachted into Mallaig.

Despite the lack of obvious tide, the sea had been doing something strange to the jellyfish, gathering them into long streams of densely packed blooms.

Rob, from Papercourt Sailing Club, who had called me a couple of times on the east coast, rang as I was traversing one of these gelatinous bands.

In my excitement I said, "Can you hear them, Rob? It's really weird."

No, he couldn't.

"It sounds like a machine gun, but much softer," I tried to explain.

The jellies were so densely packed that there was no sea room between each moon disc, and the bands stretched in a solid line a few yards wide, as far as I could see. I went across them a few times.

"And I ran into a barrel jellyfish as well. It made a stiff clunk."

Somehow, my visual excitement wasn't transmitting down the fractured phone line. We managed a sort of conversation anyway, and as ever, it was so good to be able to talk to someone whilst out on the water.

The last hour or two was blessed with a lovely lift, and the skies had cleared. Ahead of me were the clear blue seas of the west of Scotland, the foot of the Isle of Skye past Armadale, and the blue chiselled blocks of the Isles of Rum and Eigg. The Isle of Rum was blessed by a delicate stroke of white cloud, and mirrored in shape by a CalMac ferry, making its way to another distant landmark, with its merry passengers. These are the scenes about which people eulogise when they come to the west coast of Scotland, and I could see why.

Rather than the typical dash into the harbour entrance, I thought it best to wait for the big stick of lights on the outer wall, to go green. It was just as well, since a ferry came past, hot on my tail. I would have really annoyed them or worse, if I had carried on.

As we were coming into the harbour, Betty spotted another Betty. Not being the jealous type, she waved politely to the gleaming white yacht, as she bobbed all alone on the still water.

Being a little earlier than expected, I was spared the usual afternoon wind death on the water, and instead was able to enjoy a sublime windless afternoon on land. As I was packing up, a seal popped up next to our pontoon mooring point, and even came to kiss the GoPro as it was dipped into the water.

I stopped to chat to a couple next to their yacht, as I was leaving.

"Where are you heading to?" I asked.

"We've been here for a few days, so we're heading off for Tobermory tomorrow."

"It's quite a way, isn't it. And the weather doesn't look too nice," I said.

"Yeah. We're aiming for a 7am start to make sure we don't get there too late."

By chance, I joined them later for dinner, since they came into the Steam Inn where I was staying, and kindly made room for me. Pete and Jen were from Plymouth so, like me, were a long way from home, and like me were in no great rush. They were great company, calm, contented, interested and joyful.

Jen was a dentist. When I mentioned my tooth trouble, she moved around the table and said, "Let me have a look."

Enjoying the casual directness of a medic, I opened up, "It's that one. Arghhhhhhhhh."

"Hmm. It doesn't look too bad. I have got some temporary filler that might help."

In their journeying around, they had taken the train from Mallaig over to Inverness and back. In my walking along the town seafront, I had noticed the station, a single-track affair that seemed to have no right to be travelling to such a remote location.

As ever, there was some history to it. The development of a harbour at Mallaig took off in 1846, as the Herring industry began to blossom. Building of the railway started in 1897 as an extension from the West Highland railway from Fort William. It became one of the last, and most expensive routes for the next 100 years. Robert McAlpine and Sons were responsible for construction, and Sir Robert himself became known as 'concrete Bob' because of his extensive use of the material.

The most notable feature of the line is the Glenfinnan viaduct, roughly halfway to Fort William. The viaduct is a 380m long curve, and has featured in many films, including Harry Potter movies, where it can be seen carrying the Hogwarts Express.

The line secured the future of the fishing industry at Mallaig, at least initially. However, with shifting methods and port demands, landing of fish at the harbour had declined. It was still used as a transport hub for salmon farms, but transportation of tourists on their travels onwards, had become more important. It sounded like a great railway journey, but one that I would need to come back and explore later.

Tomorrow, we were heading for Tobermory.

There was to be one last stroll around this delightful little town. Orangey red sweeps of colour were brushed all across the sky, with neatly painted houses and a humble church spire etched into the backdrop, in a gorgeous sunset display. It was 10.30pm at night.

* * *

Day 57, Friday 23rd June

To Tobermory

START	08.45, Mallaig
WIND	S, 20–29mph
WEATHER	Thick cloud. 13–16°C. Rain all day
TIDE	Hard to tell. Not much
SEA STATE	Moderate
HAZARDS	Rain, wind and few landing places
FINISH	Tobermory, 18.45
DISTANCE	35 miles
SAILING HOURS	10 hours

What a day! The weather had turned foul, the first of a series of fronts that were to roll in for the remainder of June, and the whole of July, whilst Europe was scorched under baking sun and record temperatures. I was grateful for some wind, but this was going to be challenging.

Down at the pontoon, Betty was holding a carefully placed package, neatly sealed in a bag, including a note. It was from Jen and Pete. The package contained the promised Temparin for tooth repairs, and a packet of banana chips for energy. I was really touched by the thoughtful generosity.

The stretch to Tobermory looked like too much on the beat, and my back-up plans included camping on the Isle of Eigg at about 15 miles as the crow flies, or maybe somewhere on the mainland like Sanna cove (20 miles). Ron had stopped there years ago, so it should be safe enough, and I would be able to find water, but not much else. It was going to be tough.

The clear blue of yesterday had been exchanged for angry squally grey, throwing wind across white crested seas in intense rage, pumped with even greater gusto as each shower of rain came past. Pregnant clouds hung low over the hills, concealing the way forward, and only lifting slightly when they had dropped their load.

Things were going OK for the first hour or two. The 8:1 downhaul was doing the trick at depowering the sail, something I had not needed since Dover. I used to be sceptical about its value, but I could really feel the difference, now that I was on a consistent tack for hours.

The trouble with more wind when you are on the beat, is that you don't go any faster. Yesterday's conditions had been ideal in many ways – steady breeze, not too strong and fairly flat seas. Today I was going marginally slower, despite all the wind effort. It was because the wind acts against the forward movement of the boat, and neutralises its own power. And then there are the waves, which push the boat backwards as they strike, and force you up and over as they crash past. The waves don't arrive consistently but marshal their forces in sets, and if you don't respond quickly by sheeting out and bearing away, the boat can stall altogether. If that happens, you are prone to being capsized, or getting stuck in irons. It's hard work, and requires constant focus and physical effort.

After two hours, the conditions got the better of me, and I fell out. It was not a big deal in terms of time taken to return to upright, but it was a big deal as a metric for exhaustion.

After another 40 minutes, I fell out again. This time, the paddle slipped out of the cockpit, and tumbled into the sea, as I was righting the boat. Seeing my precious orange friend, out of reach, and disappearing under the waves, was a source of major panic.

"I've got to get that back," I shouted out loud.

My life depended on it, and on this occasion, there really was truth in the phrase.

"I'm sure it's supposed to float," I thought, as I stared helplessly at the submerged object.

I briefly considered jumping in to fetch it, but the idea was quickly dismissed, since it would most likely lead to a cascade of errors, with potential calamity as an end point.

It was time to run through my man overboard drill, for real. The last time I practised the procedure was instructing novices on a flat lake. But I soon discovered that it's not quite the same on a raging sea, and in a state of high anxiety, and consequently it didn't go as smoothly as I would have liked.

My paddle partner was bright (International) orange which is a colour chosen for good reason, since it is easier to spot in the sea. What's more, it slowly swam to the surface, so I was really relieved to find that I could see it as I came near. The first time I approached, I came up too short. For the second pass, I overran it. Still in panic mode, I was making a mess of this simple procedure. On the third attempt, at last, I successfully grabbed the paddle. I held on to it firmly for a while to make sure we were properly united, as if it were a rescued child.

"Boy, I'm mighty glad I have got you back in the boat."

I put an extra knot or two in my tie-on arrangement for additional security.

"How did you manage to fall out in the first place, anyway?"

No answer. I guessed that my original knot had somehow come undone.

I sailed inshore to try and find some flatter water, beating between rocks, and then headed upwind so that I could safely stop for a rest.

Suddenly you, the reader, are on board. Yes, that's you. You are now on the boat. Out at sea. Alone.

Whatever you are holding is no longer steady. It's shaking. You thought you were safe, but you are not. There are hazards all around you. You don't need to look because you know they are there. The clothes you are wearing are no longer warm and dry. They are cool and clammy. You can feel it right now. You can tell where the wind has been coming from, since you can feel it. It's not too strong through the layers, but you can feel it on your skin. Your back aches from the sitting. Your arms ache from the holding. You can feel that. Your neck is stiff because you have been looking in one direction. You can feel that too.

This is not fun. You are not enjoying this.

At least you are with Betty. You can feel the solidity of her deck on your backside. And your feet are on the floor of the cockpit. You can feel that too. The water is inches from your seat. You don't need to look down to check, since you know it is there.

You are sitting crouched on the deck with the sail flogging, making an unwelcome racket in the gale. You are still shaken from the paddle overboard episode, with the tingling after-effects making your limbs heavy, and mind thick with doubt. The tiller hangs limply overboard in its helpless 'hove to' position, matching your depressed state. Everything is wet even though it has stopped raining. Your fingers are wrinkled and white and the skin feels fragile. You can feel that. You adjust your hat, shaking a drop off the brim, and shiver as a rogue drip runs down your neck. You shiver again. The extra top layer has served you well since you are just about warm enough, but not for long if you are not careful. You are starting to feel a chill. You can feel that.

"This is too much," you say to yourself. "I don't think I can carry on."

You look around for a minute, at the sky, at the rocks not far behind you, and the angry sea. There are no signs of what to do. You are alone, stuck out in the wild wet weather. You are completely alone.

Fear is creeping up on you. You are starting to feel its chill in your chest. Your breathing has quickened slightly.

You chastise yourself, "I can't think like that."

Looking for clues as to what to do, you try and check the forecast on your phone, which is just beside you, but there is no signal. You estimate you are about halfway to Sanna cove on the mainland. That's something at least.

"What about going to the Isle of Eigg?" you think. "Urghh. Camping in the rain is no fun." You shiver again at the thought of it.

"Going back is an option, but it would be a waste of all this effort, and who knows what it will be like tomorrow," you think. You think about talking out loud, to see if that will help produce some solutions. But you keep quiet, since you are feeling subdued.

You sit for a minute longer waiting for a plan to emerge from somewhere, anywhere. Your body still aches. You are uncomfortable. You can't safely stand up and move around. You are trapped here. Stuck.

The wind is still blowing you sideways, creating an unrelenting clatter with the sail, and waves bash against Betty's side, splashing onto your lap. Betty is drifting down towards the rocks you have recently passed.

Thoughts turn to your family.

What would you say to them if they could see you now?

Would you let them know that it is all too much, that you have overstretched yourself?

Would you tell them that you don't feel you can carry on?

Would they be worried?

Or maybe they'd call the coastguard if they really knew how you felt?

Maybe they would be angry with you for getting into this mess?

It's been an age, and yet no plan is emerging.

The blindingly obvious makes it into your sludge-like mind, "I can't just stay here."

There is only one thing left to do.

Eat a sandwich.

A few mouthfuls in, you can feel something happening.

"It can't act that quickly," you think, but somehow, the bread, cheese and ham has turned into a something. A warmth, or an energy maybe. You can feel it edging around your body, like a spreading current. From your stomach, out to your limbs. It's different from the usual. It's clearer. Maybe it's because the dial said empty, before you started to add fuel. Your mind wakes up a little, like the cogs are starting to turn again.

The key turns in the lock and the door opens. "I'm going to carry on."

You can relax now. I'll take it from here. Thanks for joining, but feel free to ease back onto your reading seat. Stretch a little maybe, or take a breath in through your nose, noticing the warm still air. You are safe now. Thank you.

Having discovered the miracle of food, I kept the Tupperware box jammed between my legs, so I could fish out another sandwich without having to stop. The technique worked a treat and I managed to press on, remaining buoyant for another couple of hours. The seas grew calmer as the mainland of Ardnamurchan approached, making the sailing more comfortable and less taxing.

In a bay near Swordle Farm, a place you will never visit, I paused for another snack and a moment of onward planning. I was five hours into the journey, still warm enough and not ready to stop. It would be a reach down to the lighthouse and Sanna cove, which should be easier. What could be the harm in carrying on?

The next hour was much quicker, with gusty breezes falling off cliffs and surging across bays onto flat water. I did manage to fall out again, having failed to respond to a tumbling blast.

My learning point from that capsize, was to let off the kicker a bit more, when on a reach. That way, there was less risk of the boom being caught in the water. If the boom gets caught, you can't release any more power, so it is often "over you go". It was a useful tip to myself, one that I would continue to use for the remainder of the circumnavigation.

The Ardnamurchan Lighthouse signalled the most western point of mainland Great Britain, something I savoured for a short while before carrying on.

I rejected a stop at Sanna cove, drawn on by the fantasy of a speedy reach down the Sound of Mull towards Tobermory. It was only nine miles, but took a painful four hours of declining wind, lumpy seas and then more rain. I felt double crossed by the wind, which had pumped itself up when I didn't need it, and blown itself out when I did. The rain. Ah, the rain. After a while, you can't get any wetter, so I was getting used to that.

It was a quarter to seven in the evening, when I finally arrived, ten hours after setting off. A decidedly soggy sailor limped to a harbour pontoon and got out, pooped. I was on land, amongst civilisation, and safe. Incredibly I had made it despite my bad plan. It was kind of unbelievable. "It's amazing what you can do, and how far you can travel if you just keep going," I thought. One step at a time gets you places, regardless of how distant the destination, and how daunting the journey feels.

I was knackered, wet, and fed up, with nowhere to stay and nothing to eat.

I needed to get changed first. Having found a door code, I changed in the marina building, and left a pile of clothing under a bench, and my spray top hanging on a hook to drip. I then went into the village to explore.

Tobermory is surrounded by a wall of greenery, rising up from the waterfront, reaching up to the hilly terrain of Mull. It creates beautiful scenery in the sunshine, and lousy signal, whatever the weather. Hence, my usual digital searches for accommodation were redundant, and I had to resort to traditional house to house searching.

Despite the dour weather, there were plenty of people about, wearing more than the expected amount of tartan. Something was going on. It looked good, but it was bad news for me. Each of my many enquiries about a room for the night, delivered the same conclusion:

"Sorry, we are full. There is a clan convention in Tobermory this weekend. Didn't you know?"

No, I didn't, but I was definitely getting the idea.

I was very pleased for the MacLean clan, who were looking resplendent in their outfits as they proudly strolled along, despite the continuing rain, but I was feeling increasingly despondent. I was told there was a campsite a mile or two up the hill, which would be a back-up plan, if really, really desperate. I was beginning to feel that way. Even ridiculously priced rooms were taken.

When standing at a bar to order a drink, a voice behind me said, "Have you tried the Youth Hostel?"

Turning round to make sure I caught this valuable nugget, I said, "What hostel? No, I haven't. Is it far?"

I quickly finished my drink and dashed along the waterfront to investigate.

Ten minutes later, I was anxiously waiting in a short queue, behind a couple making a very slow, and to me, seemingly trivial query about the local surroundings. Couldn't they see my perilous situation? Didn't they know how far I had sailed today? Obviously not.

At last, they had finished, and I could find out my fate.

"Do you have a space available for tonight? Maybe tomorrow as well?"

The hostel hostess looked out from her office window, in a patient and soothing manner, making me feel immediately relaxed. Her calming disposition was definitely helped by the offer of an excellent value two-night stay, with a fresh towel as an extra. I was extremely grateful, and enormously relieved in equal measure. It was one of those situations where you feel like you want to give your saviour a kiss. Decorum and good sense got in the way, but the feeling persisted. I was saved.

In the news, interest rates went up again. There was talk about the Bank of England having missed the inflation risks. Junior doctors announced a five-day strike. Oh no. But I didn't mind, since I was safe and on dry land.

A quick shower, and a Chinese, and I was soon fast asleep, shrouded by a scattering of clothing, hung out around the end of my bunk.

* * *

Saturday 24th June

A rest day

Half awake, I could hear a rustling noise in the dormitory. "What's that?" I wondered, and then went back to sleep.

More rustling woke me up again, and this time it was joined by a light chinking sound. I opened one eye, trying to satisfy my curiosity whilst clutching on to a vestigial hope of sleep. It was a clan gentleman, addressing his outfit, made slower by his elderly and unfamiliar fingers, as they made second and third attempts to secure the sporran and chain about his person. He then went out, letting the door slam on exit, and came back soon afterwards, with an even louder slam.

Further slumber was going to be a challenge, so I lay in bed to spectate, whilst my roommate finished his personal decoration. The outfit was a lot more complicated than a pair of trackies and trainers, and much finer as well. He finally departed to join his crowd, with clunking suitcase in tow. We were to meet him later that evening.

The MacLean clan is said to be one of the oldest, reaching back to the 9th century and at one time owned major tracts of land in the Highlands and Inner Hebrides. The Isle of Mull was included in their territory, and is the location of Duart Castle (on the eastern corner of Mull) the seat of the clan, hence the location of the gathering.

Tobermory was known for many things. Most famous was that the village featured in the early noughties children's programme, 'Balamory', with the catchphrase, "What's the story in Balamory?". The line rang round in my head as if the place were familiar, echoed from my daughter's happy chants, but no vision appeared with the refrain. Now here it was. Brightly coloured and crisply painted properties, standing back politely from the water's edge in an even arc, from one end of the village to the other. It had stopped raining as well, and the sun was coming out. It was looking splendid.

The village is located on the east coast of Mishnish, the most northern part of the island of Mull. This piece of information is of little interest to you or me, but simply had to be included, because Mishnish, like Fishnish, which is further along the coast of Mull, is a wonderful name and worth repeating a few times, just for fun.

One more uninteresting fact, is that the village was founded as a fishing port in 1788, based on a design by one Thomas Telford. He was a Scottish engineer from Dumfriesshire, and not from Telford as you might imagine. He was involved in many road and infrastructure projects in Shropshire, such that the town of Telford was named after him. Well done, Mr TT.

The mission for the day was to catch up on some laundry, and then a bit of tourism before heading on for my next leg. However, on arriving at the marina building, I found the door wide open, not the usual level of security I had come to expect. An uncomfortable chill crept over me as I looked around for my precious blue spray top. It had been left to drip overnight, on a hallway hook, near some other draped sailors' outfit. But come the morning, everything had disappeared.

With a rising sense of panic, I searched around, looking for alternative places where I, or someone else, might have stowed my protective clothing. "I really need that," I said to myself, but could find nothing.

I rang a bell to summon the harbourmaster as was procedure.

"Quite a few things go missing from here," he said, without an ounce of sympathy. "Did you see the sign outside saying it is open to the public from 10am?"

No, I hadn't, even though on second viewing, it was an enormous, blaring poster, hard to miss, unless you happened to have been a demented drowned rat who had just crawled in from Mallaig.

One stab in the chest was swiftly followed by another. "It will be £36 for the two nights in the marina."

The slight respite from my gloom was to find that the bag of soggy wet sailing gear, was still stuffed under a bench opposite the washing machines. And it had effectively reserved me a place in the laundry queue. "Thank goodness no one has stolen that," I thought. "I would have been in big trouble if that had gone as well."

Clutching clean laundry tight to my chest, I headed back to a chandlery I had passed earlier, hoping that they might be able to provide a replacement spray top. Getting cold out on the water was a significant risk, and I wasn't too sure I should carry on without a substitute. Hence this shop could be mission critical.

It was a small and congested store, trying to cater to the most likely customers, not including dinghy sailors, because there were none about. Asking for some guidance, the kindly shop owner pointed to a rack of random items near the door. There was one top that vaguely matched my specifications, and only the one size. A soft waterproof outer shell, a fleecy bright yellow lining, full length front zip, wrist cuffs and a hood. This was not what I had in mind, but it was growing on me. I tried it on. My name was gradually morphing into 'Musto', because the more I walked around, zipped up and unzipped the coat, the more I felt cosy. It fitted a treat. It clearly had my name on it.

"I'm having a bit of luck here," I said to the shop owner as I was completing my purchase. "Oh, and you don't happen to have any chinagraph pencils, by any chance, do you?"

"Do you mean a string pencil?" she replied. "I think I have one in the office."

"Ah, here you are. My sister used to run the shop until she died a couple of years ago. It's been bugging me since. I haven't been sure what to do with it, so you are welcome to have it."

More luck on my part, you could say, but it felt strange to be clutching her deceased sister's memento. I wasn't sure whether it was filled with despair or anguish, but either way, respect it I must.

This was a proper string pencil. It's called a string pencil because instead of using a sharpener, you pull a thread near the point, and it reveals more delicate lead. The pencil is necessary for writing on plastic-covered material. The result is both waterproof and removable, so ideal for my purposes.

A string (or chinagraph) pencil was part of my passage planning system. I would list the conditions, hazards and timings of the day, on a preprepared sheet, and Velcro the finished product onto the deck. Each day, I tried to make sure that a wetsuit limb would not rub off crucial information, before the day was done. A morning copy was also posted on Facebook to help with communication and safety planning.

I had lost the second half of my original chinagraph pencil in Talmine, on the north coast of Scotland. The substitute system was to use a sharpie, writing on wide Sellotape stuck onto the passage planning sheet, which was then unpeeled in the evening. This laborious unsticking was a major fiddle and to be honest, had been abandoned for the last week. However, in respect of my new blue heartfelt companion, the pencil and I would religiously restore safety procedures henceforward.

In my subsequent wanderings, as well as sunshine, I discovered a couple of delights. A few streets back from the harbour and up a steep road, I was suddenly out on the moors, with the conurbation obscured by trees, as if it no longer existed. From immersion in the bustle of the water's edge, to the space and tranquillity of open green wild landscape, with not a soul in sight, felt like a miraculous transformation. How lucky the Tobermory locals must have felt, and no wonder this was a great tourist spot.

The second was the An Tobar Arts Centre / Café. It was located in a refurbished Victorian primary school next to a church. It had a splendid seated terrace overlooking the bay, a perfect spot for a summer afternoon cappuccino.

Inside I noticed a book on display, entitled "Strong winds are forecast" by Nick Ray.

"Is that the same Nick Ray who is kayaking round Scotland at the moment?" I asked the young lady who had just served me coffee.

It was, and she would know, since not only were they both Tobermory residents, but she was his Goddaughter!

Browsing the book, I wondered how my writing style might compare, should such a thing ever transpire. At 450 dense pages, it contained more words than I thought I could manage, and seemed devoid of those amazing Instagram pictures. "At least he managed to get something published," I thought, "which is a major achievement." And then a little while later, "If he can, then maybe so can I."

I found out that Pete and Jen (from Mallaig) were in town, and we arranged to meet up for a drink. I invited Gabriel along, who was one of my dorm mates from the hostel.

"We were so surprised to find out that you got here," Pete said. "The weather was awful. We had two reefs in the sail and were still struggling."

"I was pretty surprised myself, to be honest," I replied.

Jen had sent me a WhatsApp about their own troubles, and I was keen to hear about that. "What about your own adventures? What happened to the propeller?"

Pete started the story. "We were coming into Tobermory under sail and Jen was ready with the boat hook, but when I put it into gear, nothing happened. There was no movement, forwards or in reverse. Jen was shouting at me from the bow, 'what are you doing?'."

Jen continued. "We thought it was the gear box or something. In the end we had to sail onto one of those large tonnage outer moorings. It took more than one shot to pick it up though.

"Pete went into the water this morning all dressed up in pyjamas to protect him from the Lion's Mane jellies, and that's when we discovered the propeller was missing."

"The sad thing is," Pete continued, "I fitted the propeller myself!"

"Oh no!" I said. "This is making my journey sound like a doddle. What are you going to do?"

"We are looking for a place that will lift the boat so we can have a new one fitted, but they are hard to find," added Pete.

"And you wouldn't believe it, the tender motor failed on the way to the pontoon as well," said Jen, completing their catalogue of woes, all recounted with smiles and plenty of laughs.

We chatted for a while with Gabriel adding stories about Otter spotting on the Mull, his reason for staying at Tobermory.

"Hadn't we better go?" said Gabriel.

"We have managed to wrangle a pass to the MacLean clan Ceilidh this evening, and we don't want to miss it," I explained.

Gabriel had spoken to another accommodation mate, who said we could come along, so we hot footed back to the hostel to gather a couple of extra dance partners. We found our way up a different hill, following the sounds of party, and tartan clad revellers, before arriving at a large marquee in a field.

It was a lovely convivial atmosphere, and we felt incredibly welcome despite being random strangers. Roy was there, the man with the rustling sporran, and he gave us an informative and cultured tour of his outfit. He was wearing the green hunting tartan, whereas many of the ladies were in red, eschewing the more hostile cloth. Sean Connery's mother was a MacLean, and he can be seen in pictures wearing the same patterned material.

Then there was dancing. Having been to a ceilidh or two before, I roughly knew what was going on, and so did Bryony, another member of our YHA party. A lot of others didn't, though, including many of the official looking clan's folk. That made it even more fun since there was no pressure to get the steps right. Chaos ruled and everyone was having a great time. What a treat to have been able to join in. Cheers to the MacLean clan, and their conventions.

CHAPTER 14

Small boats can't
go through locks

* * *

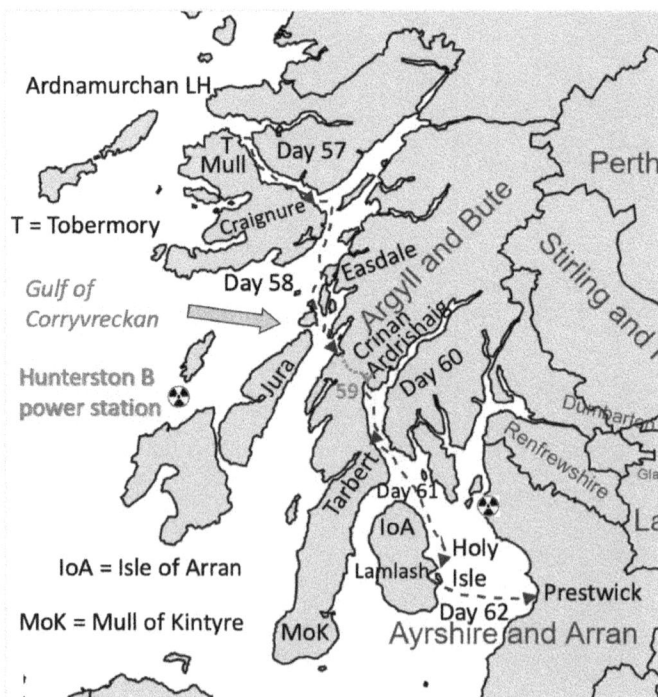

Ardnamurchan LH

T Mull — Day 57

T = Tobermory

Craignure

Easdale

Gulf of
Corryvreckan — Day 58

Argyll and Bute

Crinan
Ardrishaig

Day 60

Hunterston B
power station

Jura

59

Day 59

Perth

Stirling and

Dumbarton

Renfrewshire

Gla

Tarbert — Day 61

IoA

Holy
Isle

Lamlash

IoA = Isle of Arran

Prestwick

Day 62

MoK = Mull of Kintyre

MoK

Ayrshire and Arran

La

Day 58, Sunday 25th June

To Craignure, Isle of Mull

START	13.30, Tobermory
WIND	W, 8–12mph
WEATHER	Cloud and rain, then sun. 14–16°C
TIDE	With me till 16.00, max 0.5mph
SEA STATE	Smooth
HAZARDS	Recent storm. But, lack of wind!!
FINISH	Craignure, 19.30
DISTANCE	18 miles
SAILING HOURS	6 hours

I waited till the wind, and more importantly the rain, had passed, since it was tipping it down. Sitting in the lounge, Bryony joined me with working out the tidal flows and timings for the forthcoming Sound of Luing (next to the gulf of Corryvreckan with its alleged boat swallowing whirlpools). I think she was enjoying exercising her nautical knowledge, and it was good to have someone to help talk things through.

Down on the pontoons, I was getting ready to head off, when someone approached me.

"Hello Andrew, how are you doing?"

Looking up I said, "Oh hi, Neil."

"No, it's Sean, but good to see you," he said with his effervescent smile.

It was good to see Sean and Neil, from yacht 'Waikare', whom I had first met at Arbroath. Sadly, it was a brief encounter since it was already late, but even touching base for a few minutes makes you feel like you are connecting to old friends, part of a community of ocean dwellers.

Out on the water, paddling across the glassy green surface, I heard another call.

"Hi Andrew."

This time it was Jen and Pete from their immobilised craft.

"Look at the speed," I said, as I was paddling along. Compared to a stationary object, one or two miles per hour does look brisk. And a dinghy can be propelled by hand, whereas a yacht (without a motor, or a propeller in this case) is completely marooned.

"Do you want to stop for a coffee?" Jen asked.

Once again, I felt I needed to keep going. There was a causeway to cross between Calve Island and the mainland, before it dried.

"How is your propeller situation?" I shouted across the water.

Happily, they had managed to find a place to lift their yacht and replace the missing essentials, but they would have to wait for a week. That was one step forward at least. It was lovely to see them, to wish them well, and we would stay in touch.

Past the causeway and into the Sound of Mull, I wondered aloud, "Where on earth has the wind gone? Last night loads, and now nothing."

It was looking increasingly unlikely that I would make it to meet Tracey at Dunstaffnage Marina, north of Oban, particularly since it was a way off my main route. I made contact to let her know.

Happily, the wind arrived in the afternoon and I had a pleasant tail breeze, easing us down the Sound, past Aros and other possible emergency stopping points, till I reached Craignure.

There were a couple of dolphins about, blowing at the surface and definitely not interested in playing with my crawling craft. Luckily a ferry steered around me. Ooops, I did not see that. It was another CalMac shuttle, this one between Loch Aline and Fishnish, making the short but unexpected hop across the Sound.

Listening to the news as we trundled along, I was heartened to hear of some Russian political turbulence – the Wagner group had stormed into Moscow to make an attempted coup of sorts. Commentators said that power in Russia so often depends on war mongering and if things start to go badly, the leaders lose their position. Was this to be the start of a change? Or perhaps a new dawn? There seemed to be a glimmer of hope in this ghastly conflict.

It was another gorgeous Scottish evening at the eastern end of the Sound of Mull. The skies had brightened, leaving fluffy woollen cloud scattered around the edges of blue, dressing the graceful hills both near and far, lit by a sharp clear rain-washed light. I edged past a midstream rock, going jellyfish speed, so as to avoid disturbing the cormorants standing tall and statuesque, silhouetted in the sun as they called to their neighbours. The view across towards Oban looked benign and tempting, like a postcard apparition.

However, the wind had packed up, which was fair enough since it was long after working hours, and the tide had turned. It was time to make landfall. Heading straight into the nearest bay, I was pleased to find an unexpected campsite. And a good quality landing spot. And a nearby pub, the Craignure Inn, which was serving the necessary veg meal and chocolate brownie.

It was a 'dash and dine' affair, not in the traditional sense of going in and then scarpering without paying. My law-abiding version was to run over at top speed to catch last food orders, pay the full price, and then saunter back to my tent in a contented haze. It was well worth it. I had had a lucky day.

* * *

Day 59, Monday 26th June

To Crinan

START	10.45, Craignure
WIND	W, SW, 13–23mph
WEATHER	Sun, cloud 14–16°C. Showers
TIDE	South till 16.30, max 0.8mph
SEA STATE	Slight to moderate
HAZARDS	The gulf of Corryvreckan
FINISH	Crinan, 18.30
DISTANCE	30 miles
SAILING HOURS	7¾ hours

I ended up leaving a bit late, having been captured by some signal in a campsite tent up the hill, the comfort of a sheltered seat, plus a preoccupation with passage planning for the day. The hazards were rain showers, a south-westerly breeze making another long beat, very few places to stop, and most importantly the tides around the Gulf of Corryvreckan. Ironically, I may have been better off simply getting on with the journey, but in line with habit, I preferred to know what I was heading into.

I was further delayed by a brief landing at the end of the Isle of Mull, to put on more clothes since I was feeling a bit cold. It was a smart move. Not that I knew it at the time, but I had stopped just below Duart Castle, the historical seat of the MacLean clan.

It was a long slog. I went out past Mull, into the Sound of Lorne, beyond the Isle of Kerrera, with a view back down the Sound of the same name to Oban, and then over to mainland Scotland, skirting between more islands, and on to Easdale Island. It had been over four hours on the beat. I had a couple of on-water stops for a rest, hiding behind an island, or protruding piece of mainland, for shelter. The sun had come out, and the sandwich trick was doing its job, but it was hard work.

On landing at Easdale, the shore was covered with an endless supply of flat circular grey objects, making me think I had arrived in skimming stone heaven. I wondered what my sons would have made of the place. I later learnt that I was not the only one with the same idea. There is such a thing as the World Stone Skimming Championships which takes place annually on Easdale, no less. I had never imagined that such a competition would exist, but I was at its home.

All of this was because Easdale was one of a small group of six, referred to as the Slate Islands, located not far from my landing spot. Slate was mined extensively in the area from the 17th till the mid-20th century. It was used particularly for roofing, until cheaper and easier products, like clay tiles, came on the market. From the air, the island of Easdale shows clear evidence of past industry, where quarried material had been scooped out of the ground leaving pockmarked scars. It is into one of these puddles, that competitors sling their bouncing treasure, hoping to win a great prize, before it sinks out of sight.

Having had a bit of a rest, and spun a few of my own stones into the sea (they were good), I remembered I had other things to worry about, and needed to get a move on. The tide was running in my favour, but was soon to expire. And then there would be trouble.

The wind seemed to have softened, whilst the sea continued to look disturbed by swirls and upwellings. With seven miles of fetch to exit the channel, and only an hour to go before the waters would turn, I thought I had missed the tidal window. A passing buoy reassured me that things were still moving in the right direction, so on I trudged.

At last, I was out of the Sound of Luing and able to turn onto a reach towards Crinan. That meant I would be able to outpace any hostile tide. What a relief to be moving along at a comfortable speed, and away from the dangers of the Corryvreckan. I also had some fun trying to race a clipper that was following the same course, but there wasn't quite enough wind for me to keep up.

One last nautical mention for the day – it is quite easy to get lost in these parts. The islands and the mainland look virtually identical. Further, mainland hovers behind island, making the view from sea level appear homogenous. Too eager to reach Crinan, I followed some yachts heading north, thinking, "this looks the right way". Happily, I had learnt from experience at Beadnell on the east coast, and double checked. I was off course by more than ninety degrees, but fortunately only a mile in the wrong direction, so nothing too onerous to correct.

Crinan is not a town, or a village for that matter, but more in the hamlet domain, with the hotel making up most of the population. The Crinan Hotel was a large grand building, parked on the end of a rocky promontory, next to the lock basin entrance, and a landing dock for tall ships like the clipper I had been racing.

I wasn't at all sure where to land. Searching round the corner from the hotel, I found a floating pontoon. After doing a land-based recce, I came upon a wooded path trailing back over the promontory to the hotel. Without the path, I might have been a bit stuck. I spotted a fixed boat ramp further on from the pontoon, and a trolley underneath a shore side fender. "That might do," I said to myself. "It could also be helpful for my canal mission for tomorrow." Checking on a couple of waterside houses, no one knew whose trolley it was, so at least I was not likely to offend the fender owner. Finally, Betty was parked safely on the grass, and I could trot back to my super expensive hotel, hopefully in time for supper.

Despite being by far the priciest place on my trip, the hotel felt like it belonged to the last millennium. Curt, slightly supercilious staff were devoid of welcoming gestures, and gave the impression that their last laugh had occurred a couple of decades previously. The room I had booked was spacious and grand with a stunning view, but felt like a visit to a wealthy grandmother's house, with furniture and decoration to match. There were many low cost and easily fixable problems that remained neglected – the chain on the bath plug had fallen off, as had the hot and cold labels on the taps; the kettle had to be walked from one side of the room to another to plug it in; there were no hooks in the room, to name but a few. It felt like a ship frozen in time, washed up on a distant beach, still trying to operate as if it were a virginal cruise liner. Even the menu of Cullen Soup followed by Salmon Risotto, must have been a Delia Smith recipe from the nineties, since it was 50% cream.

There was one more thing to do before bed, which might also help digest my cholesterol-loaded dinner. I needed to do another reconnaissance trip, this time a more subversive venture. It was to work out how to manoeuvre Betty into the canal system without going through the first two locks. I'll explain a bit more in the morning. For now, I thought the options were, either:

To wheel her round on a long winding road, using the evening trolley, and then across the first swing bridge. Or,

Sail her round to a private landing I had found, roll her up the rocky ramp, and across the cinder path.

Both options would leave her ready to slide into the canal. I would then use the painter and mainsheet, tied to a canal side bollard to hold her weight, thus preventing us all tumbling into the water. The mission was to be carried out under the cover of heavy rainfall, which would hopefully throw the Scottish Canal staff off my scent. "That should work," I thought. I was determined to find a way through the system, by hook or by crook.

Day 60, Tuesday 27th June

To Ardrishaig

START	10.00, Crinan
WIND	SE, Not much
WEATHER	15–19°C. Rain, rain, and more rain
TIDE	None
SEA STATE	Smooth
HAZARDS	Locks
FINISH	Ardrishaig, 21.30
DISTANCE	9 miles
SAILING HOURS	11½ hours (technically only 1)

Breakfast was an over-elaborate affair, with table service delivered by young kilted students, being coached into the ways of moribund service by the maître d, who was issuing instructions in the corner, like a headmistress. At least it started early and there was plenty of it, since I wanted to get my grumpy self out of there, and into the rain-drenched canal system.

Waving grandma goodbye, I returned to Betty through the now dripping trees. I found the borrowed trolley, ready for phase 1 of my carefully planned campaign.

A word of explanation is needed here.

I love a canal. They are such emblematic pieces of industrial revolution infrastructure, which now bring peaceful low carbon journeys, through places you would not see or encounter in any other way. Then there is the engineering. The simplicity of water flow, gravity, locks and banks can make a whole new pathway, that could never before be imagined. A waterway that should not be, and yet there it was, to be enjoyed, admired and appreciated in all its elegant beauty. How could anyone resist?

The Crinan canal was completed in 1801, creating a short cut between Glasgow and the Inner Hebrides, principally intended for commercial vessels. Our friend Thomas Telford also had a hand in the design work. Nowadays, it is largely a tourist attraction used by leisure craft, who perhaps also like a canal, and prefer avoidance of the hazardous tip of the Mull of Kintyre.

The canal includes 15 locks, and six swing bridges. The locks were mostly in two clusters around the middle section, where there is the greatest height difference either side of the summit. There were two manned sea locks at either end, where staff take up positions to receive passing traffic, and help them on their way. Other locks were handled by the sailors themselves. The maximum height above sea level is 20 metres.

Unlike most canals, it was not fed by a river. Instead, it was an up and over affair, meaning water needs to run down from hilltop reservoirs. In 19th century days, some of these collections burst their banks on more than one occasion, causing substantial damage to the canal, the banks and the lock gates. However, when I was visiting, low summer rainfall meant that the authorities were worried about reduced draught, and excessive use of locks (which might drain more water away).

Before I set off for my circumnavigation, I had learnt about the canal and dreamed of going through it. I imagined problems and invented solutions. The battens would be removed so I could furl the sail around the mast having derigged the kicker. I could tag tail another friendly yacht into a lock. The boom would be tied up to the mast to keep it out of the way for paddling. I might be able to sail if the wind were in the right direction, and so on. I was excited to try it all out. In the end, I used none of it!

To be honest, the Mull of Kintyre didn't sound too pleasant according to Stick's stories, so there was no harm in avoiding it. But then again, neither did Duncansby Head nor Cape Wrath, but they were fine in the end.

The final consideration was meeting up with my family. Liz had booked a weekend in Prestwick, Ayrshire, and all the kids were coming up. I really, really wanted to see them. Going round the Mull would have cost me a couple of extra days, and might have meant missing them. So, the canal it was.

However, "Small boats can't go through locks" was a refrain I kept hearing, over and over again. This could be problematic.

I had diligently booked a canal transit a few days previously, and paid my licence dues. The website gave lots of detail about maximum allowable length and draught, but no minimum dimensions, despite charging an amount per metre of vessel. I thought I had better ring to check, and phoned the Crinan office the day before.

"I'm not sure about smaller vessels," he said. "Kayaks can go through though, but they need to be carried round the locks."

Followed by, "I'll ask my supervisor."

We all know where that was going to go, and a polite but intransigent 'no' inevitably came back a while later.

"Where there is a will, there is a way," I wrote in a message to Liz. She was worried the family meeting arrangements would be messed up. I didn't think she was convinced I was going to get through.

Phase 1 went according to plan. I took option two, which was to sail round past the lock entrance, to the private landing spot. The fender worked a treat in allowing me to roll Betty over the rocky lower section, and onto the grassy slope, then over the cinder track.

The hitherto untested lowering-into-the-lock method, likewise worked beautifully. It was nicely controlled slither, with neither a risk to man nor boat in the process. The grassy bank had been well lubricated by the rain. Things were going well.

My next innovation was to wrap up the boom in the sail, instead of tying it up with the main sheet, as I had imagined. That way I could paddle along unimpeded by a boom, which would have been all too eager to keep me company, as I stretched over the side. (I could not use this technique on the sea, because the boom-in-the-sail wrap, needed to be done on land.)

An official looking gentleman came out of the first swing bridge hut to see what I was up to.

"Uh oh," I thought. "This could be trouble." But a bit of 'how do you do?' satisfied my scrutineer, enough to allow a return to his nice dry smartly painted black and white building.

Before pushing off, I said out loud, "Many apologies, Betty, you have just been converted to a kayak!" Betty didn't seem to mind since we were in this together. I also had to pause, and contain my mischievous excitement for a minute or two, to allow a yacht to come chugging by, on its way to Crinan. This was the only mobile yacht I saw all day.

The next obstacle was a swing bridge. I pulled up at the pontoon and tied up.

"Where are you going?" came a cry from across the water, in an innocent sounding but strong Scottish accent.

A bit puzzled by the question, I could not quite work out the intent. We were standing next to a canal, which offered two options, namely forwards and backwards. I was not operating one of those amphibious motorised landing tenders that rise up on wheels when you reach the shore, the likes of which can be seen in posh harbours. Hence my direction options were limited to two obvious possibilities.

Maybe he was trying to say "where the hell are you going?" which would have matched the ensuing conversation a bit better, but I guess he figured that as an employee of these august waterways, perhaps he shouldn't be throwing in too many expletives.

"That way," was my thrifty reply, accompanied by the required gesture (a point).

"Are you wanting me to open the bridge?" came next.

Thinking we were getting somewhere, I said, "yes please, that would be great," in my politest English accent. Then my friendly bridge operator went back into his bothy, presumably to pull some levers.

Standing on the bank, I was feeling pleased with myself. Eagerly awaiting the grand opening, I watched on carefully to see how the mechanism would operate. Rain was falling with steady vigour but it was warm and so was I, having put on every last piece of waterproof clothing, including my nice new hooded 'Musto' top. A car came over the bridge.

"Ah, that's what he was waiting for," I said out loud. But still nothing happened.

Ten minutes into this drip stop, our busy bridge keeper came out of his bothy. I was getting impatient.

"Excuse me," I hailed across the divide. "Are you thinking of opening the bridge, because if not, I will take the mast down and go underneath?"

"You gave me a short answer," was his curt reply.

Taken aback by this foreign linguistic rule, I said, "I'm sorry about that. I didn't realise I needed to answer in a particular way?"

Then out poured a barrage of sibilant accusatory questions, as if trying to expose an undercover spy from an invading foreign force (which in truth I was).

"Have you paid for a transit?" Yes, I had.

"Have you got a pilot?"

"Sorry, what's that?"

"You need a pilot, because you are short-handed."

I could hear my interrogator, scrolling through his book of procedures.

"Small boats can't go through locks," rolled off the tongue.

"Ah, ha. I have heard that one before," I thought.

Having reached the end of his corporate checklist, and clearly abandoning procedural niceties, he threw in his own conclusion. Like a triumphant chant at the end of a demented summing up, he declared, "You gave me a short answer. I'm going to give you a short answer. I'm going inside to have lunch." True to his word, he marched into his bothy and slammed the door.

"What on earth happened there?" I wondered, feeling shocked, and at the same time slightly amused by the absurd situation. Was he looking for a longer explanation of where I was going, like round the UK? Was he trying to ask me how I managed to sneak into the lock system? Was he violently enraged by the lack of work for the day? Did he want me to try and say the name at the other end of the canal – errr lochgil …. bleah, or was it Ardrisig??? No, that would have just made things worse because neither could I quite remember which it was, nor had I figured out how to pronounce either location, without making a complete tit of myself.

I was defeated. I could not make sense of it. No matter, since there was little point in standing around being another drip. I took the mast down, and went under the bridge.

Just as I had pushed off from the pontoon on the other side, another Rottweiler came dashing out of the bothy.

"Come over here, I want to speak to you," he shouted. He was speaking in a clipped Afrikaans accent, which when issued at raised volume, sounds like you are being shot at.

"Good God. What is it with these people?" I thought.

With a few feet of water between myself and my snarling protagonist, I thought it wise to stay put.

"I can hear you OK from here," I said. "What's the matter?"

"What's your transit number?"

"Sorry, I don't know. But if you mean, have I paid for a transit licence, then yes, I have."

That clearly wasn't doing the trick.

"What's your transit number?"

"I'm sorry I don't know."

"I need to know your transit number."

Now I was getting seriously irritated.

"Look, I don't know, but you can look it up yourself." Yes, I could have looked it up on my phone, but I was in no mood to kowtow to these monsters, and it would have taken several soggy and infuriated minutes.

As I was moving to paddle off, he launched one last verbal volley, "What's your vessel name?"

"It's written on the back of the boat," I shouted back at him over my shoulder.

With that he gave up and strutted back into his office.

Boy I was angry. These guys had got under my skin and I had lost my cool, which never feels good.

After a few minutes of spitting obscenities into the canal, I managed to calm down. I knew that in some ways I was the guilty party, having broken into the waterway without following procedures. In truth, I did not think I had an alternative since in my estimation, an open approach would have led to obstruction at every turn. By the end of the day, I was proven right.

The one good thing about getting angry, is it can make you more determined. Now I was bursting with vigour. My paddling was ferocious. My conviction that I must reach 'Ardrish ... whatever', by the end of the day, was fixed in a steely light, shining bright through relentlessly raining cloud. I was going to get there, come hell or high water.

The first lock eased into view as I trickled along this silent and abandoned waterway. There was no one about. That was good.

"Ah, ha." I thought. "My first prize lies in sight."

Locks are quite simple really. You shut the gates, let in the water (or out) and then open one pair to let the vessel out. However, moving large volumes of water can be risky because of all the turbulence, especially when the flow is into the lock. Equally, it is important to keep control of the craft in the chamber to prevent damage.

In my student days, I recall a couple of young men allowing their clinker rowing boat to drift forward as the water was rising, resulting in the bow being jammed under a crossbeam. The nose was therefore held down as the water level lifted. A panicked rush to close the inlet paddle averted a total sinking, but it was close.

On another occasion, when enjoying a three-men-in-a-boat style holiday on the river Wey in Surrey – thoroughly recommended by the way – we forgot to close the downstream paddle. It took a few minutes to work out why the water level wasn't rising, but we got there in the end.

Then there is managing the vessel as it descends. Weighty objects require more handling care. One time, again on the river Wey, we took my mum out on a barge for the day. Liz had recently been on a day skipper course and was full of chat about the 'slips' she had created – it is a kind of knot that is useful for leaving a pontoon since it allows the rope to slide through the hands. Except she had tied both ends of the rope onto the barge. (She has a double first in engineering from Cambridge, by the way.)

I was enjoying operating the downstream paddle with the provided handle. But all was not well. I became increasingly alarmed as the stern of the boat rose out of the water, suspended in midair by a not-so-slippy slip. I was terrified that the whole thing would flip over into the lock, with disastrous consequences for my elderly mother, who was still sitting on board. Fortunately, the stern line broke under the weight of the vessel, which splashed down like an aquarium dolphin. A minute later, a bemused mother of mine appeared into the open, gently enquiring "Is everything alright?" and I was mighty relieved.

So, there you have it. Simples, as long as you are careful.

Except I couldn't find the lock key.

"Bother," I said. "I guess they would have given me one when I came through the sea locks."

Then the phone rang. It was the Crinan sea lock keepers.

A polite and gentle voice enquired, "You have booked a transit. Can I check what time you are thinking of coming into the sea locks?"

"Um, err ..." and various other bits of waffle followed, since I was still not ready to confess my whereabouts.

"By the way, can I check what we should do about lock keys? Where can I find one?"

The enthusiastic reply came back, "Oh, there should be one, on one of the gates in a white tube."

"Brilliant," I thought to myself. "I could be getting somewhere."

"And one other thing. There was mention of a pilot. If I were to need one, how would I go about finding one?"

There followed a complicated set up, in which I would need to ring someone, who might possibly be available tomorrow at best, and it would cost a fair bit.

"I'm not doing that," I thought.

Wandering around as we talked, I found the golden key and applied it to the mechanism, and excitedly started to wind.

The conversation concluded with, "thank you very much," and I hung up.

A moment later. "Oh shit." I had made a rookie error. I didn't need to fill up this lock till Betty was in the chamber. And now the stupid paddle wouldn't go down.

"Double shit."

I really hoped I had not broken the thing, because then I really would be in trouble. I guessed that the pressure on the paddle was too great to allow it to go back down, but the water level was not rising in the chamber either. I could not work out the paddle mechanism, since it looked different to those I had seen before. And "what were those orange blobs for?" I wondered.

This day was proving to be quite the roller coaster.

I needed some help.

I spotted a young man digging in a would-be garden, though given all the rain, it looked more like a paddy field. I explained my problem.

"I'm not sure," he said. "I wouldn't want to get into any trouble myself."

My appeals to his kinder nature drew him away from his would-be rice planting. He came over to gaze at the windlass, the water and the weird orange blob. We couldn't work it out. "Damn."

Along came a couple more official looking young men. They were from the authorities, but not coached in the ways of the cranky old men – they were polite and helpful. One was in training. It wasn't long before the famous refrain was uttered, with a downward gaze and a shake of the head, "small boats can't go through locks".

Anyway, the more trained one put things to right. He confirmed my suspicion about water pressure on the paddle, but added a key gem. "You see that orange blob on the lower gate? It's higher than the other one, which means the outlet is still open, which is why the water isn't filling up."

Now that it had been pointed out, it was obvious. One other thing that was also obvious – there was absolutely no way I was going to be allowed to go through this lock.

Fortunately, youth, innocence and kindness, possibly with a dash of respect for this elderly lunatic who was trying to get round the UK in a weighty tub, meant that they lent a hand. The main manhandling problem was that there was not just one lock, but five, marching up the hill in front of us. This was going to be hard work.

With their assistance, we fished poor patient Betty out of the canal. I then set to with a bit of rolling, whilst they went on a futile mission to find some kind of trolley. Paddy man was still about, and added some muscle to the new mission. When his mum came to pick him up, I made a point of thanking him profusely, and telling his mother what a helpful son she had.

Eventually my lock trainee duo came back, empty handed. After another hour of puffing, heaving and sliding, we were past three locks. We then managed to recruit a group of walkers, who were idly standing in the way, so the last couple were passed at a much greater speed. Finally, Betty was eased back into the water, down a grassy bank. We were at the summit. That meant seven locks had been passed, with eight to go. That was something.

"Thank you very much, guys," I said, and they ambled off to go and get dry.

There must have been some chatter on the canal wires, since a not so friendly middle-aged keeper was expecting me when I arrived at gate number eight. It soon became evident that helpfulness had long since drained away from this employee. His answers were reminiscent of David Walliams in the 'Little Britain' sketch, in which he repeatedly proclaims, "Computer says no" in a snarky tone, laced with disinterest.

I thought I would try anyway. "Would you be kind enough to lend me a hand, getting through this lock? It doesn't look like much of a drop."

With a half sigh he replied, "Small boats can't go through locks."

"Is there any way you could help moving the boat around the lock? With a trailer or something?"

"No, we haven't got anything like that. If maybe you had asked earlier, we could have looked for something."

Getting the distinct vibe, I wasn't going to get too far with this line of enquiry, I tried something else. "There is a wire fence next to the lock. How far does that go?"

Keeping up the same passionate disinterest: "It goes all the way along the locks. And there is a wall further on."

A stubborn bureaucrat can be maddening. It had been a long day and it was still raining, so my fuse was running a little short. I paused.

With a hint of disdain, or was it mockery, he asked, "So what are you going to do?"

I had a strong desire to punch him, but for me, these things never get past a flickering thought. Instead, clearly defeated by this unfulfilling encounter, I turned away and mumbled a half-hearted "I don't know."

Deflated, I walked slowly back towards Betty, wondering what to do.

There was a lane next to the locks. I could roll Betty along the road if needs be, but I would block the traffic if there was any, and it would be exhausting. "Who else might be able to help?" I wondered. "A trailer would be handy."

As if by magic, nay, even a miracle, the next vehicle to come down the road was a small truck. Suddenly reawakened, I gestured to draw their attention. In truth, the lane was so narrow that driving past would have all but involved running me over. As the vehicle drew closer, a tired, slightly tatty tradesman's motor was turning into a gleaming feathered chariot, swooping down to rescue a desperate abandoned traveller – it was a drop side van, with just enough flat surface to accommodate Betty. "This could be ideal," I thought.

What a contrast in helpfulness. It is incredible how a passerby will give so freely to someone in need. I had experienced this on so many occasions. But as soon as you employ a person, they become stingy, begrudging and devoid of humanity, when you might imagine the opposite would happen.

Lochlan and his son had been mending fences all day, and were returning home with a few spare posts and bits of wire, in the back of the van. Lochlan listened patiently, and without hesitation stepped into seamless coordinated action with his son, quietly taking great care to avoid unnecessary Betty bashing. Maybe they were motivated by a desire to circumvent authorities. Maybe they were just assisting for the love of a fellow man. Maybe they liked the sound of an impossible journey and wanted to be part of it. I didn't know, because most words were enunciated only with actions.

Together we eased Betty out of the water, through the narrow gap in the fence, and onto the flattened pile of posts. I sat up with Betty whilst we drove along, making sure she did not roll out the back. We made a fine, but ridiculous sight, trundling along, looking like a micro version of Noah's ark, rescued from the floods. It was only a few hundred yards, past locks 8, 7, 6, and finally 5, but it had saved me several hours of painful road blocking rolling. I guessed the lock keeper had gone for another break, because he was nowhere to be seen.

Past lock 5, it was time to restore aquatic order. There was indeed a plant-covered wall. It was nothing insurmountable for our local heroes, who effortlessly lifted Betty over the obstruction, and then eased her down onto a more comfortable canal surface.

Slightly overawed by the family's incredible and unassuming kindness, I was scratching around to find a way of thanking them. Unfortunately, any cash was buried in the boat somewhere, and I did not have the presence of mind to find an alternative means of expressing my huge gratitude. Instead, I fluffed a few gracious 'thank yous' and they were off, heading to a well-deserved dry home, and a cup of tea. I hope some of my appreciation landed, if not then, maybe now. Because I would like to say, "Lochlan and son, you are truly amazing good Samaritans, and the world should be proud of you."

It was 5.15pm. Although I had broken the back of the journey, literally, there was still a long way to go and potentially four more locks. The rain had eased, and then soon stopped. Round a silent corner or two, I came across a channel side pontoon and stepped out for a rest. Standing up, I spied a petrol station sign, peeping above the bank. Having been cocooned in my sloshing enclave, I was blissfully unaware of anything that might be heard or seen from an upright position. This alarming bright sight, whilst an afront to my dulled senses, did send a message. "Food," it said.

Having slid down the bank and stocked up in the shop, I stood outside dripping under the forecourt shelter for a while, stuffing my face. One mouthful only encouraged another. My haste was accelerated by a worry that the shop owners would shoo away their hobo style customer, who was spoiling the visuals. Happily, I was left to munch, dry out a little, and warm up in my own time.

By 8.30pm, lock 4 came into sight.

"The lock keepers will have gone home, and I can tackle this one without intrusion," I thought.

Another mistake. They had taken the windlass with them. Bother. Foiled again.

Looking away from the canal, I could see houses stepping down the slope, and beyond them the sea. This meant that I was at Ardrishaig, and therefore at the end of the line. That was fantastic news. There was no way I was going to return to that Godforsaken canal system on the morrow, so somehow, I had to get out and away.

Following a path between houses down to sea level, I came across a car park. Then a boat yard. "Oooh, that could be useful," I said out loud.

A gate was open and I crept in. There were some bigger boats and then smaller ones. Just as I put my hand on a likely trolley, a voice called out, "Can I help you?"

"Damn," I thought. "Busted again!"

How wrong I was, once more.

Alan set about providing unquestioning and unwavering assistance, as if he knew I was arriving, or perhaps had been ordained to help. Neither were true, but perhaps like Lochlan and son, he saw a need and felt the urge to help. The difference with the previous interaction, was that there was no Betty to be seen, and instead a man trying to nick a trolley from the boat yard. This made Alan's charity all the more remarkable. Maybe my soaked sailing gear and buoyancy aid gave him the signs of authenticity that he needed.

Either way, he unlocked the gate to the yard, walked up the path with me, hauled Betty out of the canal for the last time, onto the trolley (which happened to be a Laser trolley), down the path, making sure we didn't bash (or electrocute ourselves) on the telegraph wires, and then back to the boat yard.

"She should be safe here tonight," he said.

Then Alan waited patiently whilst I derigged, got changed, unpacked, repacked, and then drove me to the Swan Hotel in Lochgilphead (which I had booked whilst having a feed stop at the garage). What an absolute gentleman.

And what a day of extraordinary contrast between enormous obstruction, and incredible human kindness, so graciously and unflinchingly given to a total stranger. My heart was aglow, and my thanks profuse, but yet again my expressions were resoundingly inadequate for the appreciation I felt.

It was gone 10.00pm when I entered the hotel, but Stan the manager was all abuzz, and so was the bar. Stan was full of good cheer and little sleep. I drank in the happy atmosphere whilst supping on a beer, turning over the events of this absurd day in my mind. I too felt a surge of pleasure, savouring the delights of a mission completed. I had reached my goal despite having virtually all my plans laid to waste, and most of my predictions proven wrong. There was one exception, which was worth remembering – 'Where there is a will, there is a way'.

I slept well.

Day 61, Wednesday 28th June

To Tarbert

START	16.00, Ardrishaig
WIND	NW, 10–15mph from 14.00
WEATHER	Rain, then cloud then sun. 14–15°C
TIDE	Not much
SEA STATE	Slight
HAZARDS	Lack of wind
FINISH	Tarbert, 18.00
DISTANCE	10 miles
SAILING HOURS	2 hours

I had a massively late start, mainly waiting for the wind to appear, but also a chance to dry out. Having caught the bus into Ardrishaig, I hung out in the boat yard, along with my clothes.

I had a lovely, mostly sunny morning, chatting to people. Alan came down again, and demonstrated his endless generosity by helping with minor boat repairs. There was Ian, who had his own marquee, providing protection for his beloved ten-year clinker boat repair project. I ducked in under cover for an occasional spell of rain shelter, having scooped up drying clothes.

I needed to move Betty out of the way, when an incomprehensible Scottish man went out for a leisure fish. He came back later with a bucket of slimy goodies, to which I responded with the internationally recognised code of "Oooh" and "Ahhh" noises.

A man called Gordon came over for a chat. He disappeared for a while and then returned with a whole crowd, including his five children, keen to impress them with tales of sailor derring-do. I was flattered, and the children even managed to ask a few questions.

I went down to the sea lock, to admire the remainder of the canal. It all looked like a fine construction, and a fine reconstruction. Several carefully restored buildings were spaced out around Pier Square, close to the sea locks.

"I wonder if I can find out about getting a refund?" I said to myself. "After all, I have not been through any locks, and was told I was not allowed to."

I imagined the recompense procedures would be fiendishly complicated, and there was the usual question as to whether it would be worth the aggravation. Given that I had some time to spare, I thought I would give it a try.

After pushing on a few doors and following signage dead ends, I found my way into a smart compact office. To my surprise it was the South African 'what's your transit number?' man who greeted me. He was polite, efficient and civil, acting as if our shouting match of yesterday had never occurred. Remarkable.

After the paperwork was completed and refund executed in no time at all, I thought I would try my luck with launching a complaint about the swing bridge incident. I was still incensed, and thought some feedback was needed. That was no bother either. My account was diligently transcribed and edited for clarity, as we sat together calmly in the cosy office. It was all alarmingly smooth.

As we were finishing up, my efficient officious official turned to me and said, "Can I give you a piece of advice?" The question was rhetorical, of course.

"Oh dear, what's coming?" I thought. Something on the lines of, "Don't take processes for granted," or "Respect lock safety". No, I was wrong.

Instead, it was: "It would have been helpful to let us know you were in the lock system so that we could have lent a hand."

"Ok, I'll take that on board for next time," I said, keeping any rising tension under wraps, and my mind focussed on the very efficient and painless refund.

"My arse," I thought, as I headed out into the sunshine and away from the clutches of this stifling bureaucracy. At least I had the comfort of a returned transit fee, as vindication for my efforts. What a relief to be heading back to the freedom of the open sea.

I bade farewell to my boatyard buddies and headed on to Tarbert. Back out on the fine seas of Loch Fyne, with the familiarity of salt water all around, and nothing but wind and the hills of the Kintyre to trouble me, peace and tranquillity returned.

I sped along on a handsome reach. It was a meagre two hours of sailing. The sun had come out, the view into West Loch looked enticing, and there was no need to go further, so in towards Tarbert I went.

I had been to Tarbert before, with the whole family when the kids were young. We had hired a yacht from Largs, and enjoyed a wet and not too windy week. I remember sitting in a pub on the waterfront, maybe the Anchor Inn, looking out at the rain on the harbour, being glad to be inside. On this occasion I was blessed with a glorious summer's evening.

It was a slightly tricky entrance with rocks, channels and other obstructions, making a reasonable obstacle course to the pontoons themselves. Then it was a case of finding the visitor berths. Plenty of boat manoeuvring skills were required, as I beat into the inlet and then gracefully landed on a required pontoon. Shortly afterwards, a yacht, crowded with yachties, came to moor up nearby, and despite all the hands on deck, they were making a real mess of it. I was feeling a little smug as I watched. A swan, burnished white in the afternoon sunshine, and clearly impressed with my seamanship, came to give Betty a gentle nod. "I'll take that," I thought.

Checking with my pontoon neighbour, I asked, "Excuse me. Is it alright to moor up here, do you know?"

Soon I was sitting down to a cup of tea on board. Rob and Eileen were an elderly couple, who were sailing their sedate and unfussy boat called 'Possum', around the Firth of Clyde. They were warm and welcoming, and I took an instant liking to them. Hungry for more of their company, I asked if I might join them for dinner, but unfortunately, the tiny restaurant they had specially booked, was jammed.

Instead, I went to explore. At the eastern end of the waterfront walkway, there were steps and a path up to the Royal, but ruined, Castle of Tarbert. Like most castles, it commanded a great spot overlooking East Loch, the marina, the hills and Loch Fyne in the distance. I was alone, free to enjoy the evening air and softening light of a blessed Scottish summer's evening. How delightful it was.

On my previous visit, I had not realised the strategic importance of Tarbert to tenth century residents. 'Tarbert' is derived from a Gaelic word meaning 'carrying across'. There is a West Loch and East Loch, which virtually join up, but not quite. In previous times, cargo or even boats, were literally carried across from one side of the peninsula to the other. The land route had a shortcut function, missing out the Mull of Kintyre in the journey from Glasgow to the Inner Hebrides. Hence, an earlier and sweatier version of the Crinan Canal.

Reportedly King Barefoot of Norway had his longboat carried across in 1098 to signify his possession of the Western Isles, another indication of the extensive influence of the Norwegians at the time.

The castle, and its two now dismantled partners, provided a strategic guard at Tarbert isthmus, defending the lower reaches of the mull. Robert the Bruce stayed for a period in the 1300s and added strength to the fortifications. In later years, Herring fishing provided the main source of village income.

Nowadays, it is tourists and sailors. There is a seafood festival each year. There is also a collection of yacht races called the 'Scottish Series' which is not dissimilar to Cowes Week. All in all, what a lovely place and well worth a visit.

* * *

Day 62, Thursday 29th June

To Lamlash

START	11.00, Tarbert
WIND	NW, 10–19mph, then SW
WEATHER	Cloud and rain, then sun, 13–15°C
TIDE	0.3mph with me till 16.00
SEA STATE	Slight to moderate
HAZARDS	Goatfell wind shadow
FINISH	Lamlash, 16.30
DISTANCE	28 miles
SAILING HOURS	5½ hours

"Where did the morning go," I wondered. Who knows? It must have been consumed in comfort.

I met Rob and Eileen again as I was walking round to the harbour office to pay my dues. I was pleased to hear that they had had a delicious meal out. Eileen had also made a generous donation online, to one of my charities. I thanked her for that, and wished them well for their travels.

In the smart looking harbour office, I thought I would try a random request. "You don't happen to have a laminator, do you?" My passage planning sheet was starting to go soft, so I was looking for an upgrade.

"I think we do," came the reply. So, a couple of sheets were shoved into the machine and then chopped into the required size. Fantastic! What luck. They declined payment as well. My desire for administrative order was satisfied, and my planning system had had an upgrade. I would add the Velcro later, to help stick the sheet to the deck.

It was easier exiting the harbour, than coming in the night before. Round the corner heading south I was making good progress on a steady reach, bumping along at a stiff pace.

Out beyond the main shelter of the Mull of Kintyre, the wind picked up further, so did the waves, and so did my speed. It was exhilarating. There was light cloud and good visibility, only hampered by the sea spray, bouncing off the prow and then being blown into my face. A double layer of spray top was protecting me from the regular drenching, and the warmer seas of the season kept me out of chill trouble.

Looking back at the wake, I could gain a rough idea of boat speed. At this pace, the white arrow trailing behind, diverged at the thinnest of angles, only spreading to the width of Betty's transom after 20 metres or so. It was like driving a speed boat. Reviewing the tracker later, I had been touching 11.7mph or 10.2

knots without tidal assistance – my top speed so far. I had made it to the north of the Isle of Arran in an hour and half, a distance of about 12 miles. That was quick.

All good things must come to an end. This time a miscalculation contributed.

The Isle of Arran includes a large hill called Goatfell, which was covered with cloud as I approached, so I couldn't see its full height. It reaches to 874 metres which is substantially taller than most of the surrounding land. The relevance of this is the length of the wind shadow cast by an object. Sailors are told that the wind is affected to a horizontal distance of seven times the height of the obstruction, which would make about six kilometres. I was way too close to shore. I could make out yachts on the far side of the Firth of Clyde, still powered by plenty of breeze, whilst I was languishing at the mercy of swirling puffs. Bother. I even had to get the paddle out for a time.

The wind filled in when passing Brodick, and had swung round to the south-west, meaning the last 2.5 miles took a sluggish hour and a quarter. It goes to show that high speeds don't tend to last long.

Holy Isle sits at the mouth of Lamlash Bay, an imposing spear of land, leaping out of the sea. My first landing at Lamlash led to an encounter with two men dressed in Buddhist monk type attire. They were carrying supplies.

"Have you come over from Holy Island?" I asked.

In breathy tones I had a brief introduction. "We own the island, and run retreats and courses. You would be very welcome to come and visit."

I was bit nonplussed by the island owning thing, since they didn't look like your scruffy (or smart) wealthy landowners. Then there was the religious angle which was making me suspicious, but intrigued.

I later realised it was all true. The Holy Isle (as opposed to Holy Island of Northumbria), was offered for sale by a Mr and Mrs Morris back in 1990. They were approached by a man called Lama Yeshe. Being a Buddhist who promoted peace and meditation, they hoped that he might look after it well. He did. It took the Lama two years to raise the funds to purchase the Isle, and then a further few, to restore buildings to a suitable condition. Now, there is a visitable set of properties to the north, where phone-free retreats and courses are held, promoting the search for inner peace. There is a closed Buddhist female-only community to the south near the lighthouse.

The offer of a visit sounded enticing. I had a brief fantasy of stopping off on my way past in the morning, but I didn't think I had room in my schedule, since I had a family rendezvous instead. Besides, that probably wasn't the way it was supposed to be done.

I left the Buddhists on the shore and sailed off round the bay to get closer to my destination.

After my second landing, and usual boat parking and kit management faffing, I eventually found Middleton's campsite, set back from the seafront. It proved to be great value at £10 with good Wi-Fi and a laundry room. School kids were screaming about, released from class on their early Scottish summer break. I didn't mind a bit of youthful energy, but I was pleased when the racket finally went to bed at about 10.30pm.

There was one more thing to be done before going to sleep. Liz had changed the family accommodation from Ayr to Ardrossan, having upgraded from a campervan to a very nice Airbnb apartment. So, my landing spot was to head further north. Therefore, I needed to contact Prestwick Sailing Club, to see if there might be anywhere to store Betty for a day or two.

Day 63, Friday 30th June

To Prestwick

START	10.45, Lamlash
WIND	SW, 12–24mph
WEATHER	Thick cloud, rain showers, 12–14°C
TIDE	Not much
SEA STATE	Moderate
HAZARDS	Big stretch of sea, like The Channel
FINISH	Prestwick, 13.45
DISTANCE	19 miles
SAILING HOURS	3 hours

I was now south of Glasgow and Edinburgh, but still only 57% of the way around. The bad news about my journey was that I made no further progress to home on this day. That was because I was going sideways and not forwards (east vs south). The good news was that I was going to meet my lovely family. I would also meet the wonderful folk of Prestwick Sailing Club, and I would avoid the gale force winds of the coming days, wrapped up in delightful accommodation.

Unfortunately, it was raining as I was packing up. As campers will know, this makes for slower procedure, and a wet, heavy and possibly mouldy tent. I would have to try and dry it out later.

Near Betty, I found shelter to get changed. This was a covered doorway being part of a local coastguard building. I appreciated the dry spot which was providing at least some form of sailor protection, more useful, I felt, than the regular morning and evening phone calls. I waved through the window to the office worker as I left.

Out on the water, there was a slow start out to Holy Isle. Thereafter the wind and swell picked up as was forecast. Visibility was poor with heavy cloud hanging over the sea, made worse by an endless dowsing of spray, meaning my eyes were routinely awash with sea water.

Yesterday it had felt exciting. Today I was not so sure. It was a large open sea crossing, about the distance of the Channel, with little idea of where I was going other than the direction of my lowly compass. Further, I was nervous about having to travel downwind too much, since this is the most unstable point of sail. However, my tension meant that I kept pointing higher than I needed to, and increased the later need for bearing away – such is the adverse effect of unwanted worry.

I stopped a few times to correct my course, but still got it wrong. Nearing the shore, I headed for a ramp and a collection of white sticks, which I thought must be masts, but they were lamp posts. Damn. It was raining and miserable, but at least I was safe and on land.

Given all the speed, I was two hours early, so squelched into an unenthusiastic café for a warm-up, and work out what to do.

"Sorry, I don't know where that is, love," came the reply to my directions query, even though it proved to be only 150 metres along the breakwater. I suppose not everyone is a sailor!

I was surprised that someone picked up when I rang the club. It was Chris. He passed me on to David, who rang back, and talked me through all the details I needed. I still found it incredible when things worked out, and so amazing that people were willing to come down at the drop of a hat. Re-energised, I hopped back into the boat, fell out when launching through the shore break, stepped back in again, and then hopped out for the final time, a few minutes later. David was waiting below the club slipway, with a Laser trolley in hand.

What a welcome. Betty was parked safely, spars locked in the club shed, luggage retrieved, warm shower made available, schedules organised and coffee supplied, all before my family arrived. What a divine welcome.

David was a Laser sailor, like myself. He was also retired. Like myself, he had lost his mum recently. We shared stories and feelings about the death of our mothers, reflecting on the painful adjustment, and stark realisation of being in a parent-free phase of life. It was lovely to share in a spontaneous and open-hearted way, a chemistry that sometimes falls upon us without planning or forethought, making it feel all the more sincere.

Then Liz and the kids arrived. Kids still in my mind, but they are all comfortably into adulthood, and on to second or third jobs. How wonderful to see them and share lots of hugs all round. It had been a long time since I had seen any of my children, and nearly a month since I had seen Liz, so there was a lot to catch up on.

Before being escorted off to our accommodation, I needed to squeeze in a radio interview. The media doesn't wait, in my experience, so 'kiss it or miss it', I would say. This one was with Molly from West FM, but was slightly unusual since it was via WhatsApp voice note, rather than phone dialogue. It was the typical set of questions but felt a bit disjointed. Something to get used to perhaps.

The apartment in Ardrossan had been recently refurbished, and was a delightful abode with bright, well-appointed spaces. There were views from a first-floor bay window to the Isle of Arran, across frothy seas. We had a large and spacious bed, and plenty of room to hang things up to dry, including the tent.

Various goodies had arrived in the car such as a new chinagraph black pencil, and a RAM mount. The pencil would make it much easier to read my daily passage plan, since the blue one, though full of love from Tobermory, was like writing with invisible ink. The RAM mount was to be fixed to the deck to hold the GoPro. Ken Fowler had been using one, and I hoped it would allow different filming angles. I was looking forward to trying that out.

⁕ ⁕ ⁕

Saturday 1st to Sunday 2nd July 2023

To return to the bosom of my family was a joy. I am not too sure we are supposed to say that these days, but I just did. There we are. It was glorious. All those comforting habits and annoyances, that are so familiar and pleasurable for their predictability.

We stayed in, went out, explored locally, went for walks, went for a park run (I didn't since I didn't have the right shoes!!), watched TV, ate out and generally had fun.

There was a plan to catch the ferry to the Isle of Arran and walk up Goatfell, but it was too windy for the ferries, even for those huge vessels. It was blowing 25-35mph so would have been a no-sailing day for me anyway. Instead, we walked round the red sandstone harbour walls, and leant into the screaming breeze, seeing how far we could tilt.

On the Sunday, the Arran ferries were still not working – too much wind, and an additional problem of not enough staff this time (I'm not too sure what they had been doing the day before). Instead, we took a more sheltered journey over to Great Cumbrae, a small island off Largs. Sam got quite excited about the propulsion of these smaller ferries, since they didn't need to moor up when arriving at the landing ramp. They used steerable propellers at both the bow and stern, to maintain position whilst vehicles drove off (or on). Very neat.

I got excited about a piece of local history. The battle of Largs took place in 1263. This was a tactical and political coup for the Scots. I have previously made mention of the Norwegians in the Orkneys, and then at Tarbert. In 1263, King Haakon of Norway and King Alexander II of Scotland were keen to consolidate their respective territorial positions. The Norwegians had taken possession of many islands over previous centuries, ruling the Orkneys, Faroes, Outer and Inner Hebrides, and even governing land down to the so-called Southern Isles, which included the Isle of Man.

Haakon had arrived with a large fleet and moored off Largs, in the summer of 1263. King Alexander of Scotland was seriously outnumbered by his adversaries. He decided to negotiate, whilst the opposing ships waited offshore. Being a keen bureaucrat and cunning tactician, Alexander dragged out discussions until reinforcements arrived, in the form of the weather. Autumn storms blew in, which destroyed large parts of the Norwegian fleet. The ensuing land battle took place amidst much confusion and naval rescue efforts, leaving the Scots victorious. As a result of the battle of Largs, the Norwegians withdrew all the way back to the Orkneys, never to return, much to the celebration of Alexander and his followers.

I nearly forgot to mention. When on Great Cumbrae Island, we had sight of Hunterston B power station, a collection of neat white box shapes on a protrusion of land. It was another site on the nuclear power station tour. Hunterston B was an advanced gas cooled reactor, which started energy generation in 1976, but since 2022 had been closed down. The fuel is being removed for reprocessing at Sellafield. I was beginning to wonder whether any of these power stations were still working.

Returning to Prestwick, we were invited down to the sailing club, to meet other sailors and mingle for a coffee. David was there and so was the commodore, Laura. I brought my RAM mount so it could be attached to the boat. In an instant, more people arrived to help with the job. Something that I thought might take an hour of lonely fiddle, turned into 15 minutes of harmonious effortless triumph, with David leading the charge. What a wonderfully helpful and well organised club, and many thanks to David for pulling people together.

* * *

CHAPTER 15

Look! There's Ireland

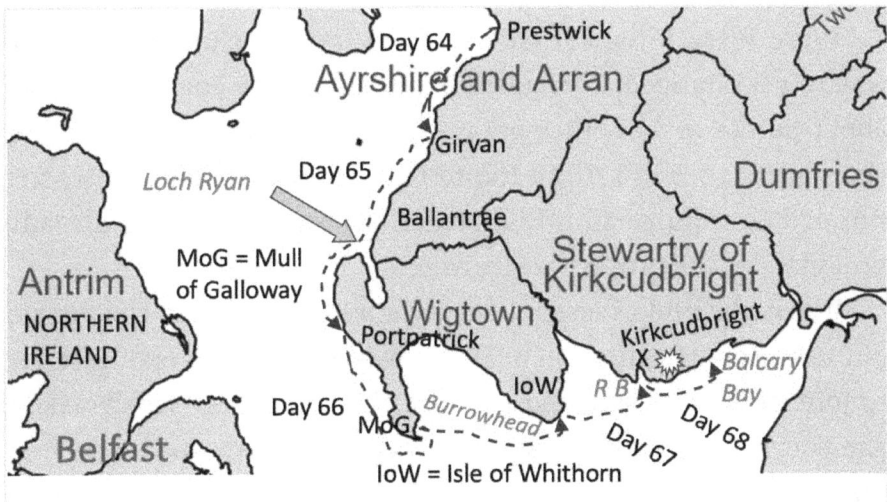

Day 64, Monday 3rd July

To Girvan

START	10.20, Prestwick
WIND	W, 18–28mph
WEATHER	Sun, cloud with showers, 12–15°C
TIDE	Against me, max 0.4mph till 14.00
SEA STATE	Moderate
HAZARDS	Strong winds and sea state
FINISH	Girvan, 15.30
DISTANCE	21 miles
SAILING HOURS	5 hours

To have been in a home away from home, and then to leave it again, felt well … err …. a wrench. Alongside the "thanks for coming up to see me", "I'll miss you" and "I love you, darling" exchanges, and parting hugs, I had a nagging thought – "Is this still a good idea?" What's more, it was still very windy, and I was unsure about conditions. I was feeling nervous, and already missing the comforts of my family and life indoors.

There were kids' courses running at the club, and on my way to get changed, I wriggled between fidgety youths learning about points of sail. They were young enough not to recognise the significance of sailing round the UK, and their tutor wasn't minded to indulge in idle distraction, more than was already provided by the group themselves.

It was the end of lesson time when I launched, so they came out to watch. On the beach, David was wearing a wetsuit, ready to join me in the sea, and retrieve the trolley. He sagely asked, "Are you sure it's not too windy?" I wasn't sure, but said it was fine. Liz, Sam, Oli and Emily were waving from the shore, collecting video content. This could be an opportunity to demonstrate that I knew what I was doing. Or alternatively make a fool of myself.

The result was somewhere in the middle. Apparently, youths were shouting "put the rudder down," as I stepped into the boat. They were right, since I hadn't noticed that it had been knocked upwards, when Betty had been rocking on the waves. Without steerage I merely drifted sideways. I took their advice without hearing it, and reset for a second and more successful departure.

Out on the water, a squall or two came through with the clouds, and then the rain stopped. Usually, the wind calms down with the passing precipitation, but unfortunately on this occasion, the breeze became even stronger. This was a bad sign, since it meant that the wind was not going to abate, and was escalating well outside my comfort zone.

After a good three hours of upwind slog and whistling wind, I paused on the water opposite Maidens Harbour, wondering about quitting for the day. Later I was told that someone had called the coastguard thinking that a windsurfer had got into difficulties. They were wrong about the vessel, but right about the trouble, because I was thinking, "this is definitely too much". However, a pause, a sandwich, a turning tide and prospect of rounding the corner at Turnberry lighthouse all helped, and I resolved to carry on.

Past the lighthouse (another Stevenson construction, by the way) I could progress on a close reach, making the travel much quicker. The seas were growing taller, and I worried about safely making it into a narrow harbour entrance, with a following swell – more of that unstable downwind trajectory. Gritting my teeth and gripping the mainsheet, I managed to find a way inside Girvan harbour walls to still waters. What a relief. The day had not been that long by usual standards, but it had felt tough.

On landing there was a threesome of spectators leaning on the harbour barrier, watching proceedings. After a while, one of the wizened gentlemen started to ask a question or two.

"Where is your support team?" he asked.

Pointing to each member of the neat assembly in turn, I replied, "you're my support team". The group shifted a little, straightened and smiles blossomed onto their faces, just for a while, before returning to observation duties.

Day 65, Tuesday 4th July

To Portpatrick

START	12.00, Girvan
WIND	SW, veering NW. 13–17mph, more later
WEATHER	Rain, then sun and cloud, 13–14°C
TIDE	Confusing. N max 2.0mph till 18.00
SEA STATE	Slight
HAZARDS	Variable wind. Complicated tides
FINISH	Portpatrick, 20.15
DISTANCE	33 miles
SAILING HOURS	8¼ hours

The wind had softened, but the rain hadn't, so I decided on a late start, encouraged by a restless night. "Maybe I will be able to catch the late tide past Portpatrick," I optimistically said to myself, when reviewing plans over breakfast. Realistically it was too far to travel on a beat, so I needed camping back-up plans. I was not keen on travelling the extra miles in and out of Loch Ryan.

Portpatrick sits on the central coastal section of the Rhin of Galloway, which forms a hammerhead shaped, double headed peninsula in the most south-western part of Scotland. The hooked bit at the bottom is referred to as the Mull of Galloway. Portpatrick looks across a 22-mile stretch of water to Northern Ireland, and is home to strong currents and lively seas. As is the case for much of the country of Scotland, there weren't many places to land, so combined with all the other hazards, I needed to consider my options carefully.

What's more, the tracker had failed yesterday. From what I could tell, the battery had gone flat, caused by a loose connection when charging. I thought I had done the necessary to restore a signal, but it was an extra layer of safety worry.

In the harbour, I met a man called James Noble and was invited on board his yacht for a chat. He had a ship hand called Gordon Monroe, who sounded more Scottish by name and by accent, but despite being younger by three decades, looked more worn out than his 93-year-old skipper. James was full of vigour.

He told me, "I still own the boat yard in Girvan, you know."

He told me about places to shelter, his system of weather checking, and stopping points in Loch Ryan, not all of which I took on board. However, to be 93 and still sailing round the lochs of Scotland in your own yacht, full of the zest of life, was an example to bear in mind for many decades to come.

After my previous wind-soaked days, by contrast, this one started off as a drudge and got worse. Tacking along the coast, I hugged the shore as much as possible to stay out of the opposing tide, even bumping into a rock at one point. It was three hours to do less than nine miles, and then another hour on to Ballantrae.

Past the conurbation, the wind picked up for a while and then died altogether. There was no way I was going to make it to Portpatrick, since it was already five o'clock and I was only a third of the way.

"Where's that NW wind that was forecast?" I kept saying to myself. Like the sailing equivalent of a mirage, it repeatedly gave the impression that it would arrive, but never did.

Luckily, I managed to get through to Liz as I was drifting about.

"Hiya darling. Thanks for picking up. I'm trying to work out how far I can get today. Do you think Dounan Bay would be possible?"

"Where is that?" said Liz.

"It's round the corner past the lighthouse," I said. I was not sure that helped!

I was really keen to catch the tides for the following day. Therefore, travelling some distance, any distance, past the northern tip of the peninsula would be an advantage. After talking things through, despite the failing light, I decided to go for it. I could camp at Dounan Bay, or maybe stay at the Corsewell Lighthouse Hotel (an adaptation from another Stevenson family construction), which was north of Dounan Bay.

A rare tip off from the Belfast coastguard prompted me to turn on my VHF radio. He told me to look out for the ferries coming out of Stranraer. I did see one heading out from Loch Ryan on its way to Northern Ireland, but it was some distance ahead and storming along, so well out of my way.

Then something happened. The mirage appeared again and this time, there was some wind with it. In addition, the tide turned in my favour, swooshing out of Loch Ryan and pushing me round the corner and down towards my goal. Boat speed increased from two miles per hour, to four, to six, to eight and maybe more, as the landscape eased past, in a surge of blinding good fortune. I could see Northern Ireland clearly across the water. Another country looking so close felt incredible. A gap in the clouds threw rays of early evening sunshine onto the water, as I grinned my gilded way down the coast. What a miraculous transformation.

Portpatrick was a cute little village with a cute little harbour, which I was extremely happy to see. Coming in through the rocky entrance, I swung round to the walled confines, to be met by a few pleasure craft strapped onto ten-metre high, slimy black walls. "Not so cute," I thought.

I shouted across to a sailor, "Does the beach stay dry at high tide?"

He did not think so. "I better go take a look," I shouted back.

Seaweed lines and dry divotted sand seemed to suggest it would be OK. The kind lady who came to help shift Betty thought it would be alright, and so did her recruited helper. In no time, Betty was parked, snug up against a wall, glowing gently in the evening light.

Then it was a short walk along the harbour's rim to the Crown Inn for a half chicken dinner (the last remaining item on the menu) and a catch-up call. I had managed to land, derig, unpack, move Betty to safety, book a hotel, and source dinner, all in 60 minutes.

"Wow, that was quick," I said to myself, still reeling in joyous disbelief at my arrival.

Further round the harbour crescent, I found a path and stomped up steep steps towards my bed. The Portpatrick Hotel is a turreted affair, occupying a commanding position, overseeing the residents below with a watchful eye, including her new visitor, Betty. I had a large room, making the accommodation seem generously affordable. Maybe the location at the bottom end of Scotland had something to do with it. I wasn't troubled to find an explanation, because the successes of the day had made me deliriously happy.

However, I also needed to think about the next day. I really wanted to get past the Mull of Galloway (the southern end of the peninsula), seeing as it featured as a major tidal obstacle in my mind.

"If I leave early, it should be possible," I told myself. Buoyed by the enthusiasm of the day, I went to sleep, tingling with the persuasive chant "we can do this" ringing round inside my head.

Day 66, Wednesday 5th July

To Isle of Whithorn

START	9.00, Portpatrick
WIND	W, then SW, 13–19mph
WEATHER	Sun and cloud, 12–15°C. Dryish
TIDE	With me 2mph, to 16.00. 3.8mph at IoW
SEA STATE	Slight then rough at Burrows Head
HAZARDS	Tide and more tide. Wind vs tide
FINISH	Isle of Whithorn, 16.30
DISTANCE	39 miles
SAILING HOURS	6 hours (80 min at Maryport)

I managed to get on the water and away by 9.00 which fitted the schedule. The wind started light enough to make me worried about progress, but filled in sufficiently to keep me flowing along with the tide. I was at the Mull of Galloway (and yet another Stevenson family lighthouse) by 11.30, impressive progress to my mind, since it was about 19 miles.

The seas were all over the place at the headland, bumping swirling and jumping in a wild and chaotic mess, whilst I was bereft of forward motion over the surface. The tracker later told me that I was doing 7-8mph past the point, hence quite similar to Duncansby Head. On this occasion, however, once I had moved round the headland, there was wind to sail by, so no need for panic paddling.

There is a Maryport Holiday Park, near Drummore, just north of the point. I say that because whenever I mentioned Maryport to anyone, they assumed I was in England. There is a much bigger Maryport in Cumbria, but I wasn't there. Instead, I happily landed in a field of caravans, but sadly, with no shop or café to provide entertainment.

Sitting on a sheltered piece of vacant decking, chewing over a standard homemade cheese and ham sandwich, I considered my options. It was too early to stop for the day. I needed to decide whether to go east from here, or south.

My predecessors had each taken a different course. Ron had stuck to the coastline from Wales, past Blackpool and then Cumbria, to reach Dumfries and Galloway. Stick, however, had rounded the Mull of Galloway and headed east, but then suddenly changed his mind and casually plunged south to the Isle of Man. The idea of a straight-line southerly route had seemed attractive in the planning stages, since it would form an admirable shortcut and a bold gesture. Faced with the cold realities of the day, things were a bit different.

The leg to the Isle of Man looked comfortably manageable, being only a little further than the stint across Luce Bay to the Isle of Whithorn, my eastern alternative. Leaving the island would be more problematic, however.

It would be about 50 miles from the Isle of Man, down to Anglesey, so further than I had travelled thus far. The wind forecast looked settled in a SW pattern for the coming days, and if it were to be a beat or fetch for 10-12 hours, out in the middle of the Irish Sea, I was not sure I would be able to manage. The alternative was to wait for a kindly weather window. "I could be stuck there for weeks," I thought, and I didn't fancy that. Besides, I wanted to see Blackpool. Because, well, Blackpool is Blackpool, and I had never been there. Hence, eastwards it was.

Part 2 of Day 66, started well. A stiffening SW breeze made for a comfortable broad reach, bumping along at 7-8mph. I passed rocky outcrops called Big Scares and Little Scares, presumably named after their unlikely location in the middle of an empty bay. For me, they were convenient waypoints.

Soon afterwards, I noticed a bad smell.

"What could that be?" I wondered. "Could it be me and my armpits? Or perhaps that cheese that has been stowed in the hull for a few weeks? Or some debris in the sea?"

More head scratching and air sniffing followed, before the obvious answer dawned on me. It was the Scares that had scared me. The smell of Guano had blown downwind, and only reached me once I had passed the rocks, giving me an odorous fright.

Onwards I sped to my destination.

I had three or so miles to go, a smidge of a distance given my hasty miles so far, but the day was not over yet. There had been so much talk about 'wind over tide' and the frightening escalation of sea state. The tide had turned but the wind direction had not, which surely would make an ideal challenging combination, and yet there was no sign of this ogre. On I went in happy oblivion, unaware of the conditions awaiting me.

Just as I thought I was within striking distance. I saw what I didn't want to see.

"Oh no, there it is," I said.

A thick band of frothy white sea, stretched out from the headland in front of me, throwing up steep waves in an angry maelstrom, whose detail appeared more and more frightening as I approached. What's more, I was unsure of the landing, remembering I needed to find my way through a rocky entrance to secure shelter. "Is it this side, or the far side of that tower?" I asked myself.

This was all bad news. It had been a long and tiring day, and a perilous ending was definitely not the kind of reception I was hoping for.

I stopped on the water to check my route, and for any forgotten hazards. I had clearly failed to notice that the tide was due to run at 3.8mph at about now, though perhaps I hadn't quite believed the reading when I first saw it. I could well believe the numbers, now that I could see the sea state in front of me. However, it was too late to do much about it.

I headed on into the marine mess. The seas I had previously encountered seemed trivial in comparison. Betty was tossed carelessly up and down over the waves, and thrown this way and that, like a plastic duck in a bathtub, filled with a toddler tantrum and too much soap. Now on the run, I was getting little assistance from the sail, which was making everything feel so much less stable. I was scared. This really wasn't fun.

I really did not want to fall out, not for reasons of pride, but for concern about survival. If I were to fall out once, it might lead to many tumbles, with sinking capability to go with it. There were rocks in front of me, the Irish Sea behind me, open mouthed and beseeching, and boiling sea all around. I really wasn't sure I could handle it. I did not know what to do. I was starting to panic.

I noticed a channel of calmer water further inshore. Too nervous to gybe around, I took a large sweeping tack, and headed in towards flatter water. But I could see in front of me, even that would soon fizzle out.

One advantage of a moment's respite was that I had a chance to collect my senses. There was no question of going back from whence I had come. Like a child's book we used to read to our children – 'We're all going on a bear hunt' – a refrain recited each time the children in the story came to an object, came back to me. It went like this: "We can't go round it; we can't go under it; we can't go over it. Oh no, we'll have to go through it."

Steeling myself for the last couple of miles, I put all my focus into keeping focussed, staying calm and keeping afloat. Back into the raging sea I went. I was crouched in the cockpit like a frightened cat, ready to leap in this direction or that, in order to stay out of the water. Up and over the waves we went, almost in control, but never feeling that way. I had to cling on.

I could now see the tower marking the harbour entrance, and a route between the rocks was coming into view. I was imploring my destination to come closer, so that I could find respite from this torment. At last, it crept within reach. Just one more gybe around, and I could head into the mini harbour and out of harm's way.

What a relief to make it to calm waters. It had been a long day, and one of the furthest distances to date. Still feeling quite jittery, I came round a breakwater, and stepped out onto a sandy shore, hugely reassured to be standing on something solid.

A local boatman gave me a hand with finding a trolley and making an introduction to the Wigtown Bay Sailing Club, whose existence I had not noticed on my digital tour of the coastline.

Being a bit of an out of the way kind of place, there were only a handful of tired, and not very seaworthy dinghies scattered on a patch of grass in front of the club. The setting provided perfect parking for me. The showers and changing facilities were in a better state than the dinghies, and were just fine.

Just as I was getting sorted, Alistair and Cat turned up. What an astonishing surprise. We had met one evening in the Fuaran Bar in Althandhu in the north-west corner of Scotland near the Summer Isles. They had been on holiday. Alistair and Cat had been keeping track of me, and had come down to welcome me ashore. Little did I know it at the time, but I would end up staying with them for three nights.

What absolute legends.

But one step at a time. After some interaction around Betty and reacquainting ourselves, we were all wondering what to do.

"Where are you staying?" was soon followed by my usual, "be careful what you offer, since I will say yes to everything" routine. Rather than rush into things, we went off to a local restaurant for a meal. The Steam Packet Inn was lovely despite its remoteness, somewhere Alistair and Cat had been to before for an anniversary meal – they seemed to be good at finding delightful, out of the way places to eat. In celebration of their previous celebration, and in appreciation of their enthusiasm for coming to meet me, I paid for their meal.

From there, the simple thing to do was to take this lost sailor home and offer him a bed for the night. I was delighted to be so generously accommodated. I was very tired.

* * *

Day 67, Thursday 6th July

To Ross Bay

START	12.00, Isle of Whithorn
WIND	S, 15–25mph. 33–48mph at 2000
WEATHER	Cloudy, 14–15°C. Dry
TIDE	With me max 2.0mph till 1500
SEA STATE	Slight to moderate
HAZARDS	Storm that night. Tricky landing
FINISH	Ross Bay, 14.05
DISTANCE	12 miles
SAILING HOURS	2 hours

The next couple of days were characterised by, 'no-go, go' days, constrained by the wildly 'yo-yo' ing wind conditions, and the wildly varying tidal heights. I had not really clocked the challenges of the west coast of the UK, nor the extreme range of the Solway Firth, which I guess is a side effect of being a southerner. I was aware of the challenges of the Bristol Channel, having kayaked down the river Wye to Chepstow, but unbeknownst to me, the Solway Firth is only a few steps behind, in terms of range. Huge flat beaches and massive height variation can mean hours of boat manoeuvring, simply to arrive or depart. Hence, getting the timing right, for both the wind and the tide, and combine that with an accessible landing spot, was quite a challenge.

Luckily, Alistair had paddled around these parts, so knew the beaches and tides of the local area. He was also kind and supportive with his advice, making the planning process so much easier.

"Not many people come to these parts," he would say, extolling the virtues of the Dumfries and Galloway peninsula. I could see what he meant.

I wasn't going to sail, but because of the planning complexities, a short hop along the coast seemed better than none, readying myself for the passage back to England. We selected Ross Bay as a destination, since it would be sheltered, and not too far inland, thus avoiding too much in-and-out distance. Ross Bay is a little dink in the coastline, near the exit to the Solway Firth from Kirkcudbright, somewhere you are unlikely to visit, but people do.

"I'm not too familiar with Ross Bay," said Alistair. "But you'd be better to get going soon, to avoid the incoming storm."

Thus, abandoning my rest day, and taking up Alistair's excellent advice and huge generosity, we set off on the ninety-minute drive back to Betty.

The Isle of Whithorn is no longer an isle, as it happens, though maps show it as such up until the 1820s. The causeway has become a main street, probably because the harbour was used for trade. In the early 1800s, the carriage of goods was often referred to as the "packet trade", since mail and small high value items were common items for carriage. The term expanded to refer to any cargo including people, with a suffix to detail the type of ship. Hence the pub on the Isle, named the "Steam Packet", refers to a trade ship from a couple of centuries ago, which plied its way between the Isle, and Liverpool perhaps.

I had passed Burrowhead the previous afternoon and coincidentally, the next day was Burrow's Day, being 7th July. The day is a Leeds Rhino's nominated event, to thank Rob for his achievements over the years. Rob Burrows loyally played for the rugby league club for 16 years up to 2017, and was part of the winning team in eight championship finals, despite being the smallest player in the super league. He was diagnosed with Motor Neurone Disease in 2019, and had continued to work tirelessly to raise funds and awareness. In 2023, the city established its first marathon run, in his honour. I felt quite humbled by his achievements, and realised my own fundraising efforts, though large in my world, were tiny in comparison to the likes of Rob. Sadly, he died in 2024.

Heading out from the harbour towards rougher seas, I remembered feeling quite anxious, although the conditions in front of me did not look too bad. Clearly the memories of the day before were still haunting me. Nevertheless, on I went, bumping out towards Ross Bay in speedy style, making it to my destination in a couple of hours – "Quick, yeah," I said to myself.

It took almost as long to find a suitable parking spot. I first pulled up on the north side of the bay. There were those weird tuffs of turf, like at Applecross, but these had a few sharp rocks scattered amongst them, hence not quite so luxurious. The tide was in, so the gaps between the grass were filled with water, meaning that a misstep sent me off balance and half falling into the sea.

The arrangement was not ideal at all, so I picked my way across a soggy and pitted overgrown field, under wire and over fence to some kind of scrapyard.

"Do you have any suggestions about where to park my dinghy round here?" I asked.

"Not really," came the reply.

"What about by that shed over there?"

"I wouldn't park there," he said. "The farmer gets very angry if people use his slipway."

Feeling slightly exasperated, I asked, "Do you have any other suggestions?"

"Some of the fishing boats park over there," he said, pointing to the other side of the bay.

"Ah, thanks. I hadn't spotted them," I said. "I'll give that a try."

Retracing my steps across the obstacle course to Betty, who was still flapping vigorously in the wind, I released her from the grassy mounds, and sailed over to the moored boats.

After untangling the centre board from mooring chains, I made landfall for the second time. The surface was definitely less weird, but again consisted of long wild grass, though with many fewer crevasses. This time I could smoothly drag Betty as far away from the water's edge as needed. She would also be sheltered from the southerly storm that was arriving in a few hours, so should be protected for the night.

Excited by the nature-soaked stopping spot, I took a David Attenborough style video. The clip revealed a lesser-rigged white laser, nesting in the marshland, as the camera approached through the parting greenery, to a backdrop of pausing, weighty commentary. We were full of contentment, believing this could be our last stopping point in Scotland. (It wasn't.)

I managed to beg a lift to Kirkcudbright from real visitors to the bay, who were staying in cottages next to the grumpy farmer's land. They had come up from Liverpool for a short break and were enjoying the bad weather. When passing the farmer's boat ramp, I could see that there were indeed notices prohibiting use without permission. I wondered what population flood was being prevented from accessing such a remote strip, but I guessed it was his space to defend.

Cat kindly picked me up after her GP surgery finished at five. I was pleased to spare my impromptu hosts an extra journey, given their enormous charity thus far. It also gave me a chance to enjoy a statutory cappuccino and carrot cake in town, whilst the weather was deteriorating outside.

Kirkcudbright is pronounced Kur-coo-brie, which took me a while to learn, since the letters bear little phonetic relationship to the sound – a Scottish Gaelic connection. It is a delightful town, straddling the mouth of the river Dee, which is both far enough away from main routes to feel peaceful, but close enough to be accessible. The town has fishing traditions, but has moved on to be an attractive destination in itself, hosting many summer festivals, a safe anchorage for yachts, and boasting a reputation of being an "Artist's town". The buildings reflected the vibrancy, being well cared for, and often painted in varying but respectful colours, giving the streetscape a lift, despite the dull skies. Something of a contrast to the homogenous grey of the east coast.

We spent a lovely evening chatting and sharing stories of family, friends, the NHS and medicine.

Alistair also showed me some of his hobby work, exploring astrophotography. I had heard of amateur astronomers discovering unspotted planets, but this was something quite different. Being a chemical engineer by background, Alistair had brought his skills to bear in capturing photographs of distant nebulae, derived from varying spectral gas emissions, light years away. I think I have got that about right.

The resultant pictures were similar to those you might see on screen savers, with multicoloured splotches and swirls, on a dark background, dotted with pin-like white stars. What seemed incredible to me, was to stand next to someone who had found a way to capture images of something unimaginably far away, yet using items that could be purchased in an earthly shop. To be in a sitting room and stare at a domestic image from far into space, felt other worldly. Mind bending, in fact. I am sure that in centuries gone by, such things would have been considered heretical. Now they were normal. I was impressed.

* * *

Day 68, Friday 7th July

To Balcary Bay

START	15.00, Ross Bay
WIND	S, 8–12mph. Nil, then E 5–10mph
WEATHER	Cloudy, 14–16°C. Dry
TIDE	Against me 2.5mph from 15.00
SEA STATE	Moderate to slight
HAZARDS	Opposing tide and no wind
FINISH	Balcary Bay, 21.30
DISTANCE	12 miles
SAILING HOURS	6½ hours

Today was to be a day off. No wait. Where was my day off?

Having spent ages planning, I eventually decided to take an extra hop along the coast, estimating the residual wind from the storm would propel me over the opposing tide. The fact that the Kirkcudbright Ranges were quiet for today, tipped the no-go, go balance, meaning I could duck under the firing schedule. They were back in action the following day.

Things started well with a super easy launch, straight off the grass and into the sea since the tide was in, even managing to keep my feet dry. I headed out across Kirkcudbright Bay on a comfortable fetch. I could see a yacht tacking out towards me, a rare sight in the last few weeks, and I wondered where it was going.

As arranged, Radio Cumbria called, for an on-the-water interview, aiming to give a more authentic feel to the conversation. Whilst I was chatting away, I was becoming increasingly worried about the declining breeze. The waters were turbulent from the storm residue and turned tide, and I was being pushed ever closer to the nearby cliffs. I even fished the paddle out whilst we were talking, to reduce the risk of being smashed onto the rocks whilst on air. That would have been embarrassing, and a little too realistic for my liking. I finished the interview by saying slightly desperately, "I just need more wind."

And then the wind disappeared altogether.

"This is ridiculous," I thought. "Fifty miles per hour of wind last night, and now nothing."

Paddling was double slow because of the tide, but I spotted a buoy and gratefully tied up, so that I could consider my options.

"Oh bugger," I said out loud.

It was warm and pleasant and still fairly early. But there was no way I could make it the next ten miles in these conditions.

I rang for some advice.

"Thanks, Alistair, for picking up. It looks like my plans have all gone wrong, and right now I really don't know what to do."

We talked about possible beaches further up the coast, that might be accessible on foot, like Mullock Bay or Port Mary. Neither of them sounded very suitable. Hopefully the shore break would not be too vicious, and I could find my way to a road. It was not looking promising. As ever, I didn't feel I could go back.

"Oh, wait a sec, Alistair. A yacht has turned up."

I hastily said my goodbyes to Alistair, as I was waving my hellos to the nearby yacht. It was the one I had seen earlier.

"Would you like a tow?" was shouted across the water.

"Yes please," I replied, a little too enthusiastically. But what the hell. I was in a fix.

Liz rang from her seat, on number one court at Wimbledon. "Are you OK? You have been stationary for a while."

"Sorry to cut you off, but I'm just grabbing a line from a passing yacht," was my pressured reply.

Mighty relieved to be making sustainable progress again, I had a shouted conversation with the crew. It was a three-generation family, who were taking a day trip along the coast, but progressing more slowly than they might, since a passenger was feeling seasick.

After a couple of hours of this, I was getting a bit restless. It was not the most comfortable arrangement. I was holding onto the rope wrapped around the mast, allowing me to adjust the length as the crafts moved closer and further away, thus giving the effect of elastic.

Like a kid on a long car journey I enquired, "Is it far to go now?" the grown-up equivalent of "are we nearly there?"!

"There is another hour or so of tide to come," shouted the grandad. He sounded like he knew what he was talking about.

It did not look that far and I thought some wind was returning. A beautiful evening was developing with glorious soft light forming over the hills. I wanted to be able to sail if I could, since motorised assistance wasn't really part of the playbook. But should I ignore the advice to my ancient mariner friend?

I didn't mean to, but in my shuffling about, I let go of the rope.

"Do you want us to come back and pick you up?" I could hear.

"Errr. Err," was all I could manage, as I was trying to adjust myself in the bottom of the wobbly boat. By the time I managed to muster an indistinct, "Yes, please. Can you come back?" they were too far away.

I quickly realised that the wind had been more apparent than real, and the tide was still out in full force. The wind was on the nose so even with paddle sailing, I was making virtually no progress. The track from the tracker on screen looked like I was going backwards and forwards along the same line, in other words, making no progress.

I was furious.

"How stupid to let go," I shouted at myself.

Paddle, paddle, paddle, tack.

Paddle, paddle, tack, I went.

Paddle, paddle, paddle, tack, panic.

The glorious fading light now looked threatening, making the silhouetted shoreline appear more ominous when transformed to a monochrome rocky barricade. I was frightened the light would disappear altogether, and Betty would come to a punctured end, all because of my own madness.

"How stupid of me to have let go of the rope," I repeated.

Fear and fury kept me working harder.

Paddle, paddle, tack.

Paddle, paddle, panic

Paddle, shout. Paddle, paddle, paddle, tack.

I seemed to be making some progress, but it was unbearably slow. It was past nine o'clock. Time was against me, and on my side, all at once. Each passing minute brought longer shadows, and thinning visibility, and at the same time, a fraction less tide. I had to keep fighting forwards.

Edging round the point, I could make out Balcary Bay in the dim light. Now that I was past the headland, the opposing tide retired its effort, and a gentle evening breeze brushed me in towards the shore.

"At last," I said. "I've made it."

The day was far from over, however.

In front of me was the yacht, parked some way offshore. It seemed to be pointing away from the wind. That seemed odd. I sailed gently past them, waved appreciatively and shouted my thanks, cheerfully wishing them a peaceful evening. Then I slithered to a stop in the underwater mud.

With a lot less sparkle in my voice, I cautiously announced an awkward reality. "Ah! They have run aground in the mud. And so have I."

That also explained the funny symbol on the Ordnance Survey map, that Alistair and I had been puzzling over in the morning. The bay was full of acres of slippery sludge.

I stepped out of the boat and disappeared up to my knees in slime. This was going to be difficult.

My new fears, in ascending order of importance, included the following:

Losing a boot in the gloop

Falling over and getting covered in grime

Getting sucked into the muck

Being trapped in the mire with a rising tide and coming to a sticky end, like the cockle pickers of Morecambe Bay, in 2004

I would need to procced with caution. I squelched around Betty, trying one form of propulsion, and then another, soon arriving at a relatively safe method of movement. Instead of standing and pulling Betty, it was best to lean and push, like driving a surfboard through reluctant waves. That way, I didn't disappear into the mud quite so much. I headed over to the nearest solid strip of shore. Then, Alistair called.

I wasn't expecting Alastair to come down to help, so was delighted to hear his cheery voice. "Whereabouts are you?" he said.

"I'm down by the water's edge. I'm nearly at the rocks," I replied.

These rocks were treble difficult. Not only were they unrelenting in their layout, they were usually dressed with a layer of slippery seaweed, and many were covered by a dense coating of barnacles, making something akin to '0' grade grinding paper. I was worried about the risk of falling, and was concerned for Betty's bottom.

It was already past 10.30 at night. With Alistair's inestimable assistance, we managed to carry, roll, shuffle Betty and all her bits, to a safe spot above the high-water mark. And then walk in the dark, back down a private driveway, owned by a crazy looking house on the corner, to where the car was parked.

Despite all this landing nonsense (the worst spot of the trip I figured), it had been the most gorgeous sunset, with the sky covered in sweeps of crimson and grey, touching elegant outlines of hills in the distance. My own foolishness stood aside Alistair's extraordinary helpfulness, without which I am sure I could not have managed. What an absurd set of contrasts.

We got back to the house at 11.30pm, and finally made it to bed at nearly one in the morning. Notwithstanding all the delays, Alistair had suggested we leave at eight in the morning, in order to catch as much bay water as possible. Smart thinking.

Or maybe it was time for me to move on!!

CHAPTER 16

Back to England with a splash

Day 69, Saturday 8th July

To Whitehaven

START	08.55, Balcary Bay
WIND	SE, veering to SW, 12–22mph
WEATHER	Cloudy, some sun, 17–22°C. Dry
TIDE	Across me, till 13.00, max 2.7mph
SEA STATE	Slight to moderate
HAZARDS	Sandbanks in middle of the Firth
FINISH	Whitehaven, 13.30
DISTANCE	17 miles
SAILING HOURS	4½ hours

The departure / disposal plan, worked a treat. Cat came down to lend a hand as well, which was hugely appreciated since it was such uncomfortable terrain. The water was being sucked out of the bay with the falling tide, as we stumbled across rocks, hurriedly carrying all the gear down to the water's edge. Our earlyish departure meant that I was spared a muddy exit. My yacht friends from the night before had already left.

It was sad to say farewell, since I had felt so welcomed and incredibly supported. Another home away from home, which was such joy to experience. The generosity of others, and the desire to support a fellow traveller, never ceased to amaze me. I am sure my departure had left Alistair and Cat with a less cluttered schedule. I hoped my stay had been of some pleasure for them as well, a dot on the horizon of memories perhaps. Alistair and Cat continued to be loyal online followers for the remainder of the journey.

And then I was gone.

The Solway Firth, for those who do not know, like the Thames Estuary, is full of sand. In fact, much of the west coast of England down to Wales, is entreated with acres and acres of coastal sand. Nautical maps go blank around these parts, since surveying will only tell a temporary picture of the forever shifting banks. It all felt quite new to me.

I passed a wind farm in the middle, and could see water colour changes ahead, with shorter smaller waves. That spelt 'shallow water' to me. I slowed down in case of a touch down, and sure enough, Betty's centre board brushed the bottom. It felt really odd to be nearly ten miles from land, and yet able to step out, and stand up in the middle of the sea (if I should want to).

And then further on, a deeper channel meant faster flow against the wind, so the waves picked up in an angry chop. I had known the channel was forthcoming and anticipated the change. I was now becoming familiar with the mood of the sea, so simply sailed on through, keeping focussed on staying in control.

Aided by a huge lift of 60 degrees as the wind veered to the south-west, I managed to make Workington. However, I did manage to miss the harbour entrance since it was too obvious, and went back to find my way in.

Edging along below dark slimy walls, I turned the corner into the domain of the Vanguard Sailing Club. There was a crescent-shaped mooring zone, mostly occupied by yachts, parked on a steep shelf of gooey mud. More mud, and more sticky mud, this time. But I didn't care. There was a ramp ahead of me, some grass, and I WAS BACK IN ENGLAND!!!!!!

Oh, my goodness. That was 43 sailing days to travel round Scotland. Brandon Pearce had taken 44 days on a paddle board, so at least I could say I was quicker (just). It felt quite unbelievable. Scotland is said to be a third of the coastline of mainland GB, so a major chunk of the distance, and a huge tick on the journey travel log.

Now, I was definitely going to take a day off.

Gowan, and then Stuart, came over to say hello. They were brothers who seemed to spend a good deal of time not doing very much, down at the sailing club. They phoned Simon the commodore, who rumbled up on his motorbike to join in the chatter, and offer advice. I wanted to check on boat security arrangements, given there was a public footpath running past the club. After a good deal of 'um-ing' and 'ah-ing,' we decided it was OK. Gowan and Stuart came back on Monday to lend a hand with launching, offering a coffee from the micro kitchen in the clubhouse. Very considerate, I thought, and much appreciated.

Simon told me that the club had been formed by the steelworks, wanting to provide recreational opportunities for workers, as was a tradition from the last century. With the closure of the plant, ownership had moved to the local council, and then on to private members. Maybe because of its beginnings, the club felt like it lacked some of the vigour of other venues - too much parking and not enough sailing perhaps - despite its excellent location on the edge of town, with easy access to plenty of safe sailing.

Maryport looked like a nice spot for a day off, and it was easily accessible by train. Any excuse to experience another piece of endearing coastal trundle track should be taken, in my view. I followed my own advice.

Before that, I took a stroll around Workington. I popped into Trespass to buy another walking top, since the zip had failed on my current version, just as I landed - fortunate timing, once again. The top was invaluable in keeping me dry from rain or spray, but not too hot.

The town was not well blessed by the weather, and, it looked tired and slightly downtrodden, a reflection of its industrial history.

Workington tells the oft familiar tale of industrial ascendancy, and later decline. Coal was an initial export trade with about

37 pits operating in the area in 1800. Local availability of low phosphorous content iron ore, and limestone, made an ideal setting for steel production. The Mossbay works only closed their doors for rail production, in 2006, having led a proud 129-year history, exporting track around the globe. "World leader in rail technology" plaques still hung in the plant as the doors shut, and there was no suggestion that this was a faded accolade. However, closure of the Bessemer converter blast furnaces in 1974 had sounded a death knell, since the costs of transporting steel significantly increased.

The Hatfield rail disaster in 2000 called for a major increase in rail production, in order to replace faulty line, thus providing a temporary reprieve for Mossbay. Corus, the owning company, were keen to move rail manufacture to Scunthorpe, nearer to steel production, then on to France or perhaps Poland, thus sadly sealing the demise of the Workington plant.

Having said that, industrial transition has been taking place over the last 50 years or more, meaning that slag heaps have been flattened, new industries have been introduced, and wind farms have replaced coal for energy production. The loss of what was, still feels painful, and casts a shadow over the town.

By contrast, there was more of a buzz in Maryport. This is the Maryport that everyone thinks of when you say the name, not the one hanging off the end of the Rhin of Galloway, from whence I had travelled. More compact and three dimensional, there was an easy view of the port from the High Street, which looked pleasant and appealing, as opposed to tangled and industrial. What's more there was a carnival going on.

"Is there a dress code for the carnival?" I asked at reception in my hotel.

"No, nothing really," came the reply. The receptionist's daughter had just popped in to say 'hi' before joining the revellers.

I too went out to soak up the vibe in the warm summer's evening. Squeezing into a bar for a beer, I found there were plenty of young people enjoying the occasion. Whilst there was a lack of layered theme, there was definitely a dress code – "not quite enough" was the format for the ladies, and short shaven head above the ears, with a mop of hair on top, for the gents. My attempts to fit in had a limited lifespan, so I cut my losses and went to bed, leaving the locals to shout and scream their way into the night.

Sunday 9th July

The sun was out, the skies clear and winds light, making perfect conditions for a rest day.

Emotionally, it felt like the descent part of a cycle ride, whereby everything is easy, joyous, effortless and relaxed, whilst relishing the success of a recent climb.

After a typical day-off morning, of thank you cards, video editing and planning, I went to explore the town.

Maryport was founded in 1749 by Humphrey Senhouse, who affectionately named the port after his wife, Mary. Echoing the success of the Lowther family in Whitehaven, the town moved into coal mining and export.

The first shipyard was built in 1765, sparked by the completion of the railway to Carlisle, and a local source of iron ore (which had also helped Workington). From 1839, John Peat started launching boats broadside into the water, as opposed to the traditional bow first approach. This was necessary because of the narrowness of the non-natural harbour, and a desire to construct larger vessels. John Peat was an early global adopter of this practice, signalling a desire for innovation. By 1916, a total of 280 ships had been built in Maryport, a measure of the industrial vigour of the town.

Tourism has become a key trade for the town. This was a significant recovery from the early parts of the 20th century, when 57% of men were unemployed, following the collapse of previously buoyant industries. What a terrible time that must have been.

Regeneration seemed to have worked, since my afternoon of wanderings was full and pleasant, and there were plenty of others doing the same. I watched cadets learn how to sail their toppers in the harbour, strolled around the sunny streets and popped into the aquarium to check out the goings on. Inside, I learnt about the life cycle of jellyfish, the process of breeding lobsters, and I caught a glimpse of flat fish swimming around a large tank – they just don't look right. It works for them though, since apparently Plaice can live as long as 50 years.

Let's not forget, the Romans had been in the area before. To the north of the town, a hillfort was excavated in 2013. The fort was built during Emperor Hadrian's time in 122 AD. Its purpose was to form a chain of defences, protecting Hadrian's wall from being outflanked from the sea.

Excavation was followed by the establishment of a museum. This was another fine feature on the tourism trail, with beautiful views from its hilltop location, and interesting, if sometimes rather slow videos, as part of the displays inside.

Having been regenerated myself, and had my fill of tourism, it was time to head off in the morning, on my own personalised tour down the Cumbrian coast.

* * *

Day 70, Monday 10th July

To St Bees

START	09.45, Workington
WIND	S, 16–23mph. Very strong later
WEATHER	Cloud then rain, 18–16°C. Dry
TIDE	1.1mph in my favour till 16.00
SEA STATE	Moderate
HAZARDS	Headwind. Rain
FINISH	St Bees, 13.45
DISTANCE	12 miles
SAILING HOURS	4 hours

Today was to be a day of drama, but in an entirely unexpected way.

After a monster breakfast, a train back to Workington, and a helping hand from Gowan and Stuart, I was away by 09.45 - not bad for me.

I was hoping for strong tides to push me round the headland of St Bees, but my flow friend didn't turn up. Instead, the sailing proved to be an increasingly weary affair, culminating in getting stuck in irons a couple of times. Then my day bag was washed overboard, as a wave ran along the boat. Somehow it had become unclipped. It took three attempts to get it back, giving me a sizeable dose of panic in the process.

I lost concentration for a moment and fell out. Shortly afterwards a huge dolphin leapt out of the water in front of me, drawing a large and showy arc in an aquarium style display. In my frantic attempt to grab some footage for the next leap, I fell out again.

"I'm not enjoying this," I said to myself. So, I went in to the beach for a rest and didn't go out again. It was the right decision despite the miserly mileage, since the wind just built and built through the afternoon, heading well into the red zone.

The beach was dotted with holidaymaking youngsters, listlessly looking for something to do. A small amount of conversation was enough to engage a large audience of youthful helpers, who speedily carried Betty up the beach, up the ramp and onto the grass – a perfect landing spot, safe from the waves and sheltered enough from the wind by the low sea wall.

There were camping facilities (no thanks), a caravan park, and a hotel (yes please), so I showered and headed off to Whitehaven on the same coastal train line as the day before. To make extra super sure of Betty's safety, I turned her nose to the wind, since it was getting really blowy.

In Whitehaven, I had a bite to eat at Wetherspoons, a stop off at Morrisons for supplies. I had a quick scout around the harbour and marina, which definitely looked more substantial than its Workington neighbour.

Interestingly, Whitehaven was the largest trading port second to London in the 1700s. Wealth then grew from coal, and later chemical industries. However, with all the industrial change, it is now Sellafield which has become the largest local employer.

Yes, Sellafield. I would pass it soon, so will mention it here as part of the nuclear update.

Sellafield is Europe's largest nuclear site, which includes more than 1000 buildings, and currently employs about 10,000 people. Its origins go back to the 1950s. It was the first to generate electricity on a commercial scale. In 1957 It was also the location of one of the world's worst nuclear incidents at the time, known as the Windscale fire – a uranium fuel rod ignited, and spread radioactive material around the environment.

After nearly 50 years, the plant ceased energy generation in 2003, and is instead focussed on fuel reprocessing and storage, with a project plan extending all the way to 2120. Hence more reliable as an industry than coal, one could argue – from an employment perspective at least.

Stepping off the train at St Bees, I felt relaxed and contented, full of food, and a dash of beer. I sauntered back to my hotel, glad not to be out on the water in the howling gale that was crashing in from the sea.

"I'll make one last check on Betty before bed," I thought.

I walked towards the sea to check where she was parked.

But Betty was gone.

I froze. The chill of the wind suddenly blew straight through me, and my brain slowed to a near stop, as if injected with fog.

"What? This can't be," I whispered to myself. Staring helplessly around at the smooth green empty grass, I could see no sign of her. I looked again as if hoping that Betty would suddenly reappear. There was still nothing.

"Could Betty have done a flier and blown away?" Disbelieving my own suggestion, I went up the slope to a downwind shelter, and found a mother sitting with her son and his bicycle.

"I've lost my dinghy …er, my sailing boat. You haven't seen, er …. any bits of boat or, …sail maybe, flying past, have you?" I asked.

A considerate and considered, "No, sorry," was returned in reply.

I went to the hotel to ask for help. A couple of gents were relaxing in the foyer. They sounded concerned by my loss, but after a few seconds started to enquire about the circumnavigation.

"I'm sorry, guys, I'd love to tell you about it, but I can't really think straight at the moment." They got the message.

I rang the Belfast coastguard, the appointed calling station for this part of the journey.

"Oh yes. You rang this morning, didn't you? The guy who's been sailing round the UK in his Laser."

"Yes, that's right."

Then, "No, sorry. We haven't heard anything, but will let you know if we do."

The receptionist lady was super helpful and found the number for the local police station and the RNLI building. There was no reply from the RNLI.

"Do you think anyone from the caravan park might have come and stolen it?" I asked.

"I don't know," she said. "I would think it's unlikely though."

The cogs of thinking were starting to operate in my head, now that the sudden shock had subsided. But the whirring was not producing many plausible explanations, or actions. Panic and desperation had taken a firm grip.

"This could be the end of the trip," I said, still speaking to the receptionist, because she might listen. "It's taken me months to pull all the kit together. If I haven't got a boat, maybe I will have to come back and finish off the trip next year."

She nodded softly and said nothing. Nothing could be said. I looked down and turned away.

I called the police who said, "Ring back in the morning if you are sure it's stolen." I couldn't be sure that a crime had been committed, but I was hoping for something a bit more sympathetic, given the level of personal crisis I was feeling.

She must have been stolen, I concluded. If someone had moved her, surely, they would have contacted me. My phone number was written on the hull, and so was the website, and they would have noticed that, surely. No one had called or emailed.

I was running out of options. I was thinking I might have to bite the bullet and go to bed. However, still buzzing from a feverish tangle of tension, huge confusion and despair, I was sure I wouldn't sleep. Instead, I went out into the wet gale, to see if I could find out who had taken my beloved Betty.

I walked towards the caravan park to have a prowl around, and see if I could find a stolen boat hanging about in full view. It seemed unlikely that a thief would leave their stolen goods lying about in full view, but what else was there to do? I went across the boat parking spot on the grass, receiving a twinge of helplessness as I passed the empty space. I strolled round the side of the RNLI building, in a dejected state.

"What!!!"

There was Betty.

She was all neatly parked up, still upside down as she should be, next to the matching cream-coloured walls of the building. All the foils etc were still locked to the foot strap.

What a monstrous relief.

But then I noticed a nasty white gel coat coloured toxic trail, marking the route over the paved forecourt. Looking more closely in the evening light, there was a hideous gash in her protective finish, exposing fibreglass, stretching over an area equivalent to the centre plate housing. And right next to that was my phone number written in large black letters.

I was furious. Incandescent with rage. All the tension of the last two hours, suddenly morphed into anger. I was staring at a whole array of profound stupidities inflicted on my innocent boat. I was in no mood to offer my would-be helper any sympathies.

"Who did this to Betty?" I shouted. Such were my profanities that I was even alarming myself, let alone any potential witness. In a lull of fury, I was grateful for the isolation of the evening, and the tempest muffling my unpleasant outburst.

Well-meaning and wise is a fine thing, but this was something else. My life depended on Betty, day after day, mile after mile on the open sea. I was very well aware that someone MIGHT come and get me if I got into trouble five miles offshore, and they MIGHT be quick enough to stop me drowning, but my very best chance of survival was with Betty. So, a nautical novice satisfying their wind-swept concern at the potential expense of my safety, did not land well.

Struggling to calm down, I rang Liz for some solace. She provided soothing words and practical sensibilities.

I also called Paul from Papercourt, for advice about the fibreglass exposure. "Not to worry," he said. "You could sail the rest of the journey like that if needs be. But why not stick some tape on it if you can."

That made one less thing to shout about.

At last, I managed to get to bed and did eventually fall asleep, thank goodness.

I never did find out who had moved Betty.

* * *

Day 71, Tuesday 11th July

To Barrow-in-Furness

START	11.45, St Bees
WIND	WSW 14–20mph, veering more W
WEATHER	Cloudy, some sun, 14–16°C. Dry
TIDE	With me after 10.00, max 0.6mph
SEA STATE	Moderate
HAZARDS	Accuracy of the wind forecast
FINISH	Barrow-in-Furness, 17.30
DISTANCE	31 miles
SAILING HOURS	6 hours

After all the tension of the evening before, this was a relatively smooth day with more than 30 miles covered.

A minor mishap or two occurred when setting off. Launching through the waves, I had frequently stuffed my gloves between buoyancy aid and splash jacket, which had worked fine up until now. Unfortunately, when out beyond the shore break, I realised that my gloves had gone. Not only that, but my pink day bag was hanging perilously over the edge of the boat, washed out by a wave again, but still clinging on with a last desperate clip. I hauled it back in, but that was a warning shot to be careful.

"Losing things tends to come in batches of three," I thought, "so there is trouble to come."

But not yet.

The other happening of the day was running out of sea near Barrow.

On a map, there is a large expanse of blue, feeding into the Northern section of the Walney Channel, that separates the Island from the mainland of Barrow-in-Furness. I had checked the clearance under the Jubilee Bridge (between Walney Island and the mainland) but had failed to register the clearance over the sand, which was hiding under its water blanket.

Having successfully negotiated rough seas over the perimeter of Duddon Sands (which fills the gap between the Lake District and Barrow), I was enjoying a stretch of flat sailing on a reach, when the sea ran out. In front of me was sand, more sand and yet more sand.

I stepped out into warm water. It was reminiscent of a summer's day beach afternoon, waiting for the tide to come and do battle with your sturdy sandcastle. Usually, the gently sploshing waves would be pool temperature, inviting you to stand your ground to the very last, hoping that on this special occasion, your construction would win. It never did.

I decided to stand my ground as well, having rejected the option of sailing round to the south channel. Instead, I booked accommodation whilst parked on my temporary beach, and then edged Betty over the yellow landscape, as the waters slowly rose for the afternoon.

Having floated off the sand, and sailed down to Barrow, I plumped for a handy landing spot on the north side of the bridge on the mainland, near an industrial looking ramp. Stepping off the boat and into the water, I discovered that it was Barrow Sailing Club, another venue I had missed on my Google preparatory circumnavigation. Not only that, but club member after club member kept appearing to lend a hand.

Gareth found a trolley and a parking spot. And when I mentioned my fright of last night, he whizzed Betty over and set about providing a temporary repair. Ash arrived, asking lots of questions and providing a healthy supply of chat, nautical stories and navigational advice, topped off with a jaunty festival hat.

Ash gave me a lift to my accommodation.

Driving out from the club, without breaking conversational stride, he said, "My wife died at the wheel with her grandson in the car. It were about a year ago. The car crashed into a wall, but luckily my grandson wasn't hurt."

"I'm really sorry to hear about that," was my equally understated reply.

"That is a hell of a lot of life events in a couple of sentences," I thought to myself.

And that was that. Conversation simply carried on as if nothing much of importance had been said.

CHAPTER 16

Day 72, Wednesday 12th July

To Blackpool

START	13.00, Barrow
WIND	W, 20–28mph, more like 35mph
WEATHER	Cloudy, 15–18°C
TIDE	Exiting the bay, max 1mph, till 14.00
SEA STATE	Moderate to rough
HAZARDS	Too much wind. Bay sands. Shore break
FINISH	Blackpool, 17.00
DISTANCE	22 miles
SAILING HOURS	3¾ hours. (20 mins stop at Piel Island)

The forecast was looking borderline. I went back to Barrow Sailing Club to join a gathering of folk including the inestimable Ash. He filled me in on tides, and hazards, whilst pouring over a wall chart in the clubhouse.

With Ash and team all lending a hand, we put in a reef by winding the sail once round the mast. I had tried to do this in East Anglia though it had simply unwound during the day, but the group effort this time looked more convincing. I hoped it would hold.

I spent a good deal of time procrastinating about whether to go, but having dithered for long enough, I decided to head out. A small group cheered me off, laughing every step of the way.

The first stretch along the Piel Channel to the south of Barrow was straightforward, being fast and flat, tonking along at a fine nine miles per hour. I took Ash's advice to stop on Piel Island, just before Morecambe Bay, in order to review whether to proceed. The Barrow boys had predicted that the 'King of Piel Island' might appear. Sure enough, whilst sitting on Betty to protect her from blowing away, munching my lunch, a man came across the qooey surface to greet me.

"You must be Andrew," he said.

"You must be the King of Piel Island," I replied, happy to engage in the Guess Who game.

Aaron had not long taken up the manager position at the tiny island's pub, called the Ship Inn, thus being anointed with this metaphorical crown. Flattered by the effectiveness of local sailing networks, and Aaron's well-wishing for the day, I gathered sufficient encouragement to send me onwards.

It was probably a bad idea, but in my defence, it is really hard to turn back.

Beyond the protection of Walney Island, the wind really picked up, and so did the sea. I soon fell out, knocked over by a gust. I was pretty sure that the mast touched the ground, which turned my anxiety up another notch or two. Murky brown waters crashed around me. The mouth of Morecambe Bay loomed large to the east, wide open and ready to swallow me up. If I were blown into the dreaded bay, there was a risk that sandbanks would rise up beneath me, to sharpen the waves and throw me out of the boat again. That could lead to mast breaking consequences. If this happened close to the shore, at least I would be washed into safety. Out at sea, as I was, it could put my life in danger.

I headed out into the teeth of the gale to find some deeper water. It was taking all my effort to stay in control.

"I'm glad we managed to put a reef in the sail," I said to myself.

And then another thought. It was a vain attempt to reassure myself that being out in a force 7 howler was an OK plan. "It's only nine miles to go."

This thought was soon followed by an awkward realisation that I had made this self-soothing gesture before – on day one no less. And that hadn't ended too well.

On I struggled. I could now see Blackpool Tower more clearly, and the thin strip of seafront which constituted the end of Morecambe Bay. That was some sort of relief. The wind was not playing nicely, and kept hounding the sea and its tiny stupid sailor.

My Tupperware box managed to fall out the back. Being very attached to my Tupperware, I went back to retrieve it, and managed to do so with one man overboard shot – well done me.

Then I fell out again.

This time it was a wave. The waves were getting bigger and less pretty, still soaked with sand, making it look like dirty dishwater, rather than a marine blue miracle. I had mistimed manoeuvres between incoming waves. Instead of crossing before or after the crest, the wave broke onto the boat and knocked me out. Stick had talked about waves breaking on his head whilst he was sailing round the UK. That sounded remarkable a few weeks ago. Then it happened to me.

Even though I could see Blackpool, I was not enjoying the ride.

At last, I was next to the tower, my intended destination. Tired and frightened by the unrelenting fury of Neptune, I could see the sanctuary of land, but had little idea of how to reach it safely. I was being thrown about in an endless battery of six-foot waves. Furthermore, I wanted to hold position between two piers, since I had a clear preference for being jettisoned headlong on to the sand, as opposed to wrapped around an iron pillar, of which there were many to hand.

"I'll be lucky if I can get in without breaking something," I said to myself, referring to both Betty and myself.

It was time to try out some of those techniques Liz and I had researched, after my calamitous day one. The idea was to release the main sheet, let the sail blow forwards in line with the boat, and use the combination of wind drag on the mast, and the power of the waves to wash me to shore in a controlled way.

It didn't work.

Apologies to Betty for my incompetence. The journey from sitting on Betty, to standing on the beach, involved quite a bit of swimming and boat chasing, in what was best described as a 'messy landing'. Fortunately, when I capsized in front of the RNLI building, everyone noticed, so I made it to the Manchester Evening News, as well as the shore. Betty nearly reached the beach before me, but in line with a great relationship, I think we will call it a draw.

I had thought Betty had arrived unscathed, since her mast was pointing out to sea, avoiding the classic masthead on the sea floor / boat / wave sandwich, with inevitable broken bits consequences. I allowed myself a few quiet moments of celebration. Sadly, I learnt later that all was not well.

Having pulled Betty and myself out of the surf, the local lifeguard, and then the local coastguard turned up, slightly berating me for not letting Holyhead coastguard know about my passage for the day. I did try and mitigate my crime by sharing that I had contacted Belfast Coastguard that morning, not realising that the responsibility had switched from one to the other, as I crossed Morecambe Bay. They weren't impressed, and went off to tell their seniors.

About 45 minutes later, having derigged and moved the boat most of the way up to the ramp over the breakwater (which was my intended destination, I would like to assure you), the RNLI turned up. A smart looking yellow booted brigade took a break from their "Saving lives at sea" shoot, to come and lend a boat-moving set of hands. This was very welcome indeed since I had had quite enough of the sea by that stage. To top that off, Betty was allowed to have a restful and secure night in the very smart RNLI shed.

However, before that, there was a problem.

"I have studied marine engineering, and once a steel tube is bent, it's permanently weakened. You ought to get that replaced." Thus spoke one of the RNLI team, as we looked along the nicely curved length of my lower mast section, as it lay peacefully resting on the mansion floor. Earlier that day, it had been straight.

Still hoping I had got away with it, I quietly mused, "I wonder how that happened?" And then, with a half sigh, "But yeah, I ought to get that replaced." The idea of a fatal fracture out at sea did not sound appealing, and wasn't a risk worth taking. The main problem was "How?"

Summoned to the nice smart upstairs office, I was confronted by the building commander and assembled crew, dotted around a nice smart table. They had now finished their nice smart filming, and were clearly done with saving lives at sea.

"How are you going to get a fix for your mast?" asked the commander.

"I don't know really. I haven't had a chance to work it out yet."

"How long do you think it will take?"

Resisting the urge to go for a straightforward "don't know", I tried to fill in some gaps. "If I order one tomorrow, I would guess it would not arrive till after the weekend, but that could be pessimistic I suppose."

"You see, this is a very busy station and if there is a shout, we need to get the vehicles out on to the water very quickly."

I wouldn't want one of those very smart and very large tractors, which have not so much as a scratch on them, running over my cute little beaten-up Betty.

Someone else chipped in, "We could move the boat to the back of the building for now."

"Thank goodness," I thought. "At least someone is a little on my side. This is feeling less like a sea rescue and more like a headmaster's office."

The commander went on, "Where were you planning to store your boat for tonight anyway?"

"I wasn't too sure, to be honest. I was heading for the tower because I knew there was a ramp over the breakwater. It's been lovely to have the support from you guys, though."

I wasn't sure that is what he wanted to hear.

"Do you think that is enough planning?" he said. He was clearly thinking about the irresponsible hooligans who paddle out to sea on a board, in an offshore breeze with no means of communication or buoyancy aid. I was in danger of being thrown into the same basket. I had a reputation to defend.

"Hey look. Today wasn't my finest, but I'm now about three quarters of the way round the whole of the UK, which is several months of sailing. And one thing I have learnt is that things just work out. And they do."

"OK. Let's make some enquiries. Let's meet again in the morning."

That was the end of the meeting. Now I felt saved. It did feel odd to have arrived in one of my most perilous states, and to be treated by my would-be rescuers as a nuisance item of debris, not up to the cosmetic mark of all the fine equipment. But, I was their guest, and grateful for the free storage space, and, they did indeed have a job to do.

I had some jobs to do as well. The easiest of which was finding a bed for the night.

You would have thought that summer season in a busy holiday destination might create booking pressure. But no. Even though it was gone 8pm, it was no bother to find a cheap, welcoming and easy reach property.

I asked the man squeezed into his reception / office box about this.

"There are a lot of hotels in Blackpool to cater for the tourists, so there is a lot of competition," he said. That seemed simple enough. I was a happy customer.

The seafront, breakwater (RNLI building) and tramway, running the full length of the water's edge from Fleetwood in the north, to Squires Gate in the South, looked smart and well kept, with jaunty decorations. In my mind, Blackpool had its down sides. Sure enough, back from the brightness of the well-resourced boundary, things looked more miserable. Though not as much as I feared. I was getting to like Blackpool.

I rang Liz to think through some options whilst I was chewing over an emergency fish and chips dinner. I rang Ash from Barrow, and he said he would see if he had any contacts at Fleetwood who might be able to loan a mast. He rang back later to say he hadn't been successful. But by that time, Liz the wizard, had suggested borrowing one from Papercourt Sailing Club. That would mean I would get to see Liz in the pickup process, and could sail the spare part back home. Paul, my inestimable techno support crew, said, "I don't think the club boats would miss it for a few weeks."

So that was the plan – go home and collect a spare. The wind looked pretty foul for the next few days, so a train journey would be welcome respite. And with my precious senior railcard, the cost would be cheaper than buying a new bit of boat.

There was a small logistics problem.

"How are you going to get it across London on public transport?" Liz asked. "There is a length restriction of two metres on the underground."

"Hmm. I don't know. Let's see," I replied, thinking, "I'm sure we can find a way." It was a good point, and I did want to test out practicalities for the return journey, so decided to carry the debris home.

Thursday 13th July

Whilst I was sitting on the forecourt outside the RNLI building, mending batten pockets like a fisherman fixing his nets, one of the guys from the night before, came up to me. "We have heard from the boat club at Squires Gate, and they should be able to look after your boat."

"That's brilliant. Thank you so much," I said. "How far is that?"

"It's a couple of miles down the coast."

"OK. I'll just finish mending the sail and then I'll be off, if that's OK? It got damaged in yesterday's landing, but it's nothing too bad."

I managed to beg another boat carrying-down-to-the-beach favour, from my hosts, in exchange for reassurance that the cuckoo would actually leave. I am sure they were relieved. With the reduction in tension from yesterday, we parted on good terms, and I also received a good luck text from the commander. My bent mast didn't cause much trouble either, on my half hour sail down to Squires Gate. The sea had settled overnight so the launching and landing was all without incident.

Tony came down to find me at Blackpool Light Craft Club, a new type of venue, not ticking any of the usual sailing / yacht club boxes. It was a patch of grass surrounded by a large fence, overshadowed by the tram terminus, sharing the plot with a modest two-storey building. It had the necessary bonus of being right next to a long concrete ramp, leading to the beach. There were a few boats parked up, most of which were on the fringes of sailable. Pulling out a prospective trolley from under a dinghy, the metal started to collapse, so we put it back, sharpish. We found another more substantial item and went off down the large expanse of beach, to find Betty.

Once again, I was touched by local responsiveness. Unlike so many others, Tony was not retired. He had dropped everything and come down at a moment's notice to help out.

Mild mannered and softly spoken, Tony was doing his best to look after the boat club, but it sounded like recruiting the assistance of others was proving a challenge.

He also shared his family struggles. There had been an uncomfortable separation and he had taken on the responsibility of looking after his own two young children with his new partner Wendy. They had moved in together and were joined by her children, so there were a lot of challenges – emotional, practical space, and financial. I felt for him, and for the family. I appreciated their huge commitment to the children, a sentiment I have shared many times before in my working life. I was honoured to have his company. He said he was intrigued, and slightly jealous of my luxurious adventure.

In case you were worried, a Laser mast pulls into two, and I was planning to transport the bottom half. However, this was still a substantial aluminium tube. For a full (or ILCA 7) rig which I was using, it is light enough to be carried in one hand, but with the impediment of being nine foot long, about the height of most ceilings. This meant that it was best to carry it parallel to the road when crossing, since walking with the pole straight ahead, would be sufficient to stop both lanes of traffic.

What's more, it rings like an organ pipe on the slightest of impacts, sending a shiver of alarm through anyone watching, myself included. How on earth was I going to squeeze this mighty weapon onto a train, let alone a tram?

Things started badly.

As usual, I was running late and needed to catch a tram to Blackpool North, and then on to Preston. Just as the tram was pulling into the stop, my phone rang. When responding to the call,

I moved, and hit a post with the mast, letting out a loud clang.

"You're not getting in here with that," said the guard, looking down at me disapprovingly. He added, "the tram is too full". He sounded like he had a few other objections up his sleeve. Waiting for another tram to find out what they might be, wasn't going to get me home, so I needed another plan.

I could walk to Blackpool South (it's on a different train line to Blackpool North), and I could still make it across London that evening. According to an earlier reconnaissance trip, the station was likely to be unmanned.

It was.

I wanted to invite some passengers to get on board with the boarding project, so introduced my lump of metal, the problem, plus a bit of unsolicited background, to a lively sounding couple on the platform. They took to the task with more enthusiasm than I had bargained for. Instead of holding the door, or giving safe passage advice, the man simply picked up the baton, and hastily thrust it into the carriage, creating a whole symphony of clonks and dongs on the way. A winced 'thank you' was mixed with a dose of relief that nothing had been broken, and no one concussed. Perhaps I would need to risk assess the passengers more carefully next time.

The ticket inspector did not notice when he came round, since the mast had been slipped under the seats. I did not think it necessary to mention its presence.

Stepping off at Preston was a slow process, gingerly angling the stick in three dimensions. I was trying to avoid touching any part of the carriage, like a "test your hand steadiness" challenge at fetes, where contact between the circular metal handle and the wobbly wire would set off an alarming buzzer.

I had two feet on the platform. There were no alarms ringing, from unwanted metal contact, or from people's faces. That was leg one of the journey completed. Success. I did my best to present a relaxed smile and a casual nod, at least trying to give myself the impression that I knew what I was doing.

Preston is a busy station and it was a busy time of day.

Having learnt from the tram incident, I figured the best mode of carriage was vertical, or so I thought. That way I could avoid a circus clown-type incident, in which a simple rotation through 180 degrees, to look for another platform for instance, could lay waste to a whole carriage load of people. I moved carefully across the concourse.

A lady came up to me in a hurry. Youthful and smartly dressed in Avanti uniform, she looked troubled and touched my arm.

"Excuse me," she said.

"Oh, here we go," I thought. "I'm in for it now."

"Excuse me," she continued in breathy haste. "Could you please put that down. It's just that those cables up there carry 25,000 volts, and I would not want you to come to any harm!"

That came with a double jolt of relief. "Phew," I thought.

Thanking her for her kindness and wise advice, I lowered the mast. Only then did I notice the sticker next to my metal holding hand, saying, 'Caution, conducts electricity. Beware of overhead cables', with one of those alarming Harry Potter scar zigzag diagrams above it.

Watching my saviour fade into the crowd, marching off to her next mission, I wondered, "Was she a conductor by any chance?" (Sorry!!!)

I had some time to kill. I discovered two things from the friendly railway staff. The first is that there is no restriction to items that can be carried, as long as it is not an electric bike, and you can fit it safely on board. That was good advice. The second was that I should reject the 1818 to London because it would be slower. That was bad advice. The one I caught was delayed by three hours having become stuck behind a broken-down Royal Mail train.

When I arrived at Euston it was 12.30am, the gates to the Northern line were closing as I, and a trickle of others, rushed to catch the last trip home. Damn it. I would not get to try out tube jousting after all.

"Now what?" I wondered. "This is gonna be a long night," I said to myself.

I had been keeping Liz abreast of the travel situation, but was getting more of the 'don't wake me up when you get home' types of messages, so a lift wasn't looking too likely.

"A night bus. Yeah, why not try a night bus," I thought. "And get as far south as possible, and then a taxi."

Having got into the groove of this mast on public transport game, I was ready for my next victim. I hovered at the back of the queue, making sure I did not disturb anyone. And then as the red doors were getting close to closing, I lowered my luggage to floor level, bent down as if creeping out of a trench, and slid the mast along the floor, accompanied by a lot of "excuse mes". The bus was very crowded and there was plenty of shuffling, before the driver could shut the doors behind me. He did tut and shake his head, half-heartedly protesting that I "shouldn't be bringing that on a bus". We headed off.

A fellow passenger recognised the piece of tubing, and struck up a sailing conversation. Ben he was called. He had been working in a bar till late. He was full of the joys of the night (and possibly some other things given his level of energy), but it was fun to have a London-based conversation about my coastal journey. He was a Laser sailor as well, and had been brought up in Aldeburgh, Suffolk. I wondered if he knew Colin and Martha whom I had met there, but he didn't. Either way, it all added to the surreal nature of the journey.

In Tooting, I reached the end of the line, and the end of the night bus schedule, so I got out. Tooting is the home of St George's Hospital medical school, where I had trained some 30 years previously, so I had a sense of familiarity. It was two o'clock in the morning, and the streets were deserted. After a couple of taxi rejections, triggered by a casual mention of the outsize luggage, I was very close to leaving the mast as litter in the street. Eventually I landed an Uber XL which could handle the nine-foot monster, by sliding it under the vast array of seats. I was relieved not to be the odious cause of significant Tooting litter, but the price of my good conscience was a large bill. At least I was home at last.

Unfortunately, I woke up Liz when getting into bed. It was 4am.

That really was one crazy journey, something to add to the long list of crazy journeys over the last few months.

* * *

Friday 14th – Sunday 16th July

The next couple of days involved catching up with Liz, the sailing club, and with Paul, who introduced me to a new mast section – thank you very much, Paul. I had a bonus catch up with my daughter Emily, who was playing in a 'Roundnet' tournament in Chiswick. I was happy to be on land, out of the gales that were wreaking havoc with anything in its way.

Luckily, my local dentist could fit me in to fix my tooth. A quick and cheap visit turned into a long and expensive one, but at least I did not have to wait a Scottish four years to have a repair. I was grateful for that.

On Sunday, I made some preparations for the next couple of days by contacting Welsh sailing clubs – there are a lot of them on the north coast of Wales. I had also been in contact with a lady, called Julie, from West Kirby who was offering to help with landing support for the upcoming sailing day. She was adding in advice about dealing with tides and the enormous beaches which are quite problematic in the area. Julie had also helped Ken Fowler on his island circumnavigations (one of my circumnavigation mentors). I was looking forward to meeting her and embracing her incredible generosity.

The journey back with replacement mast, was SOOOO much easier. It was aided by mostly functioning trains, and a cross-country route via Reading, hence no need to take the Tube.

Tony was at the platform gate to meet me when I arrived at Blackpool North. Whilst this was really appreciated, I did have a light feeling of disappointment, not to have had the chance to try out tram travel with mast in hand. It was a small price to pay, for a much more comfortable ride with Tony.

※ ※ ※

Day 73, Monday 17th July

To Wales, Rhyll

START	09.20, Blackpool, Squires Gate
WIND	W 13–22mph, veering NW later
WEATHER	Cloudy then sun. 15–18°C. Dry
TIDE	Westerly max 1.4mph till 18.00
SEA STATE	Moderate
HAZARDS	Sand & more sand. Liverpool ships
FINISH	Rhyll, 16.00
DISTANCE	35 miles
SAILING HOURS	6½ hours

There was blown sand all the way up the concrete ramp as a sign of the mighty winds of the days before. Having the trolley, albeit a pretty heavy one, was a godsend, for it was still a long drag to the sea, requiring several stops.

Tony and Wendy arrived just as I was ready to launch, making perfect timing for a farewell wave off. I handed over the trolley and compound key. I was really touched by their gentle and unassuming attentiveness, and bade them a fond farewell.

I also gave another pair of gloves a farewell, as I crashed my way through the surf.

"How did I manage to do that?" I said, chastising myself for another careless mistake.

"Was it the waves? Or focussing on the videoing whilst launching? Or did it happen when the boat was knocked over by a wave, before I got in?"

After a bit of contemplation when out on the sea, I concluded it was simply that the jacket surface was different, and was more slippery than the old one. Therefore, the stuffing-the-gloves-under-the-buoyancy-aid procedure needed to be revised. Then I realised the new jacket had zip pockets!! "That should help," I thought, mildly amused by my own stupidity. Happily, I didn't lose any more gloves after that.

I nearly lost my compass though, since the mount broke when I was opposite Southport. It was tied on with string for security reasons, and spent a good few minutes, bumping about the deck, looking ready to depart at any moment. I tried to jam it back into place, but it was too difficult. Chastened by one loss for the day, I wanted to avoid another, so put it into my day bag. I would need to navigate by line of sight and way points.

There was some kind of gas platform up ahead, and then a windfarm which acted as markers. I could see cranes in the hazy distance, which must have been a port and I guessed it was

Liverpool. A cargo ship appeared on the horizon, heading out along the shipping lane.

I reminded myself "never cross in front of a ship". They look slow but are really fast, and don't stop / can't stop / can't see you. What's more, I had had two hazards for the day and would be unwise to put myself in line for a third.

Ignoring my own advice, I went in front of it anyway, dashing into the windfarm, like a duck finding shelter amongst the reeds.

"Ha, ha, missed me," I said.

Inside the wind farm, I was surrounded by great majestic blades, winding round in perpetual circles, lined up in neat rows. It looked other worldly. Futuristic and alien to the peaceful open water, and yet in tune with nature, sucking energy from the wind, and passing it to the people, doing their bit to defend the planet from human destruction.

I was still unsure if I was supposed to sail through windfarms. I think the idea is you shouldn't, in case you crash into a turbine and damage it. This would be relevant for a cargo ship, or so I imagined, but for me it would be a no contest collision.

I had a kind of answer to my question, just as I was exiting the last row of planted metal forest. A smart red catamaran craft came racing over to me, pushing froth and bother before it. The driver slung open his window and shouted incomprehensible warble in my direction.

"Call me on channel 16," I shouted back a few times, but neither of us could understand each other.

From the non-verbals, it must have been something along the lines of "You are not allowed to sail through here. You must leave immediately," which is what I was doing anyway. He didn't seem to be picking up on my non-verbals.

As I sped off, I tutted over my shoulder to the guardians of the windfarm, "Sorry, mate, you've been asleep. And please get yourself a megaphone for next time." The catamaran went back to lurk amongst the trees.

The green hills of Wales were now clearly in sight, bringing hope of a new country, and respite from the endless sands of Lancashire. The wind had veered, giving me an extra lift, and the tide had turned, meaning progress westwards was easier than earlier. Excited by the prospect of extra miles, I greedily sailed past Prestatyn. After all, the response from the club had been a bit mealy mouthed, I thought – "we don't usually lend trolleys to visitors". Besides, Prestatyn to Rhyll would only be a few extra car minutes for Julie, and I was sure the extras would be within reach, given her helpfulness. (Prestatyn was the pick-up point I had agreed with Julie.)

I was even tempted to go beyond Rhyl, but good sense got the better of me and I landed. The tide was completely out, revealing plenty of sand, but thankfully not on the scale of Southport or Morecambe Bay. It took me at least an hour, plus assistance from a range of passers-by, to reach the high-water mark. Then I begged some help from the RNLI station to move Betty over the breakwater wall, across the promenade to a grassy bank, where she rested up for the night.

I rang Julie to make a plan. "Hi. I have overshot a bit and ended up at Rhyl. I hope that is OK for you?"

A slight pause, and then, "Thanks for letting me know."

A longer pause from me.

The hoped-for reply was something like, "Ah, OK. That is a bit further, but I will head off shortly. And I'm glad the day has gone OK." None of that materialised. I could hardly start asking for extra assistance, or step off into a whine, such as, "I thought you said you were coming to Prestatyn."

Instead, there was a brief exchange of pleasantries and, "thank you for your help", then the conversation ended.

I had seriously misread the situation.

"What happened there?" I wondered. Had I misunderstood? Or simply misheard. I didn't think so. It was a long way round from West Kirby, but I had not received any message that it was too far, and if I had, I would have completely understood. Was I starting to take advantage, or make assumptions about people's helpfulness? I hoped not. I would need to keep an eye on that. How strange. And how disconcerting. Maybe it was double payback for rejecting the Prestatyn trolley. That would teach me.

Ruminating was not going to find me anywhere to stay, however. It was a warm summer's evening, ideal for holiday season. I was staring at a Travelodge, so went over to check it out. It was full. In lieu of the room to stay, I borrowed the amply sized disabled toilet to get changed.

Panic about the possibility of having to camp started to creep in, but once again, booking.com came to the rescue, aided by Travelodge Wi-Fi. I ended up at the Crescent Hotel in town. It was conveniently located, but had a very small room, with an interesting choice of black duvet cover. The room played host to my luggage, whilst I headed off for a statutory Wetherspoon's meal deal. Things had worked out in the end.

CHAPTER 17

Ron's funeral

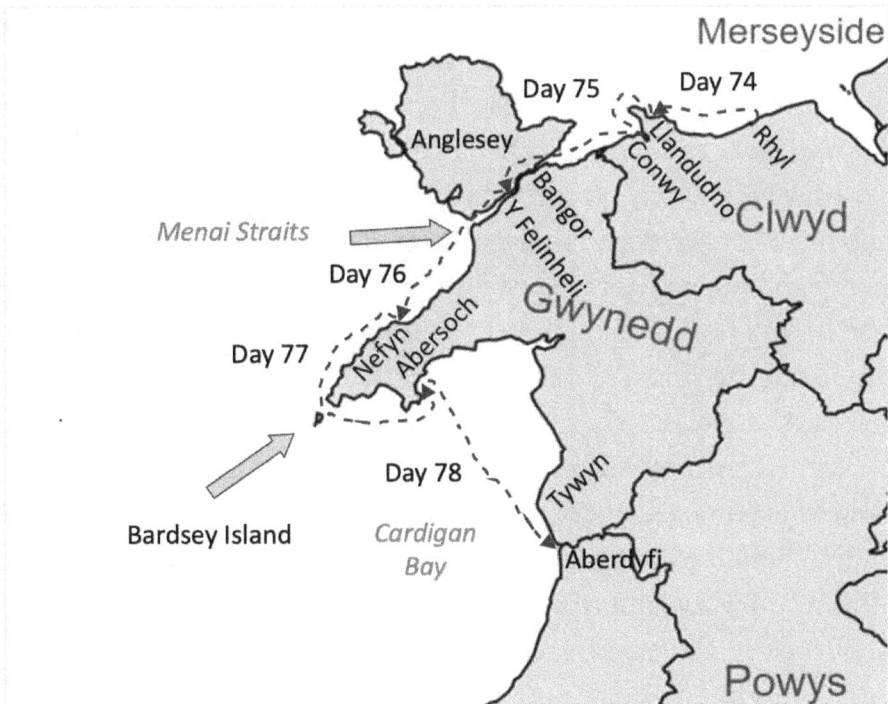

Day 74, Tuesday 18th July

To Llandudno

START	11.30, Rhyl
WIND	SE, 6–15mph
WEATHER	Cloudy and wet, 14–16°C. Light rain
TIDE	Westerly, max 1mph
SEA STATE	Slight
HAZARDS	Light winds
FINISH	Llandudno, 15.30
DISTANCE	14 miles
SAILING HOURS	4 hours

I thought I liked Rhyl. A pleasant seaside town in the warm sunshine with an easy high street and modern seascape, plus a large sandy beach, made for a comfortable summer holiday venue. Many other people thought the same. There used to be a pier (till a century ago), an ornate pavilion, a fun fair and an artificial marine lake, though only the latter remains.

However, when I returned to Betty, my mood, and opinion of the town turned down sharply. Betty had been moved, again. She had been dragged down the bank, and across the promenade and had been left, splayed out over a fence like a shipwreck, with mast angled to the skies. Worse than that, when I was close enough to check, there was a sizeable hole in the sail.

"I'm angry this morning," I said to camera. "I'm angry with the youths of Rhyl. I'm sorry, youths, but who else would do this – to muck about and drag a boat as if to sail it, but then give up when it proved tricky, and run off when they noticed some damage?"

I looked for other areas of injury. There were more sharp scratches, but as I had now learnt, no gouge occurs in the same place twice. The hole in the sail appeared enormous at first sight, but when it was rigged up and six feet further away, it had shrunk to a diddly spec. It was still a significant wound, and I would need to repair it that night, but it would be OK for the day.

Despite the gratuitous interference, an inventory check demonstrated that nothing was missing from outside, or inside the boat. Even the Welsh burgee had been left untouched. It was lying limply on the ground, as if sending a message to a passing assailant, 'Please take me, I'm yours.' How extraordinary that nothing was stolen.

John and Pete, whom I would meet that evening, wondered if it could have been drug addicts, mindlessly meddling. I would never know, but if indeed it was not the youths, "my apologies for wrongly accusing you". Either way, concerns about security had escalated several notches. Furthermore, I regretted having rejected the offer of a Prestatyn trolley, albeit a reluctant one. The incident was an important lesson.

There was to be one more breakage for the day. Just as I passed an outdoor wear shop in Llandudno after I landed, the carrying strap became irreparably detached from my day bag. I wasn't sure whether I was more disappointed, or delighted – about yet another breakage, or the amazingly fortuitous timing. I picked up a substitute, but kept the old one, which would still function as a nearly-dry bag when in the boat.

I really liked Llandudno. It occupies a long sweeping bay, with shelving shingle beach and broad bold promenade, full of strollers, many of whom were of mature years. To the north, the town is shaded by the monolithic lump of Great Orme, hosting attractions such as cable car, botanical gardens, and wait for it …. a ski and snowboard centre!! Below that is the Grand Hotel (where I stayed), and the pier which remains intact, having kept out of the way of destructive shipping (unlike other piers).

When approaching from the sea, after my languid and wet sail from Rhyl, I was pleased to see Llandudno. There was a uniform vista of seafront properties, giving an impression of a grand design. A single central ramp reached up out of the water, as if providing an entrance way, or noble staircase to the sailing club. Except the club proved the exception in the property scape, being more of a down to earth, and down in sized establishment, as if the eyeline dip was a developer's mistake. One wonders what history had enabled such an incongruous inclusion. "I got there first," was my imagined answer.

The boat park was full of Lasers, providing plenty of trolley options.

"Can I give you a hand?" said John, when I was about to wriggle Betty onto the borrowed wheels at the bottom of the ramp.

"Ooh, yes please," I said, feeling a little guilty, having already swiped the trolley and wrestled it over the locked compound gate. John had picked up my email to the club, and seemed totally at ease with the unannounced loan. Two hands were definitely better than one, when hauling Betty up the steep slope.

After sail repairs, bag repairs, and body repairs, in my grand sized and great value room, I went back to the club for a beer. John was joined by Les and Pete, and in no time, it felt like I was part of the membership, as I was effortlessly included into jollities, and our array of stories.

"Is the shore break a problem here?" I asked innocently.

"Oh yes, if there is a northerly," said Pete. "Shall we tell him about the northerly storm from '21?" he asked his colleagues.

John and Les looked at Pete to check for emotional approval before carrying on.

John started. "It was a typical race day and Les was in the safety boat. We knew there was a northerly forecast, but it looked ok and we set off to race as usual."

"I was really keen to get ahead of John and the wind was OK, so I called for another lap. But then the wind really kicked in," said Pete.

Les added to the tale. "One of the rescue boats stopped working properly, so had to return to shore. There were some youths out, so I wanted to prioritise them."

Pete continued. "John and I had both fallen out and were struggling to get back in. When Les came over, I think I was tired, or not thinking straight, but simply told Les that I would swim ashore, and told him to 'go and help John'.

"With the attention focussed on the others, no one noticed that I was stuck in the undertow on the shore." Pete paused for a moment and looked uncomfortable.

"Are you OK?" I said.

"No, it's fine," he said. "I have told this story many times before."

Having hastily gathered himself, Pete continued at his usual steamy pace. "I just couldn't get out of the surf. I was losing more and more energy, and struggling to catch some air between waves."

"Luckily, a walker spotted me and called for help, and people came down to drag me out. But if she had not called for help, I don't know what would have happened." Pete's narration, tailed off to an apprehensive stop.

"Yeah. It was a close shave," added Les. "Not our finest safety moment. You see, lots of things went wrong at the same time. It's fair to say that we have learnt a few things from it though."

"How are you now?" I asked Pete.

"It's taken a while," he said. "I thought I was OK, but my wife pointed out that I would become irritable and anxious before going sailing. That side of things is getting better though."

"These events can have quite an impact," I said, momentarily donning my psychiatrist's hat.

And then the conversation moved on to more frivolous matters, gathering together around a shared love of sailing, washed down with a beer or two. It was a joyous evening, but we were reminded that the sea must be respected.

Day 75, Wednesday 19th July

To Y Felinheli / Port Dinorwich

START	08.40, Llandudno
WIND	NW, 10–15mph
WEATHER	Cloud then sun later, 14–17°C. Dry
TIDE	Tides, all over the place
SEA STATE	Slight. Moderate at G. Orme
HAZARDS	Tides. Going down river Conwy
FINISH	Y Felinheli / Port Dinorwich, 16.15
DISTANCE	21 miles. With a few extras, ?9
SAILING HOURS	6½ hours (50 mins at Conwy)

Ash from Barrow rang me about the Swellies, wanting to keep a navigational eye on his sailing prodigy. The Swellies is an affectionate term for the turbulent middle of the Menai Straits, referring to the section between bridges which cross from Anglesey to the mainland. The straits have really complex tides, strong currents, and the Swellies have bonus hazards of a few rocky islands plonked in the middle.

"Once you get round Great Orme, head straight for Puffin Island, and then follow the markers up the channel to the Swellies. Stick to the left under the bridges, and you'll be fine," he said. It all sounded simple enough, but at the same time sufficiently complicated to need an explanation. I would have to be careful. There were stopping options at Beaumaris Sailing Club or maybe

Port Dinorwick / Y Felinheli, past the bridge, if I timed the tides accurately.

I managed an early start with the help of a Grand breakfast, and launching assistance from John and Pete who came down to give me a send-off – how incredibly kind.

With the opposing tide, and flukey headland head wind, I estimated it would take an hour and a half to pass Great Orme. It took two, and plenty of paddling – a frustrating grind. At the headland, the seas were really agitated as John had predicted, but knowing what it was, encouraged me to plough on.

Round the corner, everything settled down. The sea state and the wind direction were now in my favour and I was making a delicious seven miles per hour, so much better than the miserable one and a half mph from earlier.

"I think that's Puffin Island over there," I said to myself, but checked on Navionics to make sure. I wasn't completely sure, since the distant green hills were indistinguishable from Island, and like in the North-west of Scotland, it was hard to work out where one ended and another started.

Nevertheless, I was happy, and was making great progress. I was sure to catch the tidal window.

"There's a channel buoy," I said, and dutifully taking Ash's advice, I followed the markers.

Into the mouth of the straits I went, zooming past shoreside properties at great speed, washed along by an impressive tide, swooping past a marina that must have been Beaumaris. I took a contented video of the sun-dressed scene, naming the landmarks of this famous strait. I was on top of this journey and ahead of schedule, sporting a smug smile.

A bridge appeared on a corner. Sensing a cloud of doubt descending over the picturesque scene, I thought it best to double check my location.

"WHATTTTTT!" and then a series of screaming expletives, followed by a sudden change of course, heading straight into the nearest pontoon.

"How the hell did that happen?" I shouted at myself, enraged at my own stupidity. "How am I gonna get out of here with the tides like that?"

For I was not in the Menai Strait at all. Ash had told me that sometimes people end up going down the Conwy River by mistake, which when looking at the map, seemed like a dumb thing to do. Yet that was exactly where I was. I had been seduced by an attractive river mouth, sucked down a hapless backwater, having been deluded into thinking I was making impossibly good progress. What a fool I had been. I was seven or eight miles off course.

Still loudly berating myself whilst standing on the pontoon, I said, "I will have missed the tidal gate. That means I have lost a whole day."

To add insult to injury, a large dredging barge, looking like an enormous upturned table, blew its horn at me, demanding to moor at the spot where I had tied up. It was a choice of either oblige, or get squashed, so I moved along. This day was going badly.

With all the discontented noise coming from a stroppy sailor, David popped his head up from a neighbouring yacht. "Can I help?" he said.

The obligations of social interaction have an instant calming effect.

"Oh yes," I replied, and explained my problem.

David invited me on board so we could check out locations and tide times.

"High water is in about an hour so the flow should be slackening off. You will need to watch out for running aground as you head across to Beaumaris, though. The sands appear quite early."

I was encouraged by his calm, coupled with a dose of enthusiasm for my journey. So, in line with tradition, I decided to head off in hope. 'One step at a time and let's see where we get to,' was the mantra.

There was one more thing to tackle on the mishap list. The tracker wasn't working. This time it was lack of charge. I thought I had fixed the connection before, but obviously not, so it was time to revert to the spare.

Back online, and back on the water, I headed out on a beat, back towards Llandudno, anxious to make progress and still beating myself up on the way. The pent-up tension added vigour to the sailing, and I was into the open water in no time.

I spied another Laser dinghy out for a cruise. What a pleasure. The sun had come out and the water was glistening in reflected gaiety. We sailed towards each other, and shouted pleasantries across the waves. I needed a lot of reassurance as to the location of Beaumaris ahead of me, and he was happy to oblige. And then we parted. But that was not the last time we met. Mike, his name was, managed to track me down, and kindly came over to bid me a happy send off for my launch the following morning. What a wonderful validation.

Progress on a close, then beam reach was good. I was following the course of the A55, along the edge of North Wales, past Dwygyfylchi, Penmaenmawr, and Llanfairfechan, thinking I might need an education in how to pronounce Welsh names.

Approaching Beaumaris (it really was Beaumaris this time) I was feeling more relaxed, but equally wondering whether to try and carry on. A large dinghy, which I later learnt was a Menai Straits One Design, was sailing along, so I went closer to ask for advice.

Expecting a bemused questioning of my intentions, I was taken aback, by a direct and personal response, "It's Andrew, isn't it?"

"How did you know that?" I replied.

"We knew you were coming over this way," he replied, referring to an email I had sent.

I thought, "You are one step ahead of me, then."

And John, as he was called, was several steps ahead of me on understanding the tides.

"Just carry on down towards the pier at Bangor. And after that, Richard will come out on a paddleboard nearer the bridge, to guide you."

It sounded too good to be true, as if a wish from a fairy godmother had been granted. I thought I had missed the tidal gate by some margin, but the voice was calm and authoritative, and with hindsight, sprinkled with angelic dust. I crept away from my winged saviour towards Bangor.

Then a small motor launch drove up to me. He had sped out from the sailing club to say 'hi' and wish me well on my journey. He repeated the instructions to carry on. Now I could see the Bangor Pier, and the current running past a nearby obstacle, adding solidity to the directions. This was starting to feel like a royal escort.

Further on, Richard did indeed materialise on his paddleboard, like a gliding apparition. A morning mist over the water would have added to the visual effect, as if a man were being floated, God like, over the surface on a mission to save an imperilled seaman. He delivered his message, and then slid back to his invisible port, from whence he had come.

This was all quite surreal. If I had planned it, I would have been bobbing along with a smile, over the upwellings and turbulence under the famous suspension bridge. But none of this was my doing. I had been delivered from hades to heaven, by the gentle gestures of the Welsh community, who had strung together a cradle of seamless soft hands to guide me to safety.

Round another corner and under the road, and then the rail bridge, I was out of danger. The sun had come out. Blue skies, decorated with soft white clouds, contrasted with lush green foliage on the banks, brought back memories of a summer's afternoon idling down the River Thames. On the opposite bank, kayakers were mustering around their orange craft, ready for a practice afternoon paddle. Plas Newydd house, a large National Trust property, came into view, presenting itself through a gap in the vegetation, majestically standing back from the water's edge, separated by a well-kept lawn. This day could drift on and on.

Round one more corner was the sailing club with awaiting trolley. I needed to ascend from my reverie into the welcoming arms of yet more wonderful Welsh hospitality.

Wednesday night was race night at Y Felinheli Sailing Club, and I was invited to join the throng. Whilst tempted, I decided against it, which was probably a smart move, given the dying wind. It also meant that I could meet Cathy, who had very kindly offered to put me up for the night. She lived a short distance along the waterfront. We went past a playground, a pub and then a slate covered beach that looked like a driveway, arriving at a sun-soaked property overlooking the straits. What an idyllic spot.

Cathy had not long since stepped down from her role as Commodore at the club. Instead, she had picked up care of her charming mother, who was in the throes of dementia. Not wanting to create any extra burden, I was keen to make myself as trouble-free as possible. Sheila was as trouble-free as she could be, being endlessly light in her manner, bringing joyfulness to every interaction, despite being limited in scope of conversational repertoire. We wandered back to the club for an evening meal and to enjoy the setting sun.

There was a fine gathering of sailors for the evening. I was provided with a portion of pasta and a beer on the house, as part of a welcome. Then a gentleman turned up, whom I thought I recognised.

"Hi, it's John," he said as if we had met before. He looked very much like the sailor who had greeted me on the other side of the Menai Straits, but could this really be him. Was it his doppelganger? I thought John was from Beaumaris Sailing Club so surely, he wouldn't be coming here, unless of course he had flown over on some golden tinted guardian angel wings.

A moment or two of conversation settled my confusion. Indeed, it was one and the same person.

"How lovely to meet you again," I finally replied.

John gave a few more minutes of gentle explanation about the complexities of the Menai Straits tides, in order to try and rescue me from my other vexed question – "how on earth had I managed to get the tides right, when I thought I had got them so wrong?". His answer seemed to make sense at the time, but I would not dare to repeat it here, for fear of getting both you and me into another muddle. Let's just say, 'it's complicated'.

As the light, and the dinner were being packed up, a few of the gathering were heading to the pub, and I was invited to join them. How could I resist, particularly since it was on the very short journey to Cathy's place?

I bought a round of drinks. Listening to the pleasant summer's chatter, and a beer into the evening, I plucked up courage to ask about the unfamiliar sounds I was hearing. Most conversation was incomprehensible to my English ears, save for the occasional piece of Anglo-Saxon sentence, appearing like a sudden beacon of light through the mists of linguistic fog.

Turning to the lady standing next to me at the bar, my painfully Anglicised question, tumbled out. "Do you always speak Welsh?"

"Yes," she answered, sounding rather disgruntled. "It's compulsory in school."

Wise John settled some of my embarrassment. "The use of Welsh varies across the country," he said, "but it's stronger in the North-west."

I wasn't sure whether I felt better or worse for asking the question, but at least I had gained a drip of wisdom along the way. Which is more than I can say for my knowledge of the Welsh language. At the time of writing, I am ashamed to share that I know more Nepalese than I do Welsh, and that is only a handful of words. Something for all of us to work on perhaps?

Day 76, Thursday 20th July

To Morfa Nefyn

START	11.15, Y Felinheli
WIND	SW 10–18mph
WEATHER	Cloud then some sun. 14–16°C. Dry
TIDE	With me, max 3mph at the mouth
SEA STATE	Slight
HAZARDS	Not many
FINISH	Morfa Nefyn, 16.00
DISTANCE	22 miles
SAILING HOURS	4½ hours

Cathy and Sheila came down to bid a fond farewell, as did John, and Mike from yesterday's chance on-the-water encounter. What a fine send off, and what a special place. A good representation from women and youths, is sign of a sailing community that is doing the right things. Their recent title 'RYA club of the year' was well deserved, I was sure. I certainly felt it, and was sad to go, but the warm homely feeling it imbued would stay with me. No wonder it gives birth to some great sailors.

The straits continued to provide a delightful passage. I half regretted not stopping at Caernarfon, since the Commodore had replied to my message. The town looked inviting, with a castle beckoning me from the shore, but I felt obliged to proceed.

The tide fairly whistled me out of the mouth, near Fort Belan, into open sea, alone once more. Alone except for a dolphin who popped up by the boat for a few moments, just long enough for me to take a video of myself pointing excitedly at the water saying, "There it is. It's just there!" However, there was no sign of any sea creature in the shot.

Morfa Nefyn nestles in a long sweep of bay, facing to the north-east so protected from the prevailing south-westerly breezes. It was an easy beach for landing, and there were plenty of admiring tourists to help move Betty to her resting place, on a convenient patch of grass.

It was the last urban stopping point before rounding the tip of the Llŷn peninsula, the uppermost and more accusatory looking fingers of Welsh land, protruding into the Irish Sea. On the end of the peninsula, Bardsey Island sat alone, and isolated.

The Welsh name for Bardsey means 'Island in the currents', and its English version 'Island of the Bards'. Both were apt descriptors since the currents were indeed ferocious. Furthermore, the island had once been the location of a monastery, and it was the end point of the North Wales Pilgrim's Way. Legend has it that Bardsey Island was the burial place for Merlin the wizard.

These days, the peninsula remains a relatively unspoilt area of North Wales, making it a desirable destination for holidaymakers and conversely, a sanctuary for Welsh culture and language. One survey of schools on the Llŷn, undertaken in 2003, found that 94% of children aged between 3 and 15 could speak Welsh, an impressive application of policy for cultural preservation.

My focus was more parochial: namely, how to get round the nail-biting finger of land, safely.

I came down for a brief visit to the bar of the Bryn Nadda Hotel, before bed, and got chatting. Ken was amongst the group, and was keen to hear about my trip. Being tired from the day before, I was feeling less enthusiastic than I might have been. However, Ken's knowledge as a yachty, and previous harbour master, meant that his guidance was worth absorbing into my passage planning. The beat down to Bardsey Sound could take a while, but if I got the timing right, I should be OK, he figured. I kept my monstrous cock-up of the day before to myself, and went to bed, preferring to believe in the possible.

Day 77, Friday 21st July

To Abersoch

START	10.40, Morfa Nefyn
WIND	NW 11–15mph, backing SW 15–18mph
WEATHER	Cloudy, 14–15°C. Dry
TIDE	Against me max 2.2mph till 14.00
SEA STATE	Slight to moderate
HAZARDS	Opposing tide, wind dying
FINISH	Abersoch, 16.30
DISTANCE	31 miles
SAILING HOURS	5¼ hours (1 hour stop)

I had three more major headlands to go. There was the Llŷn, St Davids Head in South Wales, and Land's End. I probably should have counted Portland Bill, but that looked more like a pimple on the map, so didn't feature in my mind at the time. The headlands were looming large as obstacles, but beyond that, if felt like the end was creeping into sight. I kept telling people, "It's still 500 miles to go, which is a long way in a little boat."

The first headland was scheduled for today, and I was nervous. Like all of them, there would be a long beat out to a highly exposed and isolated point, where the tide and wind conditions would change dramatically, as I attempted to turn through nearly 180 degrees. Planning was therefore complicated.

Ken came down to lend a launching hand, which was really good of him.

"Hug the shore till you get to Bardsey, and you should be alright," he said. That sounded like good advice.

Round the promontory of Morfa Nefyn Bay, the sea was lumpy, but not for too long, and I carried on as instructed. On each mini promontory, the surface became roughed up again, with short sharp waves and breaking tops, making the going quite alarming. These were 'overfalls', made from fast currents over a shallow surface, a feature that I had heard described so much, but had seen little. And yet none were marked on Navionics.

The estimated time to Bardsey was about three hours, but when I paused to check my location, I was going faster than expected. This was perplexing, since the tidal flow was meant to be against me. Passing a rare fisherman's buoy, I realised that the flow was with me instead, and by some measure. That meant that I must have been the happy recipient of regular 'back eddies', something I hadn't experienced before, at least not with such clarity. It also meant that I was early, a rare and unsettling experience for me. Hence, I needed to pause.

I stopped in a small bay called Porth Ferrin, to take a break and allow the day to catch up. Scrambling to the top of the bank I was surprised to meet some youths, casually strolling along the clifftop path. They were neither dressed for the North Wales Pilgrim's Way, as would befit the route they were on, nor were they interested in an explanation as to what I was doing. The sight of a Laser dinghy parked on its side, in a deserted cove, at the bottom of a steep slope, didn't engage their attention either. I was slightly affronted, I am sorry to say, having become accustomed to minor celebrity status. I thought that a lone sailor, having landed in a tiny cove, in a remote part of Wales, would have sparked their imagination in some way. But no. They were consumed by their own company, and merely waved as they passed onwards.

It was a delightful, warm, sheltered cove, and I too became caught up with my own company. Whilst waiting, I recorded a couple of videos about the status of boat repairs, for content generation purposes. I ended up setting off late. On reflection my delay must have been fuelled by procrastination, perhaps a nervous avoidance tactic, because I was still worried about what was coming next.

As the Bardsey race came closer, the cliffs grew taller and the overfalls more vicious. I couldn't see a way around the hazards, so had to press on through each one. Betty and I had to tack through the disturbed sea, making the sections of chop more perilous, and adding to a sense of trepidation. These conditions were nothing like ones I had experienced before, and were testing my skills and my confidence. But Betty kept beating onwards, rolling over waves, or diving through the next bank, before squaring up to the oncoming barrage. Despite the challenges, we were getting closer and closer to the end of the peninsula. Betty was doing brilliantly. "We should be able to make it," I said out loud, as confidence was rising.

Then Bardsey Island emerged from round a corner, and was in front of us. We scraped our way past the headland into the sound, no more than a few feet from the rocky fingernail of North Wales. We could now bear away onto the comfort of a reach. The surface was decorated with a patchwork of roughened effects, and huge upwellings, throwing up signs of discontent as the monster of the sea ran over its disturbing underwater land neighbour.

A mile or so further on, and we could relax. There were no more angry flows. Instead, a comfortable warm tailwind was caressing us along past Hell's Mouth, around two more minor headlands and then into the safety of Abersoch Bay. We had made it. One major headland completed, and a significant step towards home.

Andy and Ben, a father and son team, were waiting for us with a trolley, when we arrived. How amazing was that?

Andy had recently retired, preferring to spend more time teaching sailing. His wife, son and his girlfriend, had come down to support endeavours of the day, so a proper family affair.

I was a bit perplexed by the concept of the Abersoch Sailing Club, since there was no building. Everything was stored on the beach, and the club effectively migrated inland when the summer season ended, like a pop-up club. It seemed to work, and I was as delighted as ever by the welcoming reception.

Betty was stored on the top of a double trailer, which I was assured would be safe (and it was), despite the hordes of listless beachgoers drifting about, looking for entertainment. "A boat on a rack could make easy pickings," I thought. But perhaps there was safety in numbers. Maybe an 'odd boat in an odd place' was a factor that had been causing trouble in recent weeks.

I was feeling a little desperate on the accommodation front, since absolutely everywhere in town was full, packed with summer holidaymakers. Penny, a university medic friend of mine, who I would meet later in Salcombe, had texted. "My brother might be heading to Abersoch for the weekend, and you could possibly stay. I'll ask him." This sounded incredibly generous, and would constitute a major rescue, if it worked out.

Penny's brother Ant soon texted to say he was delayed, and "you are very welcome to stay". How wonderfully kind to accommodate me so willingly. And what amazing good fortune, yet again.

I went into town to grab some food and a beer whilst waiting. The place was heaving, and there was not a Welsh word in earshot. It looked and sounded like Padstow in Cornwall, full of strutting youthful, or 'thinking-they-could-still-be-youthful' outdoors types, a far cry from the tempered tranquillity of the north shore. I guessed this was exactly what locals were complaining about, when they protested that North Wales culture was being diluted. However, it did look good for business – there was a sizeable queue for orders at the bar.

Ant then arrived and guided me away to his apartment, welcoming me like a long-lost friend. The rescue was stupendous, since I was offered five-star luxury, in a fantastic location, with an endless supply of kindness from Fran, and their daughters. A second dinner was on hand for an exchange of stories, and of course I had to oblige. My lucky cup was overflowing again.

Saturday 22nd July

July tempests were rolling in from the Atlantic, to dowse any suggestion of a sun scorched summer. Tomorrow was going to be another filthy wet and windy day, and I was happy to trade in a violent fight on the sea, for a day of top quality company. But I could not tarry too long, since I had another funeral to attend.

This one was for Ron, the number one Laser circumnavigator. Stick had called a few days earlier to let me know of the date, and a few days before that, to share the sad news of Ron's passing. Ron had taken his own life.

The interactions I had had with Ron had given me no clue that his time would end that way. He was gentle in manner and kindly, as well as energetic and determined. Those were characteristics that seemed to bode well for a person's happiness. I had had no inkling that such a tragic outcome might materialise. Stick filled me in with other pieces of history, which added more background. Either way, I very much wanted to join the well-wishers, to pay my respects at the event the following week. Therefore, I needed to reach a train station to carry me home. Aberdyfi / Aberdovey would be able to help. However, it would involve 28 miles of open water, crossing the top section of Cardigan Bay, in order to get there.

Before then, I had a day with Ant, Fran and family, that was filled with great walks, and wonderful conversations, carrying us down memory lanes, and onwards, onto ventures new. We paid a later visit to the South Caernarfonshire Yacht Club, where I would meet a host of enthusiastic sailing folks, young and old. Everyone was abuzz, looking forward to a great few days of top-quality sailing for their dinghy week. What's more, there was a race the following morning. I had to join in.

* * *

Day 78, Sunday 23rd July

To Aberdyfi / Dovey

START	10.45, Abersoch
WIND	SW, 14–20mph, more like 20–25mph
WEATHER	Cloudy, 15–17°C. Dry
TIDE	Not much
SEA STATE	Moderate
HAZARDS	St Patrick's Causeway, (can dry)
FINISH	Aberdyfi / dovey, 16.00
DISTANCE	28 miles
SAILING HOURS	4½ (45 mins waiting for the race)

Ant and Fran were thinking of coming out in their motorboat, to share a section of the crossing, but thought it looked too rough. It probably was, and would not have made a comfortable time for them. For me, at least, there was a healthy blow, to take me the whole way across to mid-Wales. Instead, they came down to the beach to bid farewell, under a grey and threatening sky.

Andrew and Ben were rigging up for the race, as were many others. It was breezy on the water. Being out of race practice, and unfamiliar with anyone else's company away from the land, I was feeling intimidated. "I'll just do the first beat, and then head on," I had said to Andrew.

The race was delayed by 45 minutes, since a marker had shifted. Later, some tracker observers of my journey, had wondered what had happened - for them, the blue line was going backwards and forwards on the screen, around the same spot. "Did you drop something?" I was asked.

"No. I was just hovering around the start line, waiting for a race."

Other racers shot off after the start, and I was left languishing at the back, loaded with excuses. I was relieved not to be last to the first mark, but I wasn't far off. It was an unwelcome reminder of my own racing incompetence – that's the way I saw it anyway.

Bear Grylls owns the island to the south of Abersoch Bay – St Tudwals West – so I was told, by plenty of locals. I waved as I passed, half expecting reciprocation in that fantasy way, in which you think, "because I'm thinking of you, you must be thinking of me. After all, we went to the same school, didn't we, and I'm out on a survival mission too?" He didn't wave back.

Further out into Cardigan Bay, the sea was still boiling from the day before, and it was windier than forecast. I felt vindicated in quitting the race and heading off. I had a long way to go. And a train to catch, so time was precious.

I was making good ground on a beam reach doing about eight miles per hour, but it was hard work, though not quite as bad as the Blackpool day. Up and down over the breakers, in an out with the main sheet to keep the boat flat, ducking round or over the oncoming waves. Inevitably I got it wrong on numerous occasions, and was drenched as the surf crashed into me. This was tough.

Out in the middle there was nothing to see but sea, spray and cloud all around me. I was becoming accustomed to these situations, but it was still raw. Nothing but you, Betty, and the wild elements for miles and miles. Alone and in peril. It was best not to think about it, and instead, keep going, keep focussing on the way ahead.

I took a break after a couple of hours. And then another an hour later, as I was approaching Tywyn on the coast, to see if there would be anywhere safe to land. There wasn't. I was getting tired.

Then the phone rang. Several times. Frustratingly the caller was not responding, despite shouting my replies above the sound of the wind. Someone was trying to get through. I was weary. There is only so much techno fiddling you can do, whilst bouncing about on the sea, with occasional buckets of water being thrown at you. In the end, I was defeated. I thought, "to hell with it," and carried on.

After landing, Will the harbourmaster told me that he had been watching the tracker on his phone. Having seen the blue screen boat stop, and thinking I might be in trouble, he rang the coastguard, who called me. Several times, without response. "Ah! So that's what it was!" I said.

The tracker back on the move was sufficient reassurance for my watchers to relax and leave the phone on the hook. Later still, I discovered that my headphones weren't working properly.

It was a shame to have had a rare moment of coastguard concern, and to have been unable to acknowledge the proactive approach. I thanked Will for his troubles, and when making contact on my check-in call, I thanked the coastguard as well. I would need to get the headphones replaced somehow.

When I was leaving Aberdyfi a few days later, Will also gave some excellent advice about how to get out beyond the sandbar. I could have done with some of that when coming in, since I had made a mess of it.

I had selected Aberdyfi since it was inland, and out of the direct line of surf, so compared to Tywyn should make a safer landing. I had not bargained on the sandbar being so extensive, in its role as guardian of the river mouth. Whilst helpfully providing protection for waters further inland, it was kicking up a thick band of violent surf, stretching as far as I could see.

"This looks ominous," I said to Betty as we were approaching. I sailed south, parallel to the shore, to see if there was an easier section. A central marked channel could have been a possibility, but the swell was even larger, and I was not confident about heading directly downwind in the breakers, having got it badly wrong recently. After as much surveying as seemed reasonable, I headed inland, taking the least worst line, and hoped for the best.

It wasn't good. I fell out not once, but twice. The mast head touched the bottom and bent my Welsh burgee. I lost a water bottle in the process, as well. Another one. Luckily, my frantic efforts to right the boat and prevent further damage, were successful, so no broken mast this time at least.

Slightly shaken, I headed into the flat waters of the inlet. I really had not got this surf thing sussed. Will did later say that he could see through his binoculars six-foot waves crashing over the channel markers, so maybe I was right to take another route.

The sun had started to come out. Approaching the smooth sand, and calm waters near the clubhouse, I could see onlookers watching out for my arrival. When I touched land, I could hear clapping applause, and it was for me. I was taken aback. What a fantastic reception. However, I was still feeling rattled from my shambolic arrival, and I hardly felt the ovation was justified.

Once a little more grounded, I could take on the fullness of another wonderful Welsh welcome. I had access to a shower, a place to hang my hikers for a couple of days, access to the boat park, and a beer on the house. Someone kindly came over and straightened out the burgee as well. Betty was parked up in the boat park on a borrowed trolley. There was no fence and the club seemed happy with the 'safety in numbers' approach, though I remained quietly cautious.

Last but not least, another Will very kindly offered a bed for the night on my return, so all the ducks were neatly lined up for my onward journey on Wednesday.

The funeral was on Tuesday morning, so I needed to be at home on Monday (tomorrow). My daughter was about in Birmingham that evening, so I figured that if I hurried, I could catch up with her on my way back home – a bonus visit. It was quite a time squeeze, since the trains from mid-Wales are not that quick, but I figured it would fit in. From Abersoch to Aberdyfi, and then on to Birmingham, with transitions from dry to wet to dry, I thought, "that isn't bad going for one day".

But before I leave the coast, I must say something about place names. First of all, the pairing of place names is, unsurprisingly, for the purpose of providing a Welsh and an English version. This was mildly confusing at first, particularly when Y Felinheli was translated to Port Dinorwick. For some time, I thought they were two different places, making me wonder what the speaker was talking about. Aberdyfi and Aberdovey were not so difficult since they at least sounded more or less the same. The double naming practice seems to wilt when travelling further south, until arriving at places like Mumbles, where the French had been involved! (I'll explain that one later.)

The other thing to mention is the prefix 'Aber'. As previously described when in Aberdeen, this is derived from a Gaelic word meaning mouth of the river. Hence Abersoch is at the mouth of the River Soch, Aberdyfi at the mouth of the River Dyfi, Aberaeron is at the mouth of the River Aeron, close to KeepyourAeron (Ha ha! Sorry). The convention applies inland as well, when there is a confluence between rivers such Abercyon, Aberdare and many others. Aberfan, the site of the tragic 1966 slag heap disaster in which 116 children and 28 adults were killed, must be subject to the same naming rules, but I could not find a river Fan in my searching.

Aberystwyth is on the mouth of the river Rheidol, so seems to be an exception that proves the rule. However, history says that the town was originally on the mouth of the River Ystwyth. The conurbation has effectively migrated north, round the other side of the hill separating the two rivers, and despite its shifting location, has kept its original name, thus confusing anyone who might be bothered.

Abercastle has defeated me, however. I would land there in a few days' time. There is a stream, but no river, and I could not find a name for it. The bay looks like a mouth, and there are several castles on the perimeter, so maybe someone got 'Aber' happy and became confused between castles and rivers. Who knows.

Back in Aberdyfi / dovey, Will (#2) kindly gave me a lift to the station.

The rail route was one of those single-track affairs, that took a meandering course, managing the tightrope between water's edge on one flank, and mountain side on another, dipping in and out of occasional tunnels. On through Dovey junction, Machynlleth, and finally Shrewsbury, where a slightly faster train took us to Birmingham. I love a train.

It was wonderful to see Emily, albeit for a fleeting visit. She was working as a sports psychologist, though completing her final period of supervised practice. She was sharing a top floor flat, which they had described as their penthouse suite. It was nice and light, but not quite as luxurious as the name might suggest. Her flatmate had sailed at Y Felinheli, so another crazy connection.

In the course of the conversation, Emily proudly told me that she had secured a place for Team GB, playing Roundnet. It was a new sport, a bit like volleyball, except there are only two people on each team. The net is round and laid horizontally, just off the ground, so instead of the ball going over, it is bounced onto a net, and then up to the opposing pair. Well done, Emily. I was really proud of what she had achieved.

Monday 24ᵗʰ July

The Fastnet race was on the news. It had just started. For many of the teams, the race stopped shortly after it began, because of the violent conditions, particularly near the Needles. Yachts were struggling with breakages, inadvertently activated life rafts, and crew injuries, forcing withdrawal. Pictures of the sea state made it look completely wild. A friend of mine was on board one of the most photographed yachts, where a bow man was all but submerged in an oncoming wave. It was one of those wind against tide situations, where wave heights escalate exponentially as conditions move up the Beaufort Scale. My humble brush with the sea was nothing compared to those conditions, but then again, I would have been worse than reckless to go out in such a storm.

Tuesday 25ᵗʰ July

It was nice weather down in Kent. Sixty-two miles from home to the funeral felt a long way in a car, and it was incredible to think of covering that distance in a dinghy. Stick had managed it, but I had been some way short.

The cremation was well attended to my relief, though the service was rather impersonal. The celebrant had long curling locks of hair, and looked more like a might-have-been rock star, than a borrowed man of the cloth. He delivered the required lines with just enough compassion to satisfy himself. For some reason he was also tasked with reading out speeches from Ron's elder brother, and Ron's friend 'Indian Ron', which inevitably had a puncturing effect on their heartfelt offerings. Then we were ushered out to make way for the next mournful gathering.

Stick / Neil said with a smile, "I think Ron would have found it funny."

Hilary, Ron's ex-wife, said she thought, "it was awful".

At the wake, there was a group wearing T shirts sharing the logo EGH3, which stood for East Grinstead Hash House Harriers. It was a running club. There were others from a cycling group, and then motorbikers. Ron had met Indian Ron through an advert, and they had travelled round India for a while, and continued to remain friends in the UK. No one seemed to mind the slightly old school naming convention, not least Indian Ron. Quirky was good in this space. Ron clearly liked his outdoors.

The address told us that Ron also had an economical streak, which ran deep into his childhood. There was no need to do anything flash or expensive. That explained his desire to travel round the UK on a shoestring, with a leaky boat and a leaky tent, fuelled by tins of 'all day breakfast'. He refused all offers of a bed for the night, since tent and boat needed to stay close together, as if his life depended on saving every last penny.

He told me once in shameful confidence, that he would regularly warm himself up in his tent with his gas stove, a definite 'no-no' in the camping world. Hence, he didn't have enough clothes either. For navigation he used laminated AA road maps, fitted to the deck under a perspex cover. (I used the same cut up road map idea, but I kept them in the hold, and used them for evening passage planning.) He relied on a Nokia brick phone for communication, since he went round before the smartphone era. There was no Navionics to guide him. Hats off to Ron for getting round in one piece, with such rudimentary equipment, a proper English eccentric pioneer.

Stick often said, "I have no idea how he got round, because he couldn't sail." I wasn't sure that was fair.

With a winning smile and charming manner, Stick was good company as ever. He gently chastised me for not managing to sail 30 miles upwind in a day, followed by, "I wouldn't worry about the storms coming up". Having checked the forecast, he qualified his bravado. "Hmm. Saturday looks like a rest day."

I smiled.

He offered some good advice about landing in waves. I never needed to use it, but I could have done with it for Blackpool. For those who might be tempted to follow in our footsteps, here it is – "lean right back in the boat and head in as fast as you can on a reach, and ride straight up onto the shore. Everything becomes a lot easier when you lean right out of the back."

We bade farewell to Ron for the last time, and headed onwards, each on our own separate ways. I was pleased to have got to know him better. "Thank you, Ron, for leading the way," I thought, as I drove home.

* * *

Wednesday 26th July

A few days on land allows for some catching up and planning ahead. There were repairs and kit replacements to be attended to. There was mending to do, a water bottle replacing, and my headphones had completely given up, so urgent shopping was squeezed into the schedule.

Prospective sailing clubs were contacted. The weather looked difficult with more storms coming in, and I spent a good deal of time ruminating about how to get around St Davids Head. Once again, the tides needed to be right, and stopping points planned carefully. Despite all the thinking and planning, I still wasn't sure what to do. This next headland was doing my head in.

A pleasant summer in the south-east, was transformed to a soaking wet Wales by the time I stepped off the train in Aberdyfi. Will was there to greet me. Despite the torrential rain, the village looked attractive with multicoloured riverfront housing, stepped away from the water's edge as if to hold back the steep hill behind it. An easy access beach was a short walk away, and a sea-facing section was further on for those who were so inclined. Hence, an excellent waterside location, and fantastic for sailors.

Will's house was further up a hill. He had cared for his mother for several years before she died. The property had the feel of someone from an older generation, with dark wooden panels and formal furniture, unchanged from years gone by. Will seemed to have more of an interest in sailing equipment than domestic diligence, though he apologetically tidied up a little when we came in. I didn't mind. As ever, I was delighted to be offered such a wonderful welcome, and an indoor space to sleep.

We went back down to the waterfront, and popped into the sailing club to recover my clothing. I took Will out for a meal at the Dovey Arms, which he seemed to appreciate, washed down with a beer or two, and plenty of sailing and general life chat.

* * *

CHAPTER 18

Welcoming Wales

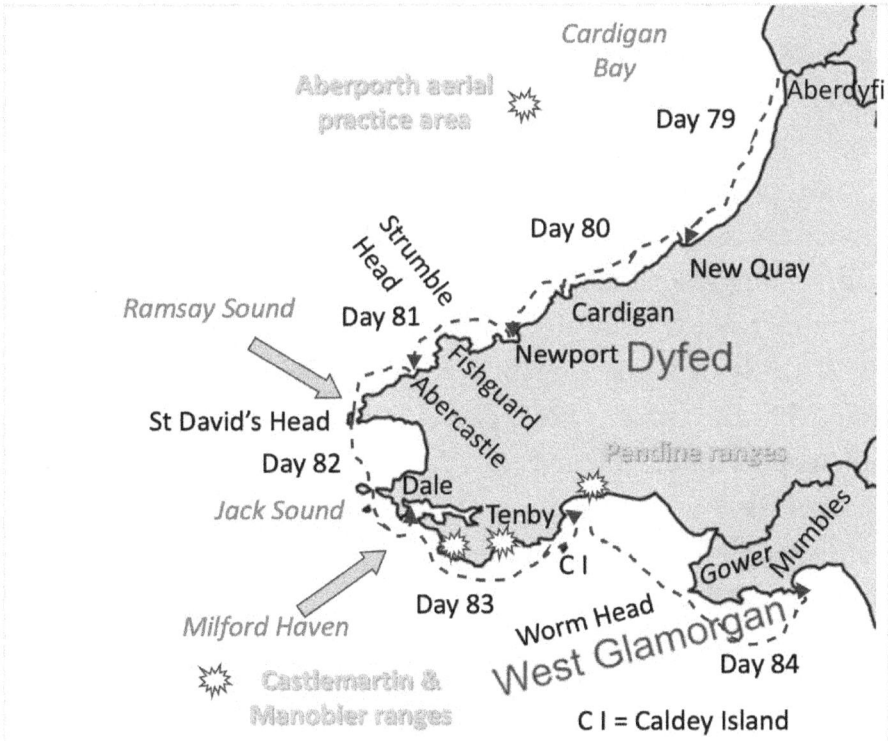

Cardigan Bay

Aberporth aerial practice area

Aberdyfi

Day 79

Day 80

New Quay

Strumble Head

Ramsay Sound   Day 81

Cardigan

Newport Dyfed

Fishguard

St David's Head

Abercastle

Day 82

Pendine ranges

Dale

Jack Sound

Tenby

Milford Haven

Day 83

C I

Worm Head

Gower

Mumbles

West Glamorgan

Day 84

Castlemartin & Manobier ranges

C I = Caldey Island

Day 79, Thursday 27th July

To New Quay

START	09.30, Aberdyfi
WIND	SW, 14–20mph
WEATHER	Rain then dry cloud, 15–17°C
TIDE	Against me till 1200, max 0.3mph
SEA STATE	Moderate to slight
HAZARDS	Rain. A long way on a beat
FINISH	New Quay, 17.00
DISTANCE	25 miles
SAILING HOURS	7½ hours

The weather had improved, but it was still raining. A small gathering had come out to bid farewell, which was much appreciated. There is usually a greater risk of forgetting something, or making a rigging mistake, if others are involved. However, on this occasion, everything went well.

With Will's excellent advice (the harbourmaster), I headed out, more or less the way I had come in. The conditions were kinder, and although I needed to proceed carefully to avoid running aground, the exit was more successful than the entrance.

With Stick's goading bravado echoing in my ear (about doing 30 miles upwind in a day), I was motivated to press on as much as I could. I picked up a response from New Quay Yacht club whilst I was on the water. The message urged me to keep going for the final five paddle-assisted miles, for by then, the wind had died.

A mini flotilla came out to greet me.

"Would you like a tow?" asked John.

"Such things should only be accepted as a last resort," I thought, and issued a "thanks very much, but I'm going to say 'no' on this occasion".

It was a lovely windless summer's evening. The Cardigan Bay Watersports centre members were readying themselves for an RYA inspection the following day, whilst preparing to run a course. I could feel the weight of procedural necessity in their activities.

I was very happy to leave Betty locked up in their beachside compound. I was then escorted round to the yacht club to meet folk. The yacht club building was fantastically located on the beginning of a breakwater, right in the centre of the village, and sized to blend into the surrounding properties.

In the bar, I was reminded, or informed, that New Quay is two words, and not one.

"We ran a sailing event here," said Chris. "One of the competitors broke his mast and ordered another one, to be couriered up the next day. It didn't arrive. When he rang to find out what had happened, the driver apologetically explained that he was in Newquay, CORNWALL. He won't be making that mistake again."

I was plied with a free beer, and a £10 note was pressed into my pocket from George, who was a veteran club member, whilst Chris offered plentiful advice about rounding St Davids Head. Then I was introduced to Neil, who stepped forward to offer accommodation for the night. Although the plethora of support was incredible, it was a little overwhelming, and I was happy to traipse off to Neil's place, for a bit more peace and quiet.

Neil and Cas had a property on the High Street, so ideal for a holiday location. Neil, like me, was adjusting to the transition of retirement, but had not stayed the moment of execution with a frivolous trip around GB. He was wondering what to do with the remainder of his life, a not inconsiderable question. We also shared the joy of having three children, so there was much to talk about. It was a soothing hour or two of gentle chatter, before I sloped off to a comfy bed, where I could continue to quietly ruminate about rounding St Davids Head.

* * *

Day 80, Friday 28th July

To Newport

START	10.00, New Quay
WIND	SW, 15–20mph
WEATHER	Cloudy, 15–17°C. Dry
TIDE	With me till 12.30. Max 1.2mph
SEA STATE	Slight to moderate
HAZARDS	Headwind. Rocky promontories
FINISH	Newport, 19.30
DISTANCE	27 miles
SAILING HOURS	5¼ + 3¾ hours

There was a bustle of people at the water sports centre. My ambition of getting away early, and out the way, had failed again. Instead, I was harangued with "sorry, who are you?" and, "I didn't know you were going to be here. No one told me". Each movement was accompanied by a "sorry", which I took to be shorthand for "sorry you are here".

I bundled Betty out onto the sand as quickly as I could, at which point, happiness was restored. Neil came down to deliver some forgotten toiletries, (oops, and thank you so much).

Chris returned to say hi and goodbye, and in so doing, told me more about the club. His dad had set it up. Chris was worried about declining membership, but he was hoping to turn it around, and this might include introducing sailability (sailing for those with a disability). I offered to provide a link to Papercourt, where sailability is well established, as a gesture of thanks for all the hospitality.

South-westerly breezes were becoming the norm, which meant tacking into the wind all day. The first couple of hours went OK, but then the tide turned and I crept along, close inshore to stay out of the current. It was hard work.

My intended destination was Cardigan, the town that gives its name to the bay. The town had a long and colourful history, reaching back to Norman times. Cardigan (Aberteifi in Welsh, because, as you have guessed, it is at the mouth of the River Teifi), had been a major port, in 1815, boasting seven times as many ships as Cardiff. Its trade was in slate, oats, barley and butter. It was also a major shipbuilding centre, up until the early 19th century. The river mouth, however, silted up, compromising its maritime usage. Further, the construction of railway linkages meant that transport by sea was less important. Industry was forced to turn to other areas.

I was planning to land somewhere in the wide sandy mouth of the river, and link up with a tentative contact who lived nearby. I was getting hesitant vibes though.

Having spent nearly five hours on the beat, I was keen to have a break. The afternoon tide was dragging me down emotionally, since I felt my progress was so slow. I really wanted to get to sand, and land. Squeezing in between Cardigan Island and the mainland, there was a stiff opposing flow. Onlookers stood watching, as I battled my way from one edge of the channel to the other, bouncing from side to side like a pinball stuck in a narrow alley, before being released to its exit.

I was in a bad mood. In fact, a really bad mood. I felt tired, having been working hard on the water. In my head, I had been feeling trapped by the constant headwinds, and the looming challenge of St Davids Head, the next in my catalogue of ominous headlands. I felt I had been making really slow progress that day. I was struggling to work out how to tackle the complicated rugged coastline, and challenging conditions over the next few days, which did not look like they were going to get any easier.

Hence, I was very grateful to take a break at Poppit Sands, on the south side of the river mouth. A coffee shop, a static seat and some signal, all helped with restoring good humour.

My Cardigan contact had gone cold, so there was no need to stay put for the night. In contrast, Andrew from Newport was being incredibly responsive and amazingly helpful.

"Should I carry on?" I wondered. It was a further nine miles, and the tide was not with me for a couple more hours.

"I reckon it will take me at least three hours," I said to Andrew on the phone. "I might not get there till seven. Do you think that would work?" (I had earlier said that I wasn't going to make it till the next day.)

"I think that should be OK," he said. He would get in touch with people at Newport.

I wasn't expecting anything, since I had given so little notice of my pending arrival. But something would be better than nothing.

Feeling refreshed and reinvigorated, I resolved to carry on.

The cherry on the cake for mood improvement, was feeling like I had a plan for progress, feeling like I was going to get somewhere.

The dark skies made it feel like dusk as I approached Newport. It was a complicated entrance since the River Nevern creeps out in a narrow shallow channel, squeezed between a long wave-covered sandbank, and the rocky edge of the bay. I was being guided in by enthusiastic boat club members, using a torchlight waving from the rocks, and the VHF radio. Except, the radio wasn't working too well, so messages were coming across in crackled fragments; I couldn't see the light; there were plenty of waves; and it is extra hard to sail through waves, whilst holding a radio. I nearly fell in. It was definitely getting dark when I made it through onto flat water, and up to the boat club.

A trolley had been brought into the water to greet Betty, and a wholesome gathering of boat club members were standing on the grass, cheering and clapping as I arrived. What an incredible reception, particularly since I had only decided to head to Newport a few hours earlier. Writing it now, it still seems remarkable. Things did not stop there.

"Where are you staying tonight?" asked Gordon, as I was derigging.

"I was going to stay with a contact near Cardigan, but she thinks it's too far, so I'm currently homeless," I replied. "To be fair, it all sounded quite complicated for her."

A slight pause and then Gordon said, "Let me get you a beer, and then we will ask around and see what is possible."

Niki came back soon afterwards with a beer, plus a plate of pasta, and an offer of staying at their place.

Niki and Gordon were in rented accommodation, since they were in the process of a house rebuild, so apologetically offered a small upstairs room. To me, it was yet more Welsh heaven.

As well as being instant good Samaritans, I was offered excellent counsel to help me attend to my headland worries. Gordon set about examining tide timetables, wind forecasts, and landing spots, embracing the nautical challenge with gusto.

"What about stopping at Abercastle?" he said.

"I hadn't considered that," I said. "Is it possible to land?"

"It's a narrow entrance, but it should be sheltered from the south-westerly breezes tomorrow. I think you'll be fine."

Being ten miles closer to St Davids Head, setting off from Abercastle really opened up rounding options. Suddenly, the obstacle had shrunk and felt so much more manageable.

That wasn't the last of the Newport generosity. A couple of days later, I received a message from Andrew, saying that a gentleman called Mike Mann had completed a driftwood sculpture in honour of my arrival. The photograph looked fantastic. When I finally took receipt of Mike's gift a few months later, I was able to appreciate the exquisite artistic detail. The wood was painted to match the green fields above Newport Bay. On the wavy sea, rode a miniature white Laser with the number 3 carefully drawn onto the tiny sail. The sailor was hanging out the side, striving for his destination, thus beautifully capturing the essence of adventure.

And after that, an auction was held to raise money for charities that I was supporting. Was there no end to the incredible generosity of Newport? Not yet.

* * *

Day 81, Saturday 29th July

To Abercastle

START	08.00, Newport
WIND	SW, 18–24mph, rising to 23–28mph
WEATHER	Sunny, 15–17°C. Dry
TIDE	With me, max 2.1mph till 14.00
SEA STATE	Moderate to rough
HAZARDS	Escalating wind. Wind against tide
FINISH	Abercastle, 11.45
DISTANCE	15 miles
SAILING HOURS	3¾ hours

With the guiding hands of Niki and Gordon, I was fuelled with porridge at seven am and rigged and ready to depart by eight. Niki's experience of rowing at Newport suggested that launching from the beach was better than from the river mouth. Her advice proved to be wise, and saved me from any rocky calamities.

My route for the day was a short stretch, out past Strumble Head, and into the inlet of Abercastle. It sounded simple enough, but proved to be quite testing.

On the tip of the headland, there is a smart white lighthouse, perched on St Michael's Island (Ynys Meicel Island) which can be accessed via a wobbly cable bridge. The lighthouse was constructed in 1908 and was one of the last to be built in Great Britan. Cut off from the mainland and run remotely, it holds a lonely position. On its day, it glistens brightly in the sunshine, looking proud and reverent, gazing out to sea.

Setting off from Newport, I was feeling nervous about the conditions. Once I left the protection of Newport Bay, the wind and the sea state quickly became pretty lively.

Heading across towards Fishguard, I could see the town, nestled in a snug corner of coastline, behind the protection of a breakwater. It was only an hour into the journey, the sun was out, but I paused on the water to consider going in. "Conditions are marginal," I thought. "But the tide is with me." So, I carried on.

At Strumble Head, just past Fishguard, things went nuts. There were enormous waves breaking in different directions.

Now you are in the boat. Yes, here we go again. You are holding the tiller and main sheet in your hands. You are tense. You are uncomfortable.

You can see the pretty white lighthouse, which tells you something, but not what to do. These waves are huge and seem to have come from nowhere. Up you go with Betty, trying to adjust your course to avoid a breaker at the top, and then bear away a fraction to try and keep the bow in touch with the water. Down you descend on the back of the mighty wall, looking for the next ascent like on a roller coaster. Except there are no tracks, no emergency break, and no health and safety inspectors. It's just you, Betty and the sea.

The wind is howling and brushing spray off the tops of the waves into your face. Wet and stinging. You check the control lines to see if you can depower the rig any more, but you have checked before, and know the answer. Your arms are straining from playing the mainsheet, and your back aches as you lean out. There is no need to keep the boat flat like in a race, but you just don't want to fall out, because heaven knows what it would be like climbing back in. You have to carry on. You are tired, and frightened and barely in control.

These wave monsters must be ten feet tall. They look enormous and threatening, as you head up the front of the next one. This time, you mistime the summit and Betty shoots through the crest and crashes down onto the wave back. You wince. "Sorry, Betty!" Something breaking would be REALLY bad. But there is no time for thinking, because you have to stay in control.

At least you are moving beyond the lighthouse. Maybe the seas will settle soon, once the worst of the tidal race has passed, since you guess that's what it's all about. You try to head inland out of the flow. But now, waves are coming at you at 90 degrees, as well as head on. This is crazy. "What's going on?" you cry, desperate to get out of here. There is nothing for it, but to tack away and head out to Ireland, away from one danger, and into another. There seems to be no end to this.

But it does end.

At last, the sea has calmed down again, and yes, you can return to your reading space. Relax. Stretch a little. Take a nice breath. Thank you.

I had made it through the worst, but still needed to figure out where to land.

The sun was out, and there were dramatic black cliffs all around, covered with a bright green topping, creating a beautiful vista.

Similar to previous occasions, it was hard to find my destination. This time, all the colours were dark, despite being well lit. I was searching for a tiny slot in the landscape, no bigger than a wrinkle. From the map, I knew the desired inlet was guarded by an island, and faced to the North-west, so it would be disguised from my line of sight, until I was in full view of Abercastle. Many times, I thought I was looking at an island, but on closer inspection, it became yet another undulation in the coastline, thus producing the cliff equivalent of a mirage. It took several approaches, aided by plenty of Navionics checks, to find the right place.

After I had landed, I noticed a slate plaque on the car park wall, celebrating the first sailor to cross the Atlantic, single handed. One Alfred Johnson, set off form Massachusetts in a fishing dory, a twin sailed craft like an oversized dinghy, completing the two-month passage on 10th August 1876. One remarkable feature of this feat was his successful landing at Abercastle. I could not help thinking that he had arrived (and not at Fishguard, for instance), more by luck than judgement. For it was a tricky spot to detect even for me, with my modern navigation aids, let alone trying to work out a safe route with a sextant and soggy maps. Nevertheless, fortune favours the brave, so they say. Huge posthumous congratulations to Alfred.

By way of a reminder of the dangers of the sea, there was an adjacent plaque. This one reported the shipwreck of steamship Leysian in the inlet in 1917. The ship had just completed transport of pack animals from the US. Perhaps, unlike Mr Johnson, they had run out of luck.

My judgement was being questioned when I came into the beach. I had sailed in on a run, and then swung round to stop, and get out. A man came charging down the gravelly surface, shouting at me.

"You're not supposed to sail in the harbour," he said. "You nearly ran into that boat."

Taken aback, and thinking better of it than to argue, I meekly replied, "I reckon I was in control."

"And I didn't catch your name by the way."

Rather than introduce himself, he preferred to repeat his complaints a couple more times, then marched back up the beach in double quick time.

Another man came down towards me, in less of a rush than the last.

"Are you Andrew?" he asked.

"How did you know that?" I asked, still shocked by my discarded anonymity.

"Oh, the guys at Newport let me know that you might be coming over." Sensing my discomfort from my most recent visitor, he added, "That's Nev by the way. Don't worry about him. He's the harbour master but he's harmless enough."

Tall, with a light-hearted manner and charming smile, David was easy company. He lent me a hand with moving items up the beach, and introduced me to Nev.

Nev was in a much better frame of mind, once he realised what I was up to. He was fixing fishing apparatus for his boat – the one he accused me of nearly crashing into. He was happy to answer questions about his hobby, so I asked him loads. He also added useful advice about traversing Ramsey and Jack Sound, so I soaked up his knowledge about that as well.

With all this sharing and caring, all was now well between us. Betty was contented too, looking up from her beachside spot between other overturned craft.

David offered the use of his outside shower room at his property up the hill. A steep path took us up to his gorgeous sun-drenched white house, on the northern side of the inlet. There was warm wind and soft grass, making perfect drying conditions, so my wet gear got a good airing. David also offered coffee, and more advice about tide times (I was asking absolutely everyone). His wife came back with her friends from a trip. And then shortly after that, David offered drinks to my friends Ann and Steve, who had arrived to pick me up, making an instant mini party. What a lovely spot and what a great atmosphere. A happy end to a testing day.

Ann and Steve were university mates, with whom Liz and I had holidayed several times. They had come over to visit some of their friends, who had kindly agreed to accommodate me on Saturday night, on the pretext that it was a worthy cause. I, of course, accepted gracefully.

Sunday 30th July

There was more foul weather on the way, so Sunday was an escape day, spent enjoying the wet Welsh coast with Ann, Steve and their friends.

In the afternoon, I was dropped off at Fishguard at a BnB for the evening, as my hosts needed to return home.

Whilst refreshed from a rest day, I was still troubled with the yo-yoing weather forecast, which led to endless rumination as to whether to sail on Monday. Conditions had been so up and down, rising to screaming gales and then dropping again to fickle winds, as one front after another came tumbling in from the Atlantic.

I rang Stick for advice.

"It's tricky," he said. "You have to work out what is in the red zone. For me, that has edged up and up over time. Now its batten breaking conditions."

I knew what he meant about the red zone, and about the margins shifting. I certainly felt more experienced and more confident about tackling extreme conditions. But the batten breaking thing? I would take that with a pinch of salt.

"I don't know for tomorrow," he said. "You could always go out and take a look. You'll know when you go out, whether it's viable."

That sounded sensible.

I rang Gordon, the enduring helping hand of Newport. He thought conditions should soften, and so would be OK. What's more, he offered to drive over and deliver me to Abercastle in the morning. "Gordon's kindness trumps a local bus service any day," I thought. How incredibly helpful yet again.

I tried to call Ken Fowler to canvass his opinion as well. He messaged back later having looked at the forecast, and suggested it looked too windy. "There might be a better day," he wrote. By then, I was set to give it a try.

I had a restless night, and woke early in anticipation of tackling St Davids Head and the sounds.

* ▲ ⊛

Day 82, Monday 31st July

To Dale

START	09.30, Abercastle
WIND	SW, 21–25mph, declining later
WEATHER	Cloudy, 16–18°C, rain showers early
TIDE	Against to 10.00. Then with, 1.7mph
SEA STATE	Moderate to slight
HAZARDS	Ramsey and Jack Sounds. Swell
FINISH	Dale, 14.00
DISTANCE	31 miles
SAILING HOURS	4¾ hours

Gordon was expertly punctual, and calmly drove his nervous passenger along the 20-minute route to Abercastle. The tide had come in. Betty was looking rested, and had had a good stay, free from harassment. A local holiday homeowner, plus Laser dinghy user, had noticed the writing on Betty's bottom. He came over to offer some adulation, which felt like a blessing for the day.

With Gordon's help, getting ready was relatively swift. I was in danger of being early again, but managed to faff about sufficiently to end up launching on time – to launch with the turning tide. I said a fond farewell to Gordon and his boundless generosity, and I was off to face the penultimate headland of the journey.

The first half hour was the most anxious making, being unsettling with its uncertainties. Soon, I eased into a routine of bouncing over the waves, and guarding against getting stuck in irons when I tacked. The wind was pretty testing but I was reassured by the knowledge that the tide would soon turn in my favour, and the wind would subside rather than increase.

Porthgain was my backout option, but it came and went without a further thought.

The anticipated three hours to Ramsey Sound shrunk to more like two, kicked on by the tide as it picked up pace near St Davids Head. A passing buoy reminded me of the accelerated speed, and for a short while I worried that I would shoot past Ramsey Sound altogether.

Ramsey Sound and Jack Sound are sneaky channels, providing a shortcut close to the mainland. However, they are dotted with rocks, washed by strong currents and drooling overfalls. The islands are, in effect, like flabby lips at the end of a dragon's upper and lower jaws, with the rocks acting like jagged teeth, half revealed at the edge of the monster's mouth, waiting to catch you. Going round the outside of this snarling trap would be possible, but would add several hours to the perilous journey.

According to my collection of Welsh advisors, I needed to watch out for Horse Rock on one side of the channel, then the famously named 'The Bitches' on the other, and finally Shoe Rock. Taken together, they called for a 'V' shaped course, through Ramsey Sound. Such was my enthusiasm for 'The Bitches', that I only just noticed Horse Rock as I was passing it. As for the rest, my route planning did the trick.

The sound exit was lined by a band of bumpy overfalls, but nothing compared to Strumble Head. I took a break when the water flattened out, to have some food and regroup.

Looking across the water towards Jack Sound, I could not make out where to go. This was partly because rain clouds were still washing into shore, meaning that I could only see a slither of grey in the distance. I checked my watch and I was in good time. The tide was adding a couple of miles per hour to my speed, so I was good to press on.

I couldn't understand why the sea state across St Brides Bay seemed so flat. This didn't make sense. It was an open mouth catching the airs of the Atlantic, and it should be lapping up the swell of the ruffled seas. I didn't mind because the crossing was quick, and a flatter sea means less drenching from the spray. An unhappy compensation was the persisting rain showers.

Skomer Island came into view, behind a moored tanker, and now I could see a small gap. "That must be Jack Sound," I said out loud.

"Just head for the middle," was Nev's advice. I could see waves breaking over rocks on either side, like saliva dripping over wetted fangs. I needed to hold my nerve and hold my course. "Betty, we can do this," I said, through gritted teeth.

More violent overfalls were waiting at the exit. Sharp breaking waves fought over each other to throw us off balance, amidst upwellings and disturbed lines of water. This was the last throw of the dice to ruin our journey. It was wild and spectacular. But Betty and I were becoming used to this sloshing nonsense. Betty floated gracefully over the surface troubles, and all I needed to do was to keep her company whilst she glided gracefully onwards.

We had made it.

Round another headland and the tide was pushing us in towards Milford Haven. Haven by name, and haven by nature, I was thinking. Then one last corner and I could see Dale and the yacht club.

I felt overjoyed coming towards the boat ramp. I felt tired but exhilarated. My excitement, and lack of attention when tacking amongst moored boats, meant that I briefly fell out since I didn't respond to a gust.

Max came out in his rib, shouting barely audible instructions, but the fact that someone was there, and had registered my presence, despite the lack of earlier communication, brought further smiles to my face.

In fact, the welcome was fantastic, and the vibe youthful and energetic. The sun had come out. Max was running a summer course, so the water was littered with learners in boats and on boards, all having a noisy good time. Young Rob had a trolley waiting, and helped land and stow Betty safely. In a quiet moment, before Sean arrived, I had a chat with Betty.

"Betty, I'm so proud of you. You have come all the way round from Abercastle. There were some big seas, weren't there, Betty? Thank you so much for carrying me through all of that. You have done so well." I gave her a little kiss.

I was really pleased to see Sean. We had met at the ILCA nationals in 2022, since he had been there to support his son Finn. We had neighbouring parking spaces so struck a conversation or two. I was feeling more aligned to those of older years, rather than the speedy youths strutting about. Back then, I had talked about the round the UK trip and Sean was encouraging of the adventure. Back then, Sean was keen that I should investigate the boat leak that I had discovered. I got that fixed.

For a long time, I had imagined coming to Dale. I wanted to reconnect. I wanted to hear about Welsh sailing and catch the flavour of local hospitality. I wanted to savour the safety of the sailing area. And now at last, here was Sean in person. As before, he was charming and engaging, and now, supplied with coffee and biscuits, to swell the occasion.

Sean had kindly taken time out from his veterinary afternoon. He gave me a quick tour of the area, driving up to the end of the promontory, so that we could take a look at Jack Sound from above. The clouds had finished their raining, and cleared off, so the sun was out. From our vantage point conditions appeared relatively benign, no doubt softened by time and distance.

Time was getting on when we returned to Sean's house. Finn and I remembered each other well. Rhia was superbly welcoming.

I was afforded what seemed like the whole of the top floor, including a sitting room, plus extraordinarily comfortable double bed. Dinner was lasagne and salad, so perfectly fitting my taste. The easy conversation, the comfortable furniture, the relatively straightforward conditions for tomorrow, with a scheduled 11.30 start, left me with a feeling of ease. I was so relieved to have passed St Davids Head and all the attendant complexities. It felt like it had been troubling me for weeks, and now it was behind me.

For the first time in ages, I sat down to watch the television. It was Matilda on Netflix, which I hadn't seen before. Good old Roald Dahl and his scripts of light and dark. I was part of the family.

Day 83, Tuesday 1st August 2023

To Tenby

START	11.45, Dale
WIND	WSW, 13–18mph
WEATHER	Cloud and sun, 13–18°C. Dry
TIDE	With me, max 2.5mph
SEA STATE	Slight, with 1m – 2m swell
HAZARDS	Complacency. Oh, and a firing range!
FINISH	Tenby, 15.30
DISTANCE	26 miles
SAILING HOURS	4 hours

I bade Sean a fond farewell when he dropped me off in the morning.

It was a new month. According to Liz, the official measurer back home, I was 78% of the way round, so had about 450 miles to go.

I can't remember much about the trip to Tenby. It must have gone smoothly.

I think it did since the tide turned as was expected, and washed me at great speed past Caldey Island, just before Tenby. I had a lovely tailwind as well.

Oh yes, I forgot to mention the ranges. There are several firing practice areas along the south coast of Wales. The government website lists firing times but does not illustrate range location, or whether firing is on land or out to sea. The areas are usually listed on Navionics but if you don't zoom in enough, the hazard does not show up, so it is very easy to miss them. Moreover, some of the ranges are privatised, and there is no link between one website and another. It seems like the military really are looking for targets! Instead, the coastguard gave useful advice, which I followed.

I rang Manorbier control station in the morning. They said it would be fine to cross if I sailed close to Castle Head, and sent them a text near the time. This would then prompt them to fire in a different direction. Given that the ranges are for firing practice, which involves a lot of missing, I was a little reassured by this plan, but not wholeheartedly so.

I followed instructions and sent a text, but received no reply. There was no reply on channel 73 either, but "maybe that's the radio not working" I thought. I later realised I had my text numbers muddled up, which is easily done when sailing along, and I had been busy texting Max! Luckily on this occasion, one error did not lead to another, and neither Betty nor I got shot.

Unfortunately, I realised I had lost my headphones at some point during the morning, presumably pulling them off inadvertently when lifting the sunglasses strap, something I feared might happen one day. Those headphones were no more than a week old. How irritating.

At Tenby the tide was coming in. Alistair of 76 happy years, greeted me on the beach because he happened to be there. He also happened to be a member of Tenby Sailing Club, so he kindly guided me to the waterfront ramp, and then past the club to the boat park. This was not really a boat park at all, but more like an elevated track next to a waterside road, used mainly by an ice cream van and the council beach attendant. It didn't feel very secure, but I followed suit and left Betty to rest, then went off to find some company and a beer.

I really liked Tenby. It was a lovely three-dimensional town, giving many varied vistas and meandering streetscapes, organised by folding lines of the cliff tops. It reminded me of Tobermory with multicoloured buildings along the seafront, except the buildings were at least an extra floor in height. So, perhaps 'Tobermory with an extra storey'?

The town layout was potentially confusing for visitors trying to find their way around. A road might head off in one direction, and then forcefully double back on itself, and end in precipitous steps dropping down to the seafront. In other places, a route would appear to form a shortcut, but the intrepid explorer might then discover that the path led you to the beach, which had unfortunately been submerged beneath the incoming tide.

A ruined Norman castle stood proud on a rocky promontory, adding splendour and separation between North and South Beach. A smart new RNLI building guarded its launching ramp below the castle, adding more drama to the scene. Wally the Walrus, having swum all the way from the Arctic, was unfazed by all this pomp, and had parked himself on the bottom of the boat slide in 2021. He was asked to move at one point though, to make way for a lifeboat.

Caldey Island is a mile from the castle by sea, so a regular stop off for summer tourists. Tourists provided useful income for the Cistercian monks (a branch of Catholicism) who own and run the island. The monks took ownership of the island in 1906, but some religious practices link back to centuries-old traditions. It reminded me of Holy Isle near the Isle of Arran in Scotland, another spiritual sanctuary off the coast of Great Britain.

I was staying at the Belgrave Hotel, a large old building on the esplanade overlooking South beach, gathered amongst other statuesque and imposing structures.

There was an in-house restaurant in the basement which seemed smart. Given that the weather was turning dark and stormy for the night, my wintery selection was 'Lamb Hot Pot'. It said 'Lamb Hot Pot with vegetables'. There was a topping of roast potatoes, together with a warm bread roll and butter, and the plate was finished off with chips. It was all very tasty, but there was a distinct lack of vegetables.

I went back to the sailing club to meet some of the locals. Tenby Sailing Club occupies a top spot in the middle of the harbour. Its three-storey stone structure was in keeping with surrounding buildings, and the first-floor bar offered great views across the water. The club website said that it was an 'integral part of the local community'. Too often, similar statements are casual boasts, but I could see what was meant after I climbed the metal stairs to the bar. It was open to the public, and was full of people.

Evening racers came in off the water, and rather than filling the tables, they were slightly squeezed into a corner. I met a guy called Steve who used to sail at Papercourt, and we shared names of folks we both knew. He had joined Tenby to enrol in a higher standard of sailing, which is fair enough since Tenby has access to a much bigger patch of water, called the Bristol Channel. It was great to make those homely connections.

I also met Blake who had been organising national sailing events at Tenby since 1976. Other people wondered how the club would manage when he finally hangs up his organisational skills. Folks like Blake are so often key drivers in helping voluntary clubs survive. Yes, it was an uncomfortable question.

On the way back to the hotel, there was Hollywood style rain, being thrown at me by gusts of wind, as if a stage crew were standing around the corner with power showers.

I ducked into Tesco's for supplies, and picked up a bag of carrots for 40p. What great value! I was pleased to get my hands on those, after the earlier hot pot stodge fest. They could go in my lunch bag with the apples, so an ideal midday snack – they are waterproof, are not easily squashed, and would probably benefit from being lightly salted. Perfect.

Back at the hotel some 20-something year old travellers tumbled into reception, close to 11:00pm with their TV equipment. They sat down and 'psssch'ed open their cans of beer, much to the annoyance of the hotel staff. The group had come down to film a drone display, that was scheduled to take place in front of the sailing club, but it was cancelled because of the weather conditions.

I was curious about the production process, having stepped into the world of online video making, and they were happy to answer questions. They said it usually takes about five hours of editing to deal with two hours of filming. That was roughly in line with my thinking, because putting the material together felt really time consuming. It also reminded me of the great work that Sam had been doing, assembling YouTube episodes. I was so grateful I was not having to do it myself. "I must ring him and thank him," I thought.

From the comfort of my room, it seemed best to wait till the wind and rain calmed down, before setting off in the morning. The Wi-Fi was finally working, and remarkably Argos had replacement headphones in store, and I could pick them up on the way to the beach. My goodness, modern living has become so immediate. Hence, everything was in order, and I could relax and settle down to a long winter night's sleep.

* * *

Day 84, Wednesday 2nd August

To Mumbles

START	12.30, Tenby
WIND	SW, nothing, then NW, 16–26mph
WEATHER	Rain then cloud, and sun. 15–17°C
TIDE	With me, max 1.2mph from 13.00
SEA STATE	Slight to rough
HAZARDS	Swell, lightning, firing range again
FINISH	Mumbles, 19.00
DISTANCE	35 miles
SAILING HOURS	6½ hours

I had vaguely considered crossing to Devon from Tenby, which would have been about 40 miles, but given the up and down wind, I thought it would be too risky.

The tide was out, and to my surprise Alistair turned up to give me a hand with launching. A trolley was certainly helpful since there was quite a way to walk. These South Wales tides have a big range, and were likely to get bigger as I approached Bristol.

It was to be a 24-hour period, with loads of overnight wind, then none, then loads later.

There was another military practice area to be avoided, whose name I can't remember. The pilot boat was parked just outside the harbour, so I stopped for a chat and to find out where to go. I was told to head for DZ2 and then go outside DZ6. These were danger markers, which are yellow blobs on nautical charts. (I had always wondered what they were!) I finally found these on Navionics, and set off on the appropriate compass bearing. I never did find the marker buoys on the water, and decided to simply carry on, hoping for the best.

Two or three miles offshore, the wind became lighter and lighter. There was still a rolling swell, giving the impression of puffs of air as the waves washed me backwards and forwards, but in fact there was no wind at all. Large rain clouds passed nearby, threatening thunder. "I certainly can't get to Mumbles like this," I said to myself.

My sister Katie rang for a chat. It was nice to hear from her, but I was not feeling very relaxed given the absence of breeze, and the discomfort of sitting under a boom, with the boat rocking from side to side. I had earlier tried to check the wind forecast, but the signal wasn't great, so I tried to ask for wind information from my sister. She helpfully supplied rain information.

I had hardly gone anywhere and wasn't going anywhere, so was seriously contemplating turning back. I needed to make a decision. I rang Liz to ask the same weather question.

"Hmm... It looks like there is plenty of wind near Ilfracombe," she mused.

"That's Devon," I said, feeling frustrated. None the wiser, I decided to stick with my plan till 14.00, and if there was no wind I would retreat, hurt and annoyed.

By this stage, I had forgotten about the military practice area, but figured that my immobility was a good excuse, not that that would help a great deal if the worst came to the worst.

In the nick of time, ripples appeared on the water, and built to a comfortable breeze, blowing me to Mumbles in the forecast direction. I was saved.

The wind grew and so did the swell. I could see some violent pointy rocks in the distance, which I later realised were called Worms Head, which is the western point of the Gower Peninsula. I estimated it would take me 30 minutes to reach the promontory, but my pace had picked up so much that I passed it in ten.

Alastair had warned me about a protruding sandbar near there, which might not be a depth problem, but could be a swell problem. Sure enough, the sea became more and more agitated, despite the fact that it was wind with tide. Having been marooned an hour earlier, I felt ill prepared for this wild ride. Large waves were breaking all around me, and there was a stiff breeze building to boot. Conditions were becoming harder and harder to manage.

I pulled on as much downhaul as I could manage, and kept the sail sheeted in a fair way, with plenty of pumping as the gusts arrived, to try and spill breeze out of the leech. I cut over the line of the sandbanks as quickly as I could, but that didn't seem to help. I ended up several miles offshore, feeling isolated, nervous and only just in control.

I wanted to head towards land (Wales, that was, as opposed to England, for I was in the Bristol channel), despite fears that a dead run would be even more challenging. On gybing round, it felt like things had settled considerably. Maybe the wind had calmed. Or perhaps I was just getting better at sailing. Either way, I was very grateful to feel back in control.

Looking at the tracker later, I had exceeded 12.5mph around Worms Head, my fastest pace so far, meaning that I had indeed been whistling along.

I had been in touch with Mumbles Yacht Club and was pleased to have received an encouraging reply. Mumbles, by the way, is said to link back to Norman times, when the French word, 'Les mamelles', meaning mammary or breasts, was used to describe the location. Presumably this referred to the undulating rocks by the lighthouse. Ah, the French!

Jo responded to my email, and said she would make contact with other club members, but did not think there would be much of a reception when I arrived. This was a cunning move. A bit like convincing yourself the movie you have taken the trouble to go and see, is not very good, your pleasure is increased by any nuggets of quality. At Mumbles, there were sacks full of welcoming gold.

The first nugget was a small pod of dolphins who joined me, just before Mumbles Lighthouse. What gorgeous creatures, who effortlessly swam along next to us, almost in touching distance, and doing so just for the fun of it. I was delighted to have their company, and was pleased to be able to catch some GoPro footage, having had so many failed attempts previously. That made one of the 'money shots' of the trip. Fortunately, all the tension of Worms Head had subsided, and I was relaxed enough to enjoy their enjoyment.

Next, having navigated round the bumpy lighthouse seas, to my delight, two dinghies came out to escort me to land. We shouted 'Hello's across the water. Jack was in a Laser, and Tim in a Topper. Their presence was doubly delightful since I received direction instructions, without which I would have definitely gone to the wrong slipway.

A crowd greeted my arrival together with trolley, chat, and lots of assistance to haul Betty up the steep concrete ramp, which was awash with waves. Jo was there coordinating efforts. She helpfully organised overnight storage for Betty in a secret gated space, in the company of other boats – Betty likes that. Then we could all relax and head off to the bar, for yet more Welsh cordiality.

Folks were impressed with my speed coming round the Gower Peninsula, and so was I. There were more sailing stories, and shared connections with Papercourt, this time through university. A group of youths came in, all dressed as lifeguards, and clearly ready to party, adding to a great vibe. But it was time to head off and relish the jewel in the crown of Mumbles welcomes – a stopover at Jo's place.

Jo and her husband were not retired, so had work to attend to in the morning. Jo was self-employed, running a business removing invasive plant species, like Japanese Knotweed, and bamboo.

I had heard about Japanese Knotweed decades ago, and learnt that it could grow from tiny fragments of root or stem, dropped, or left in the ground inadvertently. Once established it could break through walls or lift pavements. Hence it was a really destructive species, and very difficult to remove. The plant was one that sparked fear in my mind, reminiscent of the world-dominating Triffids, as imagined by John Wyndham in his famous novel. Thus, it was reassuring to meet Jo, who would calmly set about dealing with the hazardous material on a day-to-day basis. I felt that if my garden should fall victim to an invasive species, at least I could call Jo, without having to resort to drastic measures like going to live on the Isle of Wight (as was the case in the book).

The final dusting of golden friendliness came from Bertie, the three-legged family cat. Not satisfied with sniffing his way through my clothing bag, he decided to take up residence. Peering out from the blackness with his pale-yellow eyes, he purred contentedly and gave no sign of wanting to move. Maybe he was trying to say that I really shouldn't be leaving Wales. He had a good point, because Wales had been spectacular in so many ways.

Sadly, Mumbles would be the last stop on my tour of the country, for I was planning to cross the Bristol Channel the next day. Thank you, Wales, you have been so welcoming.

CHAPTER 19

The last corner in the land

* ? *

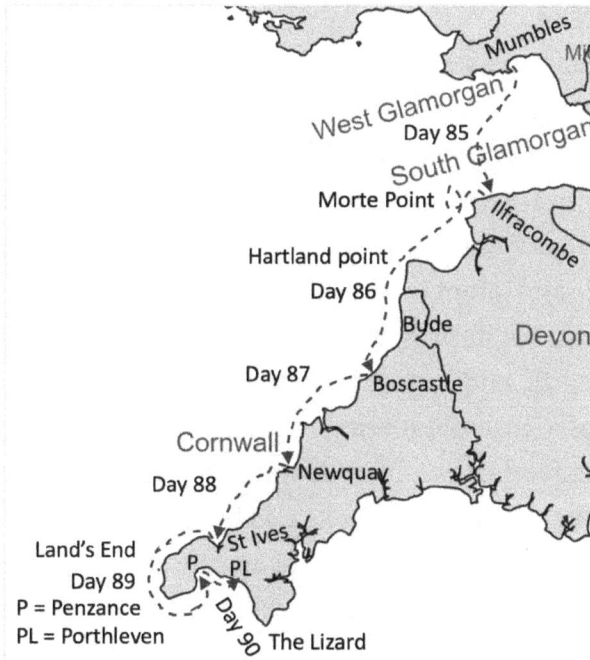

Day 85, Thursday 3rd August

To Ilfracombe

START	11.20, Mumbles
WIND	NW, 20–25mph
WEATHER	Cloudy, 15–17°C dry
TIDE	East, max 2.2mph till 15.00
SEA STATE	Moderate to rough
HAZARDS	Swell and waves, getting lost
FINISH	Ilfracombe, 14.30
DISTANCE	26 miles
SAILING HOURS	3¼ hours

It was much easier getting out from Mumbles, than it was coming in, but much lonelier. The prospect of a long open sea passage left me feeling nervous, but at least this was not the first of its kind.

The forecast was a promising north-westerly, but the wind picked up out of the shelter of Swansea Bay, then it picked up again, and then again. It was a stiff broad reach, not quite as bad as day one, but getting that way. I was building on yesterday's techniques to stay in control – loads of downhaul, with the kicker fairly loose, and plenty of sail pumping, to spill wind. I didn't know if it was an approved method, but it seemed to help. That and sheeting in and out over the waves, which now required a full range of arm movement, like taking a long oar stroke with one arm. I stayed in the boat despite the wild ride.

Measuring distance out at sea, is by the colour and size of the land ahead or behind. Moving away, the urban properties melt into the landscape after three or four miles, turning into a light smudge. Further out, the land becomes more monochrome, with grey and green, washing into one another, so that by eight miles or so, it is a wobbly line of darker grey, or maybe darker blue if the sun is out. After that, depending on the height of the terrain, the line might sink into the horizon altogether, leaving nothing but sea and sky to stare at.

The edges of both Wales and England are sufficiently upstanding, to be visible from the middle of the channel. However, a compass and Navionics were essential for correcting course, for otherwise, I would have missed my destination by several miles.

Approaching Devon, or England once more, the process was reversed. The hues became less hazy, green emerged from dark grey, and eventually some white of a town revealed itself out of the distance. By that stage, the day had been long. The excited anticipation of disembarking made me see more detail than was real. Gaps between houses or the spire of a church were imagined, confirming my misguided proximity to an end point.

At last, after several directional corrections on the water, I was approaching Ilfracombe. I had finally found the right place. With more sailing, I could confidently make out the harbour entrance, and headed in to land on the beach.

The tide was out. I stepped out onto English sand. England again, and for the last time on the trip. It felt like the end was getting closer.

There was no welcome.

Great black harbour walls towered above me, a measure of the huge tidal range that comes with the Bristol Channel. A Damien Hirst bronze statue, stood by the entrance, gazing out to sea. She was not staring down at me, but you could feel her defiant presence, as I wandered around this empty harbour goldfish bowl.

Steadily sloping sand led the way to the town and a boat ramp, so much easier to negotiate than the enormous expanses of the Solway Firth. On one wall, a fishing trawler was parked. Denuded of supporting water, its freshly painted hull was exposed, showing tangerine orange, a strip of white, and then bright blue to finish, next to the yellow floor. Resting on the sand and leaning gently against a wall, it looked more like a model in a model shop, than a hunting vessel, ready to brave the oceans.

A little further on, there were more trawlers and then yachts, neatly lined up on solid ground, and then a car, presumably making use of the smooth surface as a temporary car park. It felt quite surreal, and more like an exhibition hall than a working port.

Terrible signal and an emergency coffee delayed my meeting with Mark. We were eventually united by Betty, who was waiting patiently at the water's edge. Mark was a friend from university, who had kindly come over to provide support. Tall, and charming with a winning smile, he made everything feel easy in his presence.

We headed off into town to explore landing options, passing streams of summer tourists. Mark suggested we tried the yacht club, so went in for a beer.

The barman said, "Why not try Trevor over in the harbour office, just across the way?"

We found Trevor, who was with George, the deputy. She said, "Joe got your message and said you might be coming over." So, things had linked up after all.

"You see that ramp next to the Lime Kiln café, on the other side of the harbour?" Trevor continued, "The lock up next to it, has only been finished two weeks ago. The rowing club have a gig in there, but no one else has been using it. I'm sure the council won't mind if I give you the combination for the night."

"That sounds perfect," I said. It was.

Before heading out of town, we went to take a closer look at Damien Hirst's statue. Verity is on a 20-year loan from the artist, who himself is a resident. Some had suggested that Verity was the name of a girlfriend or muse, but it was meant as a reference to 'truth'. The figure was of a naked pregnant woman, holding a sword aloft, standing on law books, and dangling a set of scales by her side. More controversially, one side of her body had much of the skin peeled back, including from her face, exposing the musculature below, and the full form of her foetus. Verity was at once arresting and disturbing. As ever, the artist divided opinion, some finding the figure brutally disfigured, and others relishing the bold and controversial display. I couldn't help but look on in awe, admiring the brashness of the enterprise.

I had a fantastic evening with Mark and Sarah, catching up, but also enjoying a fun and sociable time with other family members, who joined for supper. Their son had yachting experience in the area, so provided advice about hazards, such as tidal races at Morte and Hartland Points. He also said I should watch out for a seaweed farm in Barnstable Bay. He had been involved with the set up, so had up to date local knowledge.

My VHF radio received drying attention on the Aga overnight. On arriving in Ilfracombe, I noticed that the protective flap covering the charging point had been left open by my bad self, so the screen was now reminiscent of a radio in the rain, from inside. Any flickers of screen life that had been evident a few hours earlier, were now extinct, and the gadget was confirmed deceased. It may have been on the way out anyway, hence the crackly reception at Newport. I would need to get hold of another one, but not before tomorrow. I was planning to press on without it.

Day 86, Friday 4th August

To Boscastle

START	10.00, Ilfracombe
WIND	NW, 14–16mph, backing WSW
WEATHER	Sun/Cloud, 14–16°C. Dry
TIDE	With me, max 2.7mph till 15.00
SEA STATE	Slight, moderate at times
HAZARDS	Tidal race at Morte and Hartland Points. Cornish cliffs. Boscastle entrance
FINISH	Boscastle, 16.00
DISTANCE	47 miles
SAILING HOURS	6 hours

Conditions looked ideal for a long day's sailing, and I was keen to make the most of it, before the wind swung back round to the gruelling south-westerlies.

An earlyish start suited Mark and Sarah, since they needed to get off to an event. Mark kindly took me on the 40-minute drive to Ilfracombe. We finished with a sneaky dash down an illicit tree-lined road, ending at the slipway. And then he sped off.

Open water swimmers were preparing for a dip, and let me use their smart new toilets. One lady was so enthused by my trip, she made a handsome online donation, which was very touching.

The tide was in. The harbour had been completely transformed by the turning of the clock. Water was now lapping at Verity's feet, roughly where we had stood the day before. It was a new day, and I was set to go. "Cornwall, here we come."

There was an onshore breeze and slight swell on the ramp, with a fairly narrow exit, so I thought carefully before launching. However, I put my centre plate down a fraction too early before

456

setting off. The rotating wave motion meant that the virginal concrete caught the back edge of my centre plate, and pulled off a slice. I only noticed, when I saw a piece of orange coloured debris in the water. In my haste to get going I thought, "I'm not going back for that. I'll have to take a proper look at the damage later."

Then I noticed that I hadn't rigged the rudder tie down properly. I paused in the harbour to sort that out.

With the broken radio in mind, I mused, "I seem to be making a lot of mistakes."

The major disaster of the day happened a few miles after setting off.

I started on a fetch, and was anxious to bend round the knuckle of North Devon, so that I could bear away and pick up speed, to make the most of the day. The tide was building at Morte Point as I was going through the race, so there were some sizeable waves, but by now I was relaxed enough to grab some footage when sailing through them.

Suddenly I realised the pink bag, containing all my essential day gear, was no longer in the boat. I looked behind me and could see it floating about 30 metres away. "How has that happened?" I shouted. The footwell was full of water from the race, and looking down, I noticed the paddle had come loose and was sloshing about, getting ready to join the bag. Now silenced by panic, I thought, "I have to get the bag back. I have to get the bag. It contains so many essential things."

However, trying to turn back in a rush, and failing to take sufficient account of the waves, I bore away too quickly, and immediately fell out. Now, Betty had turned turtle, and the paddle was floating free. Moreover, I had managed to kick a water bottle out of its holder on my way over the side, and my hat had been dislodged. It was absolute chaos.

Grabbing easy things first, I returned the soaking hat to my head, and took hold of the water bottle. The paddle was just out of reach, so a short stretch from the boat and I was back in charge of my special orange plastic friend. Next, I needed to return Betty to an upright position, and given my expertise in falling out, that didn't take long.

Sitting in my appropriately floating companion, next to a noisily flapping sail, I paused to check that nothing else was missing. Once all items were accounted for, I could then refocus on recovering the bag.

But it was nowhere to be seen. I didn't think I had taken that long to restore order. And I had successfully completed a bag overboard procedure before, so still felt sure I would find it. I was caught in that phase of mentally frozen disbelief, in which the awfulness of a potentially shocking loss has not sunk in. I was simultaneously aware that a calamity was unfolding, and yet continuing to think that everything was going to be fine. To lose my day bag would be catastrophic, since the scale of equipment jeopardy was so much greater than any previous mishap.

I was not out of the race, so the sea was still shaking violently. Desperately peering through the waves, I went downwind, zigzagging across the path I had taken. There was no sign of the bag. I looked left, I looked right, and upwind, and downwind, but there was nothing.

A stream of questions ran through my head. "Has it been blown further inshore? It was floating nicely when I first saw it. I think it was anyway? Had I taken too long getting back into the boat? Where else could it be?"

Still no sign.

"I can't keep searching forever."

I began to think it must have sunk, given that it was quite full.

"But if I can't find it, will it be safe to go on?" I asked myself. "Going back seems a bit fruitless, unless I have to."

The weather and visibility were improving, meaning that I could see Hartland Point in the distance, which was the next major landmark, despite being over 15 miles away. That meant the need for a compass was less pressing.

"I should have put the compass on the deck this morning, rather than rush off," I thought, berating myself for my errors.

After a number of further passes, the sad necessity of giving up, finally took hold. The faded pink blob had gone to join other detritus at the bottom of the sea. My apologies for leaving litter in my tracks, but I did try and tidy up.

It was a warm day, and the tide was whisking me past Morte Point, appropriately named as the graveyard for my day bag. The easy thing to do was to carry on. That had become tradition after all. So, on I went.

As I was speeding across Bideford and Barnstable Bay, keeping a lookout for the seaweed farm, I mentally listed the missing items, and tried to work out what to do to replace them. The items were as follows:

- Compass (Tacktick variety)
- Compass mount
- GoPro mounts
- GoPro leash and mouth mount
- Electronic flare
- Neck fleece
- Waterproof cap
- Spare gloves
- Sun hat from Berwick (which I had been given)
- Extra food like bananas, nuts and a sandwich
- Dry bag liner
- Dry bag itself, which was not very dry anymore.

Several miles of rumination led me to an important conclusion about the tragedy of day 86.

"It's only shopping," I said to myself.

That made events feel so much less burdensome. I had successfully cheered myself up. And I like a bit of shopping.

Quite often when a feared situation actually happens, people find themselves less troubled by the fear. I remember working with a child who was really worried about the house being burgled. When the unpleasant eventuality did occur, I thought the young person would be a lot more frightened, and was surprised to find the opposite was the case. What she told me was that she then knew what to expect, and how she and others would react. It was no longer the mysterious unknown. I guess that also happened for me. Needless to say, it doesn't work that way for everyone.

After much puzzling, I concluded that that bag had been washed out, simply because I had forgotten to strap it on that morning. Therefore, I had committed a great catalogue of errors in the last 24 hours. Perhaps it was time to take a day off before something even more serious happened.

There was one more thing to report before arriving at Boscastle. When I was reaching along past Bude, I took some video footage that I have used several times in subsequent presentations. The slide heading was "Why?" referring to the reasons for undertaking the trip.

In the video, I was a few miles offshore, with Cornwall just visible in the background. Betty was all set on a beam reach with little need for sail trim. We were making a comfortable seven or eight miles per hour, with the sea state slight, and the sun out. I was leaning out, with feet under the toe straps, keeping focussed but feeling in control. There was no one about. Nothing but land, and sea, and sky. We were alone, out at sea, at one with nature and the elements, making good speed to a known and safe destination, having travelled most of the way around mainland GB. I was the master of my own destiny, and master of the wind and waves, on board the simplest of crafts, doing the simplest of things. I felt at one with Betty and the world. We were free. We were supremely happy.

Finding the right gap in the folding cliff line of Cornwall was a little tricky, similar to Abercastle. But being a seasoned navigator by now, the quest was not too taxing.

However, the syphon-shaped narrow entrance, below tall cliffs, and between jutting breakwaters, was definitely more challenging than the Welsh experience. Swell was washing directly into the mouth, ricocheting on each precipitous wall, and being emphasised as the gap narrowed. I needed to have paddle at the ready, given that wind would be arriving from random directions, or possibly absent altogether. I really did not want to get caught up in the white froth on the rocky edges, which were only a few feet away. I was wondering if this was all a bad idea.

Round the second corner, a breakwater came into view. The tide was out, and I could see my struggle would end early, because I could step out amongst large smooth stones. I was safe from the sea.

Looking around to work out a stowage plan, I soon realised that Boscastle was a complicated landing site. Boulders, a stream, a breakwater, dense seaweed, steep walls and no safe beach. I wasn't sure what to do. Perhaps, I wasn't yet safe after all.

Fortunately, procrastination brought the tide up the stream, and helped me shape a plan. I could now move Betty past the boulders, and round the breakwater. I had to wade through a thick bed of kelp, making sure I didn't get tangled up in the slimy brown bands. This was proving to be hard work. The tide rose further, so I rolled Betty onto a tiny patch of sand, next to moored boats. That wasn't the end of it, however.

I resolved to park Betty on the top of the inner breakwater, next to some tenders. The structure was made of upright slate, and had a ramp, forming a steep and jagged path. I could roll Betty up the slope, but such was the incline that I could not let go, lest Betty would slide back down, gaining scratches and bruises on the way. I tied her painter onto a railing to hold her steady, but was still stuck, despite having only a few feet to go. Luckily, a passerby brought good sense, and muscle to the rescue, and at last Betty was parked on the top of the wall. The whole procedure had been a major struggle and taken well over an hour, despite being less than 100 metres. I wasn't looking forward to the departure!

One of the reasons for stopping at Boscastle, was because more university friends lived there, and I was hoping to see them. Unfortunately, they were away, but instead they had very kindly leant me their house for the duration.

Claire and John also left contact numbers for locals, who might be able to assist if needed. One such contact was Mary, who lived in an elegant white cottage overlooking the harbour.

When walking past, I knocked on the door by way of saying hello, though not expecting anything.

"Oh, do come in," said Mary, immediately grasping the connection.

Before I had a chance to say anything else, she said, "I'm sure you will be needing some food. My granddaughter and her husband will be here soon, but I'm sure we can stretch the food to include you. Would an omelette be OK?"

What an incredible welcome, immediately making me feel part of the occasion. There was a large sitting room window, with a view down the harbour, and I could see Betty resting in her upturned state, on the breakwater wall. Betty felt part of the party, as well.

Mary told me about the history of the cottages. They had been fisherman's dwellings for a century or so, originally owned by the local authority. After the Second World War, in 1945, the Labour Party introduced the 'Homes for all policy'. This was intended to help recovery from destruction of the Second World War, and to upgrade housing stock in general. In the next six years, 800,000 homes were built, an impressive achievement compared to recent sluggish comparisons.

As part of this policy, there was a call to end the 'outside-toilet'. Local authorities therefore offered many houses for sale, so that owners could attend to the toilet problem. Mary's house was one such purchase, now with relevant facilities welcomed into the fabric of the building.

I shared a story, about the 2004 Boscastle flood. The famous and rare event is now part of school GCSE geography lessons.

The flood was caused by an exceptional cloud burst, which parked over the catchment areas of the three rivers that converge in Boscastle. Something like seven inches of rain, fell in an afternoon in August. Steep sided valleys, usually made of non-porous slate, were already soaked from earlier in the month, meaning there was no place for the water to go. It was high tide, making the situation worse.

The river level rose by two metres in an hour, and at another point, a three-metre wave came crashing down the main road, as a blockage was released further upstream. Helped by this monster surge of water, the flood largely destroyed the central section of the village.

My story was retold from Claire. Below is a full version of events, whereas only snippets were shared at Mary's house.

Claire was returning from a day out. In the car was her seven-year-old son, and a friend of his. It had been raining hard. Very hard, so she was keen to get home.

Claire turned up a narrow lane, with steep hedges on either side. There was surface water rushing down the road washing pieces of debris with it, but nothing that the car could not manage.

Then, without warning, a huge wall of water came hurtling down the lane towards the vehicle, like a massive exaggeration of a theme park flue. It must have been caused by a field gate that had become unblocked, because with the water, there were hay bales. Not those delicate square ones that people sit on at a fete, but those huge round ones that can only be picked up by a tractor. Several of these enormous wheels, came hurtling towards them and bumped over the front of the car. Remarkably, the windscreen did not break, but the car was being washed down the lane towards the river. Claire's passengers were now terrified.

In her calm-headed retelling of the story, Claire said, "It was best to get out of the vehicle and away from the road, at this point." The car came to a stop, temporarily stuck in a ditch. She guided her passengers out of the car, onto the hedge-bank, and they scrambled to safety, away from the main stream. The road had become a river.

She noticed another vehicle further downhill. An elderly couple had opened the car door, and were slowly getting out. Except they were exiting on the road side, and not the hedge side, so were stepping into the full force of the stream. This was not a good move. No sooner had they disembarked, first one, and then the other, lost their footing, and started to slide down the lane.

After checking that the boys were OK to wait on the hedge-bank, Claire went to the couple's aid. Both had slithered down the tarmac, causing significant grazing. When she reached them, they were alive and still mobile, but not in a happy state.

Claire helped each one out of the road, and into a nearby field. Regathering the boys, they all made their way to a local farmhouse.

The elderly couple were both in need of urgent medical attention. Calling for help, the emergency service response suggested that an air ambulance would be needed. However, such was the scale of devastation down in the valley, that all the local helicopters were occupied.

After waiting two hours, the rain had abated, but the sound of choppers hadn't. The local roads were now passable, so fortunately an ambulance arrived, and transported the injured elderly pair to hospital.

Meanwhile, Claire's car had been washed away, and was jammed on the riverbank at the bottom of the hill. Like several others, including that of the rescued couple, it was full of mud and river debris, so was a write-off. Those were just two of the 150 or so vehicles that were washed away that day, some 30 of them ending up in Boscastle harbour.

Amazingly, there were no fatalities following the flood. Emergency services were praised for their impressive response. It was easy to imagine that without Claire's unsung rescue efforts, there may well have been at least two casualties. Well done, Claire, our local superhero.

After Claire was given a lift home, she thought she should ring the boy's parents, since they were abroad.

"It's been incredibly wet, and there have been some floods, but we are all OK," she said, doing her best not to worry his parents.

Sensing who was on the end of the line, the lad quickly joined in with the call, and told his parents all about events of the day, in alarming detail. They were very relieved to hear that all was fine, despite the scale of devastation in Boscastle.

After all the delightful food, company and storytelling, it was time for me to leave.

The taxi driver who came to pick me up at about 9.00pm, needed no introduction as to the location of Claire and John's house. I almost felt like a local.

There was something of an orienteering expedition to find the key, but once in I soon settled, and was quickly tucked up in bed for a good sleep. This had been my longest distance travelled so far and indeed, the longest for the trip. It felt like the sailing had been uneventful, but everything else had been the opposite. So much light and dark all in one day, but I felt satisfied.

* * *

Saturday 5th August

I had been looking forward to a day off, and it proved its worth. As an extra, I was able to borrow a car for the day, which was a massive treat. Storm Antoni was blowing in, so I would not have been able to sail anyway, meaning that timing worked out just fine, as had become the norm.

Having established a replacement kit plan, I went into Bude for a bit of shopping. I decided the following:

The electronic flair could stay where it was, on the sea floor, somewhere off Morte Point.

String would substitute for the mouth mount and leash.

I would make do with a hand-held walking compass for less than a tenner, instead of a £300 plus Tacktick effort, since I had completed my major crossings.

A couple of replacement hats from the local outdoor wear supplier, would help with sun and rain protection.

And the remaining items, including a replacement radio, would come down with Pete and Julia, whom I was planning to meet the next day. That was with the help of my delightful and glamorous shopping assistant back home. Thanks so much, Liz.

I went over to check out Bude beach, which I had seen from the sea the day before. Storm Antoni, was indeed a storm. It was one of those lean-into-the-wind-and-cover-your-eyes situations. Peering through a small gap between fingers, to prevent bits of beach being blown into my eyes, I could make out the sea roughed up so much that it had turned half white. It was definitely a day to be staying on land. That evening, I found grains of sand in my ears, my clothes, and even my shoes.

Back at Boscastle harbour, I crept over the brow of a hill to inspect tomorrow's exit. It did not look good. Much more swirling mess than yesterday, and I was really not sure how I would manage. One of the Claire and John contacts was Chris, the harbourmaster. I gave him a call. He turned out to be the brother-in-law of the sailing secretary at Papercourt (yet more connections to our local club). Chris suggested things should all calm down overnight. He said it would be relatively straightforward getting out on the ebb tide, with assistance from the flow of the river. "That's reassuring," I thought, but it certainly didn't look that way.

In the news, the women's football world cup was progressing well, with England getting into the last 16. The men's rugby world cup warm up matches were going really well for the home nations, except for England.

Interest rates had gone up again, to the highest rate in years.

I went to bed a bit earlier than usual. What joy. The tired suddenly hit me, and this time I went with it.

Day 87, Sunday 6th August

To Newquay (all one word), Cornwall

START	11.00, Boscastle
WIND	NW, 12–16mph
WEATHER	Cloud, then sun, 15–17°C. Dry
TIDE	With me max 0.8mph till 13.00
SEA STATE	Moderate to slight
HAZARDS	Harbour exit. Forgetting things
FINISH	Newquay, 15.30
DISTANCE	27 miles
SAILING HOURS	4½ hours

The big challenge was getting out of the harbour. I was quite worried about it, having been alarmed by the sea state from the evening before.

I stopped off at Mary's house to drop off some wine and chocolates, as a thank you for her impromptu generosity. Mary was delighted, and was keen to come down to see the launch.

In fact, when she later arrived at the breakwater, I put in a last-minute request. "Mary, would it be OK if I dash back and use your loo, do you think?" Luckily, the toilet was only just inside the property so easy to access. This need was out of usual abdominal character for me, but on the day, proved absolutely essential. The visit was an enormous relief! I was once again indebted to Mary for her kind nature, and she had saved me for a second time. Feeling a lot more comfortable, I returned to the gathering crowd, to reinitiate launching procedures.

Chris was there to lend support. He said he wouldn't be going out that day, since conditions were too 'bumpy', but he thought it would be OK for me. "Hmm," I thought. I was hoping to have a motorised escort, but this clearly wasn't being offered, so I resolved to press on, together with my friend 'hope for the best'.

Manoeuvring Betty back down the steep slate slope was a lot easier with several people to hand, but it was still tricky. The tide was in, so the landing obstructions were submerged. However, there were swimmers in the water, sloshing around in the swell. Fortunately, they splashed out of the way when I came into view, reducing the hazard count a fraction.

A combination of sailing, paddling and bobbing about were needed, to edge my way forward. With waves bouncing off the inlet edges, the water surface was like a gyrating jelly, devoid of any pattern, which was both really uncomfortable, but also made it harder to make progress. Swirling wind, dropped down from the cliff tops, tumbling into the harbour, arriving in random directions, in gentle puffs or vigorous blasts. One of them caught me off guard and I fell out, luckily when I was near the exit, so, far enough from the rocky walls. Unfortunately, the tumble was spotted by my onlookers, who must have been alarmed, but I was soon up and away. That was one of the most difficult landing places of the whole circumnavigation. People say that North Cornwall can be tricky, and I would agree.

A steady north-westerly breeze meant that the journey was comfortable, and quicker than expected.

I paused on the water near Padstow to admire some of the scenery and reminisce about local landmarks, that I had visited many times on childhood and adult holidays. I passed Pentire Point. I could see into the mouth of the River Camel, where it washes over the Doom Bar (which gives the beer its name), and into Hayle Bay, and Polzeath. I had stayed there many times. Onwards, round Trevose Head, there was Constantine Bay. Then further on the Bedruthan steps, all spectacular and well-trodden pieces of coastline. What a lovely trip down memory lane I was having.

I was quite perplexed coming into Newquay, because it was not how I remembered it. I kept checking on my phone to make sure. I later figured out that I had been thinking of Watergate Bay, and not Newquay. In truth, the town was new to me, hence the lack of recognition.

There was a smooth bottomed harbour at Newquay, which was filled with holidaymakers and their holiday craft, making it like a happy communal beach. Trying to look casual, I drifted onto the sand and stepped out, thinking that the tourists might be curious or even impressed. How vain I had become. What I hadn't noticed in my search for admiring glances, was that the tiller extension had been caught on the floor, and bent under the boat. It had happened before, but this time Betty had put her whole weight on the carbon fibre stick, which had given up its singular and straight alignment. It was in pieces. Just two of them, for now, but one was the requirement for effective sailing. Something would have to be done.

Just then, Pete and Julia came down the beach to greet me. Pete and Julia lived locally, and I had got to know Pete through playing squash. They had been at Boscastle in the morning, so I was expecting them, and it was fantastic to see them again.

Pete spied a man pushing an unusual contraption rolling on a pair of large fat wheels. "Excuse me, mate. Can we borrow your wheels to help move the boat?" The man was delighted to help and together we drove Betty up the slope with ease. It was a waterski trolley and was brilliant. I hadn't seen one of those before.

Newquay Sailing Club was just next to the harbour ramp, so very convenient. Instead of being the usual weather-beaten shack, in varying states of repair, it was a deep hole in a massive stone wall, protected by large locked wooden gates, more akin to the entrance to Mordor than a genteel Cornish club.

"Betty sat on the tiller extension, did she?" said Scott. He then disappeared into the bowels of the club facilities to help with repairs. First, he produced a giant rusty metal drill bit. I thought that was too thin. Then he came back with a heavy lump of metal that I thought would do just right. It needed a burr taken off the end, so Scott sunk back into the dungeon, and after a period of whirring and grinding noises, he returned victorious with a snug fitting rusty rod. My lightweight tiller extension was no longer light, but it was certainly strong.

There was a festive atmosphere in town, so we lingered to savour the evening fun. From a beach side conversation, we heard about the Newquay Rowing Club singers. We followed a few leads, and then wriggled our way into the Newquay (gig) Rowing Club, for a beer.

At the bar, it didn't take long to meet Kelvin, who introduced us to Ron and then to Phil. They were all large, bearded and booming, but very friendly. Trebillcock sounded like a classic Cornish surname, given the predominance of the prefix 'Tre-' meaning homestead, across the county. (By the way, 'Pol-' means lake or well, and 'Pen-' means hill. Hence, Trevose is a village, Polzeath is by the sea, Pentire point is a hill.) Phil spoke with a thick accent which was a little impenetrable in places, but he was enthusiastic and engaging. He gave me Gareth's contact details, the group coordinator, so I could ask if he might be able to help. What I was excited about was the idea of a Newquay men's choir, singing my Laser shanty – how amazing would that be? Just imagine!

There was a man who man who went to sea
He went to sea in his little dinghy
To sail around the British Isles,
Something like two thousand miles

Hey ho, this'll be fun,
Especially when on the reach or the run
One day when the sailing's done
He'll take his laser home.

He went to sea in his little dinghy
To raise some money for charity
First there was Place2be
Then ASF and MND

And the chorus

The boat he sailed was made for a lake
He began to think it was a mistake
And then one day a wave did come
And tried to wash him off by gum

Chorus

After a while the doc did smile
When he'd passed one thousand mile.
The folks he met were ever so kind
helping through the daily grind.

Chorus

When it's done there's a tale to tell
No more sea and no more swell
It will have been a very big test
Time for a beer and a damn good rest

Chorus

CHAPTER 19

The end

I had a reply from Gareth, and he expressed some interest, but sadly the trail went dead after a few weeks. Hence my nautical shanty is bereft of competent singers, since I would exclude myself. If you happen to know anyone who might be prepared to lend voice, to a short and jolly tune, do let me know. No auditions required!!

Day 88, Monday 7th August

To St Ives

START	11.30, Newquay
WIND	W, 8–14mph
WEATHER	Sun/cloud. 16–18–14°C. Dry
TIDE	With me from 11.00, max 0.6mph
SEA STATE	Slight
HAZARDS	Headwind
FINISH	St Ives, 17.30
DISTANCE	23 miles
SAILING HOURS	6 hours

Pete and Julia had come down to Cornwall for a weekend and had kindly offered to put me up in their accommodation, and engage with some of the mad doc's antics. They were also providing an essential delivery service. My restorative parcel of new boots, a working VHF radio and dry bags, was eagerly opened, like a stocking on Christmas morning. I now felt equipped to tackle the last major hazard - the final headland, Land's End.

I had a Radio Somerset interview at 10.30am. It lasted for longer than the usual five minutes, meandering across a range of subjects including children's mental health, my chosen charities, and the sailing trip itself. It was refreshing to engage in a wider conversation, even enjoyable, now that I had grown accustomed to the process. Surprisingly, however, none of the many radio appearances throughout the circumnavigation, led to a single donation to any of the selected charities.

Meanwhile Pete was eagerly listening to the England vs Nigeria women's world cup match on the radio. Lauren James had been given a red card, and it looked like Nigeria were set to win, but our team squeezed through on penalties.

It had been lovely to have Pete and Julia's company. I had felt really looked after, and I wished them well for their return journey. Julia also put me in touch with some others nearer the finish line including her dad, which was really supportive.

The wind had turned to a light westerly, and I feared the 23 miles to St Ives would take forever. Happily, pressure filled in, and rescued me. It was still a fair trek on a fetch, and then a beat, finally squeezing between Godrevy Lighthouse and the mainland, before easing into St Ives Bay.

I was tired on arrival. The waterfront was heaving with tourists. A cappuccino gave me a welcome boost, but that was it for welcomes, since I had failed to muster any support, even from the sailing club.

I was now familiar with the lack of notice paid by fellow pedestrians, when walking about in full sailing gear, but it was a reminder that you can wear pretty much what you like in this country, and no one will react. Perhaps I should try squirming out of the sea dressed as a mermaid, and check whether anyone bats an eyelid.

The sailing club was a short walk from the waterfront. The first boat I saw in the lightly fenced storage pen, was a Laser on a trolley. There were some tyres next to it. That meant there was one obvious course of action – shift the dingy onto the rubber, and heave the trolley over the wooden gate. The only suspicious looks I received, were from a perched seagull, who was keeping a watchful eye.

I wasn't going to be able to haul Betty over the fence, so she would have to tough it out in the open car park, which was not ideal. I borrowed a disused boat cover to complete her disguise, making her look more like a local.

Just as I was about to leave, Nick arrived, to retrieve his kayak from the compound. He helpfully allowed Betty to shuffle into the gated area overnight. That seemed much better for her, than hanging next to the pay machine for the night. I would need the gate code in the morning though, which could be a hitch.

The Sloop Inn was literally 20 yards from the sailing club. It provided good speedy food, and a beer. Then it was off to the Cohort Hostel, 15 minutes' walk away, down bustling streets and past shop-filled alleys. The hostel happened to be right next to the Co-op, which provided a perfect supply stop. "What a great town," I thought. Everything is conveniently located, and the layout is really attractive, so no wonder it is so popular for tourists.

Land's End was the last major headland, before turning to home. It had been troubling me, because like the others, conditions vary so much from one side to the other. It was more than 30 miles from St Ives to Penzance, with nowhere to stop in between, making it similar to Cape Wrath.

In theory, I could stop at Sennen Cove, which was about halfway. However, Stick had a few reservations, describing Atlantic rollers crashing onto the beach. "You'll never get off again, if you land there," he said. He had plenty of other scare stories, which helped disturb my sleep that night.

Johnny Dunnet's book "Long standing ambition", about his unsupported windsurfing round GB, was equally gloomy. He described the Land's End rounding as "traumatic", because he felt marooned on his way to St Ives (he was going the other way around). I was beginning to dread the day ahead.

Half nodding off in the hostel lounge, I was trying to work out timings for tomorrow. My analysis seemed to suggest the tide turned sooner on the south side than the north, meaning that water ran in my favour for only four hours, instead of the usual six. This was both confusing and worrying. If I missed the tidal window, I would be in trouble. If the wind died, I could get stuck, and that would mean big trouble. I needed to get going promptly in the morning.

Liz rang as I was poring over my passage plan. I was sorry to say, with the weight of weariness, and unaddressed navigational worries, I was struggling to make conversation. Liz gave up and went to bed.

I had a fitful night's sleep, fretting about what was to come.

Day 89, Tuesday 8th August

To Penzance and Corner #4!

START	09.45, St Ives harbour
WIND	W/SW, 10-15mph, little at Land's End
WEATHER	Very low cloud, 15-18°C. Drizzle
TIDE	With me at 12.00 to 16.00, max 1.6mph
SEA STATE	Slight (moderate at times)
HAZARDS	Lack of stops, small tide window
FINISH	Penzance, 17.00
DISTANCE	31 miles
SAILING HOURS	7¼ hours

I was wide awake at 0600, which was too early to get up and disturb slumbering dormitory occupants. Wanting to give myself something to do, I tried to work out where I might stay that night, should I successfully make it round. I approached both Penzance, and Mount's Bay Sailing Clubs via their contact forms, with little hope of a reply.

After a rushed breakfast, I hurried over to St Ives Sailing Club. On arrival, I realised that I had neither the gate code, nor a reply from Nick. Therefore, despite my unexpected punctuality, Betty was imprisoned, and we could go no further. For a few anxious moments, I seriously considered levering the barrier off its hinges with the lower mast section. But then, I had visions of breaking the mast, the gate, or both, so counselled myself to be patient.

Whilst waiting for a text from Nick, I took the opportunity to do some essential maintenance. The rudder tie down had become seriously frayed from scraping along the ground, so needed to be replaced. Losing control of the rudder when out at sea, would be a serious problem. I also remembered the catalogue of errors that had accumulated at Ilfracombe, when rushing to get away, so wanted to avoid repeating the same mistake.

Just when I had finished repairs, the necessary code pinged through. "Thank goodness for that," I said with a sigh of relief. There was no time to waste. With the gate to freedom now open, I undressed Betty from her mouldy cape, and redressed her with sail, boom, and rigging. She was ready to go.

I had phoned the coastguard earlier with my passage plan, but as I was leaving the compound, I had a return call. The coastguard rarely rang me, so I was given a tingle of alarm. The message made things worse.

"Have you seen the forecast?" he said.

"Yes, I have. Is there something I have missed?"

"I wanted to make you aware that visibility around Land's End is listed as very poor, in places. Had you seen that?"

"Thank you. No, I hadn't," then a small pause. "Do you have any advice about whether it is safe to go?"

"I'm afraid we don't give out advice. We just share the information. National Coastwatch will be keeping an eye out around Land's End," he said, trying to offer some recompense for his bad news. I wasn't sure how helpful that would be.

I was back on my own wit to make a decision. Looking out to sea, I could see thick grey clouds oozing past St Ives Bay. I seriously wondered whether it was safe to go. I had only a rudimentary compass on board, and I wasn't sure it would be any great use, so line of sight would be needed.

I looked up the shipping forecast, as well as the Met Office. The shipping forecast said 'visibility poor to very poor in places', so, that was in line with the coastguard's message. I wanted to check for fog, and the Met Office forecast didn't show any, which was at least some reassurance.

By now, the momentum of the day had begun to take hold, and I went with it. Under a grey and descending sky, I wiggled my way along cobbled streets, towards the sea. Ambling and disinterested tourists were already out on the seafront, and I had to work hard to avoid bashing them with the boom, as I anxiously bumped along. A group of lads were launching ribs on the slipway, getting ready for the daytime holiday activities. They were too engaged in their task, to offer a word to a solo sailor. I suddenly felt alone and foolish, amongst the crowds. Looking around for solace amongst the busy faces, I found none.

When getting ready to launch, with Betty parked on the sand, I hesitated for a few moments. "Is this wise?" I asked myself. "Clearly not," was the reply. But I headed off into the bay anyway.

Out on the water, heavy cloud hung down over the cliffs, reducing visibility, as the forecast had predicted. There was just enough gap above the grey sea, to make out a greyer land junction, which served as my guide. For nearly three hours, I tacked along the shoreline, heading in towards unsafe but visible rocks, and then out towards Ireland, and other invisible peril.

At times, the view of the land was wiped out by an especially truculent cloud, pressing down on my mood, trying to convince me to turn back. But then it would pass on, and I would nervously press on, hoping that things would not get much worse.

Near Pendeen Point, as the coast bends further south towards Land's End, the tide kicked in. I wasn't expecting that so early.

Usually, the current will wash you around obstacles, but this one had no intention of bothering with any minor obstructions, and was pushing me straight towards some foamy rocks. The alarming pace meant that I needed to bear away sharply, in order to avoid a calamitous crash, heading out to sea and into the gloom. Apparently, the sea plunges down vertically past the Point, making the area very dangerous to divers. "At least I'm on it, and not in it," I thought. I planned to keep it that way.

Having successfully passed one death-trap, I found the sea gathered pace again, and turned into tumbling overfalls with waves breaking all around me. I hadn't expected that either, thinking the main race would be opposite Land's End itself. "I've left quite a few hazards off my list today," I thought. "What's next?"

Some tide in my direction was encouraging, but the sea state felt way too much, so I headed back towards land, out of the main flow.

When I reached flatter water, I was dismayed to find that the wind had died. I wasn't expecting that either. I seemed to be getting everything wrong. Maybe the wind was caught in a phase of indecision, wondering whether to go north or south, and was tempting me to contemplate the same. But I was defiantly resolute. Having come this far, I was determined to carry on. However, time was ticking by, and I feared my rounding window would soon close. So, in line with tradition, I pulled out the paddle.

As I pushed my way towards Sennen Cove, my slow progress did give me a chance to check the next set of unregistered hazards. Visibility had improved a little, and I could now see some outcrops, off Land's End. Scrutiny of Navionics suggested it was safe to go inside them, so my course was set. Hence, having crossed yet another unplanned problem, I concluded that, despite all the rumination of the night before, my passage planning for the day had been lousy.

When the wind eventually filled in again, I was very relieved. "I might be able to make it after all," I thought, and put the paddle away.

With an increasing breeze, my speed accelerated, hustled along by the tide. I could see land turning away from me, pointing further towards France, and beyond that, a route towards home. Penzance now felt possible, and I could start to relax.

To my left, I could see a huddle of white buildings perched on the top of smudge black cliffs, which I knew were Land's End. I received a phone call. It was Sam, who had been keeping track of my progress and thought this was good moment to ring. He had managed to catch me, just as my jubilation started to fill in. What joy it was, to have reached corner #4 in all its grey glory, and doubly joyful to be able to share it with Sam.

We exchanged memories of cycle rides, setting off from the end of the land, the first to Dover, and the second, to John O'Groats. It was surreal to be there again, in memory, and in reality, this time looking up at the famous landmark from the sea.

I felt proud to have reached that point, and proud to be a father to Sam.

The rest of the sailing was relatively straightforward, and much quicker than the first half. The sea was quite lumpy over Rundles stone – which hangs like a submerged nautical pimple off the nose of England – but it did not take long to wash over that.

What's more, Paul from Penzance Sailing Club had rung me to offer a boat birth, so miraculously the contact form had worked. All of a sudden, things were working out. And, later, I received some great quality photos, from the National Coastwatch team, showing me out at sea around Land's End. Thank you very much, guys, for looking out for me.

When I landed at Penzance, Paul appeared at the harbour pontoon, with his homemade trolley. He helped with derigging, and then offered a coffee in the club.

Paul used to sail Lasers to a high standard in his youth, but now in his 70s had moved on to yachts. He also shared stories of his son's excellent exploits, competing with, and often beating Ben Ainslie, when jostling for the Atlanta Olympics. But the selector's axe fell the other way, and Lee had moved on to different things. It seems like every club had a few top-quality sailors amongst its membership.

I couldn't quite figure out what to do about accommodation, since the local options were exorbitant. When asked for advice though, Paul pointed out there was a train to St Ives, and he could give me a lift to St Erth, the connecting station.

"Perfect," I said. "That would be amazing." It meant I could return to the wonderful Cohort Hostel at £40 for the night, the comfort of familiarity, and a local train journey to boot. It did seem slightly strange to end up back where I started, after all the effort of the day. A congratulatory message from Stick, the laseraroundtheuk God, who had been keeping a watchful eye, settled my uncertainties, and I headed back to St Ives.

I went out for a beer and curry with my new dorm mate Mark, who was close to completing his John O'Groats to Land's End solo cycle ride. He had suffered a life-changing car crash, and two hip replacements, before setting out on his teenage dream ride, so had plenty to talk about. It was lovely to hear his delight at completing the challenge, and great to listen in to his long-planned adventure. His hopes for more camping had been dampened by the wet and windy weather. In contrast, my journey had been sped on by the same.

The forecast showed light winds for the next day, which would be insufficient to get round The Lizard, so I could allow myself a restful sleep, not worrying about dashing off in the morning.

● ● ●

Day 90, Wednesday 9th August

To Porthleven

START	13.00, Penzance
WIND	Southerly ish. Very little to none
WEATHER	Sun, then thick fog. 15–17°C. Dry
TIDE	Not much
SEA STATE	Smooth
HAZARDS	No wind
FINISH	Porthleven, 18.15
DISTANCE	9 miles
SAILING HOURS	5¼ hours. (slowest day so far!!)

I bade farewell to Mark, who was up and excited to be off on his last few cycling miles. He was delighted to find that it wasn't raining. For me, a lie in on my top bunk with free time and good Wi-Fi, proved a preferable option.

I really liked the Cohort Hostel. Every detail lent strength to that feeling, especially since I was enjoying the pleasures of a second night.

A small shelf ran round the edge of the bed space, so there was storage for those fiddly bits and pieces, one might otherwise lose. There were places to hang stuff to air, or dry. Each bed had its own plug socket and light, plus drawable curtain, so you could make it feel like your own den, despite eight beds to a room. There were lockable cupboards under the bunks for storage, and a small basin in the room for emergency water.

The ladder to the top bunk, and guard rail, were made of what looked like scaffolding pieces, so were solid and substantial, meaning that a night-time toilet trip did not create disturbing creaks or clunks. The scaffolding also held up chairs in the lounge, and shelves in the kitchen, giving a structural theme, but also connected to the eco credentials, which felt genuine and free of greenwashing. An upturned colander acted as the lampshade in the kitchen, which chimed with other decorative jests in the establishment. Tea and coffee were free between eight and ten in the morning, thus incentivising travellers to be up and out before the ten o'clock deadline, without need for hassle or reminder – a cunning move I thought.

The dormitories were mixed. That raised an eyebrow on first reading, but it seemed to work well as far as I could tell – there were no alarmed looks, or anxious jostling in the dormitory spaces – but, asking for female feedback would be the proper test. Either way, it was good to see some bold ideas being actioned, in a well thought out establishment.

Hostel sharing meant that I left with some no longer needed Firecamp meals, donated by a departing roommate, who had finished her walk. Thank you very much to Marion.

On my way out, I thanked the staff, and loudly sang the hostel's praises.

It was a hot, and surprisingly sweaty walk to the train station, despite a grey sky. The 10.30am chugga chugga train from St Ives was crowded with summer holidaymakers, and the intercity train to Penzance was equally stuffed, giving a festive atmosphere.

Penzance station brought back strong memories of our cycling journeys. We had taken group photos, standing by the granite station sign, under grey drizzly skies, in excited but anxious trepidation of the miles to come. On this occasion, as a seasoned sailor warmed by the rounded glow of corner #4, I was pleased to be at the end of the line to London, because for me, I was homeward bound.

The boat pen at Penzance Sailing Club was empty and dry, which gave a good opportunity to do some minor sail repairs. Luckily there were public toilets near the station which provided a very welcome stop for an emergency poo, given that my usual gastro routine had become slightly delayed. Another massive relief.

I was feeling relaxed about the journey, because it was not too far, still buoyed by the elation and relief of the previous day.

There was some wind to St Michael's Mount, then fog, and then nothing, but I didn't mind. I would get there. Thick, thick fog hung about all afternoon, obscuring everything except, sometimes, a slither of the shore. There were occasional pleasure craft, usually containing holiday fishermen, which came bobbing into view before fading away again. The radio eased the boredom of paddling.

Coming into the Cornish harbour of Porthleven, I felt like a smuggler, still shrouded in silent fog. Rowing cautiously along to avoid entrance rocks, I passed beneath stone buildings gazing suspiciously down at me, as I transported my precious cargo to shore.

At least the sun was making its presence felt, when I landed. Chattering families with idle fishing lines, and children with ice cream splodged faces, were scattered along the harbour walls. They were helping the grizzly mist turn into a gorgeous August holiday evening. But, no sooner had the sun appeared, than it started to dip below the trees, reminding me that I should get a move on. This was no longer Scotland in June, with its endless hours of daylight.

Moving across the sticky harbour floor was proving difficult. However, faffing and phone calls enticed the tide to the bottom of the slipway, where the fender could take over in transporting Betty up the concrete slope, free of mud. A passerby very kindly helped with the final lift. Betty was squeezed in amongst local craft, taking up the evening's role as tender, thus hiding in plain sight from the passing cavalry. Like flotsam, the foils and spars were dumped in a floating gig. Hopefully all would be disguised for the night, ready to be stolen away in the morning.

There was nowhere else to stay, so it was to the campsite for the night, the last of the trip as it happened. I managed to forget the hostel-donated camping meal, and it was getting late, so ended up with a supermarket dinner on the road. Dessert was a spare piece of pizza, donated by a fellow camper – how kind.

A family were tented next door in their huge fabric shed. Their two-year-old took a long look at my green slug-shaped temporary residence, as it emerged from its sausage bag. I referred to my small tent, by saying, "there is room for one man but no dog". My muddled linguistic reference was far too complicated for a toddler, but she happily repeated "no room for a dog," till she finally went to sleep. What a wonderful age to be alive.

She was also insisting it was her birthday tomorrow, despite it being her mother's. The soothing attention she received from a range of adults was all very heart warming, even when she woke with a nightmare at one in the morning. I hoped she wasn't worried about a dog.

CHAPTER 20

South-westerlies

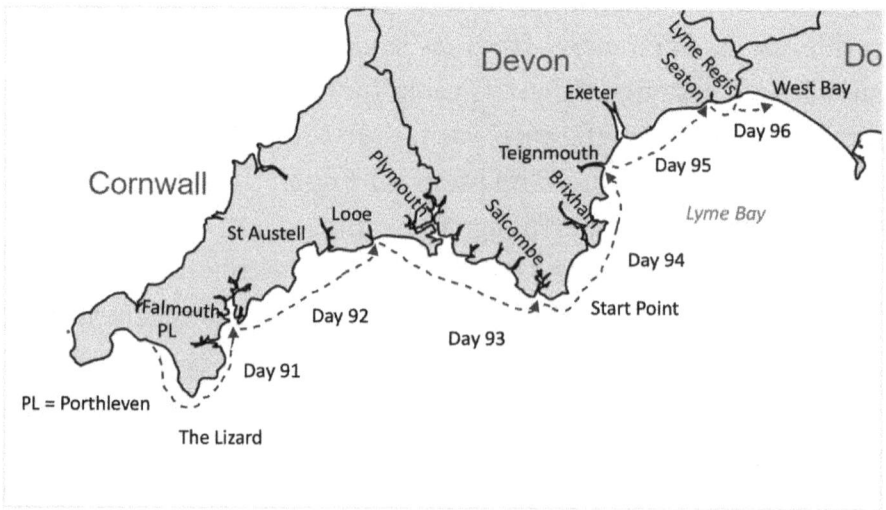

Day 91, Thursday 10th August

To Falmouth

START	10.20, Porthleven
WIND	S, 12–23mph. Light, picking up later
WEATHER	Sun/cloud, 19–21°C. FOG
TIDE	Flowing E, max 1.3mph till 15.00
SEA STATE	Slight
HAZARDS	Fog, fog, fog. No compass.
FINISH	Falmouth, 18.30
DISTANCE	36 miles
SAILING HOURS	8 hours

There was a suggestion of blue sky when packing up the tent, but that was it. "Surely the fog won't descend like yesterday," I thought, but it did.

I decanted my spars from the gig, before the rowing team arrived. The boat was filled with cheery men and women, ready to surge out onto the open sea. They were slowly followed by their sailor companion, who was struggling to make way through the inner entrance, against opposing wind and an incoming tide.

Out of the harbour, I could see the crew powering along, and felt slightly jealous as I was making next to no progress. And then they returned to base, I guessed for coffee and chat, leaving me almost stationary, and thinking I might follow suit.

The forecast had predicted mixed sun and cloud, with the wind filling from the south. There was absolutely no sign of the sun, because I had become completely encircled by fog. It grew thicker and thicker as I moved further out. This was August. It was meant to be sunny in August. I thought fog was a thing for the east coast of England or Scotland in spring perhaps. Warm wet air over cold sea is the common combination. The air was warm and moist, I guessed, but I thought the sea shouldn't be cold in this summer month. I didn't understand, but my incomprehension didn't make the fog go away.

At least some wind filled in from the South, so the forecast was at least 50% correct. I carried on into the gloom.

I had had some tasters of fog before. Previously there had been a whisper of land in sight to provide a guide, or I had a compass on deck to point the way. Now I had neither. It was a complete eerie white-out, with nothing to see, but Betty and myself. I could have been anywhere on the ocean. No one could see me.

I took a video to illustrate the thickness of the grey soup.

"I really can't see a thing," I said on tape, panning the camera round past myself, the sail and the blurred fuzz all around.

Then I spotted something up ahead, and still on camera, "Oh wait, what's that?" I said.

"Oh shit, it's the land."

It was a faint darker grey blob. Which turned into two. In fact, it wasn't the land at all. It was a couple of fishing vessels. When I came close, they enquired, "are you OK?" and "do you know where you are?" to which I replied, "sort of", and carried on. It was nice to hear their concern, however.

It was a good three hours on the beat out to Lizard Point. On the way I was guided by the sound of waves on the shore when I went too close, an occasional glimmer of shoreline under the clouds, and intermittent Navionics checks, to make sure I had not gone round in a large circle. Having embraced a few long passages before, I was fairly comfortable with the length of time on the water, recognising that 'keeping going' and eating sandwiches on the way, will get you there in the end. But the views were rubbish.

Lizard Point is decorated with plenty of rocks, such as an appropriately named lump called 'Man of War.' It is the site of many historic wrecks, so I gave the western end a wide berth, not wanting to join the underwater party. Not put off by the foghorn, mournfully sounding out to someone, and feeling more confident from a slight lift in the cloud, I ducked in between a few of the outcrops at the eastern end.

The fog was showing no sign of letting up. Necessity became the mother of invention. Without a compass, I was not sure how to pick a route that crossed shoreline indentations, on the eastern side of the Lizard. I didn't want to use sound as a guide, as I had done on the western side, since it would mean a longer route and more exposure to rocks. Hence, why not use Navionics and the wind? With the app, I could work out the desired direction. With the sail set, and the main sheet cleated in, I could then use the tell tales as the compass, adjusting my course to keep the tape guides flying. Hence the opposite of normal sailing technique. (Normally, you set a course and adjust the sail. This way, I set the sail and adjusted the course.) It worked a treat.

Nearing what I thought must be the entrance to the River Fal estuary, I could see a shape in the distance. It appeared as the line of a hill coming down to the water, and then disappearing into the sea, so nothing out of the ordinary. Except it didn't look right. The colours were the wrong way round. Through the sludge of hazy white and grey, I was expecting a darker triangle closer to the water, and lighter above it. Instead, the dark was up in the air, and lighter colours next to the water. That was odd. As usual, staring at an object does nothing for resolving the visual conundrum, and merely leads to eye strain.

I drew a bit closer.

"Oh my God. It's a bloody great cruise ship."

The long pointy bow had given the illusion of sloping land.

I quickly got onto the radio.

"Falmouth coastguard, Falmouth coastguard, this is HMS Betty, a Laser dinghy. I can see a ship in front of me off Falmouth, I think. Is it stationary?"

I was expecting to make several more appeals, and to try different channels, but within a minute, I had a reply.

"HMS Betty. This is Falmouth Coastguard. I would like to confirm that ship Calypso is at anchor. Over."

That was good news on two fronts. Firstly, the new radio was working well enough to be understood. And secondly, I was not about to be run over. I could proceed with caution.

After a few days of quiet landings, I was back in the zone of bustling, and incredibly welcoming arrivals. My contact was David. He had been a sailor at Papercourt, and had subsequently moved down to Falmouth after retirement. His recommendation was to head for Restronguet Sailing club. Having previously marked the destination as a way point on Navionics, I found my way through the fog to the landing spot, without difficulty. A couple of guys came down to the waterfront, with essential trolley in hand, and helped me park up on the grass.

David soon arrived, driving along the beach to the club. When we were heading back to his car, David pointed to a RYA plaque on the club wall with an emblematic statement declaring, "Tomorrow's champions start here". This typically brash statement, for a change, had a ring of authenticity to it, since the humble dinghy club was where Ben Ainslie had first learnt to sail. I could not help but look on in awe, ensnared by the aura of celebrity, somehow hoping that my sailing would improve if I gazed long enough at the plastic disc.

David said that the patch of water around Falmouth, known as Carrick Roads, provided one of the best sailing areas in the world. He had a point. It was a large area on the sea, yet fairly sheltered from the open water swells, with manageable tides and consistent winds, and not too much shipping. What more could one ask for?

There are several clubs on the edges of Carrick Roads (confusingly named as such given that it is an estuary). As well as Restronguet, there is Flushing Sailing Club, Mylor Yacht Club, the Royal Cornwall Yacht Club, and finally St Mawes Sailing Club, the latter being on the eastern bank (other side) of the estuary. David whizzed us round to the Royal Cornwall, to join in a gathering. People were enjoying an end of day mingle and drinks, as part of Falmouth week. Slightly to my embarrassment, he introduced me to the assembled crowd, and then passed me the microphone to say something about my adventure. I needn't have worried, since the listeners were very welcoming.

We then had a quick tour of Flushing Sailing Club. David proudly told me about his key architectural role, in rebuilding the club during lockdown. Money had been raised and the site redeveloped in a little over a year, so a phenomenal achievement. The building did indeed look spectacular and fresh. I would need to wait for another day to enjoy the views, since it was now getting dark.

Back at David's house, there were plentiful memories shared of Papercourt members, past and present. Michelle was less keen to spend time on the water, but well able to fill in details about social connections. It felt like another impressive welcome, for a fellow sailor. Michelle provided a delicious turkey pasta meal, with pavlova to finish, which sent me to food heaven and an early bed.

Day 92, Friday 11th August

To Looe

START	11.45, Falmouth
WIND	SW, 14–20mph
WEATHER	Sun/Cloud 14–20°C. Dry
TIDE	With me, max 0.5mph, till 16.00
SEA STATE	Slight to moderate
HAZARDS	Return of fog, maybe
FINISH	Looe, 16.45
DISTANCE	32 miles
SAILING HOURS	5 hours

The plan was to head to Looe. I had been there before, once when cycling from Land's End to Dover in 2014, and then again, on a windless practice Laser trip in 2021.

It's a pretty town in a steep sided valley, with an ample beach and island off the shore to add to the visual attractions. Its picturesque three-dimensional beauty has provided a draw for tourists over the centuries, meaning the town has continued to prosper once trading functions had declined.

However, when approaching the town, it was hard to let go of the school boyish sniggering thought, about the town name sounding like a lavatory. In truth, the word comes from the Cornish term 'Logh', which means deep water inlet, but you would have thought the intelligence of collective tradition could have come up with a better verbal adaptation. But maybe Looe came first. Maybe there never was a naming mistake. Because, no one quite knows when the word 'loo' arrived in the English language, or from whence it came.

Back in Falmouth, the fog had cleared at last, and the sun had come out. David dropped me off at Restronguet club, and then headed off to race his 'Folk' boat, which is a type of keeled dinghy. We tried to rendezvous on the water later, but just missed each other.

Meanwhile, dinghies were launching at Restronguet, to join the racing of Falmouth week. A few sailors came over and said hello, including a young man called Will who was learning the craft of his catamaran. I was honoured that he had seen a few of my YouTube videos, and I wished him luck for the day.

On the water, I saw boats jostling around a start line, and realised there was a minute to go. I was preparing to join in, but just as I was approaching the line, my tiller extension 'came away in my hands. Honest, guv'. It must have been weakened when at Newquay, and had simply detached itself as I was tacking.

The first job was to get out of the way of the race. And the second, to answer the question – "Should I carry on?" If it were a race, it would be game over, since with a seriously shortened tiller extension, sailing upwind would be fairly ineffective. But I wasn't in a race. Instead, I was heading to Looe, appropriately, on a run all the way. And I thought I could manage, without things getting too messy. So, on I went.

The wind picked up, making even and consistent waves, rolling neatly along the line of my course. It was delightful sailing, making steady progress past headlands and inlets. I reawakened wave surfing techniques, especially when approaching a yacht in front of me. On rising up the wave, we travelled at about the same speed, but on descending, I would pick up speed and lurch a few yards closer to my competitor. I managed to edge into the lead, not long before the yacht turned off into Fowey, defeated.

It was strange to be crossing the path of one of my practice trips. How different it was to have some wind, since I was becalmed for much of the five days on the previous visit. On that first day, I had set off from Parr Sands, in bright sunshine, full of optimism. I had ended the day's passage with sore arms, and heavy with frustration, having paddled most of the ten miles to Looe. I had wondered about two things in particular. Firstly, where on earth were the sea breezes that I was promised. And secondly, how was I going to make it round GB, if that was the pace of travel. How blessed I was, to have a kindly breeze to propel me along, when passing the south coast of Cornwall for the second time.

When I landed, the beach was full of festive sun-seeking fun, as it had been before. On this occasion, however, a couple of people appeared through the crowd to greet me, and then a couple more, and a couple more. Not only that, Callum the Commodore brought down a beer to welcome me. Darren then noticed the broken tiller extension, and to my delight said, "I think I can find someone to help sort that out." Things were getting better and better. To top it off, the gathered assembly stepped forward as if in unison, and with only the slightest of prompts, carried Betty up the beach. They marched on up to the boat park, overturning all my usual staccato landing rituals to merge into one smooth stream. Betty was carefully positioned amongst a flotilla of GP14 craft, who were packing up after a week-long sailing regatta.

When I returned to the sailing club later, prize giving and partying were in full swing, like the end of an extended summer vacation. Elegant silverware trophies, which looked like they had a fine heritage, were handed out to proud winners. Beers were purchased and passed around.

A band struck up, playing folk rock, if there is such a thing. The two musicians had nearly matching prolific beards, and nearly matching bucket hats, which were pulled down over each person's head, concealing everything but nose and whiskers. Neither person lifted their gaze from their instrument, nor took so much as a glance, or offered a shared word with the audience. They were busy with their craft. The music was doing the talking. It filled the room and the revellers with yet more zest. Nothing more needed to be said.

And then a tiller extension arrived in my hand. GOAT had been sponsoring the national event, and had very kindly donated a replacement, in exchange for promotional stickers to be attached to Betty's sides. I thought that was a very good deal – thank you, Steve from GOAT.

What a great atmosphere, what a welcoming club, and what a beautiful summer's evening, in a glorious Cornish town.

I finally peeled away after a few beers, and got to sleep rather late, tired but satisfied.

The forecast was predicting gusts of 33mph for the next day. In the interests of avoiding further breakages, I thought a rest day was in order. Besides, I was starting to plan a finish date for the end of August, so had plenty of time. There was no rush, which to me, was a great state to be in.

* * *

Saturday 12th August

Rest day

Being able to stay in the same room was a major relief, sparing me the annoyance of finding a new place, and shuffling myself and my stuff to a new venue.

My usual rest day format rolled into action. It included boat maintenance, the usual round of admin and planning, communication to upcoming stopping points, and on this occasion, a delicious midday snooze.

And finally, a double dinner before bed. A mediocre pub vegetable lasagne was topped off, and indeed topped out, by one of the packet meals that I had been given at St Ives – a very tasty Chilli con carne – cooked up with the low-tech assistance of a room-based kettle. Yum Yum, and thank you to my fellow traveller meal donor.

With much excitement, it was off to Salcombe tomorrow to see Liz and friends.

* * *

Day 93, Sunday 13th August

To Salcombe, Devon

START	09.30, Looe
WIND	SW, 14–22 mph
WEATHER	Early rain then cloud / sun, 16–19°C
TIDE	Against me, max 0.7mph till 16.00
SEA STATE	Moderate
HAZARDS	Tide in Salcombe harbour
FINISH	Salcombe, 15.00
DISTANCE	34 miles
SAILING HOURS	5½ hours

All the other dinghies had departed. I returned to find Betty, looking lonely in the exposed boat parking area, huddled next to a single club craft. The skies had turned grey and the air was filled with drizzle. The hurrying racers had been replaced by listless tourists and avaricious seagulls, guarding the waste bin. The fun and vibrancy of Friday had rolled away, and it was time to leave.

Making use of the deep-water inlet, that had given the town its name, I wheeled Betty down the slipway into the river, and headed off to complete the final 10% of circumnavigation.

With new tiller extension in hand with its bright orange bobble on the end, the day was surely going to go well. A handsome breeze pushed me along, past Plymouth and then Bigbury, past a couple more yachts, with the miles slipping easily away.

I had been in touch with Jen and Pete whom I had first met at Tobermory. They had returned to Plymouth, having completed their travels, and were delighted to exchange messages. However, they were away, releasing me from any pangs of guilt about passing them by.

Into the lumpy mouth of Salcombe harbour I went, now busy with motorised and sail craft. I wasn't sure where to land. I thought I heard some shouts, but could not see anyone or anything I recognised. There were more shouts, but still I could see nothing familiar.

"What's going on?" I wondered.

Then a lady stood up in a rib to my left, and lifted her shirt, displaying fine features beneath.

"Ha, ha," I laughed. "I recognise those," I said. For it could only be one person. It was Liz, who had come out to greet me.

Liz was being driven by Penny and Guy, and Sandy the dog, so a proper reception party. Liz felt she had waited too long for my arrival, so called for some water, and I threw her my bottle, to help quench her thirst.

Initially we landed on the beach opposite the town, but I didn't like the look of that, so headed across the water to a tiny shingle slipway, beneath the yacht club. This was perfect. Dan, Martin and Paul suddenly turned up, to give me a hand moving Betty.

We shifted her up the metal slipway, onto a safe cosy stowage area, away from wandering eyes and prying hands. They had been alerted to an arrival by Liz, and noticed the sail coming in, so leapt to the ready. How incredibly helpful.

Salcombe feels like a party town. It is populated by second homers, boat owners and people who don't mind going up and down hills.

Its history as a shipbuilding centre in the mid-1800s led to construction of several sail lofts, and much of the Victorian housing stock that still stands today. Being well located with an extensive waterfront, and beautiful hills surrounding the Kingsbridge Estuary, it draws visitors with its natural beauty. With better road links, a shift from sail to steam propulsion, the town became a resort location in the early 20th century, which has continued until today.

Our first stop on the social tour was to head up a series of steps to the yacht club. This is one of the Victorian era grand buildings. With an address of Cliff House, on Cliff Road, it is easy to imagine the superb views from splendid rooms, across the estuary.

I had hoped to catch up with Fran, whom I had approached before setting off. Her 'big adventure' in a wayfarer had occupied my thoughts a good deal, and I really wanted to meet her. Unfortunately, she was out of town. Mark, Fran's partner, was there instead. I had met him in the Royal Norfolk and Suffolk Yacht club on day 11, in a similarly spacious bar, though minus the views. He very kindly came along to greet us all, and joined in for a beer. It was lovely to meet up again, and feel the connection from east coast to south, with so many miles in between.

There was another east coast to south connection that evening. Penny and Guy's house was one of the repurposed sail loft buildings, overlooking the water, with fantastic views. They had organised a wonderful meal at their house, inviting Clodagh and Mike who were near neighbours. We had met before, on the party evening at Whitstable on day 7. Although I remembered they had a Salcombe link, I never imagined that we would meet again, so it was a real treat to renew their acquaintance. What's more, joining pieces through one conversation and then another, Liz realised that Clodagh had been in the same class in their Yorkshire school, as her younger sister. What an extraordinary set of coincidences.

All the sailing and socialising had tired me out, and I sloped off to bed a bit early. A front came through in the night, throwing rain hard at the windows, but I slept well, knowing that I had scheduled a relatively late start, after the weather had improved.

* * *

Day 94, Monday 14th August

To Teignmouth

START	12.30, Salcombe
WIND	24–35 mph early. Then SW, 14–18mph
WEATHER	Sun and cloud, 18°C. Dry
TIDE	Against me, max 1.2mph till 14.30
SEA STATE	Slight to moderate
HAZARDS	Start Point race
FINISH	Teignmouth, 19.00
DISTANCE	30 miles
SAILING HOURS	6½ hours

Liz and I had a lovely lie in, in our attic nest, waking up slowly whilst the wind was raging outside. Gentle conversation about the evening before, helped us ease from slumber, before embracing the day, and our separate journeys ahead. It was a short but intense reunion. A leisurely breakfast followed, completing the triumph of Penny's family hospitality, for which we were truly grateful. And then our ways parted once more, with sweet sorrow.

I had been warned about the sandbar of Salcombe, but had not noticed anything on arrival. Many nautical hazards have an associated tragedy. In 1916, fifteen men went out to rescue mariners, who had become wrecked near Prawle Point, four miles away. Only two of the RNLI crew survived.

In those days, lifeboats were open topped, oar powered clinkers, so not a match for the highly sophisticated vessels of today. The 15-man team made it safely out across the bar in a force nine gale, only to discover that those in peril had already been rescued by the coastguard. It was on their return journey that their boat was capsized by an enormous wave, in what was described as terrifying conditions. Things must have been bad, since they were only a few hundred yards from the shore, and yet so many lost their lives. A plaque has been erected in Salcombe to commemorate the centenary of the fourth largest loss of life in the RNLI's history.

Happily for me, things were nothing in comparison to the conditions those poor mariners faced. However, I could see breaking waves ahead of rocks, and needed to pick the right channel through the incoming tide. It gave me a taste of trouble that might have faced my forebearers, and a reminder that conditions should not be taken for granted.

Previously passing this stretch of coastline on the practice trip, I had to stop at Start Point, since I got stuck in the tidal race, when I didn't know it was a tidal race. To avoid being endlessly swirled around in the giant washing machine, I managed to beach the boat in a tiny cove below the lighthouse, until conditions changed. The experience had troubled me.

In 2023, those memories made me nervous, as I approached the headland. However, my late start meant that the current had already turned by the time I reached Start Point. Hence there was no repeat of the previous difficulty. Instead, I sailed on blissfully, between rocks and mainland, heading north into Lyme Bay with a sunny tail wind.

A pair of dolphins came to enjoy the ride. They swam alongside, almost within touching distance, ducking and diving round Betty's bow, casually undulating their tail fins to keep abreast. I have heard many yachtsmen share similar experiences. For me, the intimacy of being within a few centimetres of the surface as they played along, was something special. I could stand up and watch them from a steeper angle, or plunge my hand into the water beside Betty, to record their graceful forms swim in coordinated arcs, past Betty's scratched and beaten-up dagger board. It was as if we were at the same party, enjoying the water, the sunshine and elegant movement, together, united in our love for the sea. Those will be memories to treasure for a lifetime.

At Teignmouth, the sky turned blue, the sun turned yellow and the sand turned red.

For those who have travelled on the intercity to Penzance, the dramatic changes in terrain are plain to see. The train heads south past Exeter, and then plunges into the red zone, as it creeps along the coast past Dawlish, no more than a few feet from the sea. Alarming colours must have been enormously amplified by the frightening sea state in February 2014, when a storm smashed through train windows, and eventually destroyed the sea wall on which the tracks were resting.

Past Teignmouth, and later Totnes, the route then bends west again. The land soon morphs back into its usual palate of colours, as the rails approach the granite greys of Dartmoor, leaving the iron oxide red of sandstone behind. What a beautiful journey through millions of years of geological history, all available to view, without getting out of your seat.

On the water, the bent River Teign mouth was dotted with small boats of all kinds, out for an evening course. I called to a rib for advice about landing. It was a slightly stupid question, since there was an ideal red beach right in front of us. Helpfully, the driver pointed out a row of dinghies parked by the low sea wall, which I hadn't noticed before. It wasn't such a stupid question after all. The row of boats constituted Shaldon Sailing Club.

I borrowed a trolley and parked up amongst other Lasers in a neat row. Although Shaldon Sailing Club claims to be the third oldest in the UK, I could not find a clubhouse, either on the day, or online, later. Maybe it had shrunk rather than expanded with time. As ever, the people I met were wonderfully helpful, and seemed to be having a good time.

The real prize was finding my cousin, Ann. Ann is the senior of the three A. Hill-Smiths in the land, the third being another cousin, Alex. Together we form a small and select tribe.

Ann kindly drove over to pick me up, and then on to her daughter's house in Ashburton, where I met a blizzard of relatives, and some slices of pizza. And finally, back to Ann's place for a good sleep, amongst stored paintings and family heirlooms. What an intoxicating whirlwind of history, and a grateful stop off.

Day 95, Tuesday 15th August

To Seaton

START	12.20, Teignmouth
WIND	SW 6–9mph, but reality is better
WEATHER	Sun and some cloud, 18–20°C. Dry
TIDE	Against me, max 0.4mph till 14.00
SEA STATE	Slight to smooth
HAZARDS	Sun!!!! Light winds
FINISH	Seaton, 17.10
DISTANCE	20 miles
SAILING HOURS	4¾ hours

My usual last minute planning trick produced surprise results on two occasions for the morning. Firstly, I used a contact form for Axe Yacht Club to say I would be heading over, and was shocked to receive a reply within an hour. The second was texting Thomas, an old schoolfriend. He also replied in double quick time, reporting that not only was he in residence, but also that he would come and pick me up.

The final piece of good fortune was that the wind filled in enough to mean that I could sail, rather than paddle. I pootled gently along the coast, enjoying the sunshine, and the line of red cliffs drifting slowly by.

Passing Exeter felt like a significant landmark. I was getting ever closer to home.

Coming into the bay near Seaton, the wind more or less disappeared, but was just enough to keep me going. In front of me, a dinghy edged across towards Beer Bay, out for a casual afternoon excursion. Life felt at ease.

I could see a small amount of shore break washing onto the shingle. The sea surface was more or less glassy smooth, so I thought nothing of the hazard ahead. That was, until I jumped out.

The shingle bank was really steep, meaning that even the tiniest ripple had turned into an aggressive roller. I tried to pull Betty out of the waves, but the incline proved too much to haul a fully loaded, and fully rigged Betty, up the slope on my own. Nor did the stones provide any purchase, so my struggling resulted in small amounts of grit being shuffled towards the water, despite a lot of huffing and puffing. Innocent looking waves were punching well above their weight, as they continued to hack at Betty's stern, thrashing at the rudder, with each arrival and exit. The sail was still full, and although the breeze was light, the onshore pressure was enough to further constrain any useful escape from the water's edge.

I suddenly panicked thinking that these were exactly the kind of boat breaking conditions I had tried to avoid, and yet had failed to spot. I shouted for help towards a nearby beach sitter, something I had never done before. I had visions of another tiller extension being crushed, or worse, the rudder being snapped. The nearby beach sitter remained seated. I shouted again, but still nothing. Things felt desperate.

As if by magic, James appeared, and without asking, lent muscle to the uphill struggle. Now fully morphed into superhero, with dashing vibrant outfit, he leapt up the bank and returned with trolley, and then miraculously a tractor. Finally, Betty was dragged onto a white carpet, at the entrance to the boat park. We were saved.

James had picked up the message to the Axe Yacht Club and had kept an eye on the tracker, till we came bundling onto the shore. At that point, he dropped his suited disguise and came flying over the shingle mound to the rescue, superman-style. James, you are now an official member of the laseraroundtheuk guardian angel club, and there is quite a long list. Thank you so much, James.

Back to more mundane matters, I was to meet Thomas at Tesco. Looking around outside, I couldn't see him. Instead, I spotted an elegant motor, which was both ostentatious and totally unnecessary for the purpose, and superbly incongruous in a Seaton supermarket car park.

"There is only one person I know who could be driving that," I said to myself, and sure enough, Thomas appeared within a minute or two.

It was an exquisite English evening, celebrating fantastic surroundings, and caressed by the wonderful softness of fading August light. We ambled down memory lane over dinner, skipping through decades long past and more recent, wondering how this or that person was making their way in the world, turning over motivations or personal histories, like old ladies gossiping by the fireside. I could have stayed forever.

My bed that night was supremely comfortable, tempting me to linger. But I had to be away in the morning. I was destined to reacquaint myself with my current version of a palace, one that was ungrounded, made of plastic and called Betty. The prospect, and the transition, seemed quite surreal.

* * *

Day 96, Wednesday 16th August

To West Bay

START	12.00, Seaton
WIND	SE/S, 2–6mph
WEATHER	Sun/cloud 19–20°C. Dry
TIDE	Against me, max 1mph, till 16.00
SEA STATE	Smooth
HAZARDS	Opposing tide. No wind
FINISH	West Bay, 19.00
DISTANCE	14 miles
SAILING HOURS	6½ hours (30 mins coffee stop)

Neil from the yacht club kindly came down to help with the sendoff in the morning. My guardian angel from the evening before had clearly flown off to do other worldly things. As it happened, Neil knew Thomas from years gone by, so another connection. Neil's support was much appreciated.

Going down shingle was much easier than going up it. I tried out a new launching technique, which was to slide down the bank and jump in, only adding the centre plate when momentum had carried me a short distance offshore. That way nothing was damaged. It worked brilliantly. I would thoroughly recommend it to anyone planning a Laser circumnavigation.

On the water, it was back to paddling. I hadn't had a paddling day since Cornwall, and maybe, just maybe, this could be my last. The threatened wind didn't materialise, and in line with tradition, nor did the onshore breeze. It was paddle, paddle, paddle, with a touch of sailing in between.

Lyme Regis was a nice coffee stop with a busy beach, full of holidaymakers. Just as I was thinking of joining them, to wander along the Cobb, or go fossil hunting, I spotted a few puffs of wind beyond the breakwater, and felt obliged to carry on. My cunning self-motivational plan was to book a place to stay at West Bay, so I felt drawn to keep it, rather than waste the increasingly expensive room fees. The motivation was worth it, but I wasn't too sure about the accommodation when I eventually got there – rather a tired building, with a shared bathroom – but it would do. There was a tasty restaurant across the road, which made up for any downsides.

One good thing about West Bay was a handy sized harbour and plenty of spaces for me and my little dinghy. I found the friendly harbourmaster in the morning, who waived the fee, which I duly paid to charity.

* * *

CHAPTER 21

Portland Bill

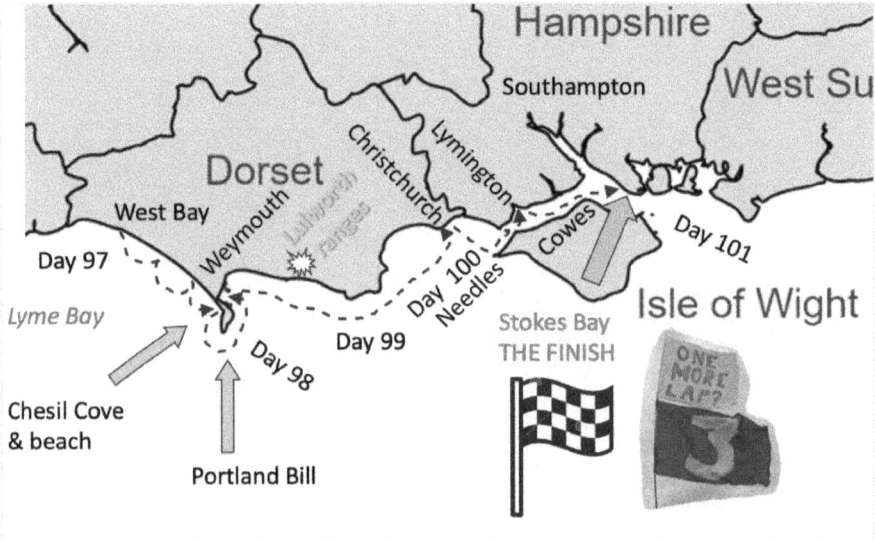

CHAPTER 21

Day 97, Thursday 17th August

To Chesil Cove

START	10.30, West Bay
WIND	ESE, 18–25mph, rising to 20–31mph
WEATHER	Cloudy 19–21°C. Dry
TIDE	With me max 0.9mph till 12.00
SEA STATE	Slight to moderate
HAZARDS	A long beat. Portland Bill maybe
FINISH	Chesil Cove, 17.15
DISTANCE	17 miles
SAILING HOURS	6 hours. (Two stops of 20 mins)

I was hoping to get around Portland Bill. I knew it would be a long beat up to the Isle of Portland, but hadn't appreciated quite how tough it would be. Chesil Beach would provide some shelter from the incoming breeze, but that was only slight respite from the relentless struggle.

Things started badly. On moving Betty along the pontoon at West Bay, my nice new tiller extension became lodged between two pieces of plastic walkway. The sail, which had blown across the jetty, was blocking my view of the boat. I only noticed the potential problem, when it was too late. The carbon fibre tube had gained a significant bend. I taped it up, but it came away in my hands later, like the last one. It was less than a week old, so the breakage was really frustrating. I thought, "I can't bear to tell Steve from GOAT, so I probably won't." I didn't. Luckily, there was enough tubing remaining, so the tiller extension was still useable.

Out of the harbour I seemed to be making good progress, as West Bay receded behind me. However, the wind gusts grew stronger as time went on. After two hours, I was knackered and needed to take a break, so beached on the fine shingle. Happily, I could just manage the steepness, and took shelter beside Betty to recuperate for a while (and eat a sandwich of course).

After setting off again, the same pattern repeated. I couldn't recall such an exhausting six hours of sailing. I found this puzzling since I was so far into the circumnavigation. Perhaps it was simply the escalating wind strength, and relentless nature of the tacking. The first couple of hours had felt more or less manageable, but things became increasingly difficult after that. I fell out to windward three times overall, when overpowered. On several occasions, I wondered if I would make it to Chesil Cove at all, let alone get round to Weymouth. The alternative of walking along Chesil Beach to Portland, or towing Betty all the way, seemed ludicrous. I had to carry on, but it was exhausting.

I was mighty glad when Chesil Cove itself came into view. It was the last stretch of pebbles, before stones turned into formidable cliffs of the Isle of Portland.

When I got closer, I began to think about the landing. Having been scarred by Seaton, I was worried about making it up the steep incline in front of me.

What took me by complete surprise when stepping out of the boat, was being met by a couple of youths at the water's edge. I immediately recognised one of them. He was Finn, son of Sean from Dale in Wales, with whom I had stayed a few weeks back. How amazing to see him again.

Thinking I was at some long lost, and far-flung corner of the earth, barricaded from the rest of the world by a huge 10-mile-long mound of shingle, I asked innocently, "How did you get here?"

"We've been doing skills week at the sailing academy, and could see on the tracker that you were coming in. We came over because we thought you might need a hand."

I certainly did, and was hugely grateful for their assistance. We chatted for a while as I was derigging. Then Finn's mother arrived, crunching down the pebble surface. She offered the prospect of a free dinner at the sailing (Weymouth and Portland National Sailing) Academy that evening, and maybe some help with sorting out a tiller extension replacement. Things were getting better and better.

Just as I was starting to make my way to the Portland Airbnb, I had more visitors to my seaside parking lot. Danni and Colin were also Laser (or ILCA) parents, supporting their daughter at the academy. Danni talked in an animated way about my exploits over the last few months, information gleaned from Facebook and YouTube. It was as if she had known me for years, and yet we had never met. I suppose being a celebrity is like that, though multiplied many times over. In short doses, I must confess, it is incredibly flattering. I gratefully accepted a lift up to the accommodation and then down to the academy, after I had dumped my stuff. I felt very spoilt.

At the academy there was so much buzz and energy, with an intense focus on learning how to race well. There were connections to people I knew everywhere. There were so many people to talk to, that I ate too slowly, and missed dessert.

One essential person to catch before departing, was Duncan from Sailingfast. He had a van full of tiller extensions, so he became my instant best friend. He kindly offered a replacement for free, but given the very short life expectancy of the last one, I insisted on paying.

Such was the unexpected social overdose, that I forgot the precious piece of kit when I stopped for a garage coffee on the way back to my accommodation. Thank goodness it was still there when I ran back a few minutes later, innocently propped in a corner. I could not possibly go back to Duncan, and ask for another one.

At 3:00am, I woke up and couldn't get back to sleep. There was nothing for it, but to return to studying tide times, and the ever-changing wind forecast. Wind seemed to be calming down by the forthcoming afternoon, but then picking up again in the evening, when storm Betty was due to arrive. The tide times did not suit that, but would it matter if I was hugging the rocky shoreline, as everyone said I should? Conditions round headlands can be so difficult, catering for so many eventualities. They just didn't fit together.

Duncan had suggested I should wait till the following day, when the wind would change to a south-westerly. This I resolved to do, and was preparing to go back to sleep, when I realised it would bring an onshore breeze, and impossible shore break. That wouldn't work. Nothing seemed to be right.

Having explored all possibilities a thousand times, I eventually went back to sleep, still devoid of a plan.

* * *

Day 98, Friday 18th August

Round Portland Bill to Weymouth

START	16.30, Chesil Cove
WIND	SE 21–28mph, dropping to 16–22mph
WEATHER	Thick low cloud. 17–19°C. Dry
TIDE	Flowing W from 14.00 max 3.5mph
SEA STATE	Moderate
HAZARDS	Tides, coming storm. The Bill
FINISH	Weymouth, 18.00
DISTANCE	11 miles
SAILING HOURS	1½ hours

"I wouldn't go," said the fisherman. A thick grey mist was hanging over the Isle of Portland, more suitable for April rather than August, and it refused to budge, despite a decent south-easterly breeze. Trying to juggle all the details of the back eddies, inner passage, Shambles Bank, wind against spring tide, and forthcoming Storm Betty, meant that my head was in a spin. I had planned to leave at 9.00, but delayed my rounding after taking an earlier fisherman's advice to wait for the wind to drop. He talked knowledgeably about conditions being "nasty" around the other side of The Bill.

"Waves were breaking over Weymouth harbour wall this morning," he said, and that was before the barricade had become lost in the mist. He gave stories of tides being simultaneously on the flood, then on the ebb and then on the flood again, all within 100m of travel. I began to feel a little sorry for the sea, and even less at ease myself.

I hung about for much of the day at the academy, having walked over from Portland. I spent the time mingling with parents of young and enthusiastic sailors. Whilst in awe of the effort and learning commitment to sailing, I was confident that the people I saw were much better sailors than myself, adding to an air of intimidation. Waiting for my wind and tide window was like waiting for an exam, in that you don't want it to happen, but you can't wait for it to be over. I was invited to stay for prize giving to share a short word to aspiring youths, about my nearly completed 'Laser around the UK' journey. Needless to say, the schedule was delayed. My anxiety to get going, before Betty (my boat), would get taken on by Betty (the storm) got the better of me, and I left.

Getting ready to do the shingle slide launch into the green sea, a third fisherman asked what I was doing. He was not enthusiastic about my intended journey.

"I don't have much choice," I said. " I'd never get off the shore tomorrow since there'll be a south-westerly blowing in", which to my mind would make ideal shore dump, boat breaking conditions. He urged me to "go and take a look" at the appropriately named Pulpit rock, but to come back if conditions were too bad. He repeated his request more than once, which was not very encouraging, but at least it was good advice. So, I set off to my doom.

Like opening an exam paper and starting to write, anxiety dissipates when you finally get going. The fear of the unknown fades because you become focussed on the conditions that are in front of you. The danger of what might be, is replaced by the hazards as they present themselves, and those hazards travel only as far as you can see, rather than the ocean of scale that you can imagine.

I did wonder what the tourists were thinking, as they looked out from the cliffs under a heavy sky, watching my little white boat beat its way past the lighthouse, just out of reach of the waves breaking on to the rocks. "I hope he knows what he is doing" might have been a thought. I didn't know everything, but I reckoned I knew enough to keep going, so round the headland we went.

My only planning mishap was to omit my sunglasses. They would have been totally unnecessary for sun protection, but would have provided helpful spray relief, for the speedy rolling reach down to the harbour wall. When I arrived there, waves were indeed breaking over defences. Oh, and in true rookie style, I went through the wrong entrance, but no one could see, because no one could see.

My joy on landing was enormous, coupled with a huge sense of relief. The exam was over with answers submitted to the examiners, and I figured that was at least a pass. Perhaps I had even earned a skills credit in the process. Not only that, having navigated round the corner, the finish line of Stokes Bay was now in sight.

A reward for my fund-raising efforts for the Andrew Simpson Foundation, was to have a trolley available and waiting when I arrived, with a handy stowage spot at the Andrew Simpson Centre. Unlike the earlier bustle and activity, the slipway was now deserted, with all the youths and parents departed. I could peacefully pack up, and warm up in the celebratory glow of a successful rounding of The Bill.

The previous day, I had dropped in to visit the centre, and meet a few of the staff. It was great to see an excellent charity at work, improving lives through sailing, and I was very much in awe of youthful passion involved.

I also had the pleasure to meet Andrew Simpson's sister, Amanda, who reminded me it was the 10th Anniversary since his early death. A huge amount of effort has been put into the foundation and a great deal of work had followed, and Amanda has been central to that. I was really impressed with all the dedication, and had huge respect for a wonderful sailor, whose legacy has lived on. It had been an honour to raise money for the foundation.

Saturday 19th August

Day off

Jill and John from Papercourt had very kindly offered the use of their flat in Weymouth, for a couple of nights, so the temptation to take a day off was too great. It was also a chance to duck the stronger breezes from Storm Betty.

As you know, I love a day off. The pressure is off but the purpose is still on. This day was no exception. The sun had come out, so it was time to don my tourist hat, and head out to see the surroundings.

I decided to revisit the Isle of Portland and take a second look at The Bill, this time from the land, and find out what storm Betty had done to the sea.

When the Portland bus disgorged its contents near the end of the promontory, it was bright but blustery. Tourists were scrambling over rocks, and were photographing the lighthouse, the waves and the turbulent sea. I followed suit. I strolled across the flat surface near the Pulpit, where I had seen observers, observing me, the day before. There was a set of footholds carved into the granite pinnacle, so the more daring visitors could put themselves at greater risk of falling off the edge, by scrambling to the top. I climbed up.

It was a fine vantage point, only feet from the crashing waves, where you can feel the full effect of the wind whistling past, with uninterrupted views all around. The sea was in its full feverish state, doing battle with opposing tide, throwing glittering waves into the air across the Shambles. I was glad to be on this personalised pinnacle, not out on the wild waters. I savoured the moment for a while, and then it was back to the bus.

By evening, the winds had subsided, and I had a lovely peaceful time, exploring the local seafront and café. Many thanks to Jill and John for allowing me to stay – it was wonderful. I hope I left the place as tidy as expected.

Day 99, Sunday 20th August

To Mudeford

START	08.45, Weymouth
WIND	SW, 12–16mph
WEATHER	Cloud then sun, 17–21°C. Dry
TIDE	With me, max 1.8mph till 15.00
SEA STATE	Slight to moderate
HAZARDS	St Alban's race. Lulworth Ranges
FINISH	Mudeford, 15.00
DISTANCE	35 miles
SAILING HOURS	6 hours

Preparations from the night before, and a taxi to the sailing academy, meant that launching was slick. Having a trolley and a place to get organised, free of sand, made a huge difference, so I was on the water by 8.45. I wanted to get away early to catch the flood tide past St Alban's Head.

A guy called 'dreadnaught' had been messaging me about St Alban's Head, warning about a tidal race, which he said was worse than Portland Bill. Since he had taken the trouble to get in touch, I rang him up to listen more carefully to his advice. However, I was a bit perplexed about his gloomy predictions, since there wasn't much of a promontory at the point in question, which I assumed was a prerequisite for a tidal race.

I set off on a steady reach, but the wind wilted as the clouds began to clear. A yacht called Bright Star was overtaking me, and we drew close for a sort of chat. "We saw you at Falmouth a few days ago," he said.

It was lovely to be noted and great to see familiar faces, although at shouting distance, conversation and visual detail was a bit thin. With their spinnaker flying, they soon eased past.

Approaching the alleged hazard at St Alban's Head, the wind died and the tide was running with me, so I figured the surface would be more or less flat. "What could possibly be the problem?" I thought to myself.

And yet up ahead, a band of waves was running right across my path, threatening to block my journey, like a log before a herd of migrating Canadian Moose. I made an attempt to avoid the disturbance by heading in towards land, but manoeuvrability had faded with the wind. I could see Bright Star taking a similar line. A yacht further ahead looked like they had turned on their motor to plough through the waves. Not having the luxury of a propellor, I decided to alter course and head straight through the watery mess. "After all," I said to myself, "I have been through worse."

The tide was pushing me onwards, and in only a few minutes, I had popped out the other side, with calm restored. I was then able to bob along nicely with the flow, pushed by an increasing breeze. Meanwhile, I could see Bright Star making its way inshore, still rocking backwards and forwards, like a wobbling weeble. That looked like an uncomfortable ride! By the time they had escaped the relentless seesaw, I was about a mile further on, and feeling very smug.

England were playing Spain in the Women's World Cup final, in a tense battle for the golden prize. I looked up an occasional update on my phone and like many, was desperately hoping that the 1-0 deficit could be levelled or better. But it wasn't to be. Tantalisingly close, but not quite there in the end. Success for the Lionesses in the Euros could not be replicated at the world stage. Well done to England's women for reaching the final though, which was a huge achievement. Stories about the game lingered on, though sadly the football was overshadowed by Louis Rubiales' forceful kiss on Jenni Hermoso.

She did eventually join in with the quiz, and the next challenge was to stop her answering all the questions before it was her turn - they were all correct. "I think we might have to put Elizabeth on mute," was the suggestion from my nephew.

Despite her intellectual vigour, she had had enough. Walking was hard, swallowing was uncomfortable and eating no longer a pleasure, but a chore. I could see what she meant. Her body was packing up, and she just wasn't enjoying being part of it. Things were only going to get worse.

I could see Brian feeling the same. Parts not working so well, frailty creeping up on him and proud independence looking perilously close to falling over. The least I could do was to honour his generosity, and help him feel part of an adventure in whatever way I could. To still feel alive and contributing.

Day 100, Monday 21st August

To Lymington

START	10.00, Mudeford
WIND	SW, 9–15mph
WEATHER	Cloud/Sun, 19–20°C. Dry
TIDE	With me max 2.6mph, till 13.00
SEA STATE	Slight
HAZARDS	Missing the tide. Shipping & ferries
FINISH	Lymington, 14.00
DISTANCE	12 miles
SAILING HOURS	3 hours

Brian organised a lovely breakfast of porridge with blueberries and bananas on top. The fruit was given the microwave treatment along with the oats, so came out hot, but the sentiment and effort were delicious. I was in no great hurry, so lingered to chat for a while and appreciate Brian's company. He courteously walked me down to the gate and I bade him a fond farewell. I hoped it had been a good stay for Brian as well as myself. Old age can be painful, and I was doing my best to stave it off for the both of us.

David kindly greeted me at Christchurch train station, and gave me a lift back to his house. He then lent a hand with rigging and launching, which was all very much appreciated. My casual start time was just as well, since the tide was coming in. There was only just enough water for Betty to float, and then sail, eking out the deeper channels as we made our way to the harbour exit.

I headed out into open waters feeling quite sad. The end was nigh. Relaxation of journey completed and time on solid ground felt enticing, but there had been so many wonderful moments and cherished memories. The kindness of strangers and passing acquaintances had been truly amazing, with memories of Erika, David, and Brian still fresh in my mind. It felt sad to leave them behind, and those many, many happy times.

Monday 28th August, a bank holiday, had been set as the final day, thus giving potential celebrants time and notice, to gather at the finish line. To avoid getting stuck the wrong side of the Needles, I figured that parking up at Lymington for a few days would reduce the risk of being late for the scheduled 16.00 arrival. Hence a short hop was required for the day's sailing.

Given the brevity of the intended journey, I felt the need for a detour over to the Needles to capture footage of this iconic landmark. The beautiful backdrop blue of yesterday had faded to dull grey and dirty white, but at least I had a bit of fun on the way, bouncing through the overfalls across the Shingles, opposite the lighthouse. And then onwards towards home.

The wind was kind and the tide kinder, whisking me past Hurst Castle, clanking channel markers and a clunking shipping container, before skipping round ferries and up to the yacht club. The sailing day was done. How busy this part of the world can be, compared to the empty silence of Scotland.

The Royal Lymington Yacht Club, being one of the larger establishments on my circumnavigation, hadn't responded to my email approach. But knocking on doors, and presenting my story to one person then another, soon led me to an out of the way space to store Betty for a few days. Youth week was due to begin, and there was much organising to be done. In small exchange for the local generosity, I lent a hand in rigging sails for new boats, in preparation for the week ahead.

Lymington is a charming town, crammed with narrow Georgian streets, sailing types and tourists. Shipbuilding had been a strong trade over the centuries, and continues to this day with a focus on yachts and leisure craft. The river is thick with moored boats of all shapes and sizes, ready to dash out into the Solent for a cruise, or a race.

Liz and I had been down to the town a few years previously, for a practice sail out to the Needles and back. We had stumbled upon a Merlin Nationals event, and such was the density of participants that it was a struggle to find a place to park, let alone unload our trailer. The gentleman helping with launching and landing had been worried about our return, fearing for some mishap. Looking back, it felt strange to have been met with such concern, over something that now felt a trivial excursion.

Having provided my helping hand at the yacht club, there was nothing more for me to do, other than drift home. Without the focus of a sailing day on the morrow, I felt slightly lost. It was strange to be going home, without a destination to aim at. I had almost finished, but I hadn't finished, so felt suspended in a happy but listless limbo, waiting for the following Monday to arrive.

Tuesday 22nd August - Sunday 27th August

The next few days passed quickly, and I found myself slipping back into daily life, without much of a thought. Rhythms of home were quickly restored.

On the Wednesday, I went down to Hayling Island to say 'hi' to some to folks, since the ILCA nationals event was on. Finn, from Wales, was competing. He had greeted me with a trolley at Chesil Beach, and I was able to return the surprise greeting. Having worked out his sail number, I spotted him arriving and found the relevant trolley, so managed to present his wheels as he came into the beach. He was delighted. A few weeks later, I sent him my Welsh burgee as a token of support for his future sailing endeavours. I think he appreciated that.

Stick was there, creating entertainment on demand, in his typical charming way. And lots of other folk, with whom I could share tales of my circumnavigation.

"You should join in with the next couple of days racing," I was told.

"Ah, my boat is in Lymington," was the most obvious excuse, but there were many others. I was much more contented to have a mingle and enjoy the atmosphere.

Day 101, Monday 28th August

To Stokes Bay. The very last day

START	10.00, Lymington
WIND	N/NW, 7–11mph
WEATHER	Cloud/Sun, 16–19°C. Dry
TIDE	Against me max 2.8mph, till 14.00
SEA STATE	Slight
HAZARDS	Opposing tide. Light wind. Being late
FINISH	Stokes Bay, 16.00. Hooray!
DISTANCE	18 miles
SAILING HOURS	4½ hours. (90 mins on Henry's boat)

"I really have to be on time," I said to myself, over and over again.

Walking down a red brick, wall lined road on the way to the yacht club, I hastened my step. My sister Fiona had contacted BBC South, who were coming to do an interview of the last day. As I paced onwards, I reflected on one of the ironies of day 101 of the adventure. Laser around the UK had been an intense focus, but it had also been an escape. Over the last few months, I had been able to loosen the shackles of time. And yet folding back into ordinary life, I realised that being organised, and being on time is an essential part of life. It is an essential part of being with a group, of being together and being coordinated, which is so fundamentally human. And without that coordination and togetherness, we are in danger of being forever alone. I, for one, would not vote for that.

Energised by the fear of being late, I was on time. I even managed to snap some selfies beforehand, with different charity shirts, ready for later publicity. Before the crew arrived, I had Betty all dressed with a Union Jack burgee, and ready to roll off the slipway for her final few miles. The interview went well, I thought. Well done me for being organised and on time! Phew!

The plans for the day were to rendezvous past Cowes, with Henry and Jacqui on their yacht, and moor up for a while. Henry was an adventure mate and a fellow doctor. We had been on several trips together, cycling from Land's End to John O'Groats with our sons, and later, kayaking down the River Wye. I had talked about the circumnavigation with him a while before setting off, and I was delighted he would be able to travel out to greet me.

Liz was bringing her Laser down to Stokes Bay, so that she could sail out and join a landing procession. My brother-in-law Julian was doing the same, transporting Oli, my middle son, in a Wayfarer. Hence a small on-the-water reception party was in the making.

Light winds and opposing tide were a risk for the day. The first couple of hours went OK. However, when crossing over to Cowes, the wind disappeared and I was caught in an anxious hour of frustrated paddling, scraping along the shoreline, threading between passing vessels and ferries. Plenty of my own puff got me past the river mouth in the end.

I found Henry and Jacqui off Osbourne Bay, and had a happy hour on board with lunch and chat, drifting on the turned tide towards the finish line.

Then it was time to go. The wind had filled in to a light but steady breeze, so easy sailing conditions.

Having set off, I went to join Liz in her Laser. Jacqui, ever the romantic, watching the scene from her Solent viewing platform, declared, "It's like Jane Austen on the water," as we approached each other.

Coming closer to land, I could see and hear a large gathering of people, cheering us in. A couple of flags were waving on an enormous extendable stick. Coming closer, I could make out a '3' on the bottom flag, which made obvious sense. What did the other one say? I could not quite read it. "Oh, ha, ha. That's funny," I said. "It must be Sam who wrote that."

It said, "One more lap."

I touched down at 15.59, so bang on time. It had been 4½ months, and 101 days of sailing to cover 2200 miles of open sea around the British Isles in my 13ft Laser. And now it was done.

My nephew Douglas was the first to step forward and give me a hug. He loves a party and is remarkably socially astute, despite his Down's Syndrome. Then Sam came over to shower me in champagne, motor racing style. And at last, Liz had freed herself from her own mini adventure, and wrapped her arms around me for a warm embrace. I had made it round safely, in my beautiful boat Betty and was home, crowded amongst appreciative onlookers, all enjoying the moment with me. What more could one ask for?

There was a large gathering of people from all sections of life. Family, friends from work, locals from squash, from the sailing club, from swimming, Sam's friends, Emily's boyfriend's parents, and even a family whom I had worked with. They had won the prize for accurately guessing the number of sailing days at the finish, and I handed them a box of chocolates, which I had carefully stowed on the boat. I was really touched that so many had come down on a bank holiday, and went round to personally thank everyone for their presence.

BBC South were there, to capture the conclusion at Stokes Bay. The interview did not take long. I was really impressed with the assembled four minutes that was broadcast later. Clips from several parts of the trip had been seamlessly pulled together in a couple of hours, something us amateurs would take weeks to edit. It was fantastic to have a TV moment, which was icing on the cake.

As the daylight started to dwindle and crowd dispersed, we were left to pack up and tow boats home. The excitement and tension of a finale had faded.

Leaving the coast, the sadness of an ending crept over me again, before the dawn of a new day and a new project had arrived. From here, there would be no more planning rituals. No more examining the weather, the tides and possible landing points, and no need for daily posts on Facebook. No more getting changed, getting launched and getting wet. Home was a reliable and safe resource instead. So much more comfortable, but so much more mundane.

My thoughts looked back from whence I had come, as if eyeing up the wake left behind from Betty's movement.

Being alone on the water had been elemental, raw and unforgiving. It was just me, the sea and Betty. There was no one else and nothing to save me. Being out on the sea with the wind in my hair and the waves all around, was cleansing. I had grown to understand more of the world we live in. Conditions I faced started to mean things, and tell stories of the ocean's own journey over rocks, round land, pushed into waves and drawn by the moon.

I had been at one with nature. That had been a very special place to be on each of the 101 days, like being back at the beginning and almost at the end, all at the same time.

As time drew on, I realised I have loved every minute of it, especially the bad bits, because the bad bits made the good bits even better.

I have loved the sailing and had grown increasingly fond of Betty. I have loved the adventure and the uncertainty of not knowing how things would pan out. And yet they did. I have loved the problem solving – figuring out how to deal with difficulties, when none of the usual resources were to hand.

I have loved the escape from the trials of everyday life. I have loved the simple rhythm of eat, sleep, sail, repeat.

I have loved landing, as well. The joy of being safely on solid ground, with sailing behind me for the day, was a relief, like a personal homecoming, repeated over and over again. The happiness of speaking to people, even for mundane tasks, was like finding treasure.

I have loved the visual capture of a journey in photos and videos. Of sharing the stories with other people. I have loved their joy and admiration of my nautical nonsense. Yes, I have to admit it, I have loved the attention.

Going round in pointless circles is the stuff of life. Sailing around mainland Great Britain and ending up where you started is definitely a glorious luxury endeavour, but gripping to me, and indeed to other people. One YouTube commentator said it was a ridiculous and attention seeking childish enterprise. My son kindly replied, saying, "Yes, we all agree it's ridiculous. But he is having a good time and so are we, and I hope you are having a good time too."

Above all, I have loved people's kindness, support and generosity. I had never imagined so much. I received so many open-hearted welcomes, from all corners of the land. It is almost too hard to fathom, in our disconnected and divided world, that such wonderful responses could be possible. And yet there it all was. A trail of connection left behind, of thoughtfulness, of giving, and through it all, of love for our fellow human beings. It was truly incredible. I remain really proud to have been witness to that.

CHAPTER 22

Epilogue

* * *

Life has returned to normal. It is a new normal in that I have retired for the second time.

I am working on a third retirement, but not just yet. I have followed through with my plan to work independently. It is odd, working because I want to, rather than because I have to, but I am not complaining. I still love the clinical contact with young people and families. I am enjoying the freedom of working to my schedule, and getting up in the morning when the time feels right. What a blessing.

However, all this freedom can be unsettling. People say that retirement involves reimagining a new life – reshaping who you are, and how you live your life. I don't think I am there yet. There are more things to try out, social connections to make, and maybe new roads to travel. Maybe even a new adventure.

Family life has fallen back into step, much as it was. Liz and myself are at home, kids in London, within easy transport reach.

There are no grandchildren as yet.

Over the 2023 winter, I delivered a number of talks about the trip, mostly to sailing clubs. It has been a lot of fun, and I have very much enjoyed sharing the stories and video material. Each talk has raised a few hundred pounds for charity. I would like to do some more.

Book writing has taken AGES. I think at least 800 hours, which is more than the sailing trip itself. I hope the product is not too bad. If you have got this far, you might have thought so. It has been fun to revisit the journey and to research places around the coast of our great countries. I have enjoyed reading back some of my own stories, since it brings the days to life in a different way to a video, or a snatched conversation with a friend. Moments like the rounding of Cape Wrath, or sailing with dolphins, or even the Crinan Canal, make me smile or laugh as I reread them. I hope they have brought joy to you as well.

Most important, however, has been the incredible generosity of those I have met along the way. I want to say it again. Time and time and time again, strangers stepped forward to help, so often when it was least expected. I don't feel I have done enough to articulate that, for it has been truly wonderful. In so many ways, the kindness of strangers, **is** the main story of the book. Thank you to everyone who helped so unflinchingly along the way.

As for Betty. Let's not forget Betty. She has been to rehab.

Before repairs were completed, I took her to an open meeting sailing event in the autumn of 2023 and came second. I usually finish further down the order so was very pleased with the result. Prior to the event, I was ready with my excuses, preparing to claim "Betty has been round GB, and is a bit tired, you know", or "the hull is in poor shape. Her bottom is still scratched to bits". However, the second-place finish suggested that excuses weren't needed, and the potential explanations were immaterial. I concluded that the number of dents and abrasions on the bottom of your dinghy makes little difference, so it might be necessary to cross that one off the potential explanations list, should you be tempted to reach that far.

Betty has now been repaired and has a lovely new shiny surface when she sits on the water. The completed map of the journey round the UK has been restored. She is raced at Papercourt Sailing Club from time to time, but she has a sister, so she can have a rest as well.

Before I finish, I have a small request. I still need some singers for my sea shanty. If anyone knows some hearty singers to offer a brief rendition of a jolly tune, do get in touch. It would be much appreciated. Contact details are on my website, which is listed in the FAQ.

One final thought.

You too can do it. Don't hold back. Now is the time. I would be happy to help you. I am sure you would enjoy it as much as I have. If I could, so can you. Think about it.

GLOSSARY

Auto-bailer

A plastic device, fitted to the underside of the hull, which will help drain water from the cockpit, when the boat is going fast enough. It is attached to a bung in the bottom of the cockpit, which means the connecting hole can be closed if speeds are slow. It is a good idea to close the auto-bailer when coming into a beach, since it is prone to being ripped off, as I discovered, when sliding the boat across sand.

Batten

Flattened fibreglass rod, which is slotted into the Leech (back edge) of the sail, to help it keep its shape.

Bear away

Changing the angle of the boat, so that it turns away from the direction of the wind. The opposite of **point up**.

Beat

A direction of sailing, which requires a series of tacks, when going upwind.

Block

A pulley, through which a rope is passed, to help it go round a corner.

Boom
A horizontal length of metal tube, which holds the sail away from the mast, so that it can keep its shape, and act to provide power. The thing you need to duck when tacking or gybing.

Burgee
A small square flag or similar, placed on top of the mast to help see where the wind is coming from.

Capsize
A dry capsize is when the boat tips over on its side, with the sail lying flat in the water. For a laser, it is quite easy to swing a leg over onto the centre board and stand on this, thus righting the boat without getting wet.

When **turning turtle**, the boat falls over completely, with the mast then pointing down to the bottom of the sea. Everything gets wet, including you.

Centreboard, Daggerboard or Centre plate
A removable board in the middle of the boat, which acts like a keel, thus helping the craft go forwards and not sideways, when the wind hits the sail.

Cockpit
The footwell in the centreline of a laser, so the sailor can sit comfortably, and for this trip, store items. The **toe strap** is in the cockpit.

Cunningham / Downhaul
A rigging set up which runs next to the mast, and pulls the front of the sail downwards, and helps depower the top of the sail, by flattening it. This is useful in stronger winds.

Ebb tide

When the tide goes out, and therefore the level of water falls. The direction of the Ebb tide depends on the precise location, and can vary hugely at different points around GB. For each particular location, however, the flow patterns repeat in consistent fortnightly cycles, as governed by the moon.

Fender

A thick inflated tube (which can come in a range of shapes and sizes), normally used on the side of a boat to prevent it being scraped, when mooring to a pontoon. For this trip, it was repurposed to be a rolling device, similar to logs, used by Egyptians when moving stones for pyramids.

Fetch

Sailing upwind, though not requiring lots of tacks (which would make it a beat).

Flood tide

The opposite of ebb tide.

Gybe(ing)

Turning the boat so that the wind changes sides (from Port to starboard, or vice versa) by pointing the nose AWAY from the wind in the process.

Hiking

Leaning out of the boat to one side, to counteract the force of the wind, and help turn wind force into forward motion.

Irons (stuck in irons)
When the boat ends up head to wind (pointing straight into the wind) by mistake, usually when it is very windy. If it's windy, it can be quite easy to fall out after being stuck in irons.

Kicker or kicking strap
Also known as the **vang**. A series of ropes and blocks, to pull the boom down and therefore change the shape of the sail. More tension makes for a flatter sail.

Knot
1 knot = 1 nautical mile per hour, or 1.15mph.

Laser / ILCA dinghy
The design was introduced in 1969 by Ian Bruce and Bruce Kirby (who died in 2021). It was the first car topping performance dinghy, so created much excitement at the time. Allegedly, the design was produced from a simple sketch rather than extensive marine engineering testing, so some aspects are a little crude, such as the angle and size of the rudder.

It is the most widely owned and sailed single handed dinghy in the world, with production numbers exceeding 222,000. The vast majority of sailing clubs in the UK have at least one Laser in the boat park.

The fibreglass hull makes it fairly robust. With a small cockpit, it is very easy to right after a capsize, since the hull will not fill with water. Combined with its relatively light weight, it makes an ideal craft for solo sailing round the UK.

There are 3 rig (sail) sizes, previously called Standard, Radial and 4.7. With the class name change to ILCA in 2019, the rigs are called ILCA 7, 6, and 4. The sail sizes are unchanged.

An ILCA 7 sail measures 7.06m2. The hull weighs 58.97kg, and when fully rigged with foils, the weight goes up to about 75kg.

Length is 4.2m, or 13ft 9in. The draft with the centreboard down is 0.79m, or 2ft 7in. With the plate up, the draft is 0.15m or about six inches.

Mainsheet
The rope used to adjust the position of the sail, by pulling it in or letting it out.

Mast
This is formed of two pieces. The bottom section for a standard rig, is made of alloy, 2.7m in length. The top section can be alloy, or latterly made of carbon fibre and is 3.2m in length. I had a carbon top section, which is stronger and less likely to break when landing.

Mast step
The hole in the foredeck, that the mast slots into in a Laser. The hole / tube below deck level, then keeps the mast upright, meaning that you can sail along.

Navionics
A subscription app that can be used on mobile phones, produced by Garmin. It gives geolocation information, gives details about tide height, tide flows, navigational points and hazards. It can be used to passage plan, calculate distances and set waypoints, and many other features.

Outhaul
Part of the rigging system, using a rope to pull the bottom of the sail flatter, which reduces its power if needed.

Overfalls

A turbulent stretch of open water, often consisting of steep and irregular waves, caused by strong current over a submarine ridge, or by meeting of currents.

Painter

A rope that is tied to the **bow** (front) of the boat, so it can be secured to a pontoon, or mooring.

Point up

Changing the angle of the boat so that it points more towards the wind. The opposite of **bear away**.

Port

The left-hand side of a boat, when looking forwards from inside the cockpit.

Reach

A point of sail where the wind is coming at roughly 90° to the direction of the boat. This is called a beam reach.

There is also a **close reach** when the wind is more like 70°, so arriving nearer the front, or a **broad reach**, more like 110° and arriving nearer the back of the boat.

Rudder

The blade in the water at the rear of the boat, used for steering.

Run

A point of sail when the wind is coming from directly behind the boat.

Shore break
Waves breaking on the shore. Usually worse on a steep beach, because they can push you forwards, and then pull you back.

Starboard
The right-hand side of the boat when looking forwards from inside the boat.

Stick Daring
Also known as Neil Peters.

Tack(ing)
Turning the boat so that the wind changes sides (from Port to starboard, or vice versa) by pointing the nose INTO the wind in the process. Tacking usually helps with going upwind.

Tell-tale
Pieces of wool or thin plastic material, attached at various points, on both sides of the sail, to help see what the wind is doing.

Tiller
The stick which is rigidly attached to the rudder, allowing it to be turned and the boat steered. Equivalent to a steering wheel in a car.

Tiller Extension
A length of tube, flexibly attached to the tiller, allowing the sailor to sit in a wide range of positions and move about the boat from side to side, and still steer.

Toe strap

A wide piece of webbing or other material, attached at each end of the cockpit (in a Laser). Feet or ankles can be placed under the strap, thus allowing the sailor to lean out of the boat (**hiking**), without falling out.

Veer

The wind direction changes in a clockwise direction. If the wind **backs**, it changes in an anticlockwise direction.

Windex

A light balanced weathervane, attached to the mast to help determine the wind direction.

APPENDIX

Beaufort scale

(up to force 10 here. The scale goes to 12)

WIND FORCE	DESCRIPTION	WIND SPEED, MPH	SPECIFICATIONS
0	Calm	<1	Smoke rises vertically. Sea like a mirror
1	Light Air	1–3	Direction shown by smoke drift but not by wind vanes. Sea rippled
2	Light Breeze	4–7	Wind felt on face; leaves rustle; wind vane moved by wind. Small wavelets on sea
3	Gentle Breeze	8–12	Leaves and small twigs in constant motion; light flags extended. Large wavelets on sea
4	Moderate Breeze	13–18	Raises dust and loose paper; small branches moved. Small waves, fairly frequent white horses
5	Fresh Breeze	19–24	Small trees in leaf begin to sway; crested wavelets form on inland waters. Moderate waves, many white horses
6	Strong Breeze	25–31	Large branches in motion; whistling heard in telegraph wires; umbrellas used with difficulty. Large waves, extensive foam crests
7	Near Gale	32–38	Whole trees in motion; inconvenience felt when walking against the wind. Foam blown in streaks across the sea
8	Gale	39–46	Twigs break off trees, generally impedes progress. Wave crests begin to break into spindrift

| 9 | **Strong Gale** | 47–54 | Slight structural damage (chimney pots and slates removed). Wave crests topple over, and spray affects visibility |
| 10 | **Storm** | 55–63 | Seldom experienced inland; trees uprooted; considerable structural damage. Sea surface is largely white |

Sea state scale

Below is the World Meteorological Organization Scale. Wave height is the highest third of the waves on the sea. The measure is from trough to crest. The full scale is included to illustrate what is best avoided!

WMO SEA STATE CODE	WAVE HEIGHT	CHARACTERISTICS
0	0 metres	Calm (glassy)
1	0 – 0.1 metres	Calm (rippled)
2	0.1 – 0.5 metres	Smooth (wavelets)
3	0.5 – 1.25 metres	Slight
4	1.25 – 2.5 metres	Moderate
5	2.5 – 4 metres	Rough
6	4 – 6 metres	Very rough
7	6 – 9 metres	High
8	9 – 14 metres	Very high
9	Over 14 metres	Phenomenal

Distance measurement

The coastline of the mainland UK can vary from under 2000 miles to 3- or even 4000 miles, or even more, depending on how you measure it. Ducking and diving into every cove makes it longer, taking a straight line across a bay, or an estuary makes it shorter.

The measurement approach that was adopted, had two phases. Firstly, a rough route was plotted, using google maps prior to the trip. Decile way points were then marked around the coast of GB. The second phase was to make daily distance calculations, based on the miles covered along that line.

The rough route plot was the most direct line, about two miles offshore, crossing obvious indentations. Most major estuaries were crossed at a fairly narrow point, such as the Thames, Firth of Forth, Bristol Channel etc.

The distance each day was formulated, based on a crude calculation. The total distance came in at roughly 2200 miles. So, each decile (10%) was 220 miles. Progress within each decile was then fairly easy to estimate, and was based on how far Andrew had travelled within that section. Complex sections might be broken into further divisions for assessing each day's official mileage. Sections with big estuaries meant he could cover a lot in a day sailing straight across, or make little apparent progress by sailing up the estuary.

No account was taken for extra distance travelled when on the beat, or against tide. No account was taken for mileage required to reach a stopping point, or to return to the hypothetical Google route line. Equally, distance going backwards (for example, the 20 miles from the Isle of Arran to Prestwick) was not added to the total miles travelled.

Courtesy of Liz Hill-Smith, official measurement systems

FAQ section

Would you do it again?
Absolutely yes. But having done it once, there is not much point in repeating the journey, since I could never be number 2 to complete the circumnavigation, and being both number 3 and number 4 doesn't sound very cool.

What are you going to do next?

Ha, ha. I don't know. First there is writing the book (going round again on paper) which has taken ages. I would like to do something else, before I am too old. Let's see.

Are you a changed person?

Yes and no. I am fundamentally the same person, with the same interests, thinking patterns and approaches to life. I have the same family and friends. But I do have a warm glow in my heart, which is a lovely feeling. It comes to life whenever I have a chance to talk about the trip. (Do please keep asking me questions.)

With all the time to think, did you come up with anything?

Unfortunately, not much really. There were no Eureka moments, or epiphanies. I think one needs a mind full of stuff, in order to make those reactions happen. Mine was largely empty of worldly troubles, being more mindful of its physical surroundings.

However, I did have one serious thought. It is this:

The fantasy of freedom is only temporary, because without the reflections from other people, we soon start to evaporate. Having spent so many hours on my own, staring at the land, I realised that I was not alone. I realised that there is nothing that we do, that does not have a social backing. Nothing that we think, or even feel, is without other people in mind. We think, we think our own private thoughts, but even then, there are other people there. In our ruminations and in our calculations and in our feelings. Everything we think, feel or do, has a social context. There is no such thing as being completely separate from other humans.

I hadn't quite realised that before.

When I have tried to share that thought with others, they have given me blank looks.

And yet it feels important.

The image of isolation on an empty green sea, feels so much less alarming when you know that people are there. Even staring at the picture, or imagining the photograph, is being part of the scene. In our minds, we carry the collective thoughts, memories and feelings of decades of social contact. Surely it is good to know that, and to remember that.

I suppose the feeling, or the image in my mind, is of a benign chorus of onlookers, concerned for a lone and isolated individual. The reality for many, is that being amongst our fellow humans on the land is not always a joyous experience.

And yet, without humans, we cannot survive. With humans we must be alive. With humans, we must resolve to deal with uncomfortable feelings and dark thoughts, because it was amongst humans that they emerged. Hiding those negativities away, is only an illusion that can never be realised. We have to find a way of being together in all of our light and dark. To feel connected and accepted. To find joy or solace in the smallest of interactions. To live, work, and care together. There is no other way.

And that is why I have resolved to go out, if I am feeling bad. To see others and to exchange looks or pleasantries. That is why, the advice for those who feel depressed, is to keep doing things and to mix with others, to create a new thread of connection, that can be sewn into a web of strength. To be with others and to be oneself, and to feel OK about that.

To me, at least, that feels important.

Is there any more content online?

Ooh yes. A series of videos on YouTube. The links are via my website which is laseraroundtheuk3. (https://www.laseraroundtheuk3. uk/). Or you can go direct to @andrewhill-smith9535 on YouTube. There is also a Facebook (https://www.facebook.com/

laseraroundtheuk/) and Instagram page with the handle laser around the UK

How much money did you raise for charities?

At the time of writing, for the three charities, I have raised over £20,000. I am planning on keeping it going and see where I get to, but it is now a trickle. Do feel free to contribute, via my website – if you type laseraroundtheuk3 into a search engine, it comes up – which has all the links to the JustGiving pages. Many thanks for thinking about it.

How much stuff did you take?

As little as possible.

Below is a breakdown of weights of things by category. The total came to 21kg but varied with the amount of food and water.

Boat maintenance – mostly spares, some tools	1
Electronics – phone, tracker, battery pack etc	1.8
Bags, and containers	2
Sailing clothes – extra layers or alternative items	2.1
Food and water	2.1
On the boat – fender, paddle, compass, and electronic flare	2.5
Land clothes – and day shoes	4.4
Sleeping – tent, air mats, sleeping bags	5.1

Where did you store your stuff?

In the hull, accessed through the hatches. The front hatch was by the centreboard, and contained camping stuff. The back hatch under the traveller contained most of the rest of the luggage. A day bag was in the cockpit.

Did it cost you much?

Not too bad I reckon.

The total was over £10,000 for the 4½ months of travel. But if you take off the typical expenses for the time period, like petrol, eating out, etc (excluding household mortgage, council tax and bills, etc), the net cost was just over £3000. That makes about £150 per week. Hence, a very cheap holiday!!

The breakdown was about

- One third on accommodation,
- One third on equipment (including electronics, and subs and camping kit, and boat stuff)
- and the final third on food, meals, transport and anything else

Was the wind mainly from the SW?

Yes and no. The chart below shows the summary. SW is the largest piece of the pie. In reality, there were more easterlies in the early parts of the trip and more westerlies later. This is a typical seasonal pattern, I understand.

Summary of wind directions

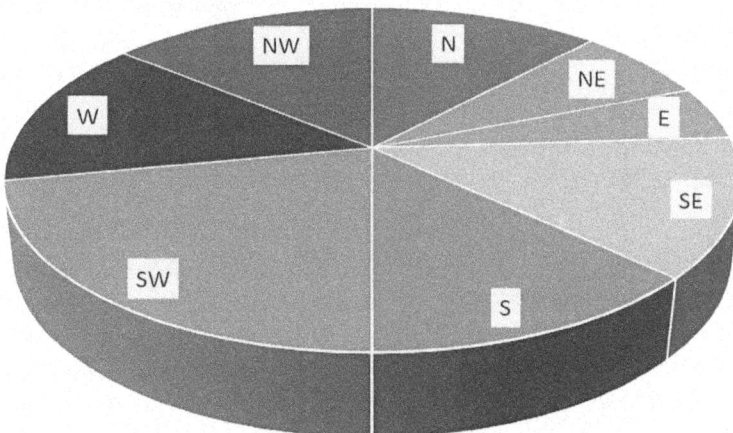

How many hours were you are sea?

It took 531 hours, at sea.

The Crinan Canal was the longest day at 11 hours, though not technically at sea. If you add that in, the total comes to 542 hours.

Excluding the Crinan Canal, the longest spells were ten hours, when crossing the Thames, or on the west coast of Scotland, going to Tobermory. There were a few short days of less than two hours, including the first.

The average time at sea, was 5.4 hours per day.

How fast did you go?

Usually, I could manage more than two miles per hour, even if there was no wind, but a few days were less!! My maximum speed was more than 12mph, when heading to Mumbles.

Average speed for the trip was a lowly 4.25mph. The maximum average was again crossing the Bristol Channel at 8mph.

www.ingramcontent.com/pod-product-compliance
Lightning Source LLC
Chambersburg PA
CBHW021131090426
42740CB00008B/743